WHO IS MARY?

THE OTHER VOICE IN EARLY MODERN EUROPE

A Series Edited by Margaret L. King and Albert Rabil Jr.

RECENT BOOKS IN THE SERIES

LAURA BATTIFERRA DEGLI AMMANNATI
Laura Battiferra and Her Literary Circle: An Anthology
Edited and Translated by Victoria Kirkham

MADELEINE DE L'AUBESPINE
Selected Poems and Translations: A Bilingual Edition
Edited and Translated by Anna Kłosowska

MODERATA FONTE (MODESTA POZZO)
Floridoro: A Chivalric Romance
Edited with an Introduction by Valeria Finucci, Translated by Julia Kisacky, Annotated by Valeria Finucci and Julia Kisacky

MARÍA DE GUEVARA
Warnings to the Kings and Advice on Restoring Spain: A Bilingual Edition
Edited and Translated by Nieves Romero-Días

LOUISE LABÉ
Complete Poetry and Prose: A Bilingual Edition
Edited with Introductions and Prose Translations by Deborah Lesko Baker, with Poetry Translations by Annie Finch

MARIE-MADELEINE PIOCHE DE LA VERGNE, COMTESSE DE LAFAYETTE
Zayde: A Spanish Romance
Edited and Translated by Nicholas D. Paige

MARGUERITE DE NAVARRE
Selected Writings: A Bilingual Edition
Edited and Translated by Rouben Cholakian and Mary Skemp

MADELEINE AND CATHERINE DES ROCHES
From Mother and Daughter: Poems, Dialogues, and Letters of Les Dames de Roches
Edited and Translated by Anne R. Larsen

ANA DE SAN BARTOLOMÉ
Autobiography and Other Writings
Edited and Translated by Darcy Donahue

MARGHERITA SARROCCHI
Scanderbeide: The Heroic Deeds of George Scanderbeg, King of Epirus
Edited and Translated by Rinaldina Russell

JUSTINE SIEGEMUND
The Court Midwife
Edited and Translated by Lynne Tatlock

KATHARINA SCHÜTZ ZELL
Church Mother: The Writings of a Protestant Reformer in Sixteenth-Century Germany
Edited and Translated by Elsie McKee

Vittoria Colonna,
Chiara Matraini, and
Lucrezia Marinella

WHO IS MARY?

Three Early Modern Women on the Idea of the Virgin Mary

Edited and Translated by
Susan Haskins

THE UNIVERSITY OF CHICAGO PRESS
Chicago & London

Vittoria Colonna, 1492–1547
Chiara Matraini, 1515–1604?
Lucrezia Marinella, 1571–1653

Susan Haskins is an independent scholar living in London. She is the author of *Mary Magdalen: Myth and Metaphor,* the coauthor of *European Art in the Victoria and Albert Museum,* and the translator of Paolo Prodi's *The Papal Prince.*

The University of Chicago Press, Chicago 60637
The University of Chicago Press, Ltd., London

Printed in the United States of America
17 16 15 14 13 12 11 10 09 08 1 2 3 4 5
ISBN-13: 978-0-226-11398-2 (cloth)
ISBN-13: 978-0-226-11400-2 (paper)
ISBN-10: 0-226-11398-1 (cloth)
ISBN-10: 0-226-11400-7 (paper)

The University of Chicago Press gratefully acknowledges the generous support of James E. Rabil, in memory of Scottie W. Rabil, toward the publication of this book.

Library of Congress Cataloging-in-Publication Data
Who is Mary? : three early modern women on the idea of the Virgin Mary / edited and translated by Susan Haskins.
p. cm. — (The other voice in early modern Europe)
Includes bibliographical references and index.
ISBN-13: 978-0-226-11398-2 ((cloth) : alk. paper)
ISBN-13: 978-0-226-11400-2 ((paper) : alk. paper)
ISBN-10: 0-226-11398-1 ((cloth) : alk. paper)
ISBN-10: 0-226-11400-7 ((paper) : alk. paper) 1. Mary, Blessed Virgin, Saint. 2. Colonna, Vittoria, 1492–1547. 3. Matraini, Chiara, 1515–1604? 4. Marinella, Lucrezia, 1571–1653. I. Haskins, Susan. II. Colonna, Vittoria, 1492–1547. Pianto della Marchesa di Pescara sopra la Passione di Christo. English. 2008. III. Matraini, Chiara, 1515–1604? Breve discorso sopra la vita e laude della beatiss. verg. e madre del figlivol di Dio. English. 2008. IV. Marinella, Lucrezia, 1571–1653. Vita di Maria Vergine Imperatrice dell'universo. English. 2008. V. Series.
BT604.W48 2008
232.91—dc22 2008038941

♾ The paper used in this publication meets the minimum requirements of the American National Standard for Information Sciences—Permanence of Paper for Printed Library Materials, ANSI Z39.48-1992.

CONTENTS

ACKNOWLEDGMENTS

I am extremely grateful to all those whose expertise I was able to turn to while preparing this volume, in particular Letizia Panizza for her advice and support, and for reading the final drafts of all the texts and for her suggestions as to where more felicitous phrasing and clarifications might be helpful. Alberta Bamonte was also extremely generous with her time, as were Adele Airoldi, Jane Bridgeman, Virginia Cox, and Alessandro Scafi. I should also like to thank Eleonora Carinci for her help. The report of the unknown reader of the manuscript was invaluable in every way. Nicholas Pickwoad unfailingly helped me throughout. I should finally also like to extend my thanks to Al Rabil for his support and encouragement, particularly in the last stages of my labors, and for his great help in securing funding for this project. My thanks also go to the National Endowment for the Humanities for their very generous grant, which enabled me to work on this volume.

Susan Haskins, London, February 2008

THE OTHER VOICE IN EARLY MODERN EUROPE: INTRODUCTION TO THE SERIES

Margaret L. King and Albert Rabil Jr.

THE OLD VOICE AND THE OTHER VOICE

In western Europe and the United States, women are nearing equality in the professions, in business, and in politics. Most enjoy access to education, reproductive rights, and autonomy in financial affairs. Issues vital to women are on the public agenda: equal pay, child care, domestic abuse, breast cancer research, and curricular revision with an eye to the inclusion of women.

These recent achievements have their origins in things women (and some male supporters) said for the first time about six hundred years ago. Theirs is thc "other voice," in contradistinction to the "first voice," the voice of the educated men who created Western culture. Coincident with a general reshaping of European culture in the period 1300–1700 (called the Renaissance or early modern period), questions of female equality and opportunity were raised that still resound and are still unresolved.

The other voice emerged against the backdrop of a three-thousand-year history of the derogation of women rooted in the civilizations related to Western culture: Hebrew, Greek, Roman, and Christian. Negative attitudes toward women inherited from these traditions pervaded the intellectual, medical, legal, religious, and social systems that developed during the European Middle Ages.

The following pages describe the traditional, overwhelmingly male views of women's nature inherited by early modern Europeans and the new tradition that the "other voice" called into being to begin to challenge reigning assumptions. This review should serve as a framework for understanding the texts published in the series The Other Voice in Early Modern Europe. Introductions specific to each text and author follow this essay in all the volumes of the series.

TRADITIONAL VIEWS OF WOMEN, 500 B.C.E.–1500 C.E.

Embedded in the philosophical and medical theories of the ancient Greeks were perceptions of the female as inferior to the male in both mind and body. Similarly, the structure of civil legislation inherited from the ancient Romans was biased against women, and the views on women developed by Christian thinkers out of the Hebrew Bible and the Christian New Testament were negative and disabling. Literary works composed in the vernacular of ordinary people, and widely recited or read, conveyed these negative assumptions. The social networks within which most women lived—those of the family and the institutions of the Roman Catholic Church—were shaped by this negative tradition and sharply limited the areas in which women might act in and upon the world.

GREEK PHILOSOPHY AND FEMALE NATURE. Greek biology assumed that women were inferior to men and defined them as merely childbearers and housekeepers. This view was authoritatively expressed in the works of the philosopher Aristotle.

Aristotle thought in dualities. He considered action superior to inaction, form (the inner design or structure of any object) superior to matter, completion to incompletion, possession to deprivation. In each of these dualities, he associated the male principle with the superior quality and the female with the inferior. "The male principle in nature," he argued, "is associated with active, formative and perfected characteristics, while the female is passive, material and deprived, desiring the male in order to become complete."[1] Men are always identified with virile qualities, such as judgment, courage, and stamina, and women with their opposites—irrationality, cowardice, and weakness.

The masculine principle was considered superior even in the womb. The man's semen, Aristotle believed, created the form of a new human creature, while the female body contributed only matter. (The existence of the ovum, and with it the other facts of human embryology, was not established until the seventeenth century.) Although the later Greek physician Galen believed there was a female component in generation, contributed by "female semen," the followers of both Aristotle and Galen saw the male role in human generation as more active and more important.

1. Aristotle, *Physics* 1.9.192a20–24, in *The Complete Works of Aristotle*, ed. Jonathan Barnes, rev. Oxford trans., 2 vols. (Princeton, 1984), 1:328.

In the Aristotelian view, the male principle sought always to reproduce itself. The creation of a female was always a mistake, therefore, resulting from an imperfect act of generation. Every female born was considered a "defective" or "mutilated" male (as Aristotle's terminology has variously been translated), a "monstrosity" of nature.[2]

For Greek theorists, the biology of males and females was the key to their psychology. The female was softer and more docile, more apt to be despondent, querulous, and deceitful. Being incomplete, moreover, she craved sexual fulfillment in intercourse with a male. The male was intellectual, active, and in control of his passions.

These psychological polarities derived from the theory that the universe consisted of four elements (earth, fire, air, and water), expressed in human bodies as four "humors" (black bile, yellow bile, blood, and phlegm) considered, respectively, dry, hot, damp, and cold and corresponding to mental states ("melancholic," "choleric," "sanguine," "phlegmatic"). In this scheme the male, sharing the principles of earth and fire, was dry and hot; the female, sharing the principles of air and water, was cold and damp.

Female psychology was further affected by her dominant organ, the uterus (womb), *hystera* in Greek. The passions generated by the womb made women lustful, deceitful, talkative, irrational, indeed—when these affects were in excess—"hysterical."

Aristotle's biology also had social and political consequences. If the male principle was superior and the female inferior, then in the household, as in the state, men should rule and women must be subordinate. That hierarchy did not rule out the companionship of husband and wife, whose cooperation was necessary for the welfare of children and the preservation of property. Such mutuality supported male preeminence.

Aristotle's teacher Plato suggested a different possibility: that men and women might possess the same virtues. The setting for this proposal is the imaginary and ideal Republic that Plato sketches in a dialogue of that name. Here, for a privileged elite capable of leading wisely, all distinctions of class and wealth dissolve, as, consequently, do those of gender. Without households or property, as Plato constructs his ideal society, there is no need for the subordination of women. Women may therefore be educated to the same level as men to assume leadership. Plato's Republic remained imaginary, however. In real societies, the subordination of women remained the norm and the prescription.

2. Aristotle, *Generation of Animals* 2.3.737a27–28, in *The Complete Works,* 1: 1144.

The views of women inherited from the Greek philosophical tradition became the basis for medieval thought. In the thirteenth century, the supreme Scholastic philosopher Thomas Aquinas, among others, still echoed Aristotle's views of human reproduction, of male and female personalities, and of the preeminent male role in the social hierarchy.

ROMAN LAW AND THE FEMALE CONDITION. Roman law, like Greek philosophy, underlay medieval thought and shaped medieval society. The ancient belief that adult property-owning men should administer households and make decisions affecting the community at large is the very fulcrum of Roman law.

About 450 B.C.E., during Rome's republican era, the community's customary law was recorded (legendarily) on twelve tablets erected in the city's central forum. It was later elaborated by professional jurists whose activity increased in the imperial era, when much new legislation was passed, especially on issues affecting family and inheritance. This growing, changing body of laws was eventually codified in the *Corpus of Civil Law* under the direction of the emperor Justinian, generations after the empire ceased to be ruled from Rome. That *Corpus,* read and commented on by medieval scholars from the eleventh century on, inspired the legal systems of most of the cities and kingdoms of Europe.

Laws regarding dowries, divorce, and inheritance pertain primarily to women. Since those laws aimed to maintain and preserve property, the women concerned were those from the property-owning minority. Their subordination to male family members points to the even greater subordination of lower-class and slave women, about whom the laws speak little.

In the early republic, the *paterfamilias,* or "father of the family," possessed *patria potestas,* "paternal power." The term *pater,* "father," in both these cases does not necessarily mean biological father but denotes the head of a household. The father was the person who owned the household's property and, indeed, its human members. The *paterfamilias* had absolute power—including the power, rarely exercised, of life or death—over his wife, his children, and his slaves, as much as his cattle.

Male children could be "emancipated," an act that granted legal autonomy and the right to own property. Those over fourteen could be emancipated by a special grant from the father or automatically by their father's death. But females could never be emancipated; instead, they passed from the authority of their father to that of a husband or, if widowed or orphaned while still unmarried, to a guardian or tutor.

Marriage in its traditional form placed the woman under her husband's authority, or *manus*. He could divorce her on grounds of adultery, drinking wine, or stealing from the household, but she could not divorce him. She could neither possess property in her own right nor bequeath any to her children upon her death. When her husband died, the household property passed not to her but to his male heirs. And when her father died, she had no claim to any family inheritance, which was directed to her brothers or more remote male relatives. The effect of these laws was to exclude women from civil society, itself based on property ownership.

In the later republican and imperial periods, these rules were significantly modified. Women rarely married according to the traditional form. The practice of "free" marriage allowed a woman to remain under her father's authority, to possess property given her by her father (most frequently the "dowry," recoverable from the husband's household on his death), and to inherit from her father. She could also bequeath property to her own children and divorce her husband, just as he could divorce her.

Despite this greater freedom, women still suffered enormous disability under Roman law. Heirs could belong only to the father's side, never the mother's. Moreover, although she could bequeath her property to her children, she could not establish a line of succession in doing so. A woman was "the beginning and end of her own family," said the jurist Ulpian. Moreover, women could play no public role. They could not hold public office, represent anyone in a legal case, or even witness a will. Women had only a private existence and no public personality.

The dowry system, the guardian, women's limited ability to transmit wealth, and total political disability are all features of Roman law adopted by the medieval communities of western Europe, although modified according to local customary laws.

CHRISTIAN DOCTRINE AND WOMEN'S PLACE. The Hebrew Bible and the Christian New Testament authorized later writers to limit women to the realm of the family and to burden them with the guilt of original sin. The passages most fruitful for this purpose were the creation narratives in Genesis and sentences from the Epistles defining women's role within the Christian family and community.

Each of the first two chapters of Genesis contains a creation narrative. In the first "God created man in his own image, in the image of God he created him; male and female he created them" (Gn 1:27). In the second, God created Eve from Adam's rib (2:21–23). Christian theologians relied principally on Genesis 2 for their understanding of the relation between man and woman, interpreting the creation of Eve from Adam as proof of her subordination to him.

The creation story in Genesis 2 leads to that of the temptations in Genesis 3: of Eve by the wily serpent and of Adam by Eve. As read by Christian theologians from Tertullian to Thomas Aquinas, the narrative made Eve responsible for the Fall and its consequences. She instigated the act; she deceived her husband; she suffered the greater punishment. Her disobedience made it necessary for Jesus to be incarnated and to die on the cross. From the pulpit, moralists and preachers for centuries conveyed to women the guilt that they bore for original sin.

The Epistles offered advice to early Christians on building communities of the faithful. Among the matters to be regulated was the place of women. Paul offered views favorable to women in Galatians 3:28: "There is neither Jew nor Greek, there is neither slave nor free, there is neither male nor female; for you are all one in Christ Jesus." Paul also referred to women as his coworkers and placed them on a par with himself and his male coworkers (Phlm 4:2–3; Rom 16:1–3; 1 Cor 16:19). Elsewhere, Paul limited women's possibilities: "But I want you to understand that the head of every man is Christ, the head of a woman is her husband, and the head of Christ is God" (1 Cor 11:3).

Biblical passages by later writers (although attributed to Paul) enjoined women to forgo jewels, expensive clothes, and elaborate coiffures; and they forbade women to "teach or have authority over men," telling them to "learn in silence with all submissiveness" as is proper for one responsible for sin, consoling them, however, with the thought that they will be saved through childbearing (1 Tm 2:9–15). Other texts among the later Epistles defined women as the weaker sex and emphasized their subordination to their husbands (1 Pt 3:7; Col 3:18; Eph 5:22–23).

These passages from the New Testament became the arsenal employed by theologians of the early church to transmit negative attitudes toward women to medieval Christian culture—above all, Tertullian (*On the Apparel of Women*), Jerome (*Against Jovinian*), and Augustine (*The Literal Meaning of Genesis*).

THE IMAGE OF WOMEN IN MEDIEVAL LITERATURE. The philosophical, legal, and religious traditions born in antiquity formed the basis of the medieval intellectual synthesis wrought by trained thinkers, mostly clerics, writing in Latin and based largely in universities. The vernacular literary tradition that developed alongside the learned tradition also spoke about female nature and women's roles. Medieval stories, poems, and epics also portrayed women negatively—as lustful and deceitful—while praising good housekeepers and loyal wives as replicas of the Virgin Mary or the female saints and martyrs.

There is an exception in the movement of "courtly love" that evolved in southern France from the twelfth century. Courtly love was the erotic love between a nobleman and noblewoman, the latter usually superior in social rank. It was always adulterous. From the conventions of courtly love derive modern Western notions of romantic love. The tradition has had an impact disproportionate to its size, for it affected only a tiny elite, and very few women. The exaltation of the female lover probably does not reflect a higher evaluation of women or a step toward their sexual liberation. More likely it gives expression to the social and sexual tensions besetting the knightly class at a specific historical juncture.

The literary fashion of courtly love was on the wane by the thirteenth century, when the widely read *Romance of the Rose* was composed in French by two authors of significantly different dispositions. Guillaume de Lorris composed the initial four thousand verses about 1235, and Jean de Meun added about seventeen thousand verses—more than four times the original—about 1265.

The fragment composed by Guillaume de Lorris stands squarely in the tradition of courtly love. Here the poet, in a dream, is admitted into a walled garden where he finds a magic fountain in which a rosebush is reflected. He longs to pick one rose, but the thorns prevent his doing so, even as he is wounded by arrows from the god of love, whose commands he agrees to obey. The rest of this part of the poem recounts the poet's unsuccessful efforts to pluck the rose.

The longer part of the *Romance* by Jean de Meun also describes a dream. But here allegorical characters give long didactic speeches, providing a social satire on a variety of themes, some pertaining to women. Love is an anxious and tormented state, the poem explains: women are greedy and manipulative, marriage is miserable, beautiful women are lustful, ugly ones cease to please, and a chaste woman is as rare as a black swan.

Shortly after Jean de Meun completed *The Romance of the Rose,* Mathéolus penned his *Lamentations,* a long Latin diatribe against marriage translated into French about a century later. The *Lamentations* sum up medieval attitudes toward women and provoked the important response by Christine de Pizan in her *Book of the City of Ladies.*

In 1355, Giovanni Boccaccio wrote *Il Corbaccio,* another antifeminist manifesto, although ironically by an author whose other works pioneered new directions in Renaissance thought. The former husband of his lover appears to Boccaccio, condemning his unmoderated lust and detailing the defects of women. Boccaccio concedes at the end "how much men naturally surpass women in nobility" and is cured of his desires.[3]

WOMEN'S ROLES: THE FAMILY. The negative perceptions of women expressed in the intellectual tradition are also implicit in the actual roles that women played in European society. Assigned to subordinate positions in the household and the church, they were barred from significant participation in public life.

Medieval European households, like those in antiquity and in non-Western civilizations, were headed by males. It was the male serf (or peasant), feudal lord, town merchant, or citizen who was polled or taxed or succeeded to an inheritance or had any acknowledged public role, although his wife or widow could stand as a temporary surrogate. From about 1100, the position of property-holding males was further enhanced: inheritance was confined to the male, or agnate, line—with depressing consequences for women.

A wife never fully belonged to her husband's family, nor was she a daughter to her father's family. She left her father's house young to marry whomever her parents chose. Her dowry was managed by her husband, and at her death it normally passed to her children by him.

A married woman's life was occupied nearly constantly with cycles of pregnancy, childbearing, and lactation. Women bore children through all the years of their fertility, and many died in childbirth. They were also responsible for raising young children up to six or seven. In the propertied classes that responsibility was shared, since it was common for a wet nurse to take over breast-feeding and for servants to perform other chores.

Women trained their daughters in the household duties appropriate to their status, nearly always tasks associated with textiles: spinning, weaving, sewing, embroidering. Their sons were sent out of the house as apprentices or students, or their training was assumed by fathers in later childhood and adolescence. On the death of her husband, a woman's children became the responsibility of his family. She generally did not take "his" children with

3. Giovanni Boccaccio, *The Corbaccio, or The Labyrinth of Love,* trans. and ed. Anthony K. Cassell, rev. ed. (Binghamton, N.Y., 1993), 71.

her to a new marriage or back to her father's house, except sometimes in the artisan classes.

Women also worked. Rural peasants performed farm chores, merchant wives often practiced their husbands' trades, the unmarried daughters of the urban poor worked as servants or prostitutes. All wives produced or embellished textiles and did the housekeeping, while wealthy ones managed servants. These labors were unpaid or poorly paid but often contributed substantially to family wealth.

WOMEN'S ROLES: THE CHURCH. Membership in a household, whether a father's or a husband's, meant for women a lifelong subordination to others. In western Europe, the Roman Catholic Church offered an alternative to the career of wife and mother. A woman could enter a convent, parallel in function to the monasteries for men that evolved in the early Christian centuries.

In the convent, a woman pledged herself to a celibate life, lived according to strict community rules, and worshiped daily. Often the convent offered training in Latin, allowing some women to become considerable scholars and authors as well as scribes, artists, and musicians. For women who chose the conventual life, the benefits could be enormous, but for numerous others placed in convents by paternal choice, the life could be restrictive and burdensome.

The conventual life declined as an alternative for women as the modern age approached. Reformed monastic institutions resisted responsibility for related female orders. The church increasingly restricted female institutional life by insisting on closer male supervision.

Women often sought other options. Some joined the communities of laywomen that sprang up spontaneously in the thirteenth century in the urban zones of western Europe, especially in Flanders and Italy. Some joined the heretical movements that flourished in late medieval Christendom, whose anticlerical and often antifamily positions particularly appealed to women. In these communities, some women were acclaimed as "holy women" or "saints," whereas others often were condemned as frauds or heretics.

In all, although the options offered to women by the church were sometimes less than satisfactory, they were sometimes richly rewarding. After 1520, the convent remained an option only in Roman Catholic territories. Protestantism engendered an ideal of marriage as a heroic endeavor and appeared to place husband and wife on a more equal footing. Sermons and treatises, however, still called for female subordination and obedience.

THE OTHER VOICE, 1300–1700

When the modern era opened, European culture was so firmly structured by a framework of negative attitudes toward women that to dismantle it was a monumental labor. The process began as part of a larger cultural movement that entailed the critical reexamination of ideas inherited from the ancient and medieval past. The humanists launched that critical reexamination.

THE HUMANIST FOUNDATION. Originating in Italy in the fourteenth century, humanism quickly became the dominant intellectual movement in Europe. Spreading in the sixteenth century from Italy to the rest of Europe, it fueled the literary, scientific, and philosophical movements of the era and laid the basis for the eighteenth-century Enlightenment.

Humanists regarded the Scholastic philosophy of medieval universities as out of touch with the realities of urban life. They found in the rhetorical discourse of classical Rome a language adapted to civic life and public speech. They learned to read, speak, and write classical Latin and, eventually, classical Greek. They founded schools to teach others to do so, establishing the pattern for elementary and secondary education for the next three hundred years.

In the service of complex government bureaucracies, humanists employed their skills to write eloquent letters, deliver public orations, and formulate public policy. They developed new scripts for copying manuscripts and used the new printing press to disseminate texts, for which they created methods of critical editing.

Humanism was a movement led by males who accepted the evaluation of women in ancient texts and generally shared the misogynist perceptions of their culture. (Female humanists, as we will see, did not.) Yet humanism also opened the door to a reevaluation of the nature and capacity of women. By calling authors, texts, and ideas into question, it made possible the fundamental rereading of the whole intellectual tradition that was required in order to free women from cultural prejudice and social subordination.

A DIFFERENT CITY. The other voice first appeared when, after so many centuries, the accumulation of misogynist concepts evoked a response from a capable female defender: Christine de Pizan (1365–1431). Introducing her *Book of the City of Ladies* (1405), she described how she was affected by reading Mathéolus's *Lamentations*: "Just the sight of this book . . . made me wonder how it happened that so many different men . . . are so inclined to express both in speaking and in their treatises and writings so many wicked insults about women and their behavior."[4] These statements impelled her to detest herself "and the entire feminine sex, as though we were monstrosities in nature."[5]

The rest of *The Book of the City of Ladies* presents a justification of the female sex and a vision of an ideal community of women. A pioneer, she has received the message of female inferiority and rejected it. From the fourteenth to the seventeenth century, a huge body of literature accumulated that responded to the dominant tradition.

The result was a literary explosion consisting of works by both men and women, in Latin and in the vernaculars: works enumerating the achievements of notable women; works rebutting the main accusations made against women; works arguing for the equal education of men and women; works defining and redefining women's proper role in the family, at court, in public; works describing women's lives and experiences. Recent monographs and articles have begun to hint at the great range of this movement, involving probably several thousand titles. The protofeminism of these "other voices" constitutes a significant fraction of the literary product of the early modern era.

THE CATALOGS. About 1365, the same Boccaccio whose *Corbaccio* rehearses the usual charges against female nature wrote another work, *Concerning Famous Women.* A humanist treatise drawing on classical texts, it praised 106 notable women: ninety-eight of them from pagan Greek and Roman antiquity, one (Eve) from the Bible, and seven from the medieval religious and cultural tradition; his book helped make all readers aware of a sex normally condemned or forgotten. Boccaccio's outlook nevertheless was unfriendly to women, for it singled out for praise those women who possessed the traditional virtues of chastity, silence, and obedience. Women who were active in the public realm—for example, rulers and warriors—were depicted as usually being lascivious and as suffering terrible punishments for entering the masculine sphere. Women were his subject, but Boccaccio's standard remained male.

Christine de Pizan's *Book of the City of Ladies* contains a second catalog, one responding specifically to Boccaccio's. Whereas Boccaccio portrays female virtue as exceptional, she depicts it as universal. Many women in his-

4. Christine de Pizan, *The Book of the City of Ladies,* trans. Earl Jeffrey Richards, foreword by Marina Warner (New York, 1982), 1.1.1, pp. 3–4.

5. Ibid., 1.1.1–2, p. 5.

tory were leaders, or remained chaste despite the lascivious approaches of men, or were visionaries and brave martyrs.

The work of Boccaccio inspired a series of catalogs of illustrious women of the biblical, classical, Christian, and local pasts, among them Filippo da Bergamo's *Of Illustrious Women*, Pierre de Brantôme's *Lives of Illustrious Women*, Pierre Le Moyne's *Gallerie of Heroic Women*, and Pietro Paolo de Ribera's *Immortal Triumphs and Heroic Enterprises of 845 Women*. Whatever their embedded prejudices, these works drove home to the public the possibility of female excellence.

THE DEBATE. At the same time, many questions remained: Could a woman be virtuous? Could she perform noteworthy deeds? Was she even, strictly speaking, of the same human species as men? These questions were debated over four centuries, in French, German, Italian, Spanish, and English, by authors male and female, among Catholics, Protestants, and Jews, in ponderous volumes and breezy pamphlets. The whole literary genre has been called the *querelle des femmes*, the "woman question."

The opening volley of this battle occurred in the first years of the fifteenth century, in a literary debate sparked by Christine de Pizan. She exchanged letters critical of Jean de Meun's contribution to *The Romance of the Rose* with two French royal secretaries, Jean de Montreuil and Gontier Col. When the matter became public, Jean Gerson, one of Europe's leading theologians, supported de Pizan's arguments against de Meun, for the moment silencing the opposition.

The debate resurfaced repeatedly over the next two hundred years. *The Triumph of Women* (1438) by Juan Rodríguez de la Camara (or Juan Rodríguez del Padron) struck a new note by presenting arguments for the superiority of women to men. *The Champion of Women* (1440–42) by Martin Le Franc addresses once again the negative views of women presented in *The Romance of the Rose* and offers counterevidence of female virtue and achievement.

A cameo of the debate on women is included in *The Courtier*, one of the most widely read books of the era, published by the Italian Baldassare Castiglione in 1528 and immediately translated into other European vernaculars. *The Courtier* depicts a series of evenings at the court of the duke of Urbino in which many men and some women of the highest social stratum amuse themselves by discussing a range of literary and social issues. The "woman question" is a pervasive theme throughout, and the third of its four books is devoted entirely to that issue.

In a verbal duel, Gasparo Pallavicino and Giuliano de' Medici present the main claims of the two traditions. Gasparo argues the innate inferiority of women and their inclination to vice. Only in bearing children do they profit the world. Giuliano counters that women share the same spiritual and mental capacities as men and may excel in wisdom and action. Men and women are of the same essence: just as no stone can be more perfectly a stone than another, so no human being can be more perfectly human than others, whether male or female. It was an astonishing assertion, boldly made to an audience as large as all Europe.

THE TREATISES. Humanism provided the materials for a positive counterconcept to the misogyny embedded in Scholastic philosophy and law and inherited from the Greek, Roman, and Christian pasts. A series of humanist treatises on marriage and family, on education and deportment, and on the nature of women helped construct these new perspectives.

The works by Francesco Barbaro and Leon Battista Alberti—*On Marriage* (1415) and *On the Family* (1434–37)—far from defending female equality, reasserted women's responsibility for rearing children and managing the housekeeping while being obedient, chaste, and silent. Nevertheless, they served the cause of reexamining the issue of women's nature by placing domestic issues at the center of scholarly concern and reopening the pertinent classical texts. In addition, Barbaro emphasized the companionate nature of marriage and the importance of a wife's spiritual and mental qualities for the well-being of the family.

These themes reappear in later humanist works on marriage and the education of women by Juan Luis Vives and Erasmus. Both were moderately sympathetic to the condition of women without reaching beyond the usual masculine prescriptions for female behavior.

An outlook more favorable to women characterizes the nearly unknown work *In Praise of Women* (ca. 1487) by the Italian humanist Bartolommeo Goggio. In addition to providing a catalog of illustrious women, Goggio argued that male and female are the same in essence, but that women (reworking the Adam and Eve narrative from quite a new angle) are actually superior. In the same vein, the Italian humanist Mario Equicola asserted the spiritual equality of men and women in *On Women* (1501). In 1525, Galeazzo Flavio Capra (or Capella) published his work *On the Excellence and Dignity of Women.* This humanist tradition of treatises defending the worthiness of women culminates in the work of Henricus Cornelius Agrippa *On the Nobility and Preeminence of the Female Sex.* No work by a male humanist more succinctly or explicitly presents the case for female dignity.

THE WITCH BOOKS. While humanists grappled with the issues pertaining to women and family, other learned men turned their attention to what they perceived as a very great problem: witches. Witch-hunting manuals, explorations of the witch phenomenon, and even defenses of witches are not at first glance pertinent to the tradition of the other voice. But they do relate in this way: most accused witches were women. The hostility aroused by supposed witch activity is comparable to the hostility aroused by women. The evil deeds the victims of the hunt were charged with were exaggerations of the vices to which, many believed, all women were prone.

The connection between the witch accusation and the hatred of women is explicit in the notorious witch-hunting manual *The Hammer of Witches* (1486) by two Dominican inquisitors, Heinrich Krämer and Jacob Sprenger. Here the inconstancy, deceitfulness, and lustfulness traditionally associated with women are depicted in exaggerated form as the core features of witch behavior. These traits inclined women to make a bargain with the devil—sealed by sexual intercourse—by which they acquired unholy powers. Such bizarre claims, far from being rejected by rational men, were broadcast by intellectuals. The German Ulrich Molitur, the Frenchman Nicolas Rémy, and the Italian Stefano Guazzo all coolly informed the public of sinister orgies and midnight pacts with the devil. The celebrated French jurist, historian, and political philosopher Jean Bodin argued that because women were especially prone to diabolism, regular legal procedures could properly be suspended in order to try those accused of this "exceptional crime."

A few experts such as the physician Johann Weyer, a student of Agrippa's, raised their voices in protest. In 1563, he explained the witch phenomenon thus, without discarding belief in diabolism: the devil deluded foolish old women afflicted by melancholia, causing them to believe they had magical powers. Weyer's rational skepticism, which had good credibility in the community of the learned, worked to revise the conventional views of women and witchcraft.

WOMEN'S WORKS. To the many categories of works produced on the question of women's worth must be added nearly all works written by women. A woman writing was in herself a statement of women's claim to dignity.

Only a few women wrote anything before the dawn of the modern era, for three reasons. First, they rarely received the education that would enable them to write. Second, they were not admitted to the public roles—as administrator, bureaucrat, lawyer or notary, or university professor—in which they might gain knowledge of the kinds of things the literate public thought worth writing about. Third, the culture imposed silence on women, considering speaking out a form of unchastity. Given these conditions, it is remarkable that any women wrote. Those who did before the fourteenth century were almost always nuns or religious women whose isolation made their pronouncements more acceptable.

From the fourteenth century on, the volume of women's writings rose. Women continued to write devotional literature, although not always as cloistered nuns. They also wrote diaries, often intended as keepsakes for their children; books of advice to their sons and daughters; letters to family members and friends; and family memoirs, in a few cases elaborate enough to be considered histories.

A few women wrote works directly concerning the "woman question," and some of these, such as the humanists Isotta Nogarola, Cassandra Fedele, Laura Cereta, and Olympia Morata, were highly trained. A few were professional writers, living by the income of their pens; the very first among them was Christine de Pizan, noteworthy in this context as in so many others. In addition to *The Book of the City of Ladies* and her critiques of *The Romance of the Rose,* she wrote *The Treasure of the City of Ladies* (a guide to social decorum for women), an advice book for her son, much courtly verse, and a full-scale history of the reign of King Charles V of France.

WOMEN PATRONS. Women who did not themselves write but encouraged others to do so boosted the development of an alternative tradition. Highly placed women patrons supported authors, artists, musicians, poets, and learned men. Such patrons, drawn mostly from the Italian elites and the courts of northern Europe, figure disproportionately as the dedicatees of the important works of early feminism.

For a start, it might be noted that the catalogs of Boccaccio and Alvaro de Luna were dedicated to the Florentine noblewoman Andrea Acciaiuoli and to Doña María, first wife of King Juan II of Castile, while the French translation of Boccaccio's work was commissioned by Anne of Brittany, wife of King Charles VIII of France. The humanist treatises of Goggio, Equicola, Vives, and Agrippa were dedicated, respectively, to Eleanora of Aragon, wife of Ercole I d'Este, duke of Ferrara; to Margherita Cantelma of Mantua; to Catherine of Aragon, wife of King Henry VIII of England; and to Margaret, Duchess of Austria and regent of the Netherlands. As late as 1696, Mary Astell's *Serious Proposal to the Ladies, for the Advancement of Their True and Greatest Interest* was dedicated to Princess Anne of Denmark.

These authors presumed that their efforts would be welcome to female patrons, or they may have written at the bidding of those patrons. Silent themselves, perhaps even unresponsive, these loftily placed women helped shape the tradition of the other voice.

THE ISSUES. The literary forms and patterns in which the tradition of the other voice presented itself have now been sketched. It remains to highlight the major issues around which this tradition crystallizes. In brief, there are four problems to which our authors return again and again, in plays and catalogs, in verse and letters, in treatises and dialogues, in every language: the problem of chastity, the problem of power, the problem of speech, and the problem of knowledge. Of these the greatest, preconditioning the others, is the problem of chastity.

THE PROBLEM OF CHASTITY. In traditional European culture, as in those of antiquity and others around the globe, chastity was perceived as woman's quintessential virtue—in contrast to courage, or generosity, or leadership, or rationality, seen as virtues characteristic of men. Opponents of women charged them with insatiable lust. Women themselves and their defenders—without disputing the validity of the standard—responded that women were capable of chastity.

The requirement of chastity kept women at home, silenced them, isolated them, left them in ignorance. It was the source of all other impediments. Why was it so important to the society of men, of whom chastity was not required, and who more often than not considered it their right to violate the chastity of any woman they encountered?

Female chastity ensured the continuity of the male-headed household. If a man's wife was not chaste, he could not be sure of the legitimacy of his offspring. If they were not his and they acquired his property, it was not his household, but some other man's, that had endured. If his daughter was not chaste, she could not be transferred to another man's household as his wife, and he was dishonored.

The whole system of the integrity of the household and the transmission of property was bound up in female chastity. Such a requirement pertained only to property-owning classes, of course. Poor women could not expect to maintain their chastity, least of all if they were in contact with high-status men to whom all women but those of their own household were prey.

In Catholic Europe, the requirement of chastity was further buttressed by moral and religious imperatives. Original sin was inextricably linked with the sexual act. Virginity was seen as heroic virtue, far more impressive than, say, the avoidance of idleness or greed. Monasticism, the cultural institution that dominated medieval Europe for centuries, was grounded in the renunciation of the flesh. The Catholic reform of the eleventh century imposed a similar standard on all the clergy and a heightened awareness of sexual requirements on all the laity. Although men were asked to be chaste, female unchastity was much worse: it led to the devil, as Eve had led mankind to sin.

To such requirements, women and their defenders protested their innocence. Furthermore, following the example of holy women who had escaped the requirements of family and sought the religious life, some women began to conceive of female communities as alternatives both to family and to the cloister. Christine de Pizan's city of ladies was such a community. Moderata Fonte and Mary Astell envisioned others. The luxurious salons of the French *précieuses* of the seventeenth century, or the comfortable English drawing rooms of the next, may have been born of the same impulse. Here women not only might escape, if briefly, the subordinate position that life in the family entailed but might also make claims to power, exercise their capacity for speech, and display their knowledge.

THE PROBLEM OF POWER. Women were excluded from power: the whole cultural tradition insisted on it. Only men were citizens, only men bore arms, only men could be chiefs or lords or kings. There were exceptions that did not disprove the rule, when wives or widows or mothers took the place of men, awaiting their return or the maturation of a male heir. A woman who attempted to rule in her own right was perceived as an anomaly, a monster, at once a deformed woman and an insufficient male, sexually confused and consequently unsafe.

The association of such images with women who held or sought power explains some otherwise odd features of early modern culture. Queen Elizabeth I of England, one of the few women to hold full regal authority in European history, played with such male/female images—positive ones, of course—in representing herself to her subjects. She was a prince, and manly, even though she was female. She was also (she claimed) virginal, a condition absolutely essential if she was to avoid the attacks of her opponents. Catherine de' Medici, who ruled France as widow and regent for her sons, also adopted such imagery in defining her position. She chose as one symbol the figure of Artemisia, an androgynous ancient warrior-heroine who combined a female persona with masculine powers.

Power in a woman, without such sexual imagery, seems to have been indigestible by the culture. A rare note was struck by the Englishman Sir Thomas Elyot in his *Defence of Good Women* (1540), justifying both women's participation in civic life and their prowess in arms. The old tune was sung by the Scots reformer John Knox in his *First Blast of the Trumpet against the Mon-*

strous Regiment of Women (1558); for him rule by women, defects in nature, was a hideous contradiction in terms.

The confused sexuality of the imagery of female potency was not reserved for rulers. Any woman who excelled was likely to be called an Amazon, recalling the self-mutilated warrior women of antiquity who repudiated all men, gave up their sons, and raised only their daughters. She was often said to have "exceeded her sex" or to have possessed "masculine virtue"—as the very fact of conspicuous excellence conferred masculinity even on the female subject. The catalogs of notable women often showed those female heroes dressed in armor, armed to the teeth, like men. Amazonian heroines romp through the epics of the age—Ariosto's *Orlando Furioso* (1532) and Spenser's *Faerie Queene* (1590–1609). Excellence in a woman was perceived as a claim for power, and power was reserved for the masculine realm. A woman who possessed either one was masculinized and lost title to her own female identity.

THE PROBLEM OF SPEECH. Just as power had a sexual dimension when it was claimed by women, so did speech. A good woman spoke little. Excessive speech was an indication of unchastity. By speech, women seduced men. Eve had lured Adam into sin by her speech. Accused witches were commonly accused of having spoken abusively, or irrationally, or simply too much. As enlightened a figure as Francesco Barbaro insisted on silence in a woman, which he linked to her perfect unanimity with her husband's will and her unblemished virtue (her chastity). Another Italian humanist, Leonardo Bruni, in advising a noblewoman on her studies, barred her not from speech but from public speaking. That was reserved for men.

Related to the problem of speech was that of costume—another, if silent, form of self-expression. Assigned the task of pleasing men as their primary occupation, elite women often tended toward elaborate costume, hairdressing, and the use of cosmetics. Clergy and secular moralists alike condemned these practices. The appropriate function of costume and adornment was to announce the status of a woman's husband or father. Any further indulgence in adornment was akin to unchastity.

THE PROBLEM OF KNOWLEDGE. When the Italian noblewoman Isotta Nogarola had begun to attain a reputation as a humanist, she was accused of incest—a telling instance of the association of learning in women with unchastity. That chilling association inclined any woman who was educated to deny that she was or to make exaggerated claims of heroic chastity.

If educated women were pursued with suspicions of sexual misconduct, women seeking an education faced an even more daunting obstacle: the assumption that women were by nature incapable of learning, that reasoning was a particularly masculine ability. Just as they proclaimed their chastity, women and their defenders insisted on their capacity for learning. The major work by a male writer on female education—that by Juan Luis Vives, *On the Education of a Christian Woman* (1523)—granted female capacity for intellection but still argued that a woman's whole education was to be shaped around the requirement of chastity and a future within the household. Female writers of the following generations—Marie de Gournay in France, Anna Maria van Schurman in Holland, and Mary Astell in England—began to envision other possibilities.

The pioneers of female education were the Italian women humanists who managed to attain a literacy in Latin and a knowledge of classical and Christian literature equivalent to that of prominent men. Their works implicitly and explicitly raise questions about women's social roles, defining problems that beset women attempting to break out of the cultural limits that had bound them. Like Christine de Pizan, who achieved an advanced education through her father's tutoring and her own devices, their bold questioning makes clear the importance of training. Only when women were educated to the same standard as male leaders would they be able to raise that other voice and insist on their dignity as human beings morally, intellectually, and legally equal to men.

THE OTHER VOICE. The other voice, a voice of protest, was mostly female, but it was also male. It spoke in the vernaculars and in Latin, in treatises and dialogues, in plays and poetry, in letters and diaries, and in pamphlets. It battered at the wall of prejudice that encircled women and raised a banner announcing its claims. The female was equal (or even superior) to the male in essential nature—moral, spiritual, and intellectual. Women were capable of higher education, of holding positions of power and influence in the public realm, and of speaking and writing persuasively. The last bastion of masculine supremacy, centered on the notions of a woman's primary domestic responsibility and the requirement of female chastity, was not as yet assaulted—although visions of productive female communities as alternatives to the family indicated an awareness of the problem.

During the period 1300–1700, the other voice remained only a voice, and one only dimly heard. It did not result—yet—in an alteration of social patterns. Indeed, to this day they have not entirely been altered. Yet the call for justice issued as long as six centuries ago by those writing in the tradition of the other voice must be recognized as the source and origin of the mature feminist tradition and of the realignment of social institutions accomplished in the modern age.

We thank the volume editors in this series, who responded with many suggestions to an earlier draft of this introduction, making it a collaborative enterprise. Many of their suggestions and criticisms have resulted in revisions of this introduction, although we remain responsible for the final product.

VOLUME EDITOR'S INTRODUCTION

THE OTHER VOICE

This introduction departs from the usual introductions to volumes in the Other Voice in Early Modern Europe series, since the present book contains not so much the writings of a particular female author but prose essays on one subject, the Virgin Mary, and the responses to the idea of her of three Italian women writers of the sixteenth and seventeenth centuries: Vittoria Colonna (1492–1547), Chiara Matraini (1515–1604), and Lucrezia Marinella (1571–1653). The three texts were written between 1540 and 1602, but even within that sixty-year span (Colonna's was published in 1557 though written in about 1540, Matraini's in 1590, and the first edition of Marinella's in 1602), approaches towards Mary changed radically. These changes were spurred on not only by the movement started in the 1530s by which the Church of Rome sought to reform its own institutions and practices, and in which both Vittoria Colonna and her friend Michelangelo Buonarotti (1475–1564) were involved, but also by the schism that took place between the Catholic Church and Protestantism after the Council of Trent (1543–65). This schism led to the Church of Rome's resurgence, the Counter-Reformation, when Catholic dogma was reasserted in response to Protestant criticisms of its beliefs and practices. Devotion to the Virgin, which was particularly encouraged by the Jesuits, was one of the strongest resources cultivated by the Counter-Reformation.

These texts are testimony to the importance of the Virgin Mary to Catholic women in Italy in the sixteenth and early seventeenth centuries. They would probably have attracted a largely female audience, and those by Chiara Matraini and Lucrezia Marinella, especially, appear to have a more female bias, even though Marinella's was dedicated to the Doge and Signoria, or Council, of Venice. (Matraini's was dedicated to her cousin, Juditta Matraini, abbess of the monastery of San Bernardo in Bologna.) Of the three writers, Colonna's somewhat austere devotion to Mary focuses on Christ in his Passion and death, while the other two present a Mary who, unlike in the gospel accounts, is constantly with Jesus throughout his life and at his death, playing a redemptive role in interceding for Christians in their passage from earth to heaven; indeed, she is a heavenly being herself, present in God's redemptive plan even before the Creation. In elaborating her role beyond that found in the canonical gospels, the authors make use of New Testament apocrypha and other noncanonical texts, texts that had been part of popular piety since the late thirteenth century and, although criticized by Church leaders, had continued to be used, particularly by laypeople. As women, the writers were not to deal with theology—the preserve of male ecclesiastics—but as laywomen, and first and foremost literary writers, they were addressing, among their audience, other laywomen, with a stress on devotion and appealing to the imagination and emotions. In so doing, they expressed their understanding of Mary as virgin, mother, miracle maker, and model for themselves and their readers. They thus contributed to "the other voice" in ways similar to those of Catholic and Protestant women in Germany, France, and Spain, whose contributions are documented in other volumes published in this series.[1]

Vittoria Colonna's presentation of Mary is a highly personal meditation by its author, a response to an image of the dead Christ lying in his mother's arms, known as the *Pietà.* Colonna dwells on Mary's emotions at her son's death and follows her mourning process. Her Mary is the humble, selfless Virgin of the gospels who is present at her son's Crucifixion and death, together with other women such as Mary Magdalen, but not with the disciples whom Mary feels should have been there, and criticizes for being absent. Mary's role in the Redemption is resumed here: as mother of the Redeemer and model of faith. It is her presence beside him, with him, through life and

1. See, for example, the Catholic writers Jeanne de Jussie (French), *The Short Chronicle* (2006); Gabrielle de Coignard (French), *Spiritual Sonnets* (2004); Cecilia Ferrazzi (Spanish), *Autobiography of an Aspiring Saint* (1996); Francisca de los Apóstoles (Spanish), *The Inquisition of Francisca* (2005); María de San José Salazar (Spanish), *Book for the Hour of Recreation* (2002); and the Jansenist Jacqueline Pascal (French), *A Rule for Children and Other Writings* (2003). Another Vittoria Colonna text, *Sonnets for Michelangelo* (2005), also appears in this series. The Protestant writers are Katharina Schütz Zell (German), *Church Mother: The Writings of a Protestant Reformer in Sixteenth-Century Germany* (2006); Marie Dentière (French), *Epistle to Marguerite de Navarre and Preface to a Sermon by John Calvin* (2004); Olympia Morata (Italian), *Olympia Morata: The Complete Writings of an Italian Heretic* (2003); and Johanna Eleonora Petersen (German), *The Life of Lady Johanna Eleonora Petersen, Written by Herself* (2005). A teaching volume including these and other (pre-Reformation) women writers has also been published as an ancillary text to the series: *Teaching the Other Voices: Women and Religion in Early Modern Europe,* ed. Margaret L. King and Albert Rabil Jr. (2007). The Other Voice in Early Modern Europe series is published by the University of Chicago Press.

at death, that gives her a redemptive role in her own right, interceding for Christians who come after her.

Chiara Matraini's "brief discourse" on the life of Mary takes her redemptive role a step further by having her be part of God's redemptive plan from before the Creation. She is the second Eve and thus the second earth from which the second, heavenly Adam (Christ) sprang. In her discussion of Adam and Eve, Matraini makes them equals in the earthly paradise, following the first account of creation in Genesis 1:26–31 rather than the second in Genesis 2:21–25; their disobedience is also a joint disobedience. In departing from the traditional view of the culpable Eve, Matraini lays the ground for Mary the "very powerful woman," the woman God promised the serpent would come to conquer evil (Genesis 3:15). She is also Wisdom (Sophia), Empress of the Universe. Matraini makes fulsome use of apocryphal texts in her image of Mary. She emphasizes the roles of Mary that might be of interest to female readers: she is a prophetess, like Elizabeth and Anna; her marriage, a symbol of the Incarnation, is a union of humankind with God; and it is through her power in instigating her son's first miracle that water is changed into wine at the marriage feast of Cana (John 2:1–11). But despite her great power Mary is humble, and thus a model for women readers. Indeed, she is so humble that it does not occur to her that it might be she who is to be the virgin mother of God. And it is through humility that she goes to the Temple for purification, though she does not need to submit to the Law that governs other women.[2] Matraini's Mary thus inculcates women with Catholic theology and practice.

Of the three works on the Virgin Mary, Lucrezia Marinella's *Life of Mary Virgin, Empress of the Universe* is the longest and written in the grandest style—appropriate, she believed, for her subject. The work's popularity is evident as it was reprinted three times following its initial publication in 1602. Marinella stresses the miraculous and marvelous in creating her epic: fictional monologues and dialogues based on the gospels or apocrypha adumbrate the New Testament story. As in Matraini, the theme of matrimony and the family is central in keeping with the Catholic Church's post-Tridentine stress on the sacrament and on family ideology. With this intent Marinella relates the story of the Virgin's conception, life, and death as a magnificent narrative replete with the miracles and marvels its heroine undergoes. To an even greater extent than Matraini, Marinella focuses on female behavior and decorum and matters of feminine interest throughout her book. Anna goes

2. See below chapter 2, notes 94 and 97, regarding women's uncleanness after childbirth and the purification laws in Leviticus.

to meet Joachim "together with some respected women," as no "respectable" woman would be allowed out without a female companion; and Mary, going to visit Elizabeth, takes "two elderly women" as chaperones; Mary's frugality is emphasized, a virtue drawn from sixteenth- and seventeenth-century secular conduct books about household management. Mary is a model for all young women, from early girlhood through to their lives as wives and mothers.

WHO IS THE VIRGIN MARY?

Who is Mary? This was a question that Christians asked as the story of Jesus—his conception, birth, infancy, preaching, teaching, death, and resurrection—was disseminated in the early Christian centuries. Michelangelo's drawing of Mary and the dead Christ, made for Vittoria Colonna in around 1540, its subject that of her *Plaint of the Marchesa di Pescara,* the first Marian writing in this volume, shows the sorrowful mother, the Mater Dolorosa, raising her arms in lamentation above her dead son, whose body is supported by two *putti,* or cherubim, and suspended between her knees.[3] This scene, never mentioned in the New Testament, the only textual evidence we have for Christ's life, represents the imagined anguish of a mother at her child's death, but in this case, in Christian terms, it also shows the Mother of God mourning her son's death, and possibly at the same time celebrating it, as through his death, new spiritual life was given to believers. The scene is also representative of the genre of devotional writings found in this collection, and thus invites imaginative meditation and reflection upon the greater story that lies behind it—Jesus's self-sacrifice for the redemption of humankind.

Mary was naturally present at the beginning of her son's life and also, according to the gospel of Saint John, at the end of it. The few references to her in the canonical gospels (those regarded by the Church as authentic) mostly concern the periods before his birth and during his early life, and yet she became the most powerful female icon in Christendom, the most depicted female figure in an art the purpose of which was to teach and explain to the faithful the origins of their beliefs. Who she was became a story elaborated throughout the early Christian period, out of the desire and need to deify her son Jesus as the Son of God, and yet believe in him as man, and in the workings out of the doctrines of the Incarnation and of original sin, and

3. Michelangelo's drawing is in the Isabella Stewart Gardner Museum, Boston. See page 51 of this volume. For a discussion of the drawing in relation to Vittoria Colonna's work, see chapter 1, note 3 below.

the idea of the Fall—the reason, it was believed, for humankind's woes, and for Christ's redemptive act on the cross. A brief discussion of Mary's cult will therefore help to set the writings within their contexts.

MARY IN THE SCRIPTURES

Mary does not appear in the gospel of Mark, the earliest account of Christ's life, written in about 66–68, which begins with his adult ministry; she is, however, referred to in chapter 6 as "Mary," Jesus's mother (v. 3), and she is also referred to in 3:31.[4] She does appear in the other two synoptic gospels, Matthew and Luke (the word "synoptic" meaning from more or less the same point of view), and it is in them that we encounter her for the first time in the lead-up to Jesus's birth. These accounts conflict, however: in Matthew's beautiful narrative of Jesus's infancy, written ostensibly from Joseph's point of view, Mary is betrothed to the latter and, before they come to live together, is found to be pregnant. Joseph's integrity prevents him from publicly humiliating her; he decides to separate from her informally, but an angel appears to him in a dream, telling him that Mary has conceived through the Holy Spirit and is to give birth to a son, whom he should name Jesus, and who will save his people from their sins (Matthew 1:21). According to verse 23, this birth of a child to a virgin is the fulfillment of Isaiah's prophecy in the Old Testament that a "virgin shall conceive and bear a son: and his name shall be called Emmanuel" (Isaiah 7:14).[5] Obeying the angel, Joseph takes his wife to his home, and "till she had brought forth her first-born son," he "knew her not" (v. 25).

Matthew's account sets the stage for Christ's miraculous birth: it states simply that Mary's conception is virginal and stresses the point that Joseph did not have intercourse with her before Christ's birth. In the genealogical list preceding this account, Jesus's descent through Joseph, son of Jacob and husband of Mary, links him directly back to Abraham and David, making the point that through Joseph, Jesus is their legitimate heir: Joseph's role in God's design is thus emphasized, paradoxically since he is not Jesus's biological father. Usually shown in Christian art as an elderly or old man, sitting alone pensively while Jesus is being born, or to the side in scenes of the magi come to adore the child Jesus, or leading the donkey bearing the

4. See below, note 8.

5. The Book of Isaiah was written in about 735 BCE. Matthew would have been using the Septuagint version of the Old Testament (i.e., the earliest Greek translation of the Hebrew Bible). The title derives from the legend of its writing by seventy (Latin, *septuaginta*) or, more precisely, seventy-two, translators sent from Jerusalem to Alexandria in the late third century BCE.

Virgin and child to Egypt, Joseph was to come into his own during the late sixteenth and early seventeenth centuries, when his cult was fostered. This is manifested in the prominent role he is given in Matraini and Marinella's texts.

In Luke's account (according to legend, dictated to him by the Virgin), Mary, betrothed to Joseph, receives a visit from the angel Gabriel. He tells her not to be afraid, and that she is to conceive and bear a son, to be called Jesus, the "Son of the Most High" (Luke 1:31–32). To her startled question as to how this might come about, since she is a virgin, the angel tells her that the Holy Spirit will come down upon her, and that the child is to be called the Son of God (v. 35). To assure her of the miraculous nature of what is about to take place, he tells her that her cousin Elizabeth, now old and beyond childbearing age, has conceived a son. (The account of Elizabeth's conception of Saint John the Baptist, with her aged husband Zaccharias, precedes the angel's annunciation to Mary [1:1–25].) Mary makes her *fiat*, or assent ("Be it done to me according to thy word"); the angel departs. Mary then visits Elizabeth in the hill country of Judea. On hearing Mary's greeting, the child leaps in Elizabeth's womb; Elizabeth asks why it should be she who is honored with a visit from the mother of her "Lord," reinforcing the concept of the divinity of Christ's conception, rather than she who should visit the Virgin. Mary praises God in the beautiful poetic song, the Magnificat (Luke 1:46–55).[6] Mary's obedience to God's will, expressed in her *fiat*, and the humility expressed in the Magnificat were fundamental to the construct she became, which was to be her legacy to her female descendants. So also was the emphasis on her virginal conception of Christ and the importance placed upon it by the Church, all to the detriment of women.

Luke's narrative gives further and different details: Caesar Augustus issues a decree for a census of the entire Roman world, and Joseph takes Mary, "his espoused wife, who was with child," from Nazareth to Bethlehem to be registered. (In Jewish law, a betrothed couple was regarded as married, so any child conceived was therefore legitimate.) There is no intimation here that Joseph had misgivings about Mary's conception. Mary gives birth "to her first-born son," a phrase that was to cause confusion from earliest Christianity, although modern scholarship notes that in biblical Greek the term

6. See below for further discussion on this point. See also the appendix for a full transcription of this prayer. Some scholars have argued that because of its strong resemblances to the language of the "Song of Hannah" (1 Samuel 2:1ff.) and because a few Latin manuscripts read *et ait Elisabeth,* instead of *et ait Maria,* that Luke originally attributed the prayer to Elizabeth rather than to Mary.

does not necessarily imply that Mary went on to have other children.[7] It is Luke's well-known account that has given rise to the countless Nativity images from earliest times, relating her wrapping of the child in swaddling clothes and laying him in a manger because the inn was full. An angel then appears to shepherds, the first witnesses of the birth of the Son of God. Mary goes to the Temple to carry out her purification rites, and Jesus is presented there. Simeon, an elderly man awaiting his own death, to take place only after he has seen "the Christ of the Lord," takes the child in his arms and chants the *Nunc dimittis* ("Now thou dost dismiss thy servant, O Lord, according to thy word, in peace" [2:29]), prophesying to Mary that a sword will pierce her soul, referring to Christ's rejection by the people and to his death (vv. 34–35).

In Matthew, the magi, or wise men, seek the newborn Jesus, inquiring in Jerusalem for the king of the Jews (2:1–2). This news perturbs King Herod, who calls together the chief priests and scribes to inquire after Jesus. Directing the magi to Bethlehem, he requests that they tell him when they find the child so that he too may come to pay homage. The magi take their gifts to Jesus but, warned in a dream, do not return to Herod (vv. 3–12). The magi are counterparts to the shepherds, but as non-Jewish, or Gentile, recognizers of the Messiah. Joseph too is warned in a dream to take Jesus and Mary to Egypt, to flee the massacre of the innocents perpetrated by Herod to kill Jesus. After Herod's death, Joseph is told in another dream to return to Israel, and the holy family goes to Nazareth in Galilee (vv. 13–23). Mary's role in Matthew's account ends here.

Luke continues the tale into Jesus's childhood. When he is twelve, Mary and Joseph take him to Jerusalem to celebrate the Passover (2:41–52). On returning they lose Jesus who, without his parents knowing it, has stayed on in the city. They look for him, finding him three days later in the Temple among the doctors, where all listening to him are astounded by his wisdom and answers. Mary, overcome, asks why Jesus has done this to them, displaying her maternal sorrow in terms entirely human: "Son, why hast thou done so to us? Behold, thy father and I have sought thee sorrowing." His reply, "How is it that you sought me? Did you not know that I must be about my Father's business?" confuses them, but should be understood in the light of his awareness of his own divine role as Messiah (vv. 48–49).

Mary seems not to have played a large part in her son's public life. And, she was to be rejected by him once more, as recounted in Luke 8:19–21, dur-

7. See *The Jerusalem Bible,* ed. Alexander Jones (Garden City, NY: Doubleday, 1966), Luke 2:7, note c.

ing his public ministry. Surrounded by large crowds, and telling parables, Jesus learns that his mother and brothers have come looking for him, and are outside but unable to reach him because of the throng. Jesus replies that his mother and brethren are those who "hear the word of God and do it," thus eschewing family relationships for those divine.[8] Joseph also vanishes, to be referred to again, in passing, when Jesus is described as "the carpenter's son."[9]

It is only in the fourth gospel, John's, that Mary is given prominence and roles not referred to elsewhere—she is present at the important episode of the marriage feast of Cana (John 2:1–11) as instigator of her son's first public act and miracle. At a certain point, the wine runs out, and she informs Jesus, "They have no wine" (v. 3); his reply is the somewhat terse "Woman, what is that to me and to thee? My hour is not yet come." Mary tells the servants to do as he tells them. Christ then instructs the servants to fill six water jars, and to give some to the chief steward of the feast who, tasting the water now changed into wine, asks the bridegroom why he has kept the best wine to the last, contrary to custom (vv. 9–10). This episode shows Mary's compassion towards her fellow-beings but also depicts her as a mediatrix, and, Christologically, the incident is regarded as prefiguring the changing of water into wine at the Eucharist, an action prompted by Mary's request. Mary is not, however, mentioned by name: she is simply "the mother of Jesus" (2:1). In John also, she follows Jesus to Capernaum (v. 12), and is present at Calvary, standing near the cross, again as "his mother," together with "his mother's sister," Mary the wife of Cleopas and Mary Magdalen (19:25). According to John, as Christ dies on the cross, he sees "his mother" and the "disciple standing, whom he loved," usually taken to be the evangelist himself, and says to Mary, "Woman, behold thy son." He then says to the disciple, "Behold thy mother." According to the evangelist, "from that hour, the disciple took her to his own," and then Christ, drinking the vinegar and hyssop, says, "It is consummated," and bowing his head, "gave up the ghost" (19:26–30). This event acts on two strata: on a human level, Christ ensures the care of his mother in the hands of his "beloved" follower, and on an ecclesiological level, Mary becomes the universal mother, and a type of "Mother Church," under whose cloak John, as a representative of humanity, is protected.

John's account is very different from those of the three other gospel

8. Similarly, in Mark 3:31–35, Christ asks the multitude who inform him that his mother and brethren are looking for him, "Who is my mother and my brethren?" He tells the listeners that they are his mother and brethren as they are doing the will of God.

9. Matthew 13:55.

writers. In the latter accounts Mary is not listed among the women who watch the crucifixion: in Matthew these watch "afar off," and are the "many women" who had "followed Jesus from Galilee, ministering unto him," among whom were "Mary Magdalen, and Mary the mother of James and Joseph, and the mother of the sons of Zebedee" (27:55–56), although in the Eastern Church the Virgin is often regarded as the "other Mary" who, with Mary Magdalen, sits "over against the sepulcher" after Joseph of Arimathea has wrapped Jesus's body in a clean shroud, placed it in his own new tomb, and rolled a large stone before it (v. 61). (The Syriac [Eastern] tradition shows Mary visiting the tomb and falling at Christ's feet on recognizing him after the Resurrection, as in the wonderful illustrations to the sixth-century manuscript of the Rabbulah Codex [Biblioteca Mediceana, Florence].) In the Western tradition the "other Mary" is the mother of James (Mark 16:1; Luke 24:10). However, in the Acts of the Apostles the Virgin is named explicitly as "Mary, the mother of Jesus" who, "with the women," pray in the upper room in Jerusalem, together with the apostles and brothers, after the Ascension (1:14). In some gospel commentaries she is also with the disciples when the Holy Ghost comes down upon them at Pentecost, and is therefore often shown in medieval and later art as the central figure as the dove descends (Acts 2:1ff.).

The so-called infancy accounts are now agreed to be later additions to the gospels, written more than eighty years after the events depicted occurred. Yet they were not the first reference made in the scriptures to Jesus's mother. In Saint Paul's Epistle to the Galatians, written probably within twenty years of Christ's death, Paul relates that Jesus was "made of a woman" (4:4), in order to assert Christ's humanity as well as his divinity. Mary, however, is not mentioned by name.[10] As we have seen, Mark's brief references to her were probably written around ten years later, and although they allude to Christ's public ministry and specific mention of Mary's name is made, her figure remains in the background, her role a minor one.

THE EARLY CULT IN THE EASTERN CHURCH

These brief, tantalizing, narratives are the germs out of which grew the enormously rich imagery—in liturgy, literature, music, and the visual arts—that accrued to the figure of the Virgin Mary, born out of ecclesiastical necessity as well as pious curiosity about her figure as the Mother of God, and fascination in Christ's, as well as her, forebears. Her legendary life was created in the

10. Paul's Epistle to the Galatians was probably written between 48 and 56.

context of the conflicts in which the fledgling Christian Church found itself with other creeds and faiths such as Judaism and paganism, and with those it regarded as heretics; these conflicts concerned the nature of Christ—whether he was both true man and true God—and the nature of evil, or, more precisely, of that original sin, which, according to believers, had put Christ on the cross. Mary's cult, at its peak in the West between the eleventh and thirteenth centuries, had its roots in the fourth-century Eastern Church in Syria, the cradle of asceticism. There, from the very inception of Christianity, which had replaced the earlier traditions of Mani,[11] much attention had been focused on the gospel accounts of Christ's birth. It was there that ideas about Mary's sexual purity, her virginity, were formed and fostered.

The infancy narratives, occurring only in Matthew and Luke, contained the germs of the story that was to form the core of Christian belief. Matthew, intent upon stressing Mary's virginity, and the birth of the promised Savior, emphasized that Joseph "knew her not till she brought forth her firstborn son; and he called his name Jesus" (1:25), thus setting in motion the debate. In seeing the birth of Jesus as the fulfillment of the prophecy in the Book of Isaiah of a virgin giving birth to salvation, Matthew had based his theory on the Septuagint translation into Greek of the Old Testament, where the original Hebrew word *almah* used to describe the young girl in Isaiah's prophecy, signifying a nubile, marriageable young woman, was translated into the Greek as *parthenos,* which connotes the physical nature of intact virginity, rather than *neanis,* meaning a nubile young girl or maiden. With this mistranslation of a single word was founded and reinforced Christianity's focus and emphasis on Mary's sexual purity as prime qualification for her role as Mother of God, Theotokos or "God-bearer," the title she would be given at the First General Church Council of Ephesus in 431. Luke too was anxious to emphasize the virginal state of the mother of God, stressing that she was a "virgin espoused" to Joseph, of the house of David, "and the virgin's name was Mary" (1:27), this miraculous event preceded by another, Elizabeth's conception of John the Baptist (vv. 5–25). But, according to Luke, Mary also underwent the purification rites carried out by Jewish women according to the Law (2:22), so it would seem that he was not propounding the view that she was a virgin *in partu* and *post partum,* or that her physical integrity had not been damaged during and after the birth of Jesus.

11. Mani (ca. 216–76) was born in Persia. He taught a radical form of Gnosticism, concerning hidden truths based on a supposed primeval conflict between light and dark. Its severe asceticism was widespread by the fourth century (Saint Augustine was an adherent for nine years), and may have influenced such later heresies as the Albigensians and Bogomils.

From Christianity's beginnings, the gospel accounts of Christ's birth were the subject of intense scrutiny, and ideas about Mary's virginity were battled over in the process of deifying Christ and establishing Mary's role as the human mother of her divine and human son. To this end, the perfection of his mother, as the unsullied vessel capable of bearing her perfect son, was a necessity and *sine qua non,* the object of much theological debate as the Incarnation, the original mystery and central tenet of Christianity, was worked out in the first centuries after Christ's death.

The earliest references to Mary came from the Greek-speaking church of the eastern Mediterranean: the first-known comment, made by Ignatius, bishop of Antioch (d. ca. 110), referred to her as the paradoxical "virgin" and "mother," stressing that through her involvement in the Incarnation, "Jesus was born of Mary and of God."[12] Mary's role in soteriology was enlarged upon during the slightly later dispute between Justin Martyr (ca. 100–ca. 165), the Greek convert and early Christian apologist, and Trypho the Jew (fl. ca. 135). Trypho had argued against the Septuagint translation of *almah* as *parthenos* and favored the word *neanis.* Justin, the first to call Mary "the Virgin" in lieu of her proper name, as a general idea, established the Eve/Mary antithesis that was to become so important in Marian theology and spirituality: in the new dispensation, the New Testament had supplanted the Old, and, just as Christ had become the "new Adam," so the Virgin was the "new Eve."[13] The heresy-hunting Irenaeus of Lyons (ca. 130–202) was to have a profound influence on theology and the concept of Mary in his doctrine of "recapitulation," the idea of all things having their origins in Christ's humanity, the Incarnation. He also enriched the Eve/Mary parallel: the first Adam had been created from the virgin earth, without labor; similarly Jesus had been born of a virgin.[14] Eve, while still a virgin, had disobeyed God and was the source of humankind's ruin; Mary, already betrothed, but nevertheless a virgin, through her obedience had been the source of her own salvation as well as humanity's.[15] And he also

12. Antioch, in Syria, was one of the first major Christian urban centers, together with Alexandria and Rome. Saint Ignatius of Antioch, *To the Ephesians* 7, 2. See *Dictionnaire de Spiritualité ascétique et mystique: doctrine et histoire,* 17 vols. (Paris: Beauchesne, 1937–95), vol. 10, col. 423.

13. Saint Justin Martyr, *Dialogue with Trypho* 87, 2; 100, 5 (*Dictionnaire de Spiritualité,* vol. 10, col. 424). See the English-language translation of the *Dialogue* by A. Lukyn Williams (London: SPCK, 1930).

14. Saint Irenaeus of Lyons, *Against the Heresies* 3, 21, 10. See Hilda Graef, *Mary: A History of Doctrine and Devotion,* 2 vols. (New York: Sheed & Ward, 1963), 1:39. Irenaeus was probably born in Smyrna but studied in Rome.

15. *Against the Heresies* 3, 22, 4 (Graef, *Mary,* 1:39–40).

saw her as the virgin Eve's advocate, or comforter, the first known intimation of Mary's role as mediatrix.[16]

With the growing asceticism of the Church and the flourishing monastic communities in the deserts of Egypt, Syria, and Palestine of the late second to fourth centuries, virginity was becoming the Christian ideal: according to Origen (d. 253), the great Greek theologian and grand master of the Alexandrian school, Jesus was the model for male celibates, while Mary was the exemplar for female virgins, a highly significant concept leading to Mary's being regarded as the model for consecrated virgins, and one that would be strongly endorsed during the peak of the ascetic movement in the following century.[17] Origen was also to have a profound effect on Mary's status and role. Of paramount importance, he was also the first to describe her as Theotokos, translated later into Latin as "Dei genetrix" or "Mater Dei," or "Mother of God."[18]

Exaltation and veneration of Mary reached its apogee in the Eastern Church in Ephrem Syrus (306–73), the most celebrated biblical exegete and writer among the Syrians. Ephrem's influence was huge, particularly on the liturgy, and, in his oft-stated view of the Virgin's perfect sinlessness, has been regarded as a witness to the Immaculate Conception. His hymns to the Virgin profoundly affected Marian liturgy, which was established in Syria in 370.[19] In the *Banquet,* his symposium on chastity—one of a rash of treatises on the superiority of the virginal life—Methodius, bishop of Lycia (d. ca. 311), compared Mary to the virgin earth from which Adam had been taken, a theme that will be seen in Matraini's text.[20] To Epiphanius (ca. 314–403), bishop of Salamis, in Cyprus, the problem of Mary's virginity was solved by Joseph being a widower and being given to the Virgin as a protector. At the age of over eighty, Joseph had six children already; intercourse for him was therefore unnecessary, it was deemed. (This is still the view of the Eastern Church.)[21]

In his most important writing, the *Panarion,* known as the "Refutation of

16. *Against the Heresies* 5, 19, 1 (Graef, *Mary,* 1:40).

17. Origen, *In Matthaeum* 10, 17 (*Dictionnaire de Spiritualité,* vol. 10, col. 425).

18. Graef, *Mary,* 1:46, who notes the more literal, but rather clumsy, translation of *Theotokos* as "she who gives birth to God."

19. Ephrem also wrote hymns on the Nativity, Epiphany, and Crucifixion, verse homilies and commentaries, and also refuted such heresies as Arianism and Manichaeism (Graef, *Mary,* 1:57–62). The term "witness" is used in the religious sense of attesting, or testifying, to a holy mystery.

20. Saint Methodius, *Symposium* 3, 4 (Graef, *Mary,* 1:47).

21. Saint Epiphanius, *Panarion* 78, 7 (Graef, *Mary,* 1:71).

All Heresies," Epiphanius also stressed Mary's perfect virginity and the association between her and the Church: virginity had begun with her, and she had had the gift of prophecy as a result.[22] Mary was the New Eve and Mother of the Living; reflecting on her death, Epiphanius was the first to attest to the concept of the Virgin's bodily assumption into heaven.[23] The "Akathistos," the most famous and beautiful Byzantine liturgical hymn in praise of the Incarnation, written in Greek probably in the early sixth century, was sung in her honor. Its authorship is uncertain but it probably belongs to the Syrian Saint Romanos Melodos (d. 518), the most renowned poet of the Byzantine period. It addresses Mary with the paradox, "Rejoice, O Bride unmarried," and extols her conception of Jesus by the Holy Spirit, for her paradoxical virginity and maternal love, and for the tenderness she shows as mother of Christ before whom she also bows in worship as the "Son of the Highest."[24] Romanos's *kontakion*, a canticle or lyric homily, again praises her perfections, celebrating her as Theotokos, its theological point to reinforce the formulation of the Third Council at Ephesus, which had identified her as the "Birth-Giver of God." In his *kontakion* for Good Friday, the epithets of Christ as the "Son of the Virgin" and "God of the Virgin" reinforce Mary's role in the redemption of mankind, the mother lamenting over her son's body.[25]

Mary's cult has been seen as taking root and flowering in the Syrian East for two reasons, one theological and the other social: the presence of a pre-Christian feminine power, in the figure of the polytheistic Syrian goddess, in a cult spread across the Greek and Roman world; and the relative freedom and respect accorded to Syrian women before the advent of Christianity.[26] These powerful female symbols, known as Ishtar in Mesopotamia, or Asherah from Canaan, or Ashtoreth, were figures later identified with Isis, Phrygian Kybele, and Greek Hera, the mother goddess, more powerful than comparable goddesses in Greek and Roman mythology. The female element in Jewish monotheism is often grammatically derived: *Hok-*

22. *Panarion* 78–79 (*Dictionnaire de Spiritualité,* vol. 10, col. 431). *Panarion* is Greek for "medicine chest."

23. *Panarion* 78, 11 (Graef, *Mary*, 1:72).

24. *Akathistos* (Greek, "not sitting" because it was sung standing). The "Akathistos" was sung in the Orthodox Church on the Saturday of the fifth week in Lent. Consisting of twenty-four stanzas, the first part was drawn on events in Christ's life, from the Annunciation to the Presentation; the second celebrated the mystery of the Incarnation. In it, Mary is described as defeating demons, giving strength to martyrs, and opening Paradise (see Graef, *Mary*, 1:127–29).

25. Romanos was the most important composer of *kontakia,* which were metrical sermons chanted to music.

26. Susan Ashbrook Harvey, "Women in Early Syrian Christianity," in *Images of Women in Antiquity*, ed. Averil Cameron and Amélie Kuhrt (London: Croom Helm, 1983), 288–98, at 291.

mah, the personification of Wisdom, is a female noun in Hebrew, and, for the same reason, the female personification of Yahweh's divine presence is the holy *Shekinah*. These grammatical terms were translated into early Syrian religious thought, creating a fertile soil for the new Christian goddess, and mother of a god, Mary.[27] But Mary's cult has also been seen as a natural development growing out of the process of the Church's self-definition in the early Christian centuries and doctrinal formulation after the Council of Nicaea, especially in relation to the concept of virginity and Christology.[28] Ascetic Christianity, its ideology deriving from the cenobitic life in Syria, Egypt, Palestine, and Asia Minor, was to supersede and transform a society that had once accepted powerful female deities into one that was highly misogynist and far more hostile toward the female than Hellenism had been, its sterile feminine imagery reflecting negatively on real women, who were, as a consequence, viewed as sources of pollution and therefore vilified. In the process of the politicization of Church practice, women now came to be seen as pale reflections of the Virgin Mary, docile, passive, humble, veiled, and silent, their lives ruled by men. In Christian hands, the feminine words *Hokmah* (Hebrew, "Wisdom") and *Sophia* in Greek, in Latin would become *spiritus,* masculine.

Mary's role became increasingly prominent in the Church's process of countering heresies. At the first ecumenical council at Nicaea in 325, in the wake of religious factionalism, the dogmatic basis of the Christian faith was set down: Mary's part in salvation was emphasized in opposition to the Arians and Gnostics in the creed of Nicaea or, as it is better known, the Nicene Creed.[29] At the Third General Council at Ephesus in 431, her divine motherhood was defined and the Nicene Creed reaffirmed. The epithet Theotokos was also upheld at Ephesus, and later at the Fourth General Council of Chalcedon in 451, which defined the two natures of Christ, human and divine in one person.[30] As a result of these triumphs over heresy, images of

27. Ibid., 289–90.

28. Averil Cameron, "The Cult of the Virgin in Late Antiquity: Religious Development and Myth-Making," in *The Church and Mary: Papers Read at the 2001 Summer Meeting and the 2002 Winter Meeting of the Ecclesiastical History Society,* Studies in Church History 39, ed. R. N. Swanson (Trowbridge: Boydell & Brewer, 2004), 1–21, at 13–14.

29. Arius (d. 336), a priest at Alexandria, had denied the full divinity of Christ; he was banished by the Council at Nicaea.

30. In 429 Nestorius (d. after 451), patriarch of Constantinople, supported those who opposed the use by Greek theologians of the increasingly popular term Theotokos, which designated the Virgin as mother of God. To Nestorius the term was incompatible with Christ's true humanity: the Virgin could only be mother of Christ the human, not divine, person. He was deposed at the Council at Ephesus.

the Madonna and child became widespread as representing official doctrine, while feasts, homilies, and hymns to Mary proliferated.[31] Mary was accorded the epithet *Aeiparthenos*, or "ever Virgin," at the Second Council of Constantinople in 553, and her divine motherhood was emphasized at the Third Council in 680–81. These councils, while intensely debating Christ's nature, also defined Mary's role and virginal status; in the effort to render her exempt from original sin, other aspects of her life, such as her own conception and her death, and bodily elevation into heaven, were matters of debate for centuries. The Immaculate Conception, its feast day kept on December 8, became dogma only in 1854, and the Assumption (August 15) in 1950.

Feast days: Days celebrating Mary, established by the Church, and called feast days, were also first known in the East. The Assumption is her principal feast, since it commemorates her death, as in the customary practice in calendars naming martyrs and saints, known as martyrologies. First mentioned before the Council of Ephesus, the Assumption was called the "Commemoration of St. Mary." In the fourth century in Antioch a feast connected to her death was celebrated on January 16; in Palestine it was observed on August 15 in the fifth century and, by around 600, on the same date in the Greek Church. The feast of her Purification was honored in Jerusalem (at that time on February 14), and attested to by Etheria, a noble lady from Galicia who made a pilgrimage to Palestine in the late fourth century.[32] The Annunciation (March 25) was first celebrated in Byzantium between 400 and 500, and in the next century the ancient Parthenon in Athens was dedicated to Mary. Around 550, feast days marking her birth (September 8) and death, or Dormition (August 15), known as the *koimesis* (Greek, "falling asleep"; Latin, *dormitio*), were also established in Byzantium, where the feasts of the Presentation of the Virgin (November 21) and Purification (now February 2) were kept in the seventh century. The feast of her conception appears to have been known in the East by the end of the sixth or during the seventh century, spreading to the West, where it was first attested in the ninth century, and where, despite controversy over the doctrine of the Immaculate Conception for several centuries, the feast (December 8) was approved in

31. See Mary B. Cunningham, "The Meeting of the Old and New: The Typology of Mary the Theotokos," in Swanson, *The Church and Mary*, 52–62, at 55.

32. Etheria's (or Egeria's) pilgrimage to Egypt, the Holy Land, Edessa, Asia Minor, and Constantinople probably took place between 381 and 384. Etheria wrote an account in a letter now called *Itinerarium Egeriae*, or the Travels of Egeria. The middle part of her account survived, and was copied in the Codex Aretinus, written at Monte Cassino in the eleventh century, but the beginning and end are lost. The Codex was found in the late nineteeth century in a monastic library in Arezzo, Italy.

1476. In the West the feast of the Purification was the first to be celebrated in Rome, during the latter half of the seventh century, followed by the Dormition, known later in the West as the Assumption, and then the Annunciation, first known in the sixth century in the East, and universal in the West by the eighth century. Mary's Nativity, originally part of the Christmas cycle as a feast of Christ, but given more of a Marian emphasis, was commemorated at the end of the seventh century in the East, and from the eleventh century in the West. The feast of the Visitation, until 1969 observed on July 2, first appeared in the thirteenth century, under the auspices of the Franciscan order, and was established for the entire Church of Rome in the sixteenth century.

MARY IN THE WESTERN CHURCH

Although slower to develop in the West, Mary's cult was to meet its champion in the fourth century in Ambrose, bishop of Milan (ca. 339–97), and by the end of the Middle Ages, Saint Bernard of Clairvaux (1090–1153) would be the catalyst of a whole new mystical devotion to her. While Irenaeus of Lyons had celebrated Mary's role in salvation and had been one of the first to assert the Eve/Mary parallel—Mary the *causa salutis* and *advocata Evae,* the "cause of well-being" and "advocate of Eve"—Ambrose was to wax lyrically about the Virgin's role in salvation: her motherhood was real, since from her Christ had received her own flesh; and since he was generated from God the Father, and was God himself, then Mary had to be the mother of God.[33] However, Ambrose did not go so far as to use the Latin equivalent of the term Theotokos (*Mater Dei*), which was rarely used in the West, since the cult of Kybele, the mother goddess, was still widespread in the western part of the Roman Empire. His metaphorical language was to pass into the canon: Mary "like a cloud rained the grace of Christ on the earth," the image of the cloud expressing both Christ's real humanity and the fullness of grace.[34] (Matraini uses Ambrose's analogy; see 95 below.) Mary was also a type of the Church, the model and mistress of virginity, and the model for mothers.[35]

A highly important contribution to Mariolatry, Mary's role as model of virginity, was born out of criticisms from the monks Helvidius (fourth century) and Jovinian (d. ca. 405), who denied the superiority of virginity over marriage—the ascetic teaching of the monks who exalted virginity to

33. Saint Ambrose, *De Incarnationis Dominicae Sacramento* 104 (Graef, *Mary,* 1:78).

34. Saint Ambrose, *De Institutione Virginis* 81 (Graef, *Mary,* 1:87).

35. Saint Ambrose, *Epistula* 63, 110–11 (*Dictionnaire de Spiritualité,* vol. 10, col. 432).

the detriment of marriage—giving them equal importance. Saint Jerome (ca. 345–419) attacked Helvidius, gathering together all the scriptural arguments in favor of Mary's virginity *post partum* and several years later, from his retreat in Bethlehem,[36] rounded on Jovinian (already expelled from Rome and condemned by Ambrose in Milan), writing two books opposing him in which he discoursed at length on Mary's virginity.[37] In a letter to Eustochium, that virgin par excellence, Jerome offered Mary as an example of virtue, and in his first book against Jovinian described Mary as the "mother of many virgins."[38] It was Ambrose, however, through his sermons, later published, who had the greatest effect on popular piety: to him Mary was the perfect woman, the virginal mother of Christ who had never known sin, and had been prefigured in numerous texts of the Old Testament and in the Shulamite, or Bride, of the Song of Songs (also known as the Canticle of Canticles). She was for Ambrose the example of the Christian life. So great was the power of his oratory in proposing Mary as the model for all the virtues that the parents of Milan were alarmed to see large numbers of their young daughters eschew marriage in favor of becoming consecrated virgins, or brides of Christ.

Mary's personal sanctity reached a definitive status through the reflections of Saint Augustine of Hippo (354–430): in his gloomy view of mankind, all were sinful. Arguing with Pelagius, the British (or Irish) monk (fl. 400–18), who opposed his teaching, stating that mankind could remain sinless through free will, Augustine called upon the example of Mary, the exception to the rule, and recipient of abundant grace from God to fully overcome sin: Mary was the sole recipient of this grace, her sinlessness achieved through grace and not the effect of her free will.[39] He was also the first Latin father to assume that Mary had made a vow of virginity.[40] For Augustine, who defined original sin in the way it was understood until modern times,

36. Saint Jerome, *Adversus Helvidium* 18 (*Dictionnaire de Spiritualité*, vol. 10, col. 432).

37. Saint Jerome, *Adversus Jovinianum* (*Dictionnaire de Spiritualité*, vol. 10, col. 432).

38. Saint Jerome, *Epistula* 22, 38, and *Adversus Jovinianum* 1, 31 (*Dictionnaire de Spiritualité*, vol. 10, col. 433). Saint Eustochium (370–ca. 419) was a noble Roman virgin and a daughter of Saint Paula (347–404), a Roman matron, who dedicated herself to a life of devotion. In 385 mother and daughter followed Saint Jerome to Palestine, settling in Bethlehem, and building four monasteries.

39. Saint Augustine, *De natura et gratia* 36, 42 (*Dictionnaire de Spiritualité*, vol. 10, col. 434). Augustine's mentor had been Ambrose, who helped him to convert in 386; he fought against Manichaeism, to which he had been an adherent for nine years, a heresy that denied that Christ had truly taken flesh from Mary. See also above, note 11.

40. Graef, *Mary*, 1:95–96. Mary's vow had already been suggested in the Eastern Church by Gregory of Nyssa (ibid.).

Mary was also a "supereminent member" and "type of the Church," thus confirming her ecclesiological role.[41] In the West, Mary's perpetual virginity was asserted at the Lateran Synod of 649.

Some of the most beautiful images in Marian art are of Mary's Assumption, such as Titian's painting of 1518 (Santa Maria Gloriosa dei Frari, Venice), where she spirals up on a cloud, a vision of swirling red and blue, supported by *putti* upwards towards the welcoming arms of God the Father in heaven, the apostles ranged below her, astonished and marveling.[42] Early Christians in the East, aware that nothing was known of Mary's post-Resurrection life or the manner of her death, and that no relics existed, created pious tales about the end of her life, of how, body and soul incorruptible, unlike other mortals, she was translated or assumed into heaven.[43] These legends appear no earlier than the fourth century, but the nucleus of the story derived from as early as the third century and, according to the scholar M. R. James, was first elaborated, if it did not originate there, in Egypt.[44] In fourth- and fifth-century apocryphal manuscripts in Syriac, Greek, Latin, Armenian, Coptic, and Ethiopian—the major languages spoken by Christians at this time—Mary did not even die. The texts, with such titles as "The Passing Away of Mary" or "The Obsequies of Mary," relate her passing or *transitus* in Jerusalem, followed by varying miraculous happenings, and finally her assumption into heaven. Although the *Transitus* was condemned as apocryphal, it became a widespread belief in the Church, both East and West.

In the West, in Gaul, the Church's teaching about the Assumption was established by Gregory of Tours (d. 594), who knew the story of the Virgin's death and accepted as historical truth the account attributed to Melitus (d. ca. 190), bishop of Sardis. Saints Albert the Great, Thomas Aquinas, and Bonaventure were all to defend the doctrine. As shown above, the earliest feasts celebrating her death were noted in the fourth century at Antioch and in the fifth century in Palestine; in the sixth century the Greek Church celebrated it on August 15, and by the end of the eighth century it was uni-

41. Saint Augustine, *Sermo Denis* 25, at 7, 8 (Graef, *Mary*, 1:97).

42. Blue is the Virgin's traditional color, usually worn with white, although she is often seen in blue and red in Venetian painting.

43. Reasons for the New Testament's silence regarding Mary's death were given in the eighth century by Andrew of Crete (d. 740): it had come too late to be included in the Scriptures, and Christ's incarnation had to be preached first (Graef, *Mary*, 1:151).

44. *The Apocryphal New Testament: Being the Apocryphal Gospels, Acts, Epistles and Apocalypses*, ed. and trans. by M. R. James (Oxford, 1924), 194. A fuller account of the legends appears below in the discussion of the *Transitus* texts.

versally observed in the West on that date. Mary's triumph over death, her uncorrupted body ascending into heaven, is crowned with the ultimate accolade "Queen of Heaven," or "Regina Coeli," an image that was first painted in the church of Santa Maria Antiqua, the earliest Christian building in the Forum of Rome, during the first half of the sixth century, where she is shown enthroned, seated by her son in heaven.

The title "Queen of Heaven" associates Mary with the "woman clothed with the sun," the vision of the Apocalypse from the Book of Revelation, an allegory foretelling the destruction of the wicked, Satan's overthrow, and the establishment of Christ's kingdom on earth. This association had first been applied to Mary by Epiphanius in the late fourth century: "And a great sign appeared in heaven: a woman clothed with the sun, and the moon under her feet, and on her head a crown of twelve stars" (Revelation 12:1), a dramatic reference that is incorporated in the mass for the feast of the Assumption. The account in Revelation continues: "And, being with child, she cried travailing in birth, and was in pain to be delivered. . . . And there was seen another sign in heaven. And, behold, a great red dragon, having seven heads and ten horns and on his heads seven diadems" (vv. 2–3). The dragon pursues the mother, after her born child, "who was to rule all nations with an iron rod" (v. 5), is "taken up" to God, clearly a reference to the Messiah, whose mother of salvation had been promised by God in the Garden of Eden (Genesis 3:15). The typological significance of the vision of the woman was to be absorbed into Mary's imagery, referring to her power over evil, the role given to her by the Church as the one predestined to bring about humanity's salvation from Eve's sin, and hence also the title given to her by early commentators, "Second Eve." In art she appeared symbolically standing on a serpent or dragon, alluding to the words of God in the Garden of Eden (Genesis 3:15), "I will put enmities between thee and the woman, and thy seed and her seed: she shall crush thy head, and thou shalt lie in wait for her heel."

The lovely imagery of the Song of Songs was also applied to the theme of the Virgin of the Immaculate Conception. It was absorbed into medieval litanies, or supplications, to the Virgin: "Pulchra ut luna, electa ut sol"—"fair as the moon, bright as the sun" (6:9); "flos campi"—"flower of the field" (Rose of Sharon, 2:1); "lilium inter spinas"—"lily among thorns" (2:2); and "Turris David"—"tower of David" (4:4). Better-known examples such as the "hortus conclusus"—"a garden enclosed" (4:12)—alluding to the concept of virginity, and the "fons hortorum"—"the fountain of gardens"—and "Puteus aquarum viventium"— "a well of living waters" (4:15)—the latter two referring to the water of redemption, are themes running through Matraini's *Brief Discourse* as well as in Marinella's *Vita*.[45]

Prayers and liturgy: One of the most famous Marian hymns, the marvelous anthem "Ave Maris Stella" ("Hail, Star of the Sea"), dates from at least the ninth century, and may have been written by Paul the Deacon (ca. 720–ca. 800), the Benedictine author of the *History of the Lombards*. The beautiful prayer, the Ave Maria (Hail Mary), based on the angel's salutation to Mary in Luke 2, became known during the eleventh century, as did the antiphon *Salve Regina* (Hail, Holy Queen), one of the most widely used Catholic prayers. The *Regina Coeli* ("Queen of Heaven"), the Easter antiphon, dates from the following century; the Angelus, which originated with the Franciscans, became a popular devotion in the thirteenth century. Liturgical devotions in the West included the Little Office of Our Lady, as well as a mass and office devoted to Mary on Saturdays.

By the end of the patristic period, Byzantines such as Saint John Damascene (d. 749) had waxed ecstatically over Mary's holiness and purity, her intercessory powers, her queenliness, and her role as mediatrix in the growing number of homilies and liturgies concerning the glorious Theotokos. These expressed a profound and rich spirituality that was translated into the iconography of Mary, in both East and West, and in the case of the West an art that was enormously influenced by Byzantine imagery.[46]

45. Such literary symbols are to be found translated in seventeenth-century art, particularly in Spain, as in the depiction of the Immaculate Conception in Murillo's several paintings of the subject, and, in Italy, in Cavaliere d'Arpino's apocalyptic *Immaculate Conception* (ca. 1602/4, Real Academia de Bellas Artes de San Fernando, Madrid). The Virgin is portrayed with a halo of stars, on a crescent moon, the serpent at her feet, and with such symbols as the *hortus conclusus*, the well, and the burning bush below her in the landscape; two angels lift her, while *putti* heads peep from under her feet, and two angels descend with a golden crown.

46. It may be useful to note that Mary was, contemporaneously in the seventh century, also of interest in the nascent Muslim world; in the Koran a somewhat different, more human and dynamic, Mary appears with greater frequency than she does in the New Testament, and in fact is the only woman in the scripture to have a book named after her, as the "Ideal Mother" of the prophet Jesus. The Prophet Mohammed died in 629; the holy book, not necessarily penned by him, but by someone with knowledge of the apocryphal writings referred to above, was written around 600. Mariam, or Mary, is mentioned thirty-five times, while Jesus is referred to seven or eight times. The text relates the Virgin's early life, her divine protection, her being fed by angels, her dedication to God at birth, and her childhood in the Temple. She is visited by Gabriel but makes no *fiat*; there is no Joseph, no inn, nor manger, and she undergoes an agonizing labor, alone, under a palm tree. The Koran attests to the virgin birth of Jesus, but regards Jesus as a human being, a messenger of God, and not God incarnate. Gabriel "arranges" for Mariam to have water gush beneath her feet and to receive dates. Returning home with the baby, she is slandered by those she meets, but not allowed to speak until the baby himself speaks from his cradle to exonerate her from all blame, thus enhancing his miraculous existence.

MARY IN THE APOCRYPHA

Although Mary's appearance in apocryphal writings has to a certain extent been discussed above, a fuller exposition may be of use to readers since much of what two of the women writers of the Marian texts translated here used or had at their disposal were writings based on the early apocryphal texts. Indeed, Lucrezia Marinella, the only one of the three to refer to her "bibliography," mentions at least one source that is apocryphal.[47] A pivotal text concerning Mary, the mid-second-century apocryphal Book of James, was the *locus classicus* of the concept of her perpetual virginity, one of the major teachings of the Catholic Church, and of the later Church dogma concerning her own conception by her parents, the Immaculate Conception.[48] It was also the site of the naming of her parents, Joachim and Anna. Written originally in Greek, the earliest text to come down to us is in Syriac, and therefore translated within the area in which Syriac was spoken.[49] Although it was prohibited in the West for propounding the tale of Joseph's first marriage, the Book of James was to be absorbed into, edited, and added to in the Gospel of Pseudo-Matthew, an apocryphal Latin text of the eighth or ninth century, the contents of which then passed into medieval devotional literature, which in turn influenced Church art, and, for the purposes of this essay, several elements in both Matraini's and Marinella's texts. Its influence on medieval and later popular piety and spirituality is unparalleled.

The Book of James: This text relates the miraculous conception of the Virgin Mary by her parents, Anna and Joachim, an elderly couple whose barrenness had been a source of inconsolable sorrow (echoing the story of Elizabeth and Zaccharias, the parents of Saint John the Baptist).[50] Joachim, "exceed-

47. I am in the process of preparing an article that will include, among other things, a comparison of the first and third editions of the *Vita* and an overview of Marinella's sources.

48. The Book of James purported to be by James, "the Lord's brother," in order to establish an earlier date for it and harness it to the gospels, but probably in fact was compiled by a later Jewish Christian writer from different sources, including the gospels of Matthew and Luke. Its first printed Latin translation appeared in 1552, when it was given the title *Protevangelium* by Guillaume Postel (d. 1581), who translated it and introduced it into Europe. The text exists in the original Greek, and there are several oriental versions, the earliest being in Syriac. There are over one hundred Greek manuscripts, some dating from the third century; but there is no early Latin version. The translation used for the summary that follows is from James, *Apocryphal New Testament,* 39–49. I also refer to the edition by J. K. Elliott, *The Apocryphal New Testament: A Collection of Apocryphal Christian Literature in an English Translation* (New York: Oxford University Press, 2005), 48–67.

49. Syriac, a type of Aramaic, was the main literary and liturgical language other than Greek. There was a strong Syriac tradition of translating Greek texts.

50. Cf. Luke 1:15–80.

ing rich," offers gifts in the Temple, whereupon the high priest Reuben states that his barrenness renders his gifts unworthy. Joachim goes into the desert for forty days (mirroring Jesus's forty days in the wilderness);[51] meanwhile, Anna laments his absence and her own childlessness. Donning her bridal clothes, she sits beneath a laurel tree in the garden, weeping even more on seeing a nest of sparrows, seemingly reproaching her for her own barren state. An angel appears and tells her—in the language of Luke's gospel—that she will conceive and bear a child; Anna promises to dedicate that child to God, to minister to him "all the days of its life." Two messengers then arrive, heralding the arrival of Joachim (who has also received an angelic visitation) with his flocks; the elderly couple embrace. Although unspecified, this greeting was later regarded as a metaphor for the human act of conception, elaborated on by Church Fathers such as Saint Augustine as being achieved without concupiscence, or desire, the sin believed by some to have led to the Fall. (Thus Mary was conceived without sin, and untainted by original sin through her Immaculate Conception, the teaching that was to be a source of controversy throughout the Middle Ages, and was only made Church dogma as late as 1854.) The following day Joachim returns to the Temple and presents his gifts.

After the Virgin's birth, Anna inquires after her child's sex. Hearing that it is a female, Anna, echoing Elizabeth's speech in Luke, says, "My soul is magnified this day." Mary's miraculousness is evident from her earliest days: able to stand at six months, she can walk seven steps and return to her mother's arms. On her first birthday, the priests, scribes, elders, and people of Israel celebrate at a great feast organized by Joachim. At the age of three, she is taken by Joachim and Anna to the Temple, where she is left; on the third step of the altar, "she danced with her feet and all the house of Israel loved her." Food is brought to her by an angel. When she reaches the age of twelve, the priests, concerned that she will pollute the sanctuary through the onset of menstruation, decide to marry her off. An angel tells Zaccharias, the high priest, to call in all the widowers, each to bear a rod, and the one whose rod flowers will become the Virgin's husband. Zaccharias gathers together the rods, goes into the Temple to pray, and returns the rods to their owners. A dove flies out of Joseph's rod and lands on his head: he has been chosen. But he refuses, excusing himself as old, and already with sons. He is, however, persuaded by the priest, and takes Mary to his house; in this account Joseph has become a builder and goes "away to build [his] buildings," leaving Mary behind. Through her relationship to Joseph, Mary

51. Matthew 4:1–11; Luke 4:1–13.

has now become of the tribe of David. This tale is similarly the *locus* of the episode of the Virgin's winning the lot to weave the "true purple and scarlet" for the veil of the tabernacle.[52] It is while she is weaving the veil that the angel announces her conception of Jesus. After staying with Elizabeth for three months during her pregnancy, Mary becomes afraid and returns home to hide herself away, and we are told, "Now she was sixteen years old when these mysteries came to pass." This is the first instance of an apparent element of shame.

When Joseph returns to find Mary "great with child," his response is similar to that related in Matthew—she has been seduced. On his accusing her, she defends her purity, insisting that she does not know how this came about. As in Matthew, it is through the agency of an angel that Joseph's suspicions are allayed. Joseph and Mary are brought before the priest, and Joseph is accused by Annas the scribe of defiling Mary. Given the "water of the conviction of the lord," they are sent separately into the hill country and return whole, and are then released. En route for Bethlehem to fulfill the census requirements, Mary's birth pangs cause them to stop at a cave—in Joseph's words, "to hide thy shame." Joseph then seeks a midwife, whom he tells of Mary's conception of Jesus by the Holy Ghost, and who witnesses the cloud and light that yield the baby. The child goes immediately to Mary's breast. The midwife's friend Salome, in disbelief, tests Mary's virginity, then withdraws her hand, having confirmed Mary's hymen is intact. Salome's hand falls into the fire as punishment, and is restored to her when she acknowledges the child as king. This detail is the origin of the idea that Mary, conceived by Anna in angelic *apatheia,* in turn conceived Jesus without her hymen being broken, and gave birth in the same way, and is the first assertion of her perpetual virginity.[53] The story of Mary's painless parturition may well have influenced the later "Revelations" of Saint Bridget of Sweden (ca. 1303–73), founder of the Brigittine order, which related Bridget's visions of Christ's birth, in which Mary gave birth on her knees, worshiping the child, the source of countless images of the Nativity (e.g., by Piero della Francesca, National Gallery, London, 1480s), a scene in which Mary had formerly, and naturally, been shown recumbent, as in Byzantine and Ro-

52. Purple was the color of divinity and royalty. In the Hebrew context it was the color of the high priest's clothes. Here the color signifies Mary's own status as the future mother of God. Zaccharias, the high priest in the Book of James, is not the same figure as Zaccharias the priest and father of John the Baptist.

53. The Book of James and the Ascension of Isaiah, a Jewish-Christian text from the end of the first century CE strongly influenced by Gnosticism, were the sources of the idea of Mary's virginity *in partu,* a theme taken up by the Fathers.

manesque art. Jesus's birth is followed by the arrival of the magi, the massacre of the innocents, and a confusing account of Elizabeth hiding Saint John the Baptist, Herod's search for the latter, and the death of Zaccharias.

The Gospel of Pseudo-Matthew: Chapters 1–17 of the Book of James were incorporated into the Gospel of Pseudo-Matthew, a Latin compilation written no earlier than the fifth century and more likely in the eighth or ninth, but with omissions and elaborations.[54] This was to be the main source for vernacular literary and visual accounts of the life of Mary from the tenth to the fifteenth century. The tenth-century Benedictine nun and poet Hrosvita of Gandersheim knew of it when she came to write her narrative poem on Mary's Nativity, which was designed to be read aloud or recited by the sisters of her convent. Similarly, it is clear from the iconography in the Arena Chapel in Padua that the Florentine artist Giotto (1266–1327) knew this work, in its later forms in the Dominican Jacobus de Voragine's compilation of saints' lives and legends, *The Golden Legend* (1297), and in the Franciscan Pseudo-Bonaventure's *Meditations on the Life of Christ* (ca. 1300), when he came to paint the fresco cycle of the Virgin's life (1305).[55] Lucrezia Marinella may well have been familiar with this cycle since she was brought up in Venice, and lived for a time near Padua.

In the Pseudo-Matthew account of Mary's early life, more details are given: Joachim, wealthy as he is in the Book of James, is now charitable, giving his money away. (This may be the source for Marinella's description of Anna and Joachim's charity, 130 below.) He marries Anna, "daughter of Ysachar," and they live together for twenty years, childless. Reuben, the high priest, again rejects Joachim's offerings; Anna laments on seeing a sparrow's nest, comparing her own infertility to the abundance in the nest. An angel promises her a daughter; and in fear and sorrow she throws herself on her bed for a whole day and night. Joachim is also visited by an angel in the wilderness, with the same promise. The angel now tells Anna to meet Joachim at the now-named Golden Gate of the Temple, which she does; Mary is born. Taken to the Temple at three years of age, Mary walks up fifteen steps, a description that becomes part of her imagery henceforth (as

54. The Gospel of Pseudo-Matthew was originally known as the *Liber de infantia* (of both Mary and Christ) or the *Historia de Nativitate Mariae et de Infantia Salvatoris* (James, *Apocryphal New Testament*, 70; Elliott, *Apocryphal New Testament*, 86). The summary of the Gospel of Pseudo-Matthew that follows is taken from James, ibid., 73–75.

55. Laura Jacobus, "Piety and Propriety in the Arena Chapel," *Renaissance Studies* 12, no. 2 (1998): 117–205, at 179. The article discusses Giotto's frescoes of the early life of the Virgin in the context of contemporaneous conduct books and devotional literature. I am extremely grateful to Laura Jacobus for providing me with a copy of her illuminating article.

seen in works by Titian and Giotto). Her beauty, chastity, wisdom, and piety are extolled. She tells the priest Abiathar of her vow of perpetual virginity, on refusing his offer to marry his son, an extraordinary departure from Jewish tradition where marriage was regarded as a God-given duty. It is therefore necessary to find a guardian for her. Men without wives are invited to compete for Mary's hand, and each is instructed to bring a rod. A dove appears, signifying Joseph is favored; he resists but is overcome, and he and Mary are betrothed.

Mary and the five other virgins in the Temple again compete with each other for the colors of the veil for the tabernacle—on Mary's winning the purple, the others, jealous, tease her as "Regina virginum," or "queen of the virgins," for which they are rebuked by an angel since it is a true prophecy. The angel appears while Mary is weaving by the fountain, and the next day returns "to complete the Annunciation." As in the Book of James, Joseph arrives home to find Mary pregnant; the virgins defend her, but Joseph laments until reassured by the angel, whereupon he begs Mary's pardon. Mary and Joseph are summoned by the priests but absolved of any wrong. En route for Bethlehem, Mary is shown a cave by an angel, and Jesus is born. Joseph brings midwives, Zelomi who believes, and Salome whose doubt withers her hand, which is healed by touching the swaddling cloth. The ox and the ass adore the child; Jesus is circumcised and presented to Simeon. This is followed by the arrival of the magi, the massacre of the innocents, and the warning to flee into Egypt.

Pseudo-Matthew's use of the Book of James ends here, with the rest of the account possibly derived from local oral legend, and not taken from a written text.[56] On the way to Egypt, Mary sits beneath a very tall palm and asks Joseph for some of the fruit, despite the height of the tree. Jesus commands the palm to give his mother of its fruit—the tree bends as low as her feet, and on its rising, he tells it to give them the water concealed beneath its roots; the bending tree appears in Matraini's account (105). When Mary and the child enter the Temple at Hermopolis,[57] all the idols fall, fulfilling Isaiah's words, "Behold the Lord shall come upon a light cloud and enter into Egypt. And all the *gods* made by the hand of the Egyptians shall be moved before his face."[58]

56. James, *Apocryphal New Testament*, 74.

57. Hermopolis, or Huiusmopolis (Heliopolis). Heliopolis (Greek, "city of the sun") was a city in Egypt mentioned by Jeremiah in an oracle of doom directed against the Egyptians (Jeremiah 43:13).

58. Quoted in James, *Apocryphal New Testament*, 75.

Transitus *tales/texts*: As noted above, Mary's post-Resurrection life, dormition, and Assumption were the subjects of several varying accounts from which basic themes can be extrapolated.[59] She is described as living with a number of virgins and/or Saint John in Jerusalem, carrying out charitable activities and comforting the apostles. As we have seen, the earliest story of her death, or dormition, or *transitus*, appears to have originated in apocryphal literature from around the fourth century on. Longing to be reunited with her son, she is warned of her death through a visitation by him or by the archangel Gabriel. In the *Transitus Mariae* of Saint John the Divine, John returns from Ephesus, and is the narrator of the account, while the apostles, summoned from all the quarters of the world where they had gone to preach Christianity, also arrive to attend her deathbed.[60] Mary is afraid that the Jews will burn her body, a trope that occurs in Marinella's account. At her death, her soul is taken up to heaven by Jesus, and her body borne by the apostles to Jehosophat for burial. There is a funeral procession, and the high priest who tries to steal the bier has his arm fixed to it, an incident also included in Marinella's text. Jesus arrives in a chariot, calls into the tomb for his mother to arise, using the words from the Song of Songs, "Rise up, my love," summoning the archangel Michael to bring her soul. She rises, falls at his feet, and blesses him. He leaves her with angels who bear her to heaven. The scene of Mary's death is often depicted with her lying on a bier, the apostles all around her, while Christ stands over it, a little girl child, sometimes shown naked, symbolizing Mary's soul, sitting on his arm.

The *Transitus* texts, as this summary suggests, contain strongly anti-Semitic elements, hostile images that laid foundations for conventional anti-Semitism in later writings and visual art, and that are echoed to some extent in both the Matraini and Marinella accounts of Mary's life. (Marinella, having described the Jews as "envious" and "wicked" [207, 215 below]—conventional epithets in the context of medieval Christian literature—then relates the Virgin's fear, at the end of her life, that they will burn her body, the theme deriving from the *Transitus Mariae*.)[61] Mary's image in early Chris-

59. For the texts of the Assumption of the Virgin, see James, *Apocryphal New Testament*, 194–227; Elliott, *Apocryphal New Testament*, 691–723.

60. The standard Greek text of the *Transitus*, "The Discourse of St. John the Divine Concerning the Falling Asleep of the Holy Mother of God," is attributed to John the Theologian, or the Evangelist.

61. See Stephen J. Shoemaker, "'Let us go and burn her body': The Image of the Jews in the Early Dormition Traditions," *Church History* 68, no. 4 (1999): 775–823. According to John the Theologian, the Virgin says to him: "'The Jews have sworn that when my end cometh they will

tianity had developed in the context of Jewish and Christian debates over her virginity, as evinced in the argument between Trypho the Jew and Justin Martyr, and in the pagan Celsus's attacks on Christianity. In the early Middle Ages, her role as propounder of anti-Semitic views intensified, becoming a standard trope of both the tradition of the Christians versus the Jews and of early Marian hagiography, seen specifically in the narratives relating the end of her life. Anti-Semitism intensified during the period of the Crusades, the ostensible purpose of which was to regain the Christian places in the Holy Land; the figure of Mary in scenes of Christ's Passion, and her apostrophizings of the Jews, can be seen as a reflection of conventional Christian belief.

While several other apocryphal stories about the Virgin Mary exist, including the legend of her last years spent in Ephesus with Saint John the Evangelist, the two major accounts from the Book of James and Pseudo-Matthew, as well as the *Transitus* tales, serve to provide details of her legend as it came down through the Middle Ages. Their purpose was to supplement the somewhat scanty data of the gospels and Acts, but also to foster and strengthen belief in such teachings as the Immaculate Conception and the Virgin Birth and to extol specific virtues such as Mary's chastity and virginity, and to provide a genealogy for the mother of God. The Book of James was central to the very idea of Mary, and what came to be known and believed about her, and through its incorporation into medieval compendia of saints' lives, such as the *Golden Legend*, or devotional works like Pseudo-Bonaventure's *Meditations on the Life of Our Lord Jesus Christ*, it became part of popular piety and belief until the Counter-Reformation and beyond, informing the works of Matraini and Marinella.

MEDIEVAL CULT

Mary's cult was at its peak between the eleventh and thirteenth centuries. A mosaic of 1140, in the conch of the central apse of Santa Maria in Trastevere in Rome, shows her enthroned beside Christ as Queen of Heaven. She holds a phylactery, which reads in Latin: *Leva eius sub capite meo et dextera illius amplexabitur me* ("His left hand beneath my head, and his right hand shall embrace me" [Song of Songs 8:3]). Christ's arm encircles Mary, while the book on his knee reads: *Veni electa mea, ponam in te tronam meam* ("Come my chosen

burn my body.' And I answered and said unto her: 'Thy holy and precious body shall not see corruption'" (James, *Apocryphal New Testament*, 202).

one, I shall place thee on my throne").[62] By the Middle Ages the allegorical association between Mary and the Bride, or Shulamite, of the Old Testament love poems, probably an epithalamium, called the Song of Songs, had become standard. Following the rabbis who had interpreted the poem as an allegory of Yahweh's love for his people, Israel, it had been a logical step for Christian exegetes to see in it Christ's love for his Church, for every individual soul, and for the Virgin Mary. Ambrose appears to have been the first Church Father to have applied verses from the Song of Songs to the Church and to Mary, the type of the Church. He also used the imagery of the Song for his teaching on Mary, the injunction "Let him kiss me with the kiss of his mouth" (Song of Songs 1:1) signifying the grace of the Holy Spirit descending on her at the Annunciation.[63] Through allegory, Mary becomes the bride of her son. While the link between Mary and the Bride had occurred in earlier exegesis, it was Saint Bernard of Clairvaux, the founder of the Cistercian order of monks, who was to bring the allegory to its full mystical splendor, which became the source of much of the imagery surrounding the Virgin. In so doing he transformed what had been Mary's gentle cult in the West, an accompaniment to or by-product of the Christological year, into one of intense fervor of love and devotion for Mary herself, spread by the order, which established abbeys all over Europe during the twelfth century.

According to the gospel writers and exegetes, Mary did not have an important part in the events of her son's Passion. But just as Christ's Passion and death naturally became a focus during the Crusades, so too did the Virgin become part of that focus, as the sorrowing mother or *Mater Dolorosa,* a trope that had first appeared in the Eastern liturgy such as Romanos Melodos's *kontakion* for Good Friday, and was taken up by the Cistercians and mendicants in the medieval West. In the cultural interaction between East and West during the Crusades, the highly wrought religious "psyche" of the East was to inform and fuse with the mystical mode of the West: the *Christus triumphans* on his cross, triumphant over death, gave way to the Byzantine *Christus patiens,* suffering and dying, wounds in his side, hands, and feet, gushing blood, as in countless crucifixes painted in Italy during the twelfth and

62. The quotation from the book on Christ's knee is inspired by the Song of Songs, and by Psalm 45, taken from an antiphon for the feast of the Assumption in the eighth-century *Liber Pontificalis,* attributed to Pope Gregory the Great (Emile Mâle, *The Early Churches of Rome,* trans. by D. Buxton [London: E. Benn, 1960], 140–41). See Marina Warner, *Alone of All Her Sex* (New York: Vintage, 1983), 122, who notes the mosaicist's error in the transcription, which should read *ponam te in tronam meam.*

63. Saint Ambrose, *De Institutione Virginis* 94, and *Expositio in Psalmium* 118, 1, 16 (Graef, *Mary,* 1:85–86, 88).

thirteenth centuries.[64] Christ's Passion in its new form gave Mary a new role, and a kind of character development, one that was often highly dramatic, such as in her portrayal lamenting over her son's dead body in the marvelously moving hymn on the Passion in the vernacular, the "Donna del Paradiso," by the Franciscan Jacopone da Todi (ca. 1230–1306), and in contemporaneous mystery plays, cycles of plays that dramatized the most important biblical stories, from the Creation to the Last Judgment.

Prompted by such writings, and by such medieval meditational handbooks as the Pseudo-Bonaventure *Meditations on the Life of Christ,* and compilations of *vitae* or lives, legendary and otherwise, of saints and holy people, most notably the *Golden Legend* of Jacobus de Voragine, Mary's iconography was also to expand: Trecento Passion scenes in fresco, sculpture, glass, and miniatures show her accompanying her son on the way to Calvary, helping to take down his body from the cross, and preparing it for burial, often in strongly emotive and dynamic images. From the late fifteenth century, she was a focal point of the *Pietà* or Lamentation, a nonbiblical devotional image, in which Christ's body lies on the ground or on an altar-like block, surrounded by a group of mourners, with Mary weeping, nearly fainting, often held up by Saint John the Evangelist or Mary Magdalen—an object of pathos. Its purpose was religious contemplation, to stir compassion in the believer's heart and to remind him or her of its source, the events of Good Friday. A more private variant, known as the *Vesperbild,* but with the same devotional purpose and usually sculpted, shows Mary alone, seated, her adult child lying across her knees, in a kind of reversion to his childhood.[65] In Michelangelo's drawing for Vittoria Colonna, Christ's dead body is held between his mother's legs, while angels support his arms, a cross between the *Vesperbild* and a Man of Sorrows, or *imago pietatis,* an image of sorrow, where the dead Christ is shown standing or being held up by angels or saints, presented to the spectator to meditate upon, pathetic but triumphant: Vittoria Colonna's *Plaint* and Michelangelo's drawing are sixteenth-century interpretations of this *Pietà* genre.

By the Middle Ages, Mary's *vita* was complete. Influenced by courtly

64. Such as that by Alberto Sozio in the Duomo in Spoleto (1187), Italy, or the Crucifix of the Master of San Francesco (ca. 1260–72, National Gallery, London).

65. The *Vesperbild* is believed to have originated in the Rhineland in the thirteenth century, influenced by the twelfth-century Latin sequences of the Virgin's lamentations beneath the cross, the *Planctus Mariae.* See Joanna E. Ziegler, *Sculpture of Compassion: The Pietà and the Béguines in the Southern Low Countries c. 1300–c. 1600* (Brussels: Brepols, 1992), esp. 28–34. The earliest *Vesperbilds* have been linked to female convents in the Rhine Valley. See *Imago Mariae: Tesori d'arte della civiltà Christiana,* ed. Pietro Amato (Rome: A. Mondadori, 1988), 19.

poetry and feudalism, she was very much the medieval lady. Also imbued with character traits, she was humble, meek, silent, and passive, the ideal woman molded to the desiderata of the Church's male hierarchy, an example for all women, and a somewhat impossible one for most. In Mary the contemporary believer, especially the female, found her model not only in holiness but also in social behavior: Mary's humility and obedience, her timidity and modesty, were all qualities appropriate to the "handmaid of the Lord," taken from the story of the Annunciation—the Christian virtues based on the value of chastity. Despite the poverty and lowliness with which the gospels had endowed her, the medieval Mary descended from illustrious blood and noble lineage, a theory derived from the medieval equation of holiness with high rank. Her beauty was extolled and conformed to contemporary canons of pulchritude: in the earliest "Life of Mary," written by Epiphanius the Monk (d. ca. 800), her complexion was pale, and she had light brown hair and eyes, black eyebrows, a straight nose, and a long face, hands, and fingers, an ideal Byzantine beauty.[66] Traveling westward, her hair became blonde or golden, her eyes blue: in the Latin *Vita Beatae Virginis Mariae et Salvatoris Rhythmica,* written by Werner the Swiss in 1172, and described as reading like a versified novel, she was a medieval German maiden, blonde, with blue eyes, highly arched brows, acquiline nose, and red, fullish lips—the author remarks on the cleanliness of her teeth and breath. (It is also here that her task of cleaning ornaments as a Temple virgin is related).[67] In 1624 Cardinal Federico Borromeo was to explicitly describe the way Mary was to be portrayed: "her complexion was the color of grain [Latin, *triticum*]. Her hair was blonde, her eyes intelligent, clear, with pupils the color of olives. Her eyebrows were arched and rather black, she had a long nose, lips bright and full of sweet words; her face not round and sharp but somewhat long, her hands and fingers similarly rather long."[68]

66. Graef, *Mary*, 1:182. She could, however, have the same features, but with black hair and dark eyes, as in the mosaic in Santa Maria in Trastevere.

67. *Vita Beatae Virginis Mariae et Salvatoris Rhythmica,* ed. A. Vögtlin (Tübingen: Literarischer verein in Stuttgart, 1888). This uses the Book of James, but is extravagantly exaggerated. It was the source of many similar works in the vernacular. In the Passion story, Mary loses control and raves hysterically, fainting at Jesus's arrest, then laments and falls into a deathlike swoon at the scourging, and screams and tears her hair at the carrying of the cross. Christ appears to her after the Resurrection, and she asks him to preserve her body from the Jews' fury. After various miracles and conversions, she ascends through various heavens to become Empress of Heaven (Graef, *Mary*, 1:259–62).

68. Federico Borromeo, *Le immagini della Beatissima Vergine* (1624), chap. V: "colore fuit triticum, referente, capillo flavo, oculis acribus, subflavas, et tanquam oleae colore pupillas in eis habens.

Mary's behavior and comportment were also those of a medieval lady. Jacobus has shown that an international consensus existed on matters of social decorum, which can be seen in devotional literature and conduct books of the time.[69] Mary becomes a Temple virgin (an element found in both Matraini and Marinella) at three years of age (according to Matraini) or seven (a highly anachronistic feature, as well as inaccurate, since women in the Jewish religion were not allowed into the inner sanctum), her tasks to keep ornaments clean, to read the Bible, and to weave and spin, much like a medieval nun.[70] In the second and third editions of her *Life of the Virgin Mary,* Marinella describes how such activities continued to be carried out by young girls—"this is still the case amongst us today" (148 below). Mary is also eloquent but prudent of speech, a requisite for the female in secular handbooks written on her behalf such as Juan Luis Vives's *Education of a Christian Woman* (1524), and a feature found in Matraini's and Marinella's characterizations. Mary's knowledge of the Bible is excellent, and she is able to expound upon it in its tropological, mystical, moral, and literal meanings (cf. 150 below).[71]

Mary is humble and obedient, her humility allowing her to praise God in her adversities (194 below). The author of Pseudo-Bonaventure's *Meditations,* addressed to a Poor Clare, explains that the pregnant virgin, always conscious of her duty to God, and being very prudent, remained silent though aware of her husband's distress; becoming distressed herself, as she did not like to deceive him, she hoped that God might deign to alleviate their marital difficulties.[72] Matraini quotes the original language of this passage almost verbatim. But in fact it is the Virgin's humility that does not allow her to presume to disclose God's plan to Joseph (cf. 93 below). In Marinella's account of the Visitation, Elizabeth does not fall to the ground as she would on greeting the Mother of God, for fear, she explains, of offending the Virgin's humility (168 below). Thus humility and courtesy, ideal feminine traits, are exemplified in this scene, humility being the chief Franciscan virtue, as well

Supercilia ei erant inflexa, et decenter nigra, nasus longior, labia florida, et verborum suavitate plena; facies non rotunda et acuta, sed aliquanto longior, manus simul et digiti longiores" (*Imago Mariae,* ed. Amato, 33).

69. See Jacobus, "Piety and Propriety," 180ff.

70. See Graef, *Mary,* 1:259–60.

71. Ibid., 1:259.

72. Jacobus, "Piety and Propriety," 190. Cf. Pseudo-Bonaventure, or Giovanni de Caulibus, *Meditations on the Life of Christ: An Illustrated Manuscript of the Fourteenth Century,* trans. by Isa Ragusa, ed. Isa Ragusa and Rosalie B. Green (Princeton, NJ: Princeton University Press, 1961), 29.

as a weapon of female subordination.[73] In fourteenth- and fifteenth-century Italy, a particular genre of image, the "Madonna of Humility," showed Mary seated on a cushion on the ground, nursing her child, as Marina Warner has noted, "the one natural biological function . . . permitted the Virgin."[74] It is an ambiguous image since it symbolizes her humanity, demonstrating her maternal power as life-giver, her milk the symbol of the gift of life, while at the same time seating her on the lowly ground (Latin, *humus,* "ground," root of "humility"). Such nurturing figures would be models for women.

When traveling to visit Elizabeth, Mary is accompanied by "two elderly women" as well as Joseph, since etiquette would never allow a lady to go out on her own (cf. 168 below). Mary dutifully, as any good wife, takes in needlework to augment the little that Joseph as a foreigner can earn while in Egypt (194 below). She spends her last days reading the psalms, meditating, and doing good works, all Counter-Reformation desiderata. In Mary the contemporary believer, especially the female, found a model not only in holiness but also in social behavior, or decorum, as would the women readers of Matraini's and Marinella's works.

By the time Vittoria Colonna, Chiara Matraini, and Lucrezia Marinella came to write their individual studies of the Virgin, there was of course a vast host of source material from which they could choose, and in which they were already probably well versed, popularizing compendia such as the *Golden Legend,* an Italian translation of which had been printed by Nicolas Jensen in Venice after 1475, and the *Meditations on the Life of Christ,* which was printed in 1527, as well as countless individual works such as Antonio Cornazzano's *Vita della Gloriosa Vergine* (1485), Pietro Aretino's *Vita di Maria Vergine* (1539), and the Dominican Luís de Granada's popular *Rosario della sacratissima vergine Maria, madre di Dio, nostra avocata* (1572).[75] From 1559, however, the only Bible to which women could have had ready access was the Vulgate, since Session 25 of the Council of Trent placed all unauthorized vernacular bibles, both the Old Testament and the New, on the Index of Prohibited Books; nonetheless, bibles and other Protestant literature might be obtained

73. See Jacobus, "Piety and Propriety," 195, where Mary is the model of courtesy in the episode of the Visitation, which encapsulates "the delicate etiquette of a meeting between two women who in worldly terms were closely ranked by their shared lineage, but were of unequal heavenly rank." See also Jacobus's insightful comments in relation to Giotto's depiction of the scene (ibid., 196).

74. Warner, *Alone of All Her Sex,* 192.

75. Pietro Aretino, a self-confessed atheist, published his *Vita di Maria Vergine* in 1539, presumably aware of a market for the genre. Luís de Granada's *Rosario* was published thirteen times between 1572 and 1593.

in Venice and Flemish cities.[76] Women would also have had access to devotional literature and summaries of the Bible in the vernacular.

CATHOLIC REFORMATION AND COUNTER-REFORMATION

Two fundamental teachings about Mary were to remain the subjects of controversy until the nineteenth and twentieth centuries, but both became part of the Church's armory in its conflicts with Protestantism during the sixteenth century. One, the story of the ending of her life, which, through various ramifications, evolved into her bodily assumption into heaven, and became dogma in 1950; the other, the Immaculate Conception, the teaching that from the first instance of conception, Mary had been preserved free of original sin, became Church dogma in 1854. The idea of original sin, that each person was stained by sin at the moment of conception, had become the standard of the Western Church through the deliberations of churchmen such as Augustine. For Mary to be untainted, as the mother of a divine as well as human son, it was deemed necessary for her own conception to be sinless, that is, that her own conception had taken place without the concupiscence, or desire, that normal human generation required. Thus Joachim and Anna procreate without passion, and Mary is conceived sinlessly. Although the idea had first appeared in the Book of James, it was ultimately endorsed by the Western Church, though not by the Eastern Orthodox Church because of its different understanding of the nature of original sin.

Saint Bernard of Clairvaux, one of the Virgin's staunchest supporters, in fact opposed the doctrine of her immaculate conception, as did other great churchmen such as the Dominican Saint Albert the Great (d. 1280), the Franciscan Saint Bonaventure (ca. 1217–74), and Saint Thomas Aquinas (ca. 1225–74), the Dominican theologian and philosopher, as they held that the stain of original sin was transmitted in every natural conception: since Mary had been conceived in the natural way, she could not be exempt from original sin. The Dominicans, following Aquinas, generally opposed the concept, but it was accepted and defended by the Franciscans, and the controversy was to continue during the fourteenth and fifteenth centuries and beyond; from the sixteenth century it was also chiefly promoted by the Jesuits. Both the doctrines of the Immaculate Conception and Mary's Assumption took on

76. William Monter, "Protestant Wives, Catholic Saints, and the Devil's Handmaid: Women in the Age of Reformations," in *Becoming Visible: Women in European History,* ed. R. Bridenthal, C. Koonz, and S. Stuard (Boston: Houghton Mifflin, 1987), 204–19, at 207.

particular importance in the sixteenth and seventeenth centuries during the Church of Rome's conflict with the Protestants, a conflict that was the source of widespread imagery of the Immaculate Virgin in seventeenth-century art, and these teachings can be seen in both Matraini's and Marinella's treatments of and emphasis on these elements.

Mary's cult itself came under intense scrutiny from the second decade of the sixteenth century until reaffirmation of its role in the revival of the Church of Rome after the end of the Council of Trent (1563). Even before 1517, when Martin Luther (1483–1546) nailed his Ninety-Five Theses upon Indulgences to the door of Wittenberg Cathedral, demands came from within the Church itself for a spiritual revival, a renewal of discipline, and for an end to the abuses, ignorance, and corruption of the clergy. Vittoria Colonna and Michelangelo were among the humanist Catholic reformers around Pope Paul III (papacy, 1534–49). While the Virgin's theological status as the Mother of God was not a matter of dispute, the Marian cult came under fire by the reformers and later by the Reformation. Luther's denial of papal authority was to lead to the Protestant reliance on the Scriptures alone. It was on this basis that he could accept the figure of Mary, but only as the instrument of the Incarnation, and as the scriptural mother of Christ. It is interesting to note that he accepted the traditional belief in her virginity *in partu,* and also the Immaculate Conception, but not dogmatically as it was not scriptural. Until his later years Luther accepted Mary's Assumption, but ultimately thoroughly rejected it.[77] Together with other reformers such as Erasmus and Calvin, he attacked Mary's glorification by the Church of Rome: in both Luther and Erasmus's view, elevating Mary would lead to idolatry and to a diminution of the rightful fervor toward Christ.[78] The French theologian Calvin (1509–64) accepted neither the Immaculate Conception nor the Assumption, and was undecided about Mary's perpetual virginity, but he defined her as the "Holy Virgin" and a model Christian; like the other reformers, he deplored her cult.[79]

Prompted by the irrevocable schism between Rome and the Protestants,

77. See Graef, *Mary,* 2:6–12, on Luther and his views on Mary.

78. Originally a conventionally devout believer in Mary, the humanist Erasmus of Rotterdam (ca. 1466–1536) became one of the most formidable voices in his demand for Church reform, particularly concerning the cult surrounding Mary: in his view Christ was the center of devotion, and the merely outer trappings, such as images, processions, relics, indulgences, and ritual, should be done away with, together with the excesses of Marian devotion. See Graef, *Mary,* 2: 2–6.

79. Ibid., 2:12–13.

which would become definitive by 1562–63, the Church called together the Council of Trent to deal with the spread of Protestantism, to make moral and administrative reforms, and to renew its spiritual life. Opening in 1546, the Council had a profound effect on Mary's cult through three separate decisions. First, in Session 4 (held April 8), the equal validity of the Scriptures as well as the unwritten traditions of the Church as sources of religious truth were asserted, thus giving, though not explicitly, canonical authority to traditional beliefs such as the tales and miracles that had informed the figure of Mary. The same decree stated Saint Jerome's Vulgate to be the only canonical text of the Bible, and declared the Church's sole right to interpret it. This of course flew in the face of humanist translations of the Bible, and it also maintained the mistranslation of *almah*.[80] Second, Mary was specifically held exempt in the decree concerning original sin, which followed Augustine's definition, but no pronouncement was made on the Immaculate Conception.[81] And, third, by implication her cult was endorsed in the twenty-fifth session (December 3–4, 1563) concerning the invocation, veneration, and relics of saints and sacred images, in which the Council stressed the efficacy of invoking saints to gain benefits from God through Christ. Harking back to Gregory the Great's (ca. 540–604) dictum of the late sixth century that the function of art was to be the Bible of the illiterate,[82] the Church now reiterated its stance on images as instruments to express elements of belief: "And the bishops shall carefully teach this—that by means of the histories of the mysteries of our Redemption, portrayed by paintings or other representations, the people are instructed and confirmed in the habit of remembering and continually revolving in the mind the articles of the faith."[83]

By the end of the Council in December 1563 Mary's place as the unassailable focus of new piety, triumph, and exaltation was assured. A major constituent of the Counter-Reformation Church's arsenal in its reassertion of traditional Catholic beliefs and practices, Mary, through word, image, and

80. *The Council of Trent: The Fourth Session. The canons and decrees of the sacred and oecumenical Council of Trent,* trans. by J. Waterworth (New York: E. Dunigan, 1848), 17–21 (April 8, 1546: Decree concerning the canonical scriptures).

81. Ibid., *The Fifth Session,* June 17, 1546, at 4: "This same Synod doth nevertheless declare, that it is not its intention to include in this decree, where original sin is treated of, the blessed and immaculate Virgin Mary, the Mother of God, but that the constitutions of Pope Sixtus IV, of happy memory, are to be observed."

82. Saint Gregory, *Epistle* 9:9: "That which the written word is for readers, so are pictures for the uneducated." Quoted in James Hall, *A History of Ideas and Images in Italian Art* (London: John Murray, 1983), 4.

83. *The Council of Trent: The Twenty-Fifth Session,* December 3–4, 1563, at 235.

act, was given a passively combative role. (It was due to her intercession, it was believed, that the Venetian fleet was victorious over the Turks at the battle of Lepanto in 1571, prompted by the rosaries recited that day.)[84] The Immaculate Conception was the theological pivot and center of devotion: Mary's virginity before, during, and *post partum* was her role in redemption. The image of her assumption into heaven proliferated in literature and art, in scenes from both gospel and apocrypha, celebrating the Catholic Church's resurgence. The cult of Mary's Seven Sorrows (referred to in all three texts in this book) spread after its endorsement by Paul V (papacy, 1605–21), a leading proponent of the Counter-Reformation.

As part of its spiritual and moral revival, the Church imposed new instruments on to the way of life of its faithful. The family, and the roles of spouses and parents, became a focus of the post-Tridentine church, and elements reflecting these aspects of social life are a feature of Matraini's and Marinella's texts. Prior to Trent the Church had attempted to gain control over the marriage ceremony, and in 1547 it reaffirmed that marriage was a sacrament rather than a civil contract, and one that conferred grace. Hitherto a legal ceremony between two people, now, according to the Tridentine decree *Tametsi* (Session 24, November 11, 1563), a marriage was valid only when it took place in the presence of a parish priest or the local ordinary, had at least two witnesses, and was undertaken with the free consent of bride and groom.[85] Matrimony required the Church's sanction, a method of social control equal to the stress on confession and penance and the behavior of the faithful. Matraini's and Marinella's texts emphasize the role of marriage and its purpose, procreation, finding in Anna and Joachim and Mary and Joseph examples of Christian marriage and fidelity, albeit that in neither case, of course, was the process of procreation exactly a practical model to follow. In the name of tradition, and despite Tridentine rejection of apocrypha, the figures of Joachim and Anna, particularly the latter, came into focus once more, becoming highly popular despite criticism from Church leaders. Bowing to pressure from the Protestants, Pius V had suppressed the feasts of the Presentation of the Virgin and of the Virgin's parents, but Six-

84. Confraternities of the Rosary had been founded in the late fifteenth century, but the fifteen Mysteries, with 150 Aves and fifteen Pater Nosters and Glorias, were developed in the sixteenth century, and the feast of the Rosary itself instituted by Pius V (papacy, 1566–72), the Dominican pope who attributed the victory to Mary's intercession.

85. *The Council of Trent: The Twenty-fourth Session*, November 11, 1563, "Decree on the Reformation of Marriage," 198. See also Brian Richardson, "'Amore maritale': Advice on Love and Marriage in the Second Half of the Cinquecento," in *Women in Italian Renaissance Culture and Society*, ed. Letizia Panizza (Oxford: European Humanities Research Centre, 2000), 194–208.

tus V (papacy, 1585–90) reestablished the first, and Gregory XIII (papacy, 1572–85) the second.[86]

Motherhood is seen as secondary in the order of things by a Church that viewed women in the following declining hierarchy of nuns, widows, and wives, a ranking determined by the Church's ideal of virginity. Motherhood was, however, also regarded as a woman's duty, her purpose. Marriage, motherhood, and grandmotherhood are exemplified by the cult of Saint Anne, fostered first in northern Europe during the fifteenth and early sixteenth centuries, and one of the objects held in particular contumely by Luther and other reformers. (A debate as to how many husbands—two or three?—and other daughters Anna might have had even took place during the sixteenth century.)[87] Saint Anne is often shown teaching the Virgin to read—inculcating the proper religious education of children as part of the new stress in Counter-Reformation family ideology. And, still in pursuit of family values, the Church of Rome also emphasized the father figure of Joseph as part of the cult of the Holy Family, which became popular from the sixteenth century, portraying Joseph as a responsible father and husband, earning a living as a carpenter, as indeed he is described in the gospels of Matthew and Luke. In Counter-Reformation literature and art, as earlier, Joseph is generally depicted as an old man holding the child in his arms, working at his table with Jesus helping him (Mary sewing nearby), or feeding or playing with the Christ child, as any man might with his child.

Despite Tridentine condemnation of works propagating erroneous dogma and apocrypha, images of the Virgin's legendary life proliferated from the late sixteenth century, such as, for example, scenes of her embroidering in the Temple,[88] her marriage, and the new theme of the "Rest on the Flight into Egypt," as depictions of Mary's domestic life became part of the

86. Émile Mâle, *L'art religieux du XVIIe siècle* (Paris: Armand Colin, 1984), 197–98.

87. Early medieval commentators in the West identified Mary's sisters as the two other Marys mentioned in the Gospels (John 19:25 and Mark 16:1). To account for their paternity, it was deemed that after Joachim's death, Anna had married Cleopas (father of Mary Cleopas), and that her third husband was Salome (father of Mary Salome). This was the theory of the *trinubium*, or the three marriages of Anna. See "Legends of St. Anne, Mother of the Virgin Mary," in *Middle English Legends of Women Saints*, ed. Sherry L. Reames (Kalamazoo, Mich.: Medieval Institute Publications, 2003).

88. See, for example, Guido Reni's *Virgin Mary Embroidering in the Temple* (1610, Quirinale Palace, Rome). Reni's cycle is in the Cappella dell'Annunziata, the papal chapel, and must therefore have been approved by Pope Paul V. It also contains depictions of the Virgin's birth and the annunciation to Joachim. Prior to this period, the Virgin had been shown sewing or spinning or reading in scenes of the Annunciation, again occupations deemed suitable for women.

wider social ideology emphasized by the Church.[89] There are also fictional elaborations of scenes: Mary sometimes assists Christ at the flagellation, is present at the descent from the cross,[90] and features in the entirely apocryphal scenes of Christ bidding farewell and then appearing to his mother first after the Resurrection.[91] Both Matraini and Marinella include this last episode, Matraini justifying her so doing with the well-rehearsed argument that the scene had not been included by the evangelists since the women who *had* seen Christ had been disbelieved; it was, however, "most certain that Jesus Christ appeared first to His Mother . . . as she had loved Him more than the others had" (111 below).[92] She was, after all, his mother. Paintings of the Virgin's death, her Assumption, and the Immaculate Conception were also part of Rome's weaponry regarding orthodoxy, the last being an object of particular devotion of the Jesuits.[93] Marinella's surprisingly intimate (since she was unmarried at the time of its writing) scene of Mary's birth—Anna giving suck to the Virgin and Joachim's heating of swaddling clothes—may have been prompted by similarly realistic portrayals of the Virgin nursing the child, an image supported by the Dominicans, particularly since they held that as Mary was not free from original sin, lactation was her inheritance; she had accepted the full human, female, condition (145–46 below).

Letizia Panizza has shown that sixteenth- and seventeenth-century women writers specialized in religious writing, finding expression and publication in the most popular genre of writing, devotional prose and poetry, as exemplified in the three writers in this volume.[94] Both Colonna's and Marinella's texts—and Matraini's to a lesser extent—show their debt

89. Orazio Gentileschi's *Rest on the Flight into Egypt* (ca. 1627, Kunsthistorisches Museum, Vienna) shows Joseph lying, exhausted by his travails, while Mary tenderly feeds her son, the realism of the scene conveyed in the veined, full breast, while the Christ child looks at the spectator as he sucks.

90. This scene had been depicted from the early Middle Ages.

91. Guercino's dramatic and moving painting of the *Resurrected Christ Appearing to His Mother,* of 1628–30, is in the Pinacoteca Civica, Cento, Italy.

92. For the history of this theme, see James D. Breckenridge, "'Et prima vidit': The Iconography of the Appearance of Christ to His Mother," *Art Bulletin* 39, no. 1 (1957): 9–32.

93. Caravaggio's *Death of the Virgin* of 1606, now in the Louvre, so shocked its patrons for its corpse-like figure, a rendering that contradicted the dogma of Mary's immortality, that they rejected it. His painting of the *Madonna dei Palafrenieri* (Galleria Doria Pamphilj, Rome) shows the Virgin, her foot on the head of the serpent, and beneath that of the naked Christ child. The concept of the Immaculate Conception is embodied in the presence of the figure of Saint Anne standing by, and the crushing of sin and heresy, the triumph over evil, is symbolized by the serpent.

94. *A History of Women's Writing in Italy,* ed. Letizia Panizza and Sharon Wood (Cambridge: Cambridge University Press, 2000), 3, 4.

to contemporary meditative practice and imagery. Spiritual exercises had been practiced from the early Church Fathers onwards; by the Middle Ages they were "codified" in several manuscripts, such as the life of Christ by Pseudo-Bonaventure and that by Ludolf the Carthusian (d. 1378), in which the ways of imagining the entire life of Christ were set forth. Every detail of the story was to be dramatized as if the meditator were present: "I think it is pleasant to contemplate this scene . . . regardless of the truth of the matter," states the author of the *Meditations*. Further, "it is possible to contemplate, explain, and understand the Holy Scriptures in as many ways as we consider necessary, in such a manner as not to contradict the truth of life and justice and not to oppose faith and morality," the purpose being to "yield devotion, increase love, excite fervor, induce compassion, allow purity and simplicity, [and] nurture the vigor of humility and poverty."[95] Ignatius Loyola (1491/5–1556), founder of the Jesuit order, described paintings as icons for meditation, and in the *Spiritual Exercises*, published in 1548, but written twenty years earlier, he stressed the importance of the imaginative pictorial realization of the subject being meditated upon through the use of all the senses: the meditator was to see, hear, and feel Christ's (or the saints') suffering through internal visualization. Under the stimulus of the Counter-Reformation and the Jesuits, its spearhead, new treatises were written, the most popular of which were the Dominican Fray Luís de Granada's (1504–88) *Book of Prayer and Meditation* (translated into Italian in 1561) and the *Spiritual Combat* (1589) by Lorenzo Scupoli or by Theatine writers. Such manuals of meditation, or inculcation of their modes of practice, may well have been sources for the three women's writing.

Colonna and Marinella, and Matraini to a lesser extent, show their debt to current stylistic techniques such as the elaboration of scenes referred to above, whereby people, *loci*, and works of art were described in detail, an example of the rhetorical *ekphrasis*, or *descriptio*, used widely in Late Antique and medieval poetry. Colonna's *Plaint* begins with a meditation on the vision she conjures for herself of the *Pietà*, a vision that was possibly prompted by a specific image, Michelangelo's drawing for her. In the *Pietà*, time is held in suspense: it exists to allow the poet to move out from that particular moment or image, and to recreate the circumstances of the Passion, based on the gospel accounts, and the source of the Virgin's grief, in highly visual terms. Mary as mother holds the body of the grown Christ be-

95. *Meditations*, 38, 5, 71–72. Ludolf the Carthusian was the author of the celebrated *Vita Christi*, a meditation on the life of Christ, the great popularity of which is attested to by the numerous manuscript copies extant in libraries and the many editions published from 1474.

tween her knees, offering him to the viewer, narrative and drama to lead to a heightened emotional response.[96] Marinella's epic style, its minutely detailed descriptive passages evoking a sense of visual immediacy, follows the precepts of Counter-Reformation writers such as Gabriele Paleotti, bishop of Bologna, on the nature and role of art, and the value of the artistic object as an incitement to piety.[97]

While all three works are different in approach and execution, two, Matraini's and Marinella's, share a common heritage and belong to a new artistic form. (The three different responses to the idea of Mary are discussed in the sections devoted to the writers individually.) Although written in the late sixteenth and early seventeenth centuries, their texts maintain essentially medieval ideologies and social customs. Despite the Council of Trent and its critics, the medieval spirit is still very much alive, but both Matraini's and Marinella's stress on the doctrines of the Immaculate Conception and the Assumption bring their works into the Counter-Reformation, the period par excellence when such teachings were triumphantly asserted. At the same time, they are both clearly set within the new spirituality that affected literary forms in that they are written in the epic genre, which celebrated heroic actions of martyrs and newly canonized saints in long extended narratives. The theology of all three is conventional contemporary Catholicism, a profoundly integral part of the authors' daily lives. Matraini's and Marinella's *Lives* are sociologically interesting, with their focus on women's behavior and domestic lives. As noted above, in its desire to keep women in the domestic sphere as wives and mothers, the medieval Church propagated its own ideal in Mary, one that had changed little by the sixteenth and seventeenth centuries. The works of Matraini and Marinella can also be seen as manuals of instruction for women since they offer narrative images and texts of Mary's life as an example of how to live devout lives, both personally and socially, in their paeans to the model proffered them by the Church.

NOTE ON SOURCES AND TRANSLATION

The three works translated in this volume appeared in several editions either during or shortly after their authors' lifetimes. In the case of Vittoria Colonna, the one chosen is the Aldine edition of 1557, which followed a year after the first edition of 1556, both posthumous, without significant

96. See below, introduction to Colonna, 52–53.

97. Cardinal Gabriele Paleotti, *Discorso intorno alle imagini sacre e profane,* in *Tratti d'arte del Cinquecento: fra manierismo e Controriforma,* 3 vols., ed. Paola Barocchi (Bari: Laterza, 1961), 2:119–509.

changes to the text. Chiara Matraini's work was first published in 1590, but that text was not available to me at the time of translation, and I made use of the undated edition of ca. 1650. I was subsequently able to compare the two editions, to find that the texts are essentially the same. The title page and author portrait are taken from the 1590 edition, as the woodcut on the title page does not appear in the later edition. The 1610 edition of Lucrezia Marinella's work, rather than either of the two earlier editions of 1602 and 1604, was chosen so that additions made by the author to the later edition could be included. The engraved title page and illustrations, however, are taken from the 1602 quarto edition, the only edition in which they appear, since the two subsequent editions are in a smaller format. Biblical quotations given in English are taken from the Douay-Rheims version of the Holy Bible, as published by the Catholic Truth Society in 1956, since the language and literary style of this translation are both evocative of and contemporary with the works here translated.[98]

Since this volume treats of a theme, the Virgin Mary, and not of a particular writer, but of three writers' different responses to that theme, a short biography and select bibliography for each opens their respective chapters, enabling readers to find easily further reading on the subject. The nature of these works has required an extensive discussion of the theological issues and literary sources that lie behind them, and this has of necessity been done at the expense of a more literary analysis, which will be supplied by those critics who may make use of this edition and translation. Again because of the volume's thematic subject matter, the dedications or prefatory material to the works translated have not been included, nor has a translation of Lucrezia Marinella's poem in *ottava rima* been provided as it is, to all intents and purposes, a separate work, although published under the same title. Equally, the annotations to Chiara Matraini's work by Don Giuseppe Mozzagrugno have not been incorporated in this translation as they are not the work of the author herself; the reader, however, should note that they offer an interesting commentary on her text. Prose translations of Matraini's sonnets and prayers have been added. The original voices have been maintained as far as possible, since they are evocative of both time and subject, and this can be done only by adhering very closely to the style of each of the writers when translating. Hence, it is to be hoped that, while there has been no attempt at pastiche, the spirit of those voices may be heard.

98. The Holy Bible, translated from the Latin Vulgate (Old Testament: Douay, 1609; New Testament: Rheims, 1582). Preface by H. E. the Cardinal Archbishop of Westminster; notes compiled by Bishop Challoner (1691–1781) (London: Catholic Truth Society, 1956).

VOLUME EDITOR'S BIBLIOGRAPHY

PRIMARY SOURCES

The Apocryphal New Testament: A Collection of Apocryphal Christian Literature in an English Translation. Trans. by J. K. Elliott. Oxford: Clarendon Press, 1993.

The Apocryphal New Testament. Being the Apocryphal Gospels, Acts, Epistles and Apocalypses. Ed. and trans. by M. R. James. Oxford: Clarendon Press, 1924.

Colonna, Vittoria. *Carteggio*. Ed. E. Ferrero and G. L. Muller. Turin: Loescher, 1889; 2nd ed. with supplement, 1892.

———. *Pianto della Marchesa di Pescara sopra la passione di Christo. Oratione della medesima, sopra l'Ave Maria . . . etc.* Bologna: Antonio Manutio, 1557.

———. *Rime*. Ed. Alan Bullock. Rome: G. Laterza, 1982.

———. *Rime de la Divina Vittoria Colonna Marchesa di Pescara. Novamente stampate con privilegio*. Parma: [Antonio Viotti], 1538.

———. *Sonnets for Michelangelo: A Bilingual Edition*. Ed. and trans. by Abigail Brundin. The Other Voice in Early Modern Europe. Chicago: University of Chicago Press, 2005.

———. *Tutte le Rime della Illustriss. et Eccellentiss. Signora Vittoria Colonna, Marchesana di Pescara*. Venice: Giovan Battista e Melchior Sessa Fratelli, 1558.

The Council of Trent. The Fourth Session. The Canons and Decrees of the Sacred and Oecumenical Council of Trent. Trans. by James Waterworth. New York: E. Dunigan, 1848.

The Holy Bible, Douay Version. Translated from the Latin Vulgate (The Old Testament: Douay, 1609; The New Testament: Rheims, 1582). Preface by H. E. the Cardinal Archbishop of Westminster. Notes compiled by Bishop Challoner (1691–1781). London: Catholic Truth Society, 1956; reprinted, Rockford, IL: Tan Books, 1971.

The Jerusalem Bible. Ed. Alexander Jones. Garden City, NY: Doubleday, 1966.

Marinella, Lucrezia. *Arcadia felice*. Venice: Gio Battista Ciotti, 1605.

———. *Arcadia felice*. Ed. Françoise Lavocat. Florence: Accademia Toscana de scienze e lettere, "La colombaria," 162, 1998.

———. *La colomba sacra. Poema heroico di Lucrezia Marinella*. Venice: Gio Battista Ciotti, 1595.

———. *L'Enrico overo Bisantio acquistato*. Venice: Gherardo Imberti, 1635.

———. *Essortationi alle donne et a gli altri, se a loro sarrano a grado. Parte Prima.* Venice: Francesco Valvasense, 1645.

———. *La nobiltà et eccellenza delle donne, coi difetti et mancamenti de gli uomini.* Venice: Gio Battista Ciotti, 1600, 1601, 1621.

———. *The Nobility and Excellence of Women.* Ed. and trans. by Anne Dunhill. Intro. by Letizia Panizza. The Other Voice in Early Modern Europe. Chicago: University of Chicago Press, 2000.

———. *Vita del serafico, et glorioso San Francesco. Descritta in ottava rima.* Venice: Pietro Maria Bertano, et fratelli, 1597.

———. *La vita di Maria Vergine Imperatrice dell'Universo descritta in prosa & in ottava rima dalla molto illustre Sig. Lucretia Marinella; et hora in questa terza impressione da lei molto ampliata . . . Dedicata al Serenissimo Prencipe, & all'Eccelsa Signoria di Vinegia.* Venice: Barezzo Barezzi, 1610. Other editions also published in Venice in 1602, 1604, 1617.

Matraini, Chiara. *Breve discorso sopra la Vita e laude della Beatiss. Verg. e Madre del Figliuol di Dio.* Lucca: Vincenzio Busdraghi, 1590.

———. *Considerationi sopra i sette Salmi penitentiali del Gran Ré e Profeta Davit.* Lucca: Vincenzo Busdraghi, 1586.

———. *Dialoghi spirituali.* Venice: Fiorante Prati, 1602.

———. *Lettere di madonna Chiara Matraini gentildonna Lucchese, con la prima, e seconda parte delle sue Rime. Con una Lettera in difesa delle Lettere, e delle Arme. Nuovamente stampate.* Venice: Nicolò Moretti, 1597.

———. *Meditationi spirituali.* Lucca: Vincenti Busdraghi, 1581.

———. *Rime e lettere.* Ed. Giovanna Rabitti. Bologna: Commissione per i Testi di Lingua, 1989.

———. *Rime et prose di Madonna Chiara Matraini gentildonna lucchese.* Lucca: per il Busdrago, 1555.

———. *Selected Poetry and Prose: A Bilingual Edition.* Ed. and trans. by Elaine MacLachlan. Intro. by Giovanna Rabitti. The Other Voice in Early Modern Europe. Chicago: University of Chicago Press, 2007.

———. *Vita della beatissima Vergine Maria, Madre, e Sposa del Figliuol di Dio. Descritta in un discorso brevemente da M. Chiara Matraini, Gentildonna Luchese. Nuovamente Ristampata, e di belle figure adornata.* Venice: Antonio Remondini, n.d. [1650].

Paleotti, Cardinal Gabriele. *Discorso intorno alle imagini sacre e profane,* in *Tratti d'arte del Cinquecento: fra manierismo e Controriforma,* 2:119–509. Ed. Paola Barocchi. Bari: Laterza, 1961.

Pseudo-Bonaventure, or Giovanni de Caulibus. *Meditations on the Life of Christ: An Illustrated Manuscript of the Fourteenth Century. Paris: Bibliothèque nationale, Ms. Ital. 115.* Trans. by Ira Ragusa. Completed from the Latin and edited by Isa Ragusa and Rosalie B. Green. Princeton, NJ: Princeton University Press, 1961.

Vita beate virginis Marie et Salvatoris rhythmica. Ed. A.Vögtlin. Tübingen: Litterarischer Verein in Stuttgart, 1888.

Voragine, Jacobus de. *The Golden Legend: Readings on the Saints.* 2 vols. Trans. by William Granger Ryan. Princeton, NJ: Princeton University Press, 1993.

SECONDARY SOURCES

Bassanese, Fiora A. "Vittoria Colonna." In *Italian Women Writers: A Bio-Bibliographical Sourcebook*, ed. Rinaldina Russell, 85–94. Westport, CT: Greenwood Press, 1994.

Becoming Visible: Women in European History. Ed. R. Bridenthal, C. Koonz, and S. Stuard. 2nd ed. Boston: Houghton Mifflin, 1987.

Breckenridge, James D., "'Et prima vidit': The Iconography of the Appearance of Christ to His Mother." *The Art Bulletin* 39, no. 1 (March 1957): 9–32.

Brundin, Abigail. "Vittoria Colonna and the Virgin Mary." *Modern Language Review* 97, no. 1 (2001): 61–81.

Cameron, Averil. "The Cult of the Virgin in Late Antiquity: Religious Development and Myth-Making." In *The Church and Mary: Papers Read at the 2001 Summer Meeting and the 2002 Winter Meeting of the Ecclesiastical History Society*. Studies in Church History, 39, ed. R. N. Swanson, 1–21. Trowbridge: Boydell & Brewer, 2004.

The Church and Mary: Papers Read at the 2001 Summer Meeting and the 2002 Winter Meeting of the Ecclesiastical History Society. Ed. R. N. Swanson. Studies in Church History, 39. Trowbridge: Boydell & Brewer, 2004.

Cunningham, Mary B. "The Meeting of the Old and New: The Typology of Mary the Theotokos." In *The Church and Mary: Papers Read at the 2001 Summer Meeting and the 2002 Winter Meeting of the Ecclesiastical History Society*, ed. R. N. Swanson, 52–62. Studies in Church History, 39. Trowbridge: Boydell & Brewer, 2004.

Dictionary of the Bible. Ed. W. R. F. Browning. New York: Oxford University Press, 1996.

Dictionnaire de Spiritualité ascétique et mystique: doctrine et histoire. 17 vols. Paris: Beauchesne, 1937–95. See "Marie (Sainte Vierge)," 10 (1980), cols. 409–82.

Graef, Hilda. *Mary: A History of Doctrine and Devotion*. 2 vols. New York: Sheed & Ward, 1963.

Hall, James. *Hall's Dictionary of Subjects and Symbols in Art*. London: John Murray, 1974.

———. *A History of Ideas and Images in Italian Art*. London: John Murray, 1983.

Harvey, Susan Ashbrook. "Women in Early Syrian Christianity." In *Images of Women in Antiquity*. ed. Averil Cameron and Amélie Kuhrt, 288–98. London: Croom Helm, 1983.

Haskins, Susan. *Mary Magdalen: Myth and Metaphor*. London: HarperCollins, 1993; New York: Harcourt Brace, 1994.

———. "Vexatious Litigant, or the Case of Lucrezia Marinella? New Documents Concerning Her Life (Part 1)." *Nouvelles de la république des lettres* (2006-1): 81–128. Part 2, (2007-1/2): 203–30.

Imago Mariae: Tesori d'arte della civiltà cristiana. Ed. Pietro Amato. Milan: Mondadori, 1988.

Italian Women Writers: A Bio-Bibliographical Sourcebook. Ed. Rinaldina Russell. Westport, CT: Greenwood Press, 1994.

Jacobus, Laura. "Piety and Propriety in the Arena Chapel." *Renaissance Studies* 12, no. 2 (1998): 117–205.

Kuryluk, Ewa. *Veronica and Her Cloth: History, Symbolism, and Structure of a "True" Image.* Cambridge, MA: Harvard University Press, 1991.

Mâle, Émile. *L'art religieux du XVIIe siècle.* Paris: Armand Colin, 1984.

———. *The Early Churches of Rome.* Trans. by D. Buxton. London: Ernest Benn, 1960.

Malpezzi Price, Paola. "Lucrezia Marinella." In *The Church and Mary: Papers Read at the 2001 Summer Meeting and the 2002 Winter Meeting of the Ecclesiastical History Society,* ed. R. N. Swanson, 234–42. Studies in Church History, 39. Trowbridge: Boydell & Brewer, 2004.

Monter, William. "Protestant Wives, Catholic Saints, and the Devil's Handmaid: Women in the Age of Reformations." In *Becoming Visible: Women in European History,* ed. R. Bridenthal, C. Koonz, and S. Stuard, 203–19. 2nd ed. Boston: Houghton Mifflin, 1987.

Nagel, Alexander. "Gifts for Michelangelo and Vittoria Colonna." *Art Bulletin* 79 (1997): 647–68.

Niccolini, Benedetto. "Sulla religiosità di Vittoria Colonna." *Studi e materiali di storia delle religioni* 22 (1949): 89–109.

Oxford Companion to the Bible. Ed. Bruce M. Metzger and Michael D. Coogan. New York: Oxford University Press, 1993.

Oxford Dictionary of the Christian Church. Ed. F. L. Cross and E. A. Livingstone. 3rd ed. New York: Oxford University Press, 1997.

Panizza, Letizia, and Sharon Wood, eds. *A History of Women's Writing in Italy,* 1–9. Cambridge: Cambridge University Press, 2000.

Pelikan, Jaroslav. *Mary through the Centuries: Her Place in the History of Culture.* New Haven: Yale University Press, 1996.

Rabitti, Giovanna. "Chiara Matraini." In *Italian Women Writers: A Bio-Bibliographical Sourcebook,* ed. Rinaldina Russell, 243–52. Westport, CT: Greenwood Press, 1994.

Richardson, Brian. "'Amore maritale': Advice on Love and Marriage in the Second Half of the Cinquecento." In *Women in Italian Renaissance Culture and Society,* ed. Letizia Panizza, 194–208. Oxford: European Humanities Research Centre, 2000.

Schiller, Gertrud. *Ikonographie der christlichen Kunst.* Vols. 1, 4:2. Gütersloh: Gütersloher Verlagshaus G. Mohn, 1966.

Shoemaker, Stephen J. "'Let Us Go and Burn Her Body': The Image of the Jews in the Early Dormition Traditions." *Church History* 68, no. 4 (1999): 775–823.

Warner, Marina. *Alone of All Her Sex: The Myth and the Cult of the Virgin Mary.* New York: Vintage, 1983.

Ziegler, Joanna E. *Sculpture of Compassion: The Pietà and the Beguines in the Southern Low Countries c. 1300–c. 1600.* Brussels: Institut historique belge de Rome, 1992.

I

VITTORIA COLONNA'S *PLAINT OF THE MARCHESA DI PESCARA ON THE PASSION OF CHRIST*

EDITOR'S INTRODUCTION

The daughter of Fabrizio Colonna, a member of the powerful Roman clan, and Agnese di Montefeltro, daughter of Federico II, duke of Urbino, Vittoria Colonna (1490/92–1547) was born at Marino outside Rome. She married Ferrante d'Avalos, the Marchese di Pescara, in 1509. Widowed and childless in 1525, she dedicated herself to scholarship, poetry, and religious devotion, writing sonnets that reveal the intense anguish she felt at her loss in the Petrarchan verse form. After ten years' mourning, Colonna's first publication, a single sonnet, appeared in the second edition of Pietro Bembo's collection of poetry. Her *Rime* (1538) was the first collection of poetry by a woman printed in the vernacular in Italy in her own name. She had intellectual friendships with leading writers, artists, and reformers, and carried on correspondences with such personalities as Marguerite of Navarre (1492–1549), the sister of Francis I (1494–1547) and a figure within the reforming circles in France, Paolo Giovio (1483–1552), and Pietro Bembo (1470–1547), with whom she also exchanged sonnets, and who was one of her most fervent admirers. From 1530 on she was influenced by the evangelical reformer Juan de Valdés (1498?–1541), and the Capuchin vicar-general Fra' or Friar Bernardino Ochino (1487–1564). Together with the English Cardinal Reginald Pole (1500–58), she gathered together a group of reformers, the Spirituali, at Viterbo, where she lived from 1541. In 1544 she returned to Rome, where she died in the Benedictine convent of Sant'Anna. She met Michelangelo Buonarotti (1475–1564) in Rome in 1538, and they subsequently exchanged sonnets and letters. The first woman to achieve literary preeminence in the vernacular, she was also the most published and

Figure 1. Girolamo Muziano, *Portrait of Vittoria Colonna* (detail). Galleria Colonna, Rome. Photograph copyright Alinari/Art Resource, New York.

praised Italian woman writer of the sixteenth century, and role model for later Italian women writers such as Chiara Matraini.[1]

A meditation on Christ's Passion, Vittoria Colonna's *Plaint* or prose lament was composed between 1539 and 1542, and probably originally as a letter to Ochino since there are first-person addresses in the manuscript copy.[2] The Fra' was Colonna's friend and spiritual mentor until, accused of heresy, he fled to Geneva in 1542. The precise circumstances in which the work was written are unknown, but it has been suggested that Colonna may have been inspired by the drawing of the *Pietà*, given to her by Michelangelo, around the same date.[3]

The Plaint was published first in Venice in 1556, together with a further prose meditation by Colonna on the Virgin Mary, the *Oration on the Ave Maria*.[4] (The edition used for the present translation is the Aldine edition of

1. Major works: *Rime de la Divina Vittoria Colonna Marchesa di Pescara. Novamente stampate con privilegio* (Parma: [Antonio Viotti], 1538); *Litere della Divina Vettoria* [sic] *Colonna Marchesana di Pescara alla Duchessa de Amalfi, sopra la vita contemplativa di santa Catherina, Et sopra della attiva santa Maddalena non più viste in luce* (Venice: Alessandro de Viano. Ad instantia di Antonio detto il Cremaschino, 1544); *Pianto della Marchesa di Pescara sopra la passione di Christo. Oratione della medesima, sopra l'Ave Maria...etc.* (Venice: Aldus [Manutius], 1556); *Tutte le Rime della Illustriss. et Eccellentiss. Signora Vittoria Colonna, Marchesana di Pescara. Con l'Espositione del Signor Rinaldo Corso, nuovamente mandate in luce da Girolamo Ruscelli* (Venice: Giovan Battista et Melchior Sessa Fratelli, 1558); *Carteggio*, ed. Ermanno Ferrero and Giuseppe L. Müller (Turin: Loescher, 1889; 2nd ed., with suppl., 1892); *Rime*, ed. Alan Bullock (Rome and Bari: Laterza, 1982); *Sonetti in morte di Francesco Ferrante d'Avalos, marchese di Pescara; edizione del ms. XIII.G.43 della Biblioteca Nazionale di Napoli*, ed. Tobia R. Toscano (Milan: Mondadori, 1998); *Sonnets for Michelangelo: A Bilingual Edition*, ed. and trans. by Abigail Brundin (Chicago: University of Chicago Press, 2005).

For biography and bibliographical references, see Fiora A. Bassanese, "Vittoria Colonna," in *Italian Women Writers: A Bio-bibliographical Sourcebook*, ed. Rinaldina Russell (Westport, CT: Greenwood Press, 1994), 85–94; Rinaldina Russell, "Vittoria Colonna's Sonnets on the Virgin Mary," in *Maria Virgine nella letteratura italiana*, ed. Florinda M. Iannace (Stony Brook, NY: Forum Italicum, 2000), 125–37; *Sonnets for Michelangelo*, ed. and trans. by Brundin.

2. See Abigail Brundin, "Vittoria Colonna and the Virgin Mary," *Modern Language Review* 96, no. 1 (2001): 61–81, at 70 and note 19.

3. See Alexander Nagel, "Gifts for Michelangelo and Vittoria Colonna," *Art Bulletin* 79 (1997): 647–68, for an illuminating analysis of the drawing, and its relationship to the *Plaint*, and the context in which both were probably created. Benedetto Niccolini links the *Pianto* and Michelangelo's *Pietà* for Vittoria Colonna in "Sulla religiosità di Vittoria Colonna," *Studi e materiali di storia delle religioni* 22 (1949): 89–109, at 96–97. See also Brundin, "Vittoria Colonna and the Virgin Mary"; and *Sonnets for Michelangelo*, ed. and trans. by Brundin.

4. The 1556 edition was the first of five sixteenth-century editions. The other work included in the 1556 edition was an anonymous "Oration made on Good Friday, on the Passion of Christ." See Sylvia Ferino-Pagden, *Vittoria Colonna: Dichterin und Muse Michelangelos* (Vienna: Kunsthistorisches Museum, February–May 1997), exhibition catalog no. II.31, at 201. See also *Sonnets for Michelangelo*, ed. Brundin, 24.

1557.)[5] In the *Oration*, Colonna uses the Hail Mary for a line-by-line discussion of her own relationship with the Virgin Mary, stressing the Virgin's integral role with that of her son in the Redemption, and her role as mediatrix. Colonna also wrote several sonnets concerning the Virgin among her *rime spirituali*, and discussed her in letters to her cousin, Costanza d'Avalos Piccolomini, duchess of Amalfi.[6]

Colonna's *Plaint* is a highly personal meditation ("I see the sweet mother," "For me," "I believe"), and is her response to the *Pietà*, an inner vision she has of the Virgin Mary seated below the cross, with the dead Christ lying in her arms, a scene either imagined or an image actually before her. The language is direct, highly wrought, and poetic. Dwelling on the Virgin's emotions on her son's death, Colonna follows the Virgin's mourning process ("I believe that the Queen of Heaven mourned him many ways"): first in passionately grieving for Christ's dead humanity, in the form of "the beautiful body," qualifying his physical aspects, such as his hair, "cherished by her with such care," his eyes, mouth, and hands, now "torn" and bloody, while further pathos is rendered by the simple words, "and His feet," at the end of the sentence; then, moving on to contemplate his divine aspects, his mercy, justice, charity, obedience, humility, and patience, a rhetorical juxtaposing of spiritual and physical that Colonna maintains throughout the lament. Having been his bearer in life, the Virgin is his bearer in death, paradoxically desiring to be incorporated in his side and with him in his sepulcher. Colonna's Mary is the humble, selfless Virgin of the gospels—her humility makes her desire to compensate for humanity's ingratitude—and yet she is Queen of Heaven, her key role in the Redemption. Colonna builds paradox upon paradox, the Virgin thanking God for giving her such an obedient son; her duty causing her pain; the Holy Spirit making her delight in suffering; her thanking God for his own sacrifice; all her virtues, which once nourished her, now consume her. Each is constructed around the central paradox of Christianity: Christ's suffering being humankind's joy, his death humanity's redemption.

The *Plaint* is modeled on the ancient tradition of the *Improperia*, Christ's

5. *Pianto della Marchesa di Pescara sopra la passione di Christo. Oratione della medesima sopra l'Ave Maria. Sermone di M. Benedetto Varchi recitato alla Croce...etc.* (Bologna: Antonio Manuzio, 1557).

6. The letters are published as *Litere della Divina Vettoria* [sic] *Colonna Marchesana di Pescara alla Duchessa de Amalfi, sopra la vita contemplativa di santa Catherina, Et sopra della attiva santa Maddalena non più viste in luce* (Venice: Alessandro de Viano. Ad instantia di Antonio detto il Cremaschino, 1544). They also reveal the importance to Colonna of Saints Mary Magdalen and Catherine of Alexandria as role models. See Brundin, "Vittoria Colonna and the Virgin Mary," 76–80. See also *Sonnets for Michelangelo*, ed. Brundin.

Figure 2. Michelangelo Buonarotti, *Pietà* (ca. 1540), drawn for Vittoria Colonna. Photograph courtesy Isabella Stewart Gardner Museum, Boston, Mass.

reproaches spoken from the cross, part of the service for Good Friday: "O my people, what have I done to thee? Or wherein have I aggrieved thee? Answer me. Because I led thee out of the land of Egypt, thou hast prepared a Cross for thy Savior; I gave thee to drink wholesome water from the rock: and thou gavest me gall and vinegar."[7] Almost as though on behalf of the Virgin, in her own impassioned voice Colonna apostrophizes all those absent from the Crucifixion, the disciples and apostles, and the various gospel characters whom Christ had cured, saved, forgiven, and comforted, or, like Lazarus (the prefiguration of the resurrected Christ), raised from the dead. Lazarus's sister, "a woman and weak," here Mary Magdalen, is greater than him "in courage and love" for having been present.[8] While admonishing those who were not there, Colonna moves further outward, addressing and admonishing the reader and offering homilies. Through "differing reasons and various loves," the physical and mental torment the Virgin undergoes is expressed by use of frequent alliteration ("which made her toss and turn from pang to pang"), and repetition, such as the word "alone" (Italian, *solo*), underscoring the Virgin's "lonely" tasks of thanking Joseph of Arimathea, comforting Mary Magdalen, and satisfying John.[9] These rhetorical strategies prompt an emotional effect, alliteration forcing the reader to pay attention to the Virgin's torment.

Colonna's is an intricate, intellectual analysis. Based on the mind's tendency to begin from a particular situation, in this case the sight of the Virgin with the dead Christ, Colonna examines this mental image through Mary's thought processes, finally arriving at a resolution, using the trinity of meditative powers—memory, understanding, and will. She considers the debt owed by the Christian to the Virgin, the figure of true faith, whose own loss is his or her salvation, and something that neither he nor she can ever repay. Colonna rehearses the entire gamut of Catholic teaching concerning the Virgin's redemptive role. Mary is that pillar of faith (a metaphor often applied to her) and model of faith ("Only faith kept her in life, and she kept faith alive"), who provides the world with faith. As in Michelangelo's drawing, Colonna's Virgin presents her son sorrowfully, as the Redeemer, and yet possibly triumphantly: she proffers him to the believer. Through her sacrifice as Christ's mother, humanity is redeemed and presented with the true

7. The reproaches are addressed by Christ to his unfaithful people, and form part of the Good Friday liturgy of the Catholic Church. Drawn from passages in the Old Testament, they are sung during the Veneration of the Cross.

8. See note 29 below.

9. "Essa sola si doleva del suo danno, dell'ingratitudine delli altri . . . essa sola havea da ringratiar Joseph, da sodisfare Giovanni, da confortare Madalena" (*Pianto*, 9).

faith, possible only through that sacrifice. Despite her close collaboration with reformers, Colonna retained her orthodox Catholic beliefs, especially that of the fundamental role of Mary in mankind's salvation, as can been seen in the *Plaint*: redemption is through faith, and also through the sacraments, "our so many graces" flowing from "the sacred side" of Christ (i.e., the Eucharist), and through belief in the salvific power of Christ's death.

PLAINT OF THE MARCHESA DI PESCARA ON THE PASSION OF CHRIST . . . (BOLOGNA: ANTONIO MANUTIO, 1557)

Friday and the late hour prompt me to write of my sorrow at seeing the dead Christ in His mother's arms and, if obedience did not give me strength, I would deem myself most cruel in being able to write of it, although much more ungrateful were I not to give it consideration.[10] I see the sweet mother, her heart full to the brim with most burning love, tied by so many chains in the love of her Son that they cannot be expressed in ordinary language. Neither can we understand how she made herself a resting place for her dead Son, indeed for her own Lord and Father and for herself and her entire good, a resting place from past bitter travails and torment; not only to hold Him dead, but to make of her own, almost dead body, a sepulcher in that hour, of whatever living remained in her: so entirely was her body entombed with Christ's.

It seems to me the grief, which all day long the Virgin had stored up in her heart, so as to consume that most noble part,[11] and that fire of love and torment her high-mindedness had scorned to display outwardly, and which had consumed and penetrated the depths of her soul, now, in touching Christ's sacred body, grew with infinite abundance, and flowed through her eyes in bitterest tears, and through her lips in more burning

10. In the Christian Church, Friday traditionally commemorates Christ's Passion, and is observed by abstinence from meat or by other acts of penitence or charity. Colonna's meditation follows the traditional practice of affective piety, in which the meditator has before either him or her an image, or visualizes internally a real scene or scenes, and by concentrating on these images—the most appropriate, and affective, of which are of Christ's sufferings and those of the saints—is brought to a heightened sense of that which is represented, which in turn provokes feelings of horror, shame, and remorse in the meditator. Such works as the late fourteenth-century Franciscan Pseudo-Bonaventure's meditations on the Life of Christ set patterns for meditational practice.

11. The heart was regarded from antiquity as the seat of emotions. It was also seen as the superior organ since it was the center of emotional and spiritual life. According to Saint Augustine, the heart was the root of moral life or conscience. In the New Testament it is the dwelling place of Christ (Ephesians 3: 17).

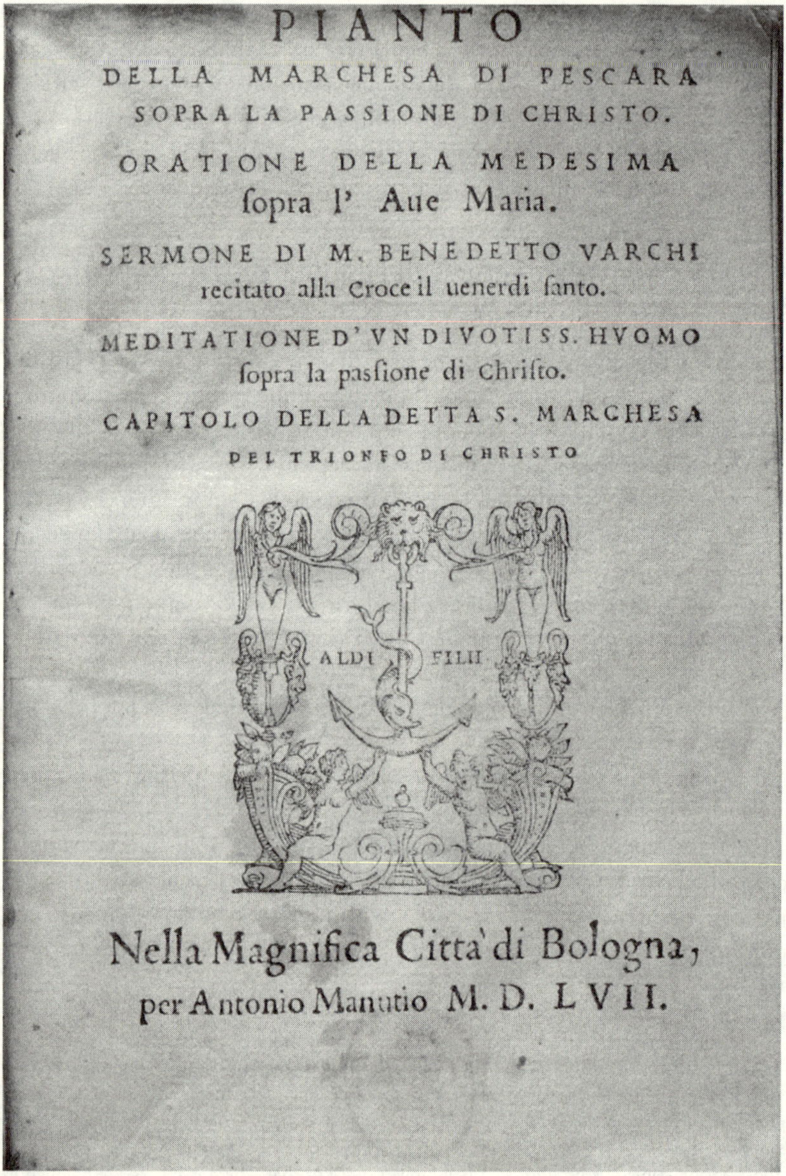

PIANTO
DELLA MARCHESA DI PESCARA
SOPRA LA PASSIONE DI CHRISTO.
ORATIONE DELLA MEDESIMA
ſopra l' Aue Maria.
SERMONE DI M. BENEDETTO VARCHI
recitato alla Croce il uenerdi ſanto.
MEDITATIONE D'VN DIVOTISS. HVOMO
ſopra la paſſione di Chriſto.
CAPITOLO DELLA DETTA S. MARCHESA
DEL TRIONFO DI CHRISTO

Nella Magnifica Citta' di Bologna,
per Antonio Manutio M. D. LVII.

Figure 3. Title page of the 1557 edition of the *Pianto della Marchesa di Pescara sopra la passione di Christo.*

sighs. Whence her tears washed and warmed Him in such a way that He appeared truly alive. Apart from his divinity, which had never left Him, I believe He had His usual great majesty and grace, indeed to an even greater degree, because whereas in others death is a violent act that injures them, in Christ, who had summoned and desired it with so much sweetness, it was an act so gentle, sweet, and pitiful that it softened every hard heart and inflamed every cold mind, so that death's ugliness was not only beautiful in this most beautiful face, but pride turned into great sweetness, darkness into clear light; and that frightening blackness, which hurts the eyes of whoever looks at it, made resplendent and beautiful through Christ's purity, gave happy assurance to whoever looked. O how desirable was that face, which in other dead people it seems one should shun! How many would wish to be under His mortal rule, to be united with the true Author of life!

I believe that the Queen of Heaven mourned Him in many ways: first as a human being, seeing this most beautiful body, created from her own flesh, entirely torn; and that hair, cherished by her with such care, having brought Him torment, which, full of His precious blood, fell around His face; the closed eyes that gave Him perpetual light; the mouth, as reward for such great and so much teaching, full of the bitterness of vinegar; the hands, which had blessed her as her Lord, and served her as a son, wounded; and His feet.[12] And I believe, limb by limb, she mourned Him, remembering how they had served Him and how they had acted on her and our behalf on earth. But then, raised to a loftier thought, I believe that she was contemplating the sacred pierced head as the rich vessel in which all wisdom, divine and human, was gathered. The closed eyes in which were the sun of justice and mercy; the brow at whose command angels tremble and the elements obey; the wounded hands, which created the heavens, and thus the feet, which trod the stars; the closed lips, out of which breathed the fervor of the holy spirit; bloodless the body, which displayed the white and holy garb of pure innocence.[13]

Then she meditated upon, even saw depicted in the divine face, the vestiges of charity, obedience, humility, patience, and peace in the divine face, saw first charity in its true seat, when He said: "Forgive them, for they know

12. The lacerations referred to are the wounds suffered through the flagellation and piercing of Christ's side during his Passion and Crucifixion. Christ's hair is full of blood from his crowning with thorns, and his mouth full of the vinegar given him on the cross. See Matthew 27, Mark 17, Luke 23, and John 19 for the relevant accounts of Christ's Passion.

13. Having meditated upon what has taken place to Christ's human form, Colonna now moves on to more metaphysical contemplation.

not what they do";[14] patience in saying, "My God, my God, why hast thou forsaken me?" That is, why do you make me sacrifice myself, when through love and patience I would prefer not to provide it so soon, but endure it much more slowly?[15] Obedience, "Into thy hands I commend my spirit;"[16] and peace, when He said, "Woman, behold thy son;"[17] and humility: "It is finished;"[18] and thanking the Father, bowed His head, and let His spirit go with so much gentleness that although these virtues departed with the soul, which, endowed with a thousand heavenly graces, obeyed the Father in His duty, their imprint remained on the sacred body until His resurrection, to live then with Christ glorified, in a better life.

All this shone forth in Christ's face more to the Madonna than to others, as she suffered more passionately. She was still thinking over what He had felt in that hour, and although she saw His closed eyes in that most sacred body, she knew that His soul's eyes opened the gates of Limbo to the Holy Fathers.[19] His lips were closed, but His more celestial ones were saying: "Lift up your gates, O ye princes."[20] She reflected that her weeping was the cause of joy to so many souls dearest to her, who had awaited so long that blessed day. But this did not allay her pain: rather it increased in her, because it made her duty, that of redeeming her descendants, even greater.[21]

And I believe that Christ's most bitter torment, while she watched, the enormous anxiety of giving Him succor, the continuous beseeching the Father to alleviate it, the varying sufferings, which made her toss and turn from pang to pang, almost took her outside herself, indeed entirely engrossed her

14. Luke 23:34: *ignosce illis quia nesciunt quid faciunt.* Colonna refers to Christ being the source of charity, exemplified in his call to God the Father to forgive his enemies, those crucifying him, for their actions.

15. *Deus meus, Deus meus, cur me dereliquisti?* On the cross, Jesus calls out to God the Father, "Eli, eli, lamma-sabachthani?" (cited from Matthew 27:46; Mark 15:34), and dies.

16. Luke 23:46: *in manus tuas commendo spiritum meum.*

17. John 19:26: *Mulier ecce filius tuus.* In the disciple John's account of the Crucifixion, Jesus entrusts John to the Virgin's care and his mother to John's.

18. John 19:30: *consumatum est.*

19. The "soul's eyes": understanding and faith opened the way to heaven. In Latin theology, the souls of those who died before the coming of Christ remained in Limbo, the *limbus patrum.* Christ's coming opened the gates of Limbo for the Patriarchs. Whether or not Limbo existed is a matter of theological opinion on which the Church has made no definitive pronouncement; in 2007 the Vatican's International Theological Commission announced that the traditional view of Limbo reflected an "unduly restrictive view of salvation."

20. Psalms 23:7: *Adtollite portas principes vestras.*

21. This refers to the paradox of Mary's suffering: Christ's death is the source of mankind's joy, since it brings redemption to mankind. The Virgin's anguish grew greater as her duty—to save mankind—became greater.

in torment and overcame her with so many evils that she was never free to think of giving way and grieving. Now that she had Him in her arms and, in the meanwhile, was seeking, one by one, through the infinite causes of His torment, like someone who, to escape death, grasps a sword that cuts his hand, so she, feeling herself swoon, grasped Christ's body, which sustained her, with its even greater wound.

O how lovingly she kissed His most holy wounds; and how in her mind she enclosed herself within the sacred side, whence she knew that the sacraments of our so many graces had flowed.[22] With what true love, I believe, she wanted everyone in the entire world to be able to see what she saw, so that they might enjoy such immense grace. And had the angels not compensated for man's ingratitude, I would feel great compassion for those who could have been there, but were not.

Alas, Peter, you heard Christ pray that your faith would not fail, come and turn your bitter tears into sweet ones.[23] And you, James, who do not eat, waiting for Christ to be brought back from the dead, come and seize the true nourishment in His sweet wounds.[24] And you, Philip, who wished to see the Father, come now and see Him remove humanity's garb to reveal the precious brocade of His divinity.[25] And you, Andrew, who did not believe that He filled so many people with so few loaves, come and see that open side, which can fill, indeed fills all good people, as many as fit in the world.[26] And let Matthew come and see Him naked, the One who took away the weight of earthly riches to give him celestial and eternal ones; he would see clearly that He did not praise poverty to not love it, since He embraced it until death.[27] I would call Thomas so that he might come and touch the

22. Mary envisions herself enclosed in Christ's side; the sacraments referred to are the blood and water flowing from Christ's side, which, together with his body, are symbolized by the bread and wine received in the sacrament, or mystery, of the Eucharist, or communion.

23. In the New Testament, Simon Peter appears to have a special undefined position in the group of Christ's twelve male disciples, which assumes some kind of leadership after the Resurrection (Acts 1–12). In Matthew 26:34, Jesus foretells that Peter will deny him three times before cockcrow (cf. Mark 14:29–31; Luke 22:33–34; John 13:36–38).

24. The son of Zebedee, James, together with his brother John, was called by Jesus while fishing with their father (Matthew 4:21; Mark 1:19; cf. Luke 5:10).

25. One of the twelve disciples, Philip was among those who brought Nathanael (see note 36 below) to Jesus (John 14:8–9; Acts 8:5–13); he asked Jesus to show the Hellenistic Jews the Father (John 14:8).

26. Andrew, brother of Simon Peter, and one of the twelve disciples. A disciple of John the Baptist before his call (John 1:40 ff.), in John 6:8–9 he points out the boy who had the loaves and fishes that were distributed.

27. Matthew, or Levi, was one of the Twelve (Mark 2:14; Luke 5:27, 29), and was called from the tax collector's table (Matthew 9:9–13; Mark 2:13–17; Luke 5:27–32). He invited Jesus to

holy wounds, as I am sure that this sweetness would increase love and faith in him so that he would not want to touch again, but because many profited by his incredulity, I will let him be.[28] But I will indeed call Lazarus, who does not understand that his sweetest sister, a woman and weak, surpasses him in courage and love, precedes him in gratitude, and is superior to him in all the virtues.[29] Alas, Lazarus, that Lord who wept for you, and who in your death made a greater sign of love than He had ever done in others' [deaths], do you not come to mourn and bury Him, to make of yourself and with your body, resurrected by Him, a burning light with the fire of charity, to give visible and natural and divine light to the person who gave it to you? Will you not gratify at least with great laments that powerful voice, which called you back from Limbo to this life?[30]

Why does the publican not come to honor himself at least by burying the good thief, to thank him for accompanying his Lord to His death? Perhaps through humility he would not have dared to touch Christ.[31] Where

---

dine with his friends—publicans and sinners—and Jesus accepted, prompting the Pharisees to accuse him of being a friend of such people (Matthew 11:19; Luke 7:34).

28. Thomas is also one of the Twelve. In John 20:19ff., Christ appears to the disciples after he has appeared to Mary Magdalen at the tomb; Thomas, not present with the other disciples, will not believe that they have seen him until he sees the print of the nails, and puts his finger into them, and into the wound in Christ's side. Christ returns a week later, telling Thomas to place his finger into the wounds, to which Thomas answers, "My Lord, and my God" (John 20:24–29); his disbelief gave rise to the expression "doubting Thomas."

29. In the New Testament Lazarus is the brother of Mary and Martha of Bethany, a household that, from the text, Christ appears to have often visited (Luke 10:38–42; John 11:1–45, 12:1–8). But according to early, and incorrect, exegesis, Lazarus was also the brother of Mary of Magdala, or Mary Magdalen, whose gospel character (Luke 8:1–4, 23:55–56, 24:1–11) had been conflated by the late sixth century with those of Mary of Bethany and an unnamed sinner in Luke 7:37–49. This aspect, as it does in Colonna's *Plaint,* forms a strong element of Lazarus's character. His "sweetest sister" is Mary Magdalen; by her "courage and love," Colonna is referring to Mary Magdalen's going to the tomb, alone and before dawn, which was seen by various commentators as a mark of courage since, according to Saint Bernard of Clairvaux, women were afraid of the dark and dared not venture forth. Colonna's reference to "woman" as "weak" derives from the misogynistic ecclesiastical male view of the supposed fragility of the female sex, weak because of Eve's temptation by the serpent (Genesis 3:1–7).

30. Colonna apostrophizes Lazarus for not coming to bury and mourn Christ, since a few days before the Passion Jesus had raised him from the dead (John 11:1–45).

31. The publicans of the New Testament were agents and collectors of taxes on behalf of the Roman administration (Matthew 5:46, 9:10ff.; Mark 2:15ff.; Luke 5:29; 7:29, 34; 19:2–10). The good thief, together with the bad thief, was crucified with Jesus (Luke 23:33–43). When the bad thief railed at Jesus for not saving them, which he could have done had he indeed been the Christ, the good thief rebuked him, saying they had deserved their punishment, and asking Jesus to remember him when He entered heaven.

is the man born blind, who does not open his eyes to so much light, since the lost light was restored to him with so much kindness by this Sun?[32] Why does the Samaritan woman not come to drink anew at the fountain of life? Why does she not now lead all of her Samaria, if she truly recognized Him?[33] What is the Canaanite woman doing if she is not showing here the greatness of her faith, so magnified by Him?[34] Why does the centurion, who judged his house unworthy of being entered by Christ when He was alive, not come now to adore Him dead?[35] Where is the true Israelite, Nathanael, whom Christ told was without guile, and that he would see such a great thing?[36] Why does Zacchaeus not run so that he will no longer have to climb the tree to see Him?[37] For all the rabble has left Him alone, and He is abandoned by His brothers and by the others.

Let all Jerusalem come: she will not be anguished to find the palms, or the clothes strewn in the streets, and to sing, "Blessed is he that cometh, etc.,"[38] whose leaders have treated him so well that they will find Him naked on the ground, nails around His head instead of palms, the mother prostrate

32. Jesus cured the man born blind (John 5:3, 9:1). There is a play on words in the Italian, *luce* and *lume,* both signifying light, and the word "sun" meaning light-giver, as well as God as sun, taken over from the classical Jupiter as sun god.

33. In John 4:1–42, Christ talks with a woman of Samaria who comes to draw water from a well. The Jews regarded the Samaritans as a heretical and schismatic group, and the disciples were scandalized to find Jesus talking to one, and a woman to boot. She attests to her belief in him as the Messiah, and goes off to tell her fellow countrymen.

34. In Matthew 15:22–28, a Canaanite woman beseeches Jesus to drive a devil out of her daughter, but he ignores her. The disciples beg him to send her away, but the woman comes again, demonstrating her faith, and Christ heals her daughter.

35. A centurion was an officer in command of 100 (*centum*) men. The centurion of Capernaum (Matthew 8:5ff.; Luke 7:2ff.) asked Jesus to cure his sick slave; feeling unworthy that Jesus should enter his house, he expressed his belief that Jesus could cure by word alone. Jesus said that he had not found such faith before, even in Israel.

36. Of Cana, Nathanael was brought by Philip to Jesus; Nathanael said to Philip, "Can any thing of good come from Nazareth?" Philip replied, "Come and see." Nathanael's unbelief was overcome by Jesus's knowledge of him, and he confessed that Jesus was the Messiah (John 1:45–51, 21:25). Jesus recommended Nathanael for his lack of guile (John 1:48), and promised him that he would see greater things than this, "the heaven opened, and the angels of God ascending and descending upon the Son of Man" (v. 51). He was one of those who saw Christ appear at the Sea of Galilee (John 21:1).

37. Zacchaeus was the chief tax collector of Jericho who, curious, went to see Jesus. A small man, he had to climb a tree in order to catch sight of Jesus, who called him down from the tree. Jesus invited himself to dinner at Zacchaeus's home, and the latter was moved to return his ill-gotten gains and give to the poor (Luke 19:1–10).

38. John 12:13: *Benedictus qui venit &c.* Colonna shows her irony and anger: she contrasts the isolation of Christ at the Crucifixion with the events of Palm Sunday (John 12:12ff.), when the

on the ground instead of the clothing, and with few friends weeping, instead of saying "Hosanna to the son of David."[39] Where is the widow who does not come, with her son returned to life, to mourn in gratitude for the compassion that the merciful Lord had for her? Why does she not help the holy mother grieve, she who has lost that Son, by whom her own son was so sweetly restored to her?[40] Let the adulteress come, with the assurance that she will not be stoned by the Hebrews, now that all the stones of their harshness have been thrown upon Him, who saved her from death.[41] Why does she who, by only touching the sacred hem, became spotless from the unclean sickness of her blood, not come to wash herself in the pure precious blood?[42] Well, Martha, since you gave Him hospitality, how late you are in burying Him![43] And when you had nothing else, He still left you free with His grace, the gift of your resurrected brother.[44] Do you think perhaps that it is enough for Magdalen to be there? Do you not know that she has buried Him in her heart and left you continually the care of the things of the world? She is truly there, mourning and serving Christ. She accompanies the Mother with such humility and with such a passionate love that she will

---

multitude took branches from palm trees and bore them as a triumphal greeting at Christ's entry into Jerusalem, the palm being a symbol both of victory and martyrdom.

39. The "nails around His head" refer to the crown of thorns placed on Jesus's head; instead of the day of exaltation, Jesus is now deserted; his mother is prostrate on the ground in place of the garments strewn by the multitude; and only the Virgin, Saint John, Mary Magdalen, Joseph of Arimathea, and Nicodemus are present instead of the multitude praising, "Hosanna to the son of David" (Matthew 21:9; cf. Mark 11:9).

40. In Luke 7:11–15, Jesus brings back to life the son of a widow in Nain, a village in Galilee.

41. In John 8:3–11, the scribes and Pharisees bring a woman taken in adultery to Jesus, declaring they are about to stone her according to Mosaic law. This is to test Jesus's fidelity to the Law; Jesus stoops to write something in the sand, then says that anyone among them who has not sinned should cast the first stone. After they have gone, Jesus tells the woman that he does not condemn her, and tells her to sin no more.

42. A woman who had had an issue of blood for twelve years and had spent all her money on doctors, came up behind Jesus and touched the hem of his robes, knowing that she would be cured. Jesus asked who had touched him, and the disciples denied doing so. The woman tremblingly confessed her action and its result, to which Jesus told her that her faith had made her whole, and to go in peace (Matthew 9:20–22; Mark 5:25–34; Luke 8:43–48).

43. Martha gives Jesus hospitality (Luke 10:38–42), and when she criticizes her sister Mary for sitting listening to him instead of helping her to serve, Jesus tells Martha that she is anxious and troubled, but that Mary has chosen the good part in listening to his words. In later exegesis Martha and Mary became the symbols of the active and contemplative life (see chap. 2, note 107, regarding the active and contemplative life).

44. According to most commentators, the Mary and Martha of the account in Luke are the same as the Mary and Martha of Bethany, whose brother Lazarus is raised from the dead by Jesus (John 11:1–46, 12:1–11).

be consoled before anyone else, to bear witness to the divine Judge of her faithful soul and of her bitter sorrow.[45]

The High Priest has not come to pay his respects to Him, when He rather had so much respect that He went to the house to ensure that his faith was not lacking, and thus more deservedly to bring his daughter back to life. Why does he not come to kiss that hand with which He raised the said young girl from death to life?[46] Why do the nine lepers, who have had time enough to correct their faults, not thank Him, if they did not thank Him then?[47] And that one who did adore Him, perhaps it seemed to him that such a brief service would be sufficient to gain an eternal reward, since he does not now respond to this obligation?[48] Why does the one who prayed to Him for help in his lack of belief, and obtained as much as he

45. Colonna asks Martha if she thinks it is sufficient that Mary Magdalen (her sister, in this case) is alone present at the Crucifixion. The Magdalen referred to here is the tripartite figure that Mary of Magdala became after her exegetical conflation with Mary of Bethany and the sinner in Luke's gospel (7:7). The "care of the things of the world" is what Christ apportions Martha when he apostrophizes her for criticizing Mary who has chosen the better part, the role of disciple and contemplative. Mary Magdalen, although here the sister of Martha, is, however, also portrayed in her true role at the Crucifixion, where, according to John, she is present by the cross and, according to the other gospels, stands nearby watching. She goes to the tomb early on Easter Day, to find angels who tell her that Christ has risen, and in John 20:1–18, he appears to her first. Colonna refers to the traditional justification for Christ's appearing first to Mary Magdalen, a question that vexed commentators from earliest Christianity: Mary Magdalen had loved him most. Her description of Mary Magdalen as companion of the Virgin after the Crucifixion derives from medieval texts such as Jacopone da Todi's *Lauda*, the Pseudo-Bonaventure *Meditations on the Life of Christ*, and Saint Mary Magdalen's *vita*, or life, in Jacobus de Voragine's late thirteenth-century compilation of saints' lives, the *Legenda Aurea* or *Golden Legend*. See Susan Haskins, *Mary Magdalen: Myth and Metaphor* (New York: Harcourt Brace, 1994), for an overview of the images of Mary Magdalen.

46. Jairus is the high priest of the synagogue in Capernaum. He comes to Jesus, begging him to cure his daughter who is on the point of death. On their way, Jesus's robe is touched by the woman with the issue of blood. Jairus's servants arrive to inform him that his daughter is dead, but Jesus takes Peter, James, and John to the house and, assuring those gathered there that Jairus's daughter merely sleeps, goes with her parents into the room where the child lies, and bids her rise. Jesus then tells her parents not to relate this event to anyone, but to give the girl something to eat (Mark 5:21–43; Luke 8:40–56). In Matthew 9:18–26, the episode is related, but Jairus is unnamed; he is simply "a certain ruler."

47. In Luke 17:12–19, ten lepers come to meet Jesus in a village in Samaria, asking him for mercy. He tells them to go and show themselves to the priests, and they are cured. One, a Samaritan, turns back, praising God, and falls on his face before Jesus, thanking him. To which Jesus responds, "Were not ten cleansed, but where are the nine?" (v. 17), noting that only the stranger has thanked him. As in the Old Testament, the term "leprosy" in the New Testament may designate a wide variety of minor skin infections.

48. I have been unable to find the source of this reference.

wanted, not come to help Him?[49] Where are the daughters of Jerusalem, who truly show that they have wept through natural compassion since their sorrow passed so briefly?[50] Now it would be right to weep over Him, that is, over that lacerated body. It is fitting that tears of charity be sprinkled when the fount of clemency went to die for us. And if you do not all come now, you will never be able to see Him again, adore Him, and thank Him. That time is fulfilled when He deigned to dwell on earth: "walk while you have the light,"[51] and if you have seen Him truly alive, in no other act has He shown His humility more, indeed all of His extraordinary graces united together, than seeing Him in the arms of Mary who, alive, will show you how much you must weep and mourn the dead Christ.

O how envious will I always be of those who were there, and how much compassion to whoever was able to be there and was not. I do not call the Father Eternal to such a great spectacle, because I know that He watched over it, being entirely pleased with Him;[52] nor even the Holy Spirit who, if that flame can appear to burn with greater love, I know that it burns and kindles with clear intense love in Christ's charity. I call not the angels, as I know that they were there; indeed, I believe that they wanted to take on human form to mourn their Lord in that deed. I do not call those happy souls in Limbo, as I know that they rejoice with His blessed soul, but I cry out with a sorrowful voice to so many ungrateful men who gave Joseph and Nicodemus alone the triumph and glory of the most beautiful work that could ever be done.[53] O most happy Joseph, you were loving with the same love: you were given the body of the One who could give Paradise to all living souls; you wrapped Him in your winding sheet, the One who bound Lucifer, loosened us from eternal suffering, broke down the Tartarean gates, opened Par-

49. Mark 9:16–26. Jesus encounters a man whose son is afflicted by a "dumb spirit." Jesus tells the man, "all things are possible to him that believeth." The father replies, "I do believe, Lord. Help my unbelief." His son is cured.

50. Luke 23:27–28. On his way to his Crucifixion, Jesus is followed by a multitude, among them women, lamenting him. He calls upon them not to weep for him, but for themselves and their children.

51. John 12:35: ". . . *ambulate, dum lucem habetis*."

52. God reiterates his pleasure in his son: "in whom I am well pleased" (Matthew 3:17, 12:18, 17:5; Mark 1:11; Luke 3:22).

53. Joseph of Arimathea was a wealthy man and member of the Sanhedrin. He was also a disciple of Jesus and obtained Jesus's body after his death, wrapped it, and laid it in his own family tomb (Matthew 27:57–60; Mark 15:43–46; Luke 23:50–54; John 19:38–42). Nicodemus also helped in Jesus's burial, bringing spices (John 18:39).

adise, and freed the world.[54] You alone consoled the afflicted mother, who alone kept faith alive in her holy breast, whence she alone carried out the duty of mercy, humility, and perfect charity, as well as the act of true gratitude. She alone mourned her loss, the ingratitude of others, and the blindness of the Hebrews.[55] She alone had to thank Joseph, satisfy John, comfort the Magdalen, sustain herself through obeying Him, whom she would have followed with such joy had she been allowed.[56]

Now, who could believe how lovingly she thanked the heavenly Father, who had brought such torment to an end, and who had made her the mother of such an obedient Son? And with what burning love she thanked the Holy Spirit who, through extraordinary love, made her delight in this suffering? And with what wonderful joy she thanked incarnate Wisdom and her most loved Christ who, with so much humble obedience, completed His own sacrifice? And with what great love she thanked the angels, who were there to compensate for mankind's failings? And I believe that through her deep humility concerning things spiritual, she thanked the sun, which had been hidden, the earth that trembled, the stones that were shattered, the air that was perturbed and, further, those bodies that rose to accompany and serve Him.[57] And she would have wished to call the entire world to adore Him in that state of such profound humility, as God had deigned to take on our humanity and, from highest Heaven, to live on our lowly earth: which seemed a wondrous thing.[58] Further, Christ's blessed soul had been with His body,

54. The Tartarus were the infernal regions of ancient Greek and Roman mythology; the Tartarean gates were the gates of hell.

55. The "blindness of the Hebrews," that is, in not believing in Christ as the Messiah and son of God.

56. Colonna imagines the Virgin with the normal duties of a mother after the burial of her son, that of being consoled, and thanking the consolers and mourners such as Joseph of Arimathea; at the Crucifixion the disciple John stood at the other side of the cross (John 19:25–26). From the cross, Christ gives the Virgin John as her son, and says to John, "This is thy mother." She also has to comfort the weeping Magdalen, who, according to Mark, Matthew, and Luke, was one of those who witnessed the Crucifixion, but in John's account stands by the cross with the Virgin, John, and Mary the mother of James and Joses, and Mary of Cleopas.

57. Colonna refers to the paradox of the Virgin's thanking God for making her the mother of such an obedient son in that he follows the command of God the Father to sacrifice himself for the sake of humanity. She imagines the Virgin thanking the elements, which had, according to the gospel accounts, behaved empathetically at the moment of Christ's death—the pathetic fallacy. The "bodies" are of those who had died before Christ's coming, and are in Limbo and hell.

58. The Virgin's humility (Latin, *humilitas,* from *humus,* "ground"). In Christian terms humility is understood as submissiveness before God, and came to be regarded as a virtue, modeled on

now that it was no longer there, she consented to support that mortal flesh, as she had before, to show a supreme degree of love to ungrateful humanity.[59] It is as if a king went to a gentleman's house to visit him, and he was not there, and only one of his servants was present, how the latter, realizing that it was his duty to acknowledge so much courtesy, would struggle to honor him, as he would not see himself as equal in merit or value in doing what his master would have done. Thus it seemed to the Virgin, seeing the absence of Christ's blessed soul, which alone was sufficient to honor God's immense greatness, saw that the great task of undertaking so large a debt belonged to her alone. Therefore she would have wanted to melt away, be consumed, even immolate herself in the fire of love, and in her tears of compassion to remove ingratitude from the world and herself, and to render God the humility and worship that were due to Him.[60]

I believe also that she went with hand and mind, seeking most reverently the noblest places inhabited by that holy soul, and touched His heart, which seemed to her to beat now and then; and the more still it felt, the more hers became disturbed with more sorrowful anxiety and torment. And similarly, she felt all His limbs, which show whether there is life or not, with chilly hope and burning sorrow. And she deceived herself thus in order to hold Him in her arms for so long, since she knew well where His blessed soul was; nor would she have wanted to bring it back from so worthy a work on account of any of her own happiness. On the contrary, she gave deepest thanks to that which pained her greatly. So that differing reasons and various loves tormented her, and it was from that greatness of love, to which every impossible thing is easy, almost obliged to divide the indivisible, that her spirit left with Christ's soul, and her soul remained to honor God and mourn His dead body, since God was present in Christ's soul and body.

And I see that all those virtues, which, like the soul's food, could feed her, were now flavored with sorrow's poison, so that rather than nourishing her, they consumed her. Love, humility, patience, obedience, all gave her sorrow. The more she loved, the more she sorrowed, knowing the goodness of her Son. The humbler she was, the more she punished herself, seeing God's greatness so humiliated. The more forbearing she wished to be, the more distressed she became, that body seeming to her to symbolize Christ's

---

Christ's example, when he humbled himself and became obedient to death (Philippians 2:8). Medieval theology saw it as the root from which all other virtues grew. It later came to be seen as a virtue opposed to pride.

59. This refers to Christian teaching that Christ was made incarnate.

60. Colonna transforms the Virgin's role by having her compensate for mankind's ingratitude to God.

unconquerable endurance. The more she wished to obey, the more she remembered that He had been obedient until death, so that those virtues that had helped her in the past now wounded her. Her shield had wounded her; the cure was further suffering. Only faith kept her in life, and she kept faith alive by reinvesting the whole world with it, the world that was now deprived of it. Therefore, since all the treasure that the Christian can obtain is born of true faith, and having received it from the Virgin Mary, without whom it would have been extinguished, we should then consider how great is our obligation to her; so great, in fact, shall we find it that this our mortal life will not suffice a thousandth part to satisfy it.

II
CHIARA MATRAINI'S
BRIEF DISCOURSE ON THE LIFE AND PRAISES OF THE MOST BLESSED VIRGIN AND MOTHER OF THE SON OF GOD

EDITOR'S INTRODUCTION

Born in Lucca to Benedetto Matraini and Agata Serantoni, Chiara Matraini (1515–1604?) was a year old when she lost her father, and was brought up by her uncle. Little is known about her family, except that it participated in the famous "straccioni" or "ragamuffin" rebellion in Lucca in 1531. At sixteen Matraini married Vincenzo Cantarini and bore a son, Federico. By 1542 she was widowed, and in 1547 appears to have caused scandal by her relationship with a married poet, Bartolomeo Graziani. In the 1550s Matraini had taken up her literary career, publishing her first book, *Rime e prose*, around 1555.[1] She also translated from the Latin an oration attributed to Isocrates (*A Demonico*, 1556), and had literary friendships with famous men such as Benedetto Varchi (1503–65), Lodovico Dolce (1508–68), and Lodovico Domenichi (1515–64), the last her teacher and admirer. Her poetry was modeled on that of Vittoria Colonna, and the first of her two collections (1555) consisted mainly of love poetry, reflecting the tenor of her earlier life. In 1560 she

1. Major works: *Rime et prose di Madonna Chiara Matraini gentildonna lucchese* (Lucca: per il Busdrago, 1555); *Meditationi spirituali* (Lucca: Vincenti Busdraghi, 1581); *Considerationi sopra i sette Salmi penitentiali del Gran Ré e Profeta Davit* (Lucca: Vincenzo Busdraghi, 1586); *Lettere di madonna Chiara Matraini gentildonna Lucchese, con la prima, e seconda parte delle sue Rime. Nuovamente stampate, etc.* (Venice: Nicolò Moretti, 1597); *Breve discorso sopra la Vita e laude della Beatiss. Verg. e Madre del Figliuol di Dio* (Lucca: Vincenzio Busdraghi, 1590); *Dialoghi spirituali* (Venice: Fiorante Prati, 1602); *Rime e lettere*, ed. Giovanna Rabitti (Bologna: Commissione per i Testi di Lingua, 1989); *Selected Poetry and Prose: A Bilingual Edition*, ed. and trans. by Elaine MacLachlan. Intro. by Giovanna Rabitti (Chicago: University of Chicago Press, 2007).

For biography and bibliographical references, see Giovanna Rabitti, "Chiara Matraini" in *Italian Women Writers: A Bio-bibliographical Sourcebook*, ed. Rinaldina Russell (Westport, CT: Greenwood Press, 1994), 243–52; Janet Smarr, *Joining the Conversation: Dialogues by Renaissance Women* (Ann Arbor: University of Michigan Press, 2005); Chiara Matraini, *Selected Poetry and Prose*, ed. and trans. by MacLachlan.

Figure 4. Woodcut of Chiara Matraini, from the 1590 edition of the *Breve discorso sopra la Vita e laude della Beatiss. Verg. e Madre del Figliuol di Dio. Di M. Chiara Matraini, Gentildonna Luchese.* Unnumbered folio. Reproduced by kind permission of the Biblioteca Marucelliana, Florence.

seems to have begun a relationship with a judge, Cesare Coccapani. In 1581 she published the *Meditationi spirituali*. Lucca was a center of Church reform, but there is little of the reform in Matraini's *Life of the Virgin*, even though she was apparently suspected of links with heretical circles.[2] But it is clear that Counter-Reformation ideology led her to write works on major religious themes, such as the *Considerationi sopra i sette Salmi penitentiali* (1586) and the present text, the *Breve discorso sopra la Vita e laude della Beatiss. Verg. e Madre del*

2. See Rabitti, "Chiara Matraini," in *Italian Women Writers*, ed. Russell, 243–52.

Figliuol di Dio (1590), both of which are entirely in keeping with the spirit of the Counter-Reformation.

Matraini's *Brief Discourse on the Life and Praises of the Most Blessed Virgin and Mother of the Son of God* was her most widely read work. First published in Lucca, it was reprinted in Venice in an undated edition of ca. 1650, with a slightly different title, and illustrated with woodcuts.[3] Dedicated to the author's cousin Juditta, abbess of the monastery of San Bernardo in Pisa, the first edition also contains annotations in an appendix and a sonnet to the author by Don Giuseppe Mozzagrugno, a Neapolitan and canon regular of the church of San Salvatore, Lucca, as well as a reply from Matraini. Matraini wrote much poetry addressed to the Virgin in other later writings such as the *Dialoghi spirituali*, and a further work on the Virgin, which was published in her volume of letters in 1597, in fact in the form of a letter to Mary.[4]

Written as a kind of long personal prayer, Matraini's prose narrative of the Virgin's life concerns God's providence and "unconquerable love," first in creating humanity and second in sending his own son to earth for its salvation, through the instrument of the Virgin Mary.[5] The Redemption plan is stated from the outset, with Lucifer's envy of the human race prompting the rest of the action, and with Mary always in God's mind, before time and before the Creation. Throughout the work runs the imagery of water in its different manifestations, symbol of the Redemption, specifically through the sacrament of Baptism.

Matraini's narrative is based on the infancy account in Luke, with the inclusion of two references to Matthew's account. She employs many of the conventional Marian metaphors and allegories found first in the early Christian Fathers such as Ambrose, so just as there is a first and second Adam, there are first and second Eves, and in replacing the first, Mary is now the second Eve, and also the second earth from which the second, heavenly, Adam sprang. An extremely important feature, however, of Matraini's account of the Fall is the placing of Adam and Eve as equals in the earthly Para-

3. *Vita della beatissima Vergine Maria, Madre, e Sposa del Figliuol di Dio. Descritta in un discorso brevemente da M. Chiara Matraini, Gentildonna Luchese. Nuovamente Ristampata, e di belle figure adornata* (Venice, Padua, and Bassano: Gio. Antonio Remondini, n.d. [1650?]). Both this and the 1590 edition have been used for this translation.

4. "Alla beatissima Vergine, e madre del Figliuol di Dio," in *Lettere di madonna Chiara Matraini gentildonna Lucchese, con la prima, e seconda parte delle sue Rime . . . Nuovamente stampate* (Venice: Nicolò Moretti, 1597), fols. 32r–34v. This work contains much the same imagery.

5. It addresses the Virgin Mary as, for example, on one occasion, "O most compassionate Virgin ... I pray to you" (108), and the work ends in the word "Amen." There is a prayer to Mary as intercessor, "advocate of us wretched sinners" (74), and exhortation to emulate her, the "Queen of Heaven" (118).

dise ("God placed man . . . in company with a beautiful and pleasing woman" [77; cf. Genesis 1:26–31]); their *joint* disobedience is through their desire to be like God and for immortality, promised them by Satan. This is in contrast to the conventional use of Genesis 2:21–5 and Genesis 3:1–24, in which Eve is taken from one of Adam's ribs, a secondary creation, and then tempted by the serpent. In Matraini's version, there is no temptation or blaming of Eve, no sexual theme. In departing from the traditional view of the culpable Eve, Matraini lays the ground for her Mary, that "very powerful woman" who, ever virgin, is the woman God promised the serpent would come to conquer evil (Genesis 3:15), and the Woman clothed with the Sun (Revelation 12:1). She is also Wisdom, *Sophia*, "the very wise Virgin," the mother, daughter, and bride of Christ. She is the Church. Her body, incorruptible at death, is raised to heaven, where she is exalted as Empress of the Universe, the intercessor between humanity and God.

The structure is chronological, consisting of a narrative built around the gospel incidents, the rhetorical *amplificatio*, interspersed with quotations from the relevant verses in Luke and adumbrations from Genesis, Proverbs, and Ezekiel in Latin. The imagined dialogue between Mary and Gabriel is based on Luke 1, as is Mary's reply, "Behold the handmaid of the Lord." Elizabeth addresses the Virgin with the second line of the Hail Mary, and there are allusions to the Magnificat and the Hail, Holy Queen. Like Colonna, Matraini uses the *Improperia* to write of Christ's Passion ("lips from which salvific and holy teachings full of truth used always to issue are now given vinegar and most bitter gall to drink" [109]), meditating on his body and the Virgin's torment by her loss. Matraini also provides extended commentaries, and addresses short homilies to the reader (such as when the magi go to honor Christ, "we too are invited to adore God" [101]), or in the case of the finding of Christ in the Temple, the reader is advised to "follow the holy footsteps of the Virgin Mary, our guide and advocate, and we will doubtless find Him within the temple of our hearts where He lives willingly through grace" [107]). The language is unadorned but on occasion consciously archaic in its inversions—for example, "Great and marvelous was the joy" (96).

Little, as we have seen, is known of Mary's life, and Matraini, like many before her, and like her near-contemporary Marinella, uses apocrypha to fill the lacunae, to expand and expound on gospel events such as the massacre of the innocents, where she shows particular gusto in relating the bloody scenes, in the rhetorical *descriptio* that enhances the narrative, or again in the almost graphic account of the circumcision, the first of the Virgin's Seven Sorrows. Although her parents are unnamed, the Virgin is said to be descended from "illustrious and royal blood," and goes through the childhood created for her by the Book of James: she is left in the Temple at three, rather oddly and specifically "as a virgin," or, as an earlier reference states, "this most noble and consecrated Virgin" (78); a husband, Joseph, is chosen for her by divine intervention. Incidents from the Pseudo-Bonaventure *Meditations* and the *Golden Legend* amplify the sense of the Virgin's piety in scenes such as the Annunciation, where she is described as being "accustomed to seeing Angels on other occasions," so seeing one now does not trouble her, merely what he has to say (83). Aware that the appearance of Christ to his mother after his Resurrection is not referred to in the gospels, Matraini offers an ingenious reason—the evangelists' purpose was to bear witness only to the facts of the Resurrection—but she is sure that Christ would have appeared first to his mother, since she had loved him most (111). Similarly, she uses apocrypha to tell of Mary's dormition, and to incorporate the Church's teaching about the Virgin's assumption and coronation in heaven.

Employing the beautiful garden imagery from the vision of Paradise found in Genesis, Matriani refers to Mary as the "chosen and fertile virgin ground," with its symbolism of fruitfulness, wherein the fruits, Faith, Hope, and Charity, the theological virtues, are nourished by the rivers of Justice, Fortitude, Prudence, and Temperance, the cardinal virtues (79, 80). Virginity is here fruitful, setting Mary apart from all other women. Using Ambrose's metaphor of Christ as the fount of divine love sent to water the infertile earth of human generation, Christ is also the dew coming down from the purest heaven of the Virgin Mary (94). Mary is also the "ample and very deep river," the "living fountain" (107), who, as intercessor between man and God, obtains the "water of mercy" from the "infinite sea" (108). It is through the Virgin Mary's prayers that Christians may arrive in heaven (Mary's intercessory role was in particular anathema to the Protestants). Matraini invokes the Song of Songs as Mary ends her life on earth: Christ beckons her in the words of the Bridegroom: "Come from Libanus [Lebanon], my spouse, come from Libanus, come" (*Song of Songs*, 4:8), and she is taken to join her heavenly bridegroom and son.

Mary is the fulfillment of prophecies. Matraini stresses her immaculate conception, without giving details, and the mystery of Christ's conception, all accompanied by prophecies and portents, such as the Sibylline oracle, to emphasize the miraculousness of Christ's birth, the spring of living water turning into oil, and the collapse of the Ara Pacis (96). Mary is also a prophetess (89), as are Elizabeth and Anna (86–87 and 102), things that would have been of interest to the female reader. There are also nice homely touches, imaginative speeches or thoughts put into the mouths and minds of characters, such as the long peroration concerning Joseph's natural emotional turmoil over Mary's pregnancy and her chastity (of both of which Matraini stresses Joseph is certain), related in a naturalistic way, and the scene of Mary in Egypt, thinking of Bethlehem where she had been born, brought up, and had given birth to Christ (105), now the *locus* of the massacre of the innocents. (In relating Joseph's doubts over Mary, Matraini departs from Luke to use Matthew's account, no doubt to heighten the drama.)[6] And quaint geographical descriptions lend color to her subject, such as in the story of the magi, who ride on "certain animals called dromedaries, which because they are very fast when they run, by divine will they traveled in thirteen days from the East to Jerusalem, said to be situated in the middle of the entire earth" (99–100).[7]

The reasons given for Mary's marriage (81–82) are accompanied by the Church's view on the sacrament: the purpose of "most holy marriage," ordained by God, is as a symbol of the Incarnation, and union of mankind with God, followed by the "blessing of offspring." Mary and Joseph's marriage, however, is solemnized by a vow of perpetual virginity, and their offspring results not from "conjunction," but through the Holy Spirit. Joseph's purpose is to protect and support Mary and to help her to look after the child Jesus, and act as an escort whenever needed, the actions of any proper husband (81–82).

Described as "a strong column," Mary is "so powerful in supporting the weight of her enormous adversities" (109) that she remains standing beside the cross, and it is through her power as the instigator of her son's first miracle that water is changed into wine at the marriage feast at Cana (John 2:1–11). The episode is seen as a symbolic precursor to the sacrament of the Eucharist, and thus empowers Mary in the eyes of Christian believers, something that Matraini celebrates in her meditation on Mary as (noted above) the "living fountain," the mediatrix who is subsequently the "most invincible warrior" against evil (114). Despite her great power, Mary is humble, and in this way a model for women readers. Her humility is too great to allow her to tell Joseph how she became pregnant as it is a mystery of God; her indomitable "forbearance," part of the fortitude with which she is endowed, keeps her silent. She merely "[begs] the Lord humbly" to put things right to prevent the destruction of their marriage (93)—fortunately, an angelic visitation to Joseph reinstates his faith in her. Again, so humble is Mary that it has not occurred to her that it might be she who is to be the virgin mother of God (84). It is through humility that she goes to

6. Matthew 1:18–21.

7. The story of the magi is the second instance of Matraini's use of Matthew's account.

the Temple for her purification despite the fact that she has no need to, in submission to the Law that governs other women (102). And it is humility, according to Matraini, that is the way for all to reach the "highest throne of God" (114).

Matraini's narrative is a thorough recapitulation of Counter-Reformation Mariolatry, a celebration of the Virgin as the Church Militant through her holy life on earth, and the Church Triumphant through her immense glory in heaven. Her great power is likened to an "army set in array" (117); she is the "triumphant Woman" in heaven (117). Through her actions Mary is also the model of the active and contemplative life, the Christian way of combining the active life, as in good works and charitable deeds, with the contemplative life of prayer and meditation ("through good works and most holy examples" [117]) propounded by the Church. She is a model of steadfastness or fortitude—while the others ran away, she remained at the cross, a not entirely accurate, but, by the seventeenth century, a conventional rephrasing of the gospel accounts.[8] Mary's death prompts Matraini to dwell on the Church's teaching regarding the Christian's preparation for death, through the sacraments of Penance, Communion, and Extreme Unction. Mary on earth had been accompanied by seven "maidens," the four cardinal and three theological virtues: her human counterpart is exhorted to abide by these to reach heaven, with Mary the protectress, guide, and advocate whom the reader should seek to emulate (118).

Interspersed with Matraini's discourse on Mary's life are prayers and sonnets addressed to the Virgin, all of which have been rendered into prose in this translation. While the first prayer and first sonnet are invocations to the Virgin to assist the writer, who describes herself elsewhere in the *Brief Discourse* as "lacking in eloquence" (81), to celebrate her subject in poetry ("teach me to speak of your holy beauty" [76]), the rest precede meditations on the biblical or apocryphal events of Mary's life in the main text, adumbrating and amplifying what is to follow. In annotating Matraini's meditations, I have not provided glosses to these sonnets and prayers, except where material contained in them is not reflected in the meditation that follows.

The penultimate sonnet (*To the gracious Star, and most faithful Guide of all the sailors of the stormy sea of this world*) is moving and personal, concerning as it does the end of the Virgin's life, a theme that parallels the approaching end of Matraini's own life—she was around seventy-five years of age when the *Brief Discourse* was published. Praying to Mary, the "shining Star of our wandering and pilgrim souls," the author asks to be guided "from the rocks" and

8. Mary is present at the Crucifixion only in John's gospel (19:25–27).

"frightening tempest she finds herself in alone" to arrive in the Virgin's "secure harbor" (118).

It may be of interest to note that Matraini's piety during the latter part of her life led her to commission a painting of the Emperor Augustus and the Sibyl from Alessandro Ardenti, in which she had herself depicted as the Cumaean sibyl, to hang over an altar she also commissioned in her parish church of Santa Maria Forisportam in Lucca. In her will of 1576, she stipulated that the painting be finished by Francesco Cellini of Lucca. The painting remained *in situ* until the twentieth century, when it was removed to the national museum of the Villa Guinigi, Lucca.[9]

BRIEF DISCOURSE ON THE LIFE AND PRAISES OF THE MOST BLESSED VIRGIN AND MOTHER OF THE SON OF GOD, BY MADONNA CHIARA MATRAINI, GENTLEWOMAN OF LUCCA . . . IN LUCCA BY VINCENZIO BUSDRAGHI, 1590[10]

Prayer to the most blessed Virgin, Mother of God, advocate of us wretched sinners

O most beautiful and excellent Virgin, who was ordained before all time, in the supreme and divine council of the highest and individual Trinity, to be evermore Virgin and Mother of the great Monarch and King of the Universe, almighty God and Redeemer of the entire world. O Empress of the angels, who sits in the highest and lofty throne next to most high God above all other creatures, clothed in that infinite light, which gives splendor to the sun, crowned by stars of excellent dignity, with which through divine grace you are worthy to be adorned. O most gracious Empress of Heaven, advocate of all those who faithfully call to you, I beg you on account of that profound humility that makes you ascend so high to God, that you will incline toward my humble and most fervent love, and purify these my impure lips of all worldly filth, and open them in your holy and most deserved praises, so that satisfying in part the great debt that I have because of the many favors that, without any worthiness, I have received from you, I do not appear entirely ungrateful to you. Open, Queen of Heaven, open, kindly and gra-

9. See Irma B Jaffe, with Gernando Colombardo, *Shining Eyes, Cruel Fortune: The Lives and Loves of Italian Renaissance Women Poets* (New York: Fordham University Press, 2002), chap. 4, "Chiara Matraini (1515–1604), The Poet as Sibyl," 112–14, for details. My thanks to Virginia Cox for referring me to this essay.

10. This translation makes use of both the 1590 Lucca edition and that printed in Venice, undated but likely ca. 1650. (See note 3 for the full citation of this edition.) Where there are discrepancies between the two editions, that of Lucca would appear to be the more reliable.

BREVE DISCORSO
SOPRA LA VITA
E LAVDE DELLA
BEATISS. VERG. E MADRE
DEL FIGLIVOL DI DIO.

DI M. CHIARA MATRAINI,
Gentildonna Luchese,

Con alcune annotationi nel fine, del R. Don Giuseppe Mozzagrugno Napoletano, Canonico Regulare del Saluatore.

IN LVCCA Appresso Vincenzio Busdraghi, 1590.
Con licentia De' Superiori.

Figure 5. Title page of the 1590 edition of the *Breve discorso sopra la Vita e laude della Beatiss. Verg. e Madre del Figliuol di Dio. Di M. Chiara Matraini, Gentildonna Luchese.* Reproduced by kind permission of the Biblioteca Marucelliana, Florence.

cious dispenser of all earthly and heavenly graces, your most generous hand to me, your faithful, poor, and beseeching servant, full of all knowledge and of all human goodwill, and bestow on me a spark of such abundant graces, which descend continually from you over those who, with devout affection, ask you, beg you, since you are that sea from which flow all rivers and the fountains of gifts from almighty God, by whom you have been made the treasurer of Paradise; and see how I have placed all my hope in you and how I would always long to praise your most holy name. Amen.

To the Safest Star of All Sailors of This World

O Virgin, only Star of the Sea, much more, sun of my deep nights, unveil, I pray to you, your light, beautiful above all others, in these fearful waves. And this small boat, wandering and weak, turn to your wide fruitful banks of divine grace and virtue whence never ever came the dark tempest of error. And for that humility on account of which God elected you to such a height, in His divine counsel, by which you were virgin and His mother, I beg you to teach me to speak of your holy beauty in such a way that it may be ever pleasing to your divine Son and everlasting Father.[11]

The supreme and most singular graces of Mary the Virgin, Mother of God, the supreme, almighty Creator and Redeemer of the World

As the divine and supreme Good, unconquerable love, beginning without beginning, and end without end of all things, wished to share His priceless boundless blessings with others, in the beginning He created the angels, who were perfect by nature, endowed with every beauty, and replete with wisdom. Among them great Lucifer stood out, and he was given this name because of the light that shone from him.[12] Knowing that the Son of God was to take on human nature, and therefore that, through divine will, human nature would be united with the Eternal Word, and that it was to be exalted above all the choirs of Angels, and that many men were to make themselves their equals in glory, and perhaps even greater, blinded by excessive arrogance in his own excellence, Lucifer was indignant at the thought of having anyone superior to himself. As if a being might exist of himself alone, and not through God his Creator, he thus wished to make himself similar to

11. The appellation "Star of the Sea" derives from the anthem "Ave Maris Stella" ("Hail, Star of the Sea"), one of the most popular Marian hymns, probably written in the ninth century. It derives from the meaning of the Jewish form of her name, Mariam, and also refers to the play on words of her name, in Latin "Maria," and the Latin word for "sea," *mare*.

12. Lucifer (Latin, "light-bearer"). As in Luke 10:18, the name was used to refer to Satan, the prince of the fallen angels, by Saint Jerome and other Fathers of the Church.

Him in his dominion. And, thus, swollen in Pride (he thought: "This man, whom God is to make, together with other men, is of a nature less noble, not at all worthy and inferior to our own, so that it is not suitable that he be made equal to us in glory"),[13] Lucifer decided to make for himself another kingdom, one that would be separate from that of God on high. As he was a rebel and most ungrateful enemy to his divine and infinite Creator, he was banished from Heaven, and sank down into the abyss of Hell, with all those who followed him, with no hope of ever leaving it, with all those who followed him. But that supreme Good, that infallible Mind, which never neglects His first grand design or His most excellent will to bestow His infinite wealth again on others, after the fall of the King of the Angels, once more created humankind in His image and likeness, so that it might know His supreme and infinite love, and once knowing it, it might love God, and loving God, it might possess Him, and possessing Him, might finally be made blessed by Him.

In the beginning, God placed man among the delights and joy of the earthly Paradise in company with a beautiful and pleasing woman, with free possession of all earthly things, except for the fruit of the Tree of Knowledge of good and evil. This God forbade them, saying to them that they were not to eat of it because, were they to do so, they would die. But proud Lucifer, ever enemy to human nature, unable, through envy, to bear their so very great happiness, with extraordinary craftiness went in the guise of a serpent to give them to understand that if they ate the forbidden fruit, they would become as gods, immortal.[14] Then, spurred by this hope, they disobeyed the commandment of their just and most kind Lord, who punished them, with a punishment they deserved.[15] But first He said to the sly and evil serpent: "I will put enmity between you and the woman, and your seed and hers: so that you will set the traps and cast the nets of your deceptions around her foot and she will trample and crush your head with it."[16]

13. This interpolation is in Lucifer's voice. For pride, see note 71.

14. Genesis 3:1–6.

15. Genesis 3:7–24. Matraini's account of the first man and woman is interesting in that it follows the creation account of Genesis 1:26–28, where God creates "man to his own image: to the image of God he created him: male and female he created them," rather than Genesis 2:7–17, where God creates Adam first, commands him not to eat of the tree of knowledge of good and evil, and creates Eve from Adam's rib (vv. 21–24). The latter account is more commonly used, where Eve is created second, as "companion and helper" to Adam, and in which she is tempted by the serpent, her desire being for knowledge. Matraini makes them equal and equally culpable.

16. Genesis 3:15: *Inimicitias ponam inter te, & mulierem, & semen tuum, & semen illius ipsa conteret caput tuum, &c.*

But who was that so very powerful woman, to whom the Lord was referring, saying that she would break the head of the ancient and death-dealing serpent with her foot, if not that most excellent Virgin, who had been chosen before time to be the way of the truth and of life, who had to come to free humankind from Satan's unhappy servitude, and from eternal death, Satan who himself was made a slave through the sin of disobedience? For she was then that so very prudent Virgin, and most powerful lady, who was able, and knew how, through divine grace, to overcome pride and infernal Lucifer's power over the human race with the holy foot of her profound humility.[17] She alone, from within her mother's womb, saint above all saints, was always without the slightest stain of sin. She alone, therefore, was destined to become Mother of God and Tabernacle of the Holy Spirit, so that the Church of Rome sings those beautiful words, from the eighth chapter of the Book of Proverbs: "The Lord possessed me in the beginning of his ways, before he made any thing from the beginning. I was set up from eternity, and of old before the earth was made. The depths were not as yet, and I was already conceived: before the hills I was brought forth."[18]

O how ancient and exalted was the lineage of this most noble and consecrated Virgin, and how peerless her divine graces! Since in her, her conception was singular, her birth divine, and the patterns of her peerless virtues marvelous; in her purity she was even purer than Adam before he sinned. And in the Angel's affirmation of her grace she was superior to the angels who cannot increase, or even diminish their first gift of God, while the blessed Virgin has always been able to increase it, even without ever lacking it.[19] And in truth, it was fitting for the great King of the Universe to endow her with all the graces and perfections as, having done everything concerned with the world's beauty and ornament, so much the less would He fail to endow His Mother with all the graces that she could receive within herself, as He intended to found and construct in her His most holy Church. And it was also fitting that such a unique Son in His goodness, might, and wisdom should make His Mother peerless and excellent in every gift and grace, endowing her with every rare virtue and excellence, since the Mother's honor was reflected in the Son. He had, besides, to observe the given

17. The Virgin's "holy foot" alludes to the "Woman clothed with the Sun" (Revelation 1:20) who crushes the dragon.

18. Proverbs 8:22–26: *Dominus possedit me in initio viarum suarum, antequam quidquam faceret à principio ab eterno ordinata sum, & ex antiques, antequam terrafieret, nundum erat abysso, & ego iam concepta eram, [. . .] & ante omnes colles ego parturiebar.* [. . .] indicates text omitted by Matraini.

19. This refers to the angel's salutation of the Virgin in Luke 1:28, "Hail, full of grace," the origin of the prayer the Hail Mary (Latin, *Ave Maria*), in use from the eleventh century.

Law to honor His parents.[20] Accordingly, God made her not only most excellent in her soul but also most noble in her body: since she was born of illustrious and royal blood, her most profound humility would show greatly in her, so that she would be more praised and admired, and exalted by God in His heavenly glory.[21]

Thus was born this most beautiful and immaculate Virgin, nobler than all the other creatures of earth and sky, to the great joy of the Angels, and to all humanity, who received free will so immediately from God on high, as we must believe, so that she could always gain merits, so much so that in her childhood she surpassed the use of reason of any person whomever in this world (except for Jesus Christ, her Son), and at scarcely three years of age she entered (as a virgin) God's Temple. There she dedicated herself entirely to its service, in prayer, fasting, and meditation, and keeping her mind ever fixed on heavenly things, and despising earthly ones, from which she was always far removed, caring only to please God and to be in the love and service of His divine Majesty.[22] She was that most gracious Virgin who, having already gathered in her noble and generous breast every excellent desire for heavenly things, and from whose beautiful hands flowed sweet fruits and holy works, was rightfully compared to the paradise of pleasures.[23]

The Garden of Pleasure is made.[24] Therefore that chosen and fertile virgin ground, over which purest Heaven abundantly spread all the divine graces, more than on any other most worthy creature whatsoever, from which was

20. The fifth commandment, "Thou shalt honor thy father and thy mother."

21. The idea of the Virgin's descent from "illustrious and royal blood" probably relates to Luke's attempt to establish her lineage, through marriage to Joseph, to the house of David (1:27), despite the Virgin's own lowly origins in the gospel accounts. In the apocryphal second-century Book of James, or *Protevangelium*, she is described as "of the tribe of David" (*The Apocryphal New Testament: Being the Apocryphal Gospels, Acts, Epistles and Apocalypses*, ed. and trans. by M. R. James [Oxford: Clarendon Press, 1924], 43). Her noble status here has probably more to do with the medieval equation of holiness with high-ranking birth.

22. The entirely apocryphal account of the Virgin's early years is related in the Book of James (James, *Apocryphal New Testament*, 41–43). Her entry into the Temple goes against all Jewish belief and practice, since no Jewish women were allowed into the inner court of the Temple or to be dedicated to its service. The custom of virgin priestesses, or vestal virgins, was pagan. Mary's life in the Temple is recounted in Jacobus de Voragine, *The Golden Legend: Readings on the Saints*, 2 vols., trans. by William Granger Ryan (Princeton, NJ: Princeton University Press, 1993), 2:152–53.

23. The word "paradise" is probably of Persian origin (*Zeud, pairidaeza*), denoting an enclosed park or pleasure ground. In the Septuagint, it occurs in Genesis 2 as the Greek rendering of the garden planted by God in Eden.

24. Ezekiel 36:35: *Facta est hortus voluptatis*. The biblical quotation should read, *Facta est ut hortus voluptatis*. The full quotation reads, "They shall say: This land *that was* untilled is become as a garden of pleasure."

formed the second heavenly Adam, entirely different from and contrary to the first one, and to which (instead of Eve) was given that Ave, which was the beginning of our salvation.[25]

It was in the midst of this earthly and so delightful paradise of the Virgin Mary, the tree of supreme Wisdom, whose roots spread greatly in the soil of her deep humility, that the fruit of immortal life was produced on which her spiritual soul alone fed itself. As if in perpetual spring, there were always on this happy ground the greenest grasses, wonderful and singular virtues, perfumed flowers of heavenly thoughts, magnificent plants of holiest wishes, in whose beautiful greening foliage the divine Spirit's holy and gentle breeze continually breathed, which always turned her to wish for other greater things. The brightness of Faith, the flowering of Hope, and ardor of Charity were the fruits of that garden. Their plants were continually bathed by four very full rivers, which watered this so very rich and fruitful garden, such as the source of Justice, Prudence, Fortitude, and Temperance.[26] Their fruits grew so tall through being watered by these rivers that with their canopies they reached the great architect of the stars, where the pure and happy birds sweetly sang those sweetest hymns of her lofty and heavenly thoughts, from the early morning of her life until the evening of her death, hymns that it was fitting to sing with whole and perfect harmony before the supreme Sun, which awakened Him. There also emanated from those sacred and most choice plants so many beautiful and unusual flowers of devotion, which rose directly into the presence of God, the high and sublime, on whom she, the blessed Virgin, as the eagle does on the sun, always fixed her gaze from her high and divine meditations. Finally, she was that garden, and that plant that showed its singular beauty and unique fertility in the holy field of the Church Militant, through her holy life, and in the Church Triumphant through her immense glory.[27] We should therefore ask this most Holy Virgin to always pray for our salvation before her most kind Son, and to conceal us beneath the shade of the very wide branches of her mercy, from the great heat of God's anger, God the just and most powerful.

25. The second Adam is Christ. The Eva/Ave play on words was a common medieval conceit that used the Latin form of Eve, Eva. *Ave* was the first word of Gabriel's address to the Virgin Mary at the Annunciation, and symbolized the reversal of Eve's fall through the Incarnation.

26. Faith, Hope, and Charity are the theological virtues, and Justice, Prudence, Fortitude, and Temperance the cardinal virtues, as classified by Aristotle and Plato, and taken over by Christians.

27. The Church Militant was the body of Christians still on earth as opposed to those in purgatory or in heaven. Christians in heaven constituted the Church Triumphant.

Prayer to the glorious Virgin

What prized gift of praise could I ever bring, O Virgin, and unique Bride, to your holy nuptials, lacking in eloquence as I am? If you, rich in grace, first of all, grant me a sweet sound, choice expressions, and clear words to my tongue, so that I may know how to sing today before your heavenly throne; thus, just as the Sun, shining Star of God, penetrates so many bodies and so many heavens, to show its splendors, so may you wish that your great light reveals your immense glories and our everlasting honors through my dull, helpless shadow.

While, in her holy virginity of body and mind, the most pure Virgin was carrying out her marvelous and worthy works in God's Temple, the time came for all the prophecies of the divine prophets and wise sibyls to be fulfilled, the prophets and sibyls who had prophesied and predicted that a virgin would conceive the Son of God.[28] Now that she had reached the age of thirteen,[29] it pleased the high and divine Majesty that the Virgin Mary should marry Joseph, of the tribe of Judah, and He desired this to be done for many various and worthy reasons. First, so that it symbolized the mystery of the divine union between Jesus Christ and His most Holy Church, who is the Bride and Mother of all the faithful. Second, so that her purity might not be defamed and that she would not incur punishment according to the Law, which was that young girls, who gave birth before they were married, had to be stoned.[30] Third, so that there was no doubt that Jesus Christ was born of a legitimate marriage and also to conceal His will about His birth from His enemies. It was also very appropriate for her to marry Joseph since, because he was just and chaste, he would be the best witness to her own ineffable purity: and also because he could support and comfort her in the nourishment and

28. In ancient times sibyls were women who supposedly uttered the oracles and prophecies of a god. Later, there were thought to be ten sibyls who lived at different times and places in Asia, Africa, Greece, and Italy. Many Christian commentators drew arguments in defense of Christianity from them, particularly concerning the birth of Christ. The Sibylline oracles was the name given to collections of supposed prophecies emanating from sibyls or seeresses. Because of the oracles' great influence in religious affairs, during the second-century BCE Hellenistic Jews in Alexandria composed texts in the same form, and Christians did the same in the second and third centuries, as a form of proselytizing. These were known and used in the Middle Ages, as can be seen in their incorporation in the *Golden Legend*.

29. Thirteen was the traditional age for young girls to marry in biblical times.

30. Matraini is here applying stoning, the punishment for adulteresses according to the Law, to mothers of illegitimate babies.

care of her little Son, and because he was a safe escort in going from place to place to provide her with whatever she needed.[31]

Therefore the Lord revealed to the High Priest, through His heavenly Ambassador, that he should gather together there all the men of the House of David and give a staff to each and, to the one whose staff flowered, the Virgin Mary would be given as bride. When he had done this, Joseph's staff produced flowers and a dove was seen on top of it, by which sign it was clearly recognized that he had been ordained by divine providence as bridegroom of the most holy Virgin, for whose worthy association and marriage God greatly exalted the most pure Virgin.[32] He thereby made her singular and peerless above all married women, so that the betrothal was celebrated by her and Joseph with a vow of perpetual virginity, inseparable companionship, and spiritual love, which returned them to the first state of innocence, and fulfilled the purpose of the first intention, for which God had ordained most holy marriage, which was a symbol of the holy Incarnation, and union of humankind with the Eternal Word; and from this followed the blessing of offspring, not by means of conjoining but through the works of the Holy Spirit.[33]

Prayer to the one and only Bride of most High God

O most beautiful and gracious Virgin, Bride of the great Monarch and King of the Universe, uniquely endowed with all the earthly and celestial graces, above all divine and immortal creatures, dressed in the light of the divine immense Sun, and crowned by the most effulgent rays of eternal glory, in which so much gracious and exceeding beauty always gazes upon your inalterable lover, splendid and sempiternal God, I beg you, most powerful Queen of Heaven, in the triumph and celebration of your sacred and most sumptuous nuptials, that He may wish to throw a small part of that bread of life, which you always enjoy in so much abundance, into the low and impoverished lap of this, your faithful servant, and generously give, so that I

31. The *Golden Legend* gives similar reasons why "the Lord wanted his mother to be married" (1:197).

32. The story of the Virgin and her suitors appears in the Book of James (James, *Apocryphal New Testament,* 42) and in the Gospel of Pseudo-Matthew (ibid., 73–74).

33. The Virgin's vow of perpetual virginity is non-gospel. The idea of her perpetual virginity was first stated in the Book of James (chap. xix; James, *Apocryphal New Testament,* 46–47), and became Church tradition through the Fathers of the Eastern Church and in the West from the fifth century.

may rejoice still more over so much and so worthy favor, and come to give thanks, honor, and praise to both of you most happy Spouses.

Salutation to the most excellent Virgin, Bride of God

Hail Mary, blessed soul, above all others beautiful, humble Virgin, who so pleased the supreme Sun that with His holy light, He made you immaculate mother. Hail, Queen of Heaven, crowned with stars, who is the goal of our exile and weeping, whence you have trodden and crushed the wicked ungrateful head of the ancient serpent. Answer, I beg you, your humble servant; behold (though I do not merit it), I turn my prayers to you and my grand desire, which is, as you know, only to hold the world worthless, and to love your Son, and His assured blessed gifts, and to honor you, noble Virgin.[34]

When the appointed time came, in which the immense fount of divine love—the Son of God—was to descend from Heaven, and come to water the infertile earth of human generation, and lodge and place Himself in the holiest cloister and virginal womb of the Virgin Mary, He sent before Him (as was fitting for someone of His greatness) that worthy celestial Ambassador, called the Archangel Gabriel, in a form visible to her, of a most elegant and upright young man clad in white garments, to announce His arrival to her and all the other things He had commanded him. On descending into Galilee, in the town of Nazareth, the Angel entered the Virgin's bedchamber, where she was, far from all worldly cares, her mind elevated in its usual and lofty meditations. Greeting her with the reverence due to the Bride and Daughter of the great magnificent Monarch and King of Heaven, he said to her: *Hail, full of grace, the Lord is with thee: Blessed art thou among women.*[35] The most wise Virgin was disquieted by the Angel's words, not because of the strangeness of his presence, however, as she was accustomed to seeing angels on other occasions, but she was perturbed by this greeting, as by something never heard.[36] She wondered what kind of greeting this was, so unusual, so lofty, and so joyful, because although she knew that in a short time the Son

34. This sonnet is based on the prayer Hail, Holy Queen (see volume editor's introduction, 20).

35. Luke 1:28. The angelic salutation is of course the beginning of the Hail Mary.

36. See *Golden Legend*, "The Annunciation of the Lord" (1:198), on Mary's often seeing angels. The *Meditations on the Life of Christ* states: "But she was perturbed and did not reply. It was not guilt that confused her or the sight of the angel, for she was accustomed to seeing him often. But . . . she was perturbed by . . . his salutation, because he had not greeted her in that way before." See Pseudo-Bonaventure, or Giovanni de Caulibus, *Meditations on the Life of Christ: An Illustrated Manuscript of the Fourteenth Century. Paris, Bibliothèque nationale, Ms. Ital. 115*, trans. by Isa Ragusa, ed. Isa Ragusa and Rosalie B. Green (Princeton, NJ: Princeton University Press, 1961), 17.

of God would be incarnate in a virgin, it never occurred to her, in her soul or into her pure mind, that it would be she, the one who would conceive and give birth to the Son of God.[37]

With her mind on this thought, she made no reply to the Angel. But, seeing her so disturbed, he said to her:

> Fear not, Mary, since you have found grace with the Lord; be not astonished that I have called you full of grace since, as the first woman lost divine grace, together with all the rest of posterity, so you have found it again for yourself and for all humankind. Therefore you will conceive, and give birth to the Son of God on high, who will bring salvation to all humanity, and who will be called Jesus, which means savior, giver of life, and destroyer of death. This will be not through any external way, common to other women, but by internal grace and virtue of the Holy Spirit.[38]

He further said to her that her Son would be the natural and essential Son of God most High, the Father Eternal, great in Power, Wisdom, Justice, and Mercy, qualities that belonged only to God on high.[39] And that He, God the Father, would give Him the throne of David, not the earthly one but the heavenly one, not temporal but eternal, and that He would reign in the house of Jacob, whose kingdom would be without end. Which means to say, among the Chosen Ones in the present circumstance through grace and, in the future, through glory and, he said, in the house, that is, the family of Jacob, as this house alone was wholly accepted by God for His people; it was also the one from which the Twelve Tribes of Israel sprang.[40] But because the most Holy Virgin had made a vow of perpetual virginity and had been joined to Joseph in this vow, she therefore replied to the Angel: "How can

37. In Christian terms, humility is understood as submissiveness before God, and came to be regarded as a virtue, modeled on Christ's example, when he humbled himself and became obedient to death (Philippians 2:8). Medieval theology saw it as the root from which all other virtues grew. It later came to be seen as a virtue opposed to pride, Lucifer's sin.

38. Luke 1:30–31. The word "external," the translation of Matraini's term "estrinseco," signifies through an external agent, that is, sexual intercourse with a man. In the Book of James (James, *Apocryphal New Testament,* 43), Mary wonders, "Shall I *verily* conceive of the living God, and bring forth after the manner of all women?"

39. The word "essential" in this context refers to Christ's intrinsic nature with God the Father.

40. The Hebrew Bible asserts that the Israelites descended from the twelve sons of Jacob (their births recorded in Genesis 29–35), each of the twelve being the ancestor of the tribe named after him.

this be, that I, not knowing a man, can conceive a son?" and she said this, thinking that she could not be, according to human nature, both a virgin and a mother.[41]

But the Angel, to remove all doubt from her, explained to her how she could be a virgin and fruitful, as he told her that all those things that were impossible to humans were very easy to God. And then he said also:

> The celestial Spirit will come down upon you, and will fill you Himself, without violating your virginity. And you will therefore conceive through the power of the Holy Spirit. But do not fear, Mary, that this most sacred conception will not take place in a human way, but in a divine way, through the power of the Holy Spirit rather than according to Adam's nature.[42]

And because he wanted to make her even more certain that what he had said to her would come to pass, he revealed to her how (through divine grace) her cousin Elizabeth, who was naturally infertile and old, had already conceived and was six months' pregnant. Then the Virgin, hearing this, and convinced with strong faith, said: *Behold the handmaid of the Lord; be it done to me according to thy word.*[43] To which reply, immediately, in an instant, in a moment, the Son of God, through the Holy Spirit, descended (in the guise of the most shining ray of sun, which pierces a closed window of the purest glass without harming it) into her virginal womb, as the worthy dwelling place of the great King of the Universe.

O wise, gracious, and most obedient Virgin, as your gentle and kind words have penetrated all the celestial spheres today, and pierced through all the choirs of Angels, they have arrived there before the most sacred and triumphant tribunal of God on high, where they have been registered in that most secret archive of Paradise; and calling yourself the handmaid of the Lord, your most humble obedience so greatly pleased God's majesty that it was the powerful reason that those banished for rebelling returned home and that those who remained deprived of their inheritance made themselves

41. Luke 1:34: "And Mary said to the angel: How shall this be done, because I know not man?"

42. Luke 1:35: "And the angel, answering, said to her: The Holy Ghost shall come upon thee, and the power of the Most High shall overshadow thee. And therefore also the Holy which shall be born of thee shall be called the Son of God." The angel assures the Virgin that she will conceive through divine intervention rather than through sexual intercourse ("Adam's nature").

43. Luke 1:38.

richer than they had been before.[44] Today the long war is ending, and today the peace so yearned for is being concluded. Today the banners are being raised in Paradise and, as a sign of joy, the vacant seats are being prepared to receive the lost and scattered sons; today for you, Virgin and Mother, the crowns are being set in order, as you have faithfully said: *Behold the handmaid of the Lord; be it done to me according to thy word.*[45] On hearing these words of consent, the Angel reverently took his leave and joyfully and promptly returned to Heaven.

To the lofty Queen of the Virgins, and Mother of most High God

O Virgin, who before time was chosen in Heaven, by God, as His daughter and bride, and made by Him, above all other glorious creatures, holy and perfect, you were conceived in the maternal womb as a white lily and as a rose, protected by high hedges and hidden from every wicked and imperfect mortal view. Therefore I praise and thank the Lord together with you, and beg you, O Virgin, that because of the so many high and immense graces that He granted you, you will beg Him (as long as there is time left in my life) to grant me that I may be His faithful servant and true lover.

After the Angel had departed, the most chaste Virgin was wholly filled with the most fervent rays of God the Incomprehensible and, burning with His infinite love, she clearly perceived (through His inner light) His lofty and profound mysteries, and saw through the power of the Holy Spirit His greatest will. Accordingly, she understood and knew that He desired in her presence to bless John the Baptist in his mother's womb. So that without further delay, and despite her tender age, she began to ascend the great hill of Judea, to visit her cousin Elizabeth.[46] Her words of greeting were no sooner heard by Elizabeth than, urged by the great fervor of her holy and prophetic spirit, Elizabeth said in a loud voice, *Blessed art thou among women, and blessed is the fruit of thy womb, Jesus,* as she understood in that moment the divine mysteries, through the revelation of her son who, having joy of his Lord, moved and celebrated in his mother's womb to pay reverence in the best manner that he was able.[47] Elizabeth therefore understood the entire mystery of the in-

44. This refers to the Virgin's role in salvation, through her giving birth to Jesus, the savior of mankind, thus redeeming the fallen angels who had rebelled and the souls in Limbo who had been deprived.

45. Luke 1:38: *Ecce ancilla Domini fiat mihi secundum verbum tuum.*

46. Luke 1:39 notes that Mary "rising up in those days, went into the hill country with haste into a city of Juda."

47. Matraini quotes here from the Hail Mary, which incorporates the angel's salutation in Luke 1:28 and Elizabeth's greeting in Luke 1:42: "And she cried out with a loud voice, and said: Blessed art thou among women, and blessed is the fruit of thy womb." Elizabeth is seen

carnation of the Son of God through the spirit of prophecy since, from the Virgin's womb, Jesus sent John the Baptist the spirit of sanctification, which cleansed him from original sin and confirmed him in the spirit of grace, so that he might know his Lord. And Elizabeth marveled that the Mother of God had come to visit her, and said (as it seemed to her more reasonable that the Virgin, because of her divinity, should be due a visit):[48]

> O how does this come about, that the Mother of my Lord should come to visit me? Because I know very well that you are the Mother of God, who is incarnate in your womb, that you are blessed above all other women for having believed entirely in the Angel's words when you said, with the consent of faith, *Behold the handmaid of the Lord; be it done to me according to thy word*, for at that hour you conceived the Son of God, whom you will name Jesus.[49]

Then, the blessed Virgin, seeing that Elizabeth's words were in harmony with the Angel's, pondered on the great dignity to which the Lord had raised and honored her above all other creatures, and began to thank Him in a spirit of humility and to magnify Him in her learned and celebrated canticle for the so very many most excellent graces and particular benefits she had received from Him: *My soul doth magnify the Lord. And my spirit hath rejoiced in God my Savior.*[50] It was as if she said, "O Elizabeth, do not think that I rejoice in myself only for the graces and singular dignities for which you have so praised me, since my soul magnifies the Lord alone, and my spirit rejoices in Him alone, who (without my meriting it) has filled me and endowed me with so many heavenly gifts and unique excellent things." From these words, all full of truth and profound humility, we must take worthy and beneficial example and know our own lowliness and the excellence of the Divine Majesty, and thus humbly praise and thank Him whenever we receive any favor from Him, as we are always bound to, rejoicing in Him alone, who is sole

---

as a prophetess because she understood and proclaimed the Incarnation. Fifteenth-century French, German, and eastern European images show the child John the Baptist kneeling and making reverence in his mother's womb while the child Jesus blesses him from his mother's womb.

48. Matraini is of course incorrect—the Virgin was never regarded as being divine; she was the human mother of the son of God.

49. Luke 1:43: "And whence is this to me, that the mother of my Lord should come to me?"

50. Luke 1:46–47: *Magnificat anima mea Dominum, & exultavit spiritus meus in Deo salutari meo.* Mary's praises form part of the Magnificat, the canticle of vespers in the Western Church chanted since the sixth century, and also in the Greek Church (see appendix).

giver and dispenser of all heavenly and earthly goods, and not rejoice in them in ourselves, as if we had received them through our own efforts.

Continuing her joyful and most celebrated canticle, the humble and holy Virgin added, *Because he hath regarded the humility of his handmaid; for behold from henceforth all generations shall call me blessed,*[51] showing that although she had all those worthy and excellent virtues that she could receive in herself through divine grace, nevertheless the Lord regarded the virtue of humility more highly in her than all the other graces with which she was uniquely endowed. And since she had received almost all the dignities that she was to have, she knew in her mind that she would obtain still more that remained. For this reason, the most wise Virgin states that in times to come, she will be called blessed by all the generations. But because some people might ask in what way the Virgin would be called blessed by all the generations—as the Saracens and Muslims deny that she is the Mother of God[52] and the evil Jews blaspheme her—we should, however, remember that there have been four generations in this world. That is, the first one, Adam's, which was without man and without woman; the second, Eve's, who was indeed born of mankind, but without woman; the third, then, joint, that is of both man and woman; and the fourth, of woman without man, which was that of Jesus Christ, born of woman without man;[53] and by those generations, she will always be called blessed, meaning, that is, that the part shall stand for the whole.[54] Since in all the generations there has been someone who believed in Jesus Christ, and that the Virgin Mary was His Mother, and, achieved in such a way, we should understand that all the generations of the world had to call her blessed above all women. Then the Virgin, showing the reason why these generations would call her blessed, added these words: *Because he that is mighty, hath done great things to me; and holy is his name.*[55] The gifts that the omnipotent and most liberal King of the Universe made to His most blessed and virgin Mother were truly

51. Luke 1:48: *Quia respexit humilitatem ancillae suae, ecce enim ex hoc beatam me dicent omnes generationes.*

52. From the ninth century the term Saracen (Latin, *saraceni*), probably originally referring to nomads of north Arabia, came to be applied to all Muslims, particularly those against whom the Crusaders had fought.

53. The four generations are: Adam, that is, the Creation; Eve's creation from Adam's side (Matraini seems oddly to be reverting to Eve's secondary creation according to Genesis 2, rather than the more egalitarian account in Genesis 1 [see above, note 15]); human procreation; and the Virgin birth.

54. This rather obscure sentence probably means: "The whole generation being understood in its representative of one believer, or part."

55. Luke 1:49: *Quia fecit mihi magna qui potens est, & sanctum nomen eius.*

incredible and magnificent, so that she was worthy of all hymns and honors, above all earthly and heavenly beings.

First, He destined her to be adorned with every excellence and singular virtue above all other creatures; second, He kept [her] from whatsoever sin, even in her mother's womb, above all the saints, hastening in her uniquely the use of reason, so that she should merit it sooner than any other saint. Fourth, He gave her grace, to keep (with conjugal faith) the vow made of her virginity in her marriage.[56] Fifth, that she should conceive as a virgin, and be a virgin in giving birth, and a virgin remain after the birth. Sixth, that after the conception and birth she would be His Mother, Daughter, and Bride. Seventh, that after she was filled with the Holy Spirit, she was a prophetess.[57] Eighth, that she knew Him very closely and helped Him for a long time. Ninth, that she acquired the crown of martyrdom, above and beyond all the Apostles and martyrs.[58] Tenth, that in her death she was privileged from decay of her most holy body. Eleventh, that after her death she was exalted and placed above all the choirs of Angels. Twelfth, that she was mediatrix between humankind and Jesus Christ her Son. Therefore it was with good reason that the Virgin said that she would be called blessed by all the generations, since she knew and acknowledged, for she was not ungrateful for them, the great favors and marvelous and singular graces she had received from God most High, who raises the humble and low and strengthens the weak and impotent. His name is so infinitely holy that it sanctifies whoever devoutly invokes it with humble contrition.

After the Immaculate Virgin had praised and magnified the Lord for the many worthy favors she had received from Him particularly and generally, she continued to celebrate Him, saying: *And his mercy is from generation unto generation, to them that fear him,*[59] giving thanks to Him on behalf of humankind for having exercised His mercy (upon the faithful among them) through means of His only begotten and most loved Son. She thanks Him again on behalf of the Holy Church for the favors it was to receive through the coming of Jesus Christ, and which He has redeemed, exalted, and replenished with spiritual wealth, and for those who would be humble and fearful of God, whom He would raise from misery, and would give grace to generation af-

56. Either Matraini or the printer has omitted God's third gift. The Virgin did not of course make a vow of virginity.

57. In many religions, prophets were intermediaries with deities, usually operating through some means of divination. Filled with the Holy Spirit, the Virgin could be described as a prophetess, and her words in the Magnificat as prophecies.

58. The Virgin's martyrdom was the Passion and death of her son.

59. Luke 1:50: *Et misericordia eius a progenie in progenies timentibus eum.*

ter generation of the Jews until the last generation of the world if, however, they were ready to obey His divine Majesty with reverence and love, being mindful of such a memorable and unexpected favor. Because those who give show themselves according to the disposition of those who receive. But because the first disposition is true humility, the root and foundation of each virtue, it is necessary for humanity first to make itself available to the grace and mercy of Jesus Christ, its blessed Lord; the most holy Virgin also celebrated her Son's power, saying: *He hath shewed might in his arm: he hath scattered the proud in the conceit of their heart,*[60] as she foresaw in her mind that her Son would demonstrate so many great and wonderful works that they would exceed all human capacities. And she refers to Him as arm, that is, the great valor and power of His eternal Father, from whom He proceeded and in her descended, and because the Devil was also to be overcome by this so very powerful and valorous arm, sin be extinguished, and eternal death killed, He would finally triumph over all His enemies and be Lord of all the world, of all the centuries, and the entire universe.

The Lord God also scatters and abases those who behave proudly, and exalts the humble, of pure and honest heart, as we have infinite examples from ancient and modern history. The Lord scattered the evil and obstinate Jews who, through their own pride and greed, wished not to receive the favor of Christ's mercy and redemption, nor, through humility or fear, make themselves open to it, but, rejecting and despising Him, then finally put Him to death. Whence Jesus Christ not only punished them, with the pain of removing from them the fruit of the Redemption and the Kingdom of God, but also castigated them with punishing them in their senses, as He scattered them and made them subject to eternal damnation both in the present and in the future. The very wise Virgin again predicted their ruin and destruction, with the following words: *He hath put down the mighty from their seat, and hath exalted the humble.*[61] And all that she predicted came to pass because righteous God deposed them from the thrones of judicial, priestly, and royal ranks, and gave their kingdom to the Christians, such as the poor and humble Apostles and converted Gentiles. And thus were the scribes and Pharisees deposed from Moses' throne whence, seated unrightfully, they made judgments, oppressing and encroaching upon unhappy and sorrowful widows and abandoned children, prolonging trials and, through greed, certifying contrary to their written Law. Almighty God deposed them also from the high throne or dwelling of the most spacious and beautiful city of Jerusalem, which, through their impiety, was

60. Luke 1:51: *Fecit potentiam in brachio suo dispersit superbos mente cordis sui.*

61. Luke 1:52: *Deposuit potentes de fede, & exaltavit humiles.*

turned upside down, ruined, and burned, with its very rich Temple, which had been built there, and from all the other cities of Judea. And finally they were banished from the entire Land of Promise forever, and poverty and vile servitude were imposed upon them, while in their place all the humble and faithful Gentiles were greatly exalted, giving to us in addition the glorious Virgin: *He hath filled the hungry with good things; and the rich he hath sent empty away.*[62]

The immaculate Virgin consequently wished to show the poor starving Gentiles, who were longing for spiritual well-being and for the Gospel teaching that would fill them through Christ's holy preaching made to them, how through that powerful arm of the great eternal Father, His Son, they would be exalted by Him, and filled with the spiritual well-being of which they had been deprived. The immaculate Virgin also made special mention of Abraham in the last of her canticles, when she said: *He hath received Israel his servant, being mindful of his mercy: As he spoke to our fathers, to Abraham and to his seed for ever.*[63] She showed how Israel had received the Child promised her according to the Law, and of whom the patriarchs and prophets had already spoken, and as Adam, Enoch, Noah, Abraham, and all their generations had reiterated in other ages and centuries, since He had been promised in the first age of the world to our father Adam, in the second to Noah, in the third to Abraham, in the fourth to David, Isaac, Jeremiah, and others, and in the fifth to Daniel, to Haggai, to Zaccharias, and Malachi.[64] But in the sixth age, God fulfilled all that He had promised to the above-mentioned ancient Fathers since He sent them His only begotten Son incarnate, reminding them of His mercy, as the most Holy Virgin had said, who with these words ended her lofty and most divine canticle. Staying for the space of three months in Zaccharias's house to help and support her kinswoman Elizabeth, after that period she returned home to Nazareth.[65]

To the most long-suffering Virgin

O Virgin, mother and daughter, concerning Christ's miraculous and divine birth, what kind of marvel will it seem to your chaste spouse [Joseph], who is already close to knowing about

62. Luke 1:53: *Esurientes implevit bonis, & divites dimisit inanes*. Christianity replaces Judaism; Ecclesia, or the Church, replaces Synagoga or the Synagogue. Christ is the perfection of religious revelation. To Christians, the Old Testament is imperfect (the Old Testament being the covenant between God and mankind by Moses and the Ten Commandments), and the New Testament is the new covenant made by Christ with God.

63. Luke 1:54–55: *Suscepit Israel puerum suum recordatus misericordiae suae. Sicut locutus est ad patres nostros Abraham, & semini eius in saecula.*

64. These are all prophets said to have foretold the coming of Christ.

65. Luke 1:56.

the high and profound mystery, which, through humility, you have kept a secret from him and concealed from him until the Angel of God tells him about it?

Having returned from visiting Elizabeth, the Virgin stayed in her parents' house, quite removed from all the world's fallacies, as she was so consumed with divine love that she was zealous to do nothing other than take pleasure in the thought of her Lord and creator, who had created her, and given her so many most singular graces, and had made her mother of Himself, and showing daily ever clearer and more evident signs of her greatest virtue and most singular perfection. And while she was staying in such worthy and joyful circumstances, Joseph, her chaste bridegroom, came to Nazareth to celebrate the wedding, and then to lead her with him to live in his holy house. Becoming aware that she was pregnant, and still unaware of the secret of the divine mystery, he was greatly troubled in his thoughts, and wholly astonished and wondering at such a novel and unexpected situation. Nor did he know in this respect what to do, not because he assumed anything less than virtuous of her, since he believed more in Mary's honor and chastity than in her pregnancy, and in grace rather than in nature, and preferred to believe that a virgin could conceive without a man rather than that the Virgin Mary could sin; but he suspected that if he mentioned it to others, she would have to bear great blame and punishment for it since, according to the Law, adulteresses were stoned.[66] If (on the one hand) he remained silent about it, and she was seen by others to be pregnant, he would be blamed for it and derided by everybody. On the other hand, considering what had been written, namely, that a virgin from the Tree of Jesse (from which Mary descended) was to be born, and that a virgin would give birth, if she were that virgin, he was unworthy to know her, let alone live with such an excellent and peerless creature.[67] He gravely suspected this, and all the more because, since her conception of the Son of God, her face shone with such divinity that it was scarcely possible to behold her without trembling. Entirely confused, Joseph was therefore caught between these thoughts, and finally resolved for all these reasons to secretly steal away from the Virgin.[68] Although she had no-

66. John 8:3–11.

67. The Tree of Jesse was the visual depiction of Jesus's descent from the royal line of David in the form of a tree springing from Jesse, David's father, and ending in Jesus or the Virgin and Child, while intermediary descendants are depicted on foliage branching out of each other.

68. The two gospel accounts of the Virgin's conception of Jesus are conflicting. In Matthew, she is betrothed to Joseph, and "before they came together, she was found with child, of the Holy Ghost" (1:18). Here Joseph was "not willing publicly to expose her, [and] was minded to put her away privately" (v. 19), but told by the angel that the child she bears "is of the Holy Ghost" and that he is to be named Jesus, Joseph takes "unto him his wife [and] knew her not

ticed his disquiet many days before, the Virgin had not however wanted to show her awareness of it and, as she was always very wise, she remained silent, showing in the invincible virtue of her forbearance that she had within her that strong and indomitable King, whom she had conceived.[69]

Similarly, we read that while the house of the Lord was being built, a hammer was never heard, nor an ax, nor other iron tools, so that from this we may consider how when God is building reasoning mankind so grace may inhabit it, this spiritual edifice is built without the lash of whips, and the hammer should not resound, nor the ax its impatient voice, but remain quiet with silence and happy with what pleases His divine Majesty.[70]

The very wise Virgin wished not to reveal to her husband Joseph the lofty and divine mystery of the Incarnation of the Son of God so that she did not exceed the bounds of her usual profound humility, which to others might possibly have appeared the opposite,[71] if she had said that she was bearing the Son of God. She wished rather to be in danger of being left by him, as he had already decided to do, but she begged the Lord humbly to be so kind as to put things right and free her husband and herself from such great torment.[72] Therefore, while Joseph was sleeping between such thoughts, the Angel of the Lord appeared to him in a dream, saying that he should not leave the Virgin, nor even look upon her with any suspicion, as she was pregnant by the Holy Ghost, and would give birth to a Son, who should be named Jesus. O how we should honor that heavenly, divine, and most holy name, who proceeded from the essence of the great Eternal Father, sent by Him from Heaven to earth through the Angel; this is that Eternal Word of the Father most High, who was always known only to Himself, and whom He Himself alone knew eternally. This is that idea of His that He has shown to Himself alone, according to the profound fullness of His divinity, through which He has made His greatest desire clear and evident to the world. And through which we obtain true wisdom and all our well-

---

till she brought forth her firstborn son" (vv. 20–25). In Luke's account, Joseph's "espoused wife" is "with child," who is her "firstborn son" (2:5, 7), and Joseph appears not to feel any concern about the situation. Joseph's suspicions concerning Mary's pregnancy are elaborated in the Book of James (James, *Apocryphal New Testament,* 44). In the *Meditations* this becomes "How Joseph Wished to Leave the Lady Secretly" (26–30).

69. *Meditations*, 29.

70. 3 Kings 6:7: "And the house, when it was in building, was built of stones hewed and made ready: so that there was neither hammer nor axe nor any tool of iron heard in the house when it was in building."

71. That is, the vice of pride, the counterpart of which was humility. The first of the deadly sins, pride was traditionally believed to have been the sin of the fallen angels and Adam.

72. *Meditations*, 29.

being. This is that most holy name, which already the ancient patriarchs and prophets so wished to know and see, the One to whom the blessed Angels in Heaven always say, *"Holy, Holy, Holy, Lord."* This is that saving name, which the Angel announced to the Virgin Mary, and revealed to Joseph with his declaration when he said, "You will call the name of this one Jesus, which means savior."[73] Awakened, therefore, and reassured of the grandeur of the mystery by the heavenly Ambassador, Joseph was calm and filled with joy, and returned to his house in company with his most worthy Bride, where they lived with incredible chastity, providing and serving her with the reverence proper to so supreme a creature.

To the most excellent Queen of all the Virgins

Today, from your unsullied Heaven, chaste Virgin, will descend divine and celestial dew, today, from your mists in obscure night, with burning ardor will come forth the supreme Sun, so that the soul may arise to new light, to a more beautiful day, with a thousand angelic spirits around.

The time was drawing near for the great Son of God, that dew so very gentle and beloved, to come down from the purest Heaven of the Virgin Mary, a dew that was to make fruitful the sterile earth of human nature with many worthy and holy deeds.[74] Wishing to know how many cities, castles, and men there were in his empire, the Emperor Octavian sent out a proclamation that every man was to go to the city where he had been born, and there offer a silver piece to the value of ten *dinari*, on the back of which was the image of Caesar.[75] And this money was called a census since before they offered it to the chief of the province, they placed it on their heads, declaring themselves in the presence of all the people to be subject to the Roman Empire. For this reason, the most Holy Virgin and her husband Joseph left Nazareth to go to Bethlehem, where they had been born, to obey the emperor's order. On their arrival, they were unable to find somewhere to stay there as the town was already full of foreign people coming and going for the same reason; therefore they had to set themselves down near the common road, beneath a certain roof that was there, where country people used

73. Matthew 1:21. Jesus is the Greek form (*Ihsous*) of the Hebrew name Joshua (literally, "Yahweh saves").

74. The metaphor of Christ as the dew that waters the earth derives from the Christian Church's use of water as a symbol of life and purification. The name of the Garden of Eden is probably connected with the Babylonian *edinu*, a plain, but also suggests in Hebrew "delight." The Garden was once believed to have been one hundred miles north of Baghdad.

75. Matraini has confused the emperor's name here. Octavian took the name Augustus when he became caesar (Luke 2:1).

(according to some) to tie their animals when they went to trade. For that reason, troughs had been set up there, which are called mangers, where Joseph set the ox and ass to eat, the animals they had brought with them to lighten their labors. The Virgin Mary thus remained here in her lofty and usual meditations. Behold, in the middle of the night there appeared near her, like a new dawn, that immense Sun that gives light to the sun and to the entire universe, that Word of the Eternal Father, blessed Jesus, whom she had conceived in her virginal womb without the stain of sin, and to whom she gave birth without pain.[76]

Thus from the second earth of the Virgin Mary was the new Adam born, in every way opposite to and different from the first one, since only sin, misery, and death to himself and all humanity had come from the first, whereas peace, life, and the glory of the human race had come from this one. She was that earth that produced the precious fruit of the exalted earth, and that source of milk and honey that has irrigated and flooded the entire earth.[77] She was that happy earth of the earthly Paradise, which yielded the wood of life, from which then issued forth so many sweet and saving fruits of piety and charity, since the Savior was born of her, coming from the high breast of the Eternal Father in which He had been concealed, and foreshadowed in the Law, and from the Mother's womb, in which He had been formed.[78] That divine and saving rain of blessed Jesus Christ, who would save His people, as the Angel had told her, had therefore come down to earth.[79] So that there was never a birth more joyful, more joyous, and more overflowing with every well-being and gladness than that of the blessed Virgin Mary, and mother of Jesus Christ, who was conceived by her without sin, borne without fatigue, and given birth to without pain. This was that saving birth in which all the ancient Fathers in past times had rejoiced, and in Heaven the Angels, who were present at the wondrous birth of God on high (made man to save humankind), exulted in, and who sang joyfully, with sweet melody, *Glory to God in the highest: and on earth peace to men of good will.*[80]

76. Luke 2:7.

77. References to milk and honey are to be found in the Wisdom books of the Old Testament (Proverbs 24:13–14; Ecclesiasticus 24:18–20).

78. "Foreshadowed in the Law" refers to Christian teaching that the coming of Christ was prefigured in the Old Testament.

79. The cloud, and the rain that falls from it, was a favorite metaphor and image of Saint Ambrose. In the *De Institutione Virginis* (2:81), he writes: "O the riches of Mary's virginity! like a cloud she rained the grace of Christ on earth!" See Hilda Graef, *Mary: A History of Doctrine and Devotion*, 2 vols. (New York: Sheed and Ward, 1963), 1:77.

80. Luke 2:14.

And the shepherds, having been brought the glad tidings of the Son of God's coming, went to adore Him with great faith and reverence.[81] But more than all the others, [He was adored by] the immaculate Virgin, His Mother, and for this, future generations will be blessed, as they are grateful for such a great and wonderful favor. Great and marvelous was the joy felt throughout the world on the birth of the invincible and great defender of the entire Chosen People, as He was to be the conqueror over our powerful enemies and giver of all graces. And so shared was this joy by all and everything that even insensible things showed signs thereof.[82]

So that a spring of living water was seen that day to transform itself into oil, and to flow all day as far as the Tiber.[83] And because the greatest peace had come to the world that ever could come there, on the same day that the great heavenly and earthly Pacifier appeared, the most beautiful Temple of Peace, which the Romans had had built, collapsed unto its foundations. Apollo's oracle had told them that the Temple would endure until a virgin gave birth and, as they believed such a thing to be impossible, and therefore that it would never end, they had written on its door the words "Eternal Temple of Peace."[84] On that same day, the Emperor Octavian similarly saw a circle of gold around the sun in which there was a beautiful young girl with a little child on her lap. This was that same Augustus Octavian who, as his people, wishing to worship him since they had been in a tranquil and peaceful state for a long time through his labors, and to acknowledge that all their well-being came from him alone, did not wish to accept being worshiped unless he knew that there was no other greater than himself and worthier of such adoration. The Sibyl then showed him the little Child in the Virgin's arms, saying to him: "This one is greater than you, and worship this one." And, as he looked at it [the vision], a voice was heard (without seeing where it came from), which said: "This is the altar of Heaven." Marveling at such a wondrous sight, Octavian then knelt and reverently adored Him, and no longer wished to be worshiped otherwise by the Romans.[85]

81. Luke 2:8–20.

82. In the Fourth Eclogue of the Roman poet Virgil (70–19 BCE) is related the birth of an heroic child who will inaugurate the Golden Age.

83. *Golden Legend*, 1:40.

84. The Emperor Constantine (d. 337) attempted to appropriate Virgil's Fourth Eclogue as the prophecy of Christ, born of a virgin (l.6: *Iam redit et virgo*). The Ara Pacis is the monumental altar in Rome, consecrated in 13 BCE after the victorious return of Augustus from Spain and Gaul, in celebration of the peace he had established within the Empire.

85. *Golden Legend*, 1:40. The emperor consulted the Tiburtine sibyl about Christ's birthday as the Senate wished to elect him a god since he had brought peace to the world, but the sibyl told

Thus born in the manger, Jesus was not only worshiped by the Virgin, the Angels, Joseph, and the shepherds, but also by the ox and the ass, amongst which, in His humility, He had wished to be born since, however lacking in reason, due to boundless nature, they recognized their Lord and, kneeling (in so far as they could), they made reverence to Him; and, as there was nothing fit to warm Him otherwise in the great cold, they warmed Him with their breath.[86] His Virgin Mother took Him with great love and devotion, and wrapped Him in a little piece of cloth, which she usually wore on her head, enclosing in a little space the One who could not be contained in all the heavens, and embraced that immense Sun, which surrounds the earth, the sea, and the heavenly spheres. And thus she was that singular Star who bore the supreme and infinite Sun.

Today, chosen and beautiful Virgin, with how much sweet and ardent eagerness you clasp in your arms the One who encircles the sea, the earth, and the sky. Today, supreme Star, you carry the eternal and infinite Sun, who is virginal, your fruitful issue. Today, you contemplate and sweetly kiss the longed-for and joyful face of God, and you find satisfaction only in loving Him. Please, if you still care about earthly tenderness, look upon my yearning, and among so much universal pleasure, give me a sweet song to praise you.

To the one and only Virgin, Mother of the Son of God

One can truly say that you are the sweet and holy Virgin, always close to joy and sorrow, and weeping. Behold, after so much rejoicing, when eight days have scarcely passed, you have pain and suffering, for your Son sheds His blood, and you shed tears, and become bloodless, feeling His wound in your soul, He who is your hope and life.

As it was the eighth day since the immaculate Virgin had given birth with incredible joy to the Son of God, she went to the Temple with her Son in her arms, and Joseph, her husband, to have Him circumcised, and to obey the will of the Lord, who had sent word to Joseph that He was to be called by the name Jesus. When she had brought Him there, she placed Him in the hands of Simeon the Prophet, who long before had prophesied and longed for His arrival, where He bore the bitter pain of the circumcision, spilling copious amounts of His most precious blood. The Virgin Mary, seeing the delicate flesh of her tender Son, and most loved by her beyond all else, cut with the

---

him that a king had been born that day who would be more powerful than him, and Augustus accordingly refused his own deification.

86. *Meditations*: "The ox and the ass knelt with their mouths above the manger and breathed on the Infant as though they possessed reason and knew that the Child ... needed to be warmed" (33). The *Golden Legend* relates that they "went to their knees and worshiped him" (1:41). Praises of the ass are common in Renaissance literature. It is a symbol for humility—this is why it "kneels," is obedient, and is willing to perform everyday tasks that others will not do.

flint knife, was also wounded in her heart by incredible pain, so great that it exceeded that of all other mothers who had experienced it, as she knew how much more tender and delicate her sweet Son's constitution was than those of all the others, since He had been begotten by the Holy Spirit.[87] Nevertheless, on the other hand, she also comforted herself, thinking of that most holy name of Jesus, which He had to have, which meant having to be Savior of the world. And while this circumcision was unnecessary for Him, He wanted nevertheless to bear it to show His true and perfect humility, and fulfill in Himself the Law that He had given to others, and also to satisfy the Jews who, had He not been circumcised, would have been scandalized by Him. And thus He had spilled His most precious blood for us not only as an adult, but also in his childhood.

Blessed Jesus was therefore circumcised first at His birth, with Simeon's flint knife, and then with poverty's knife all the days of His life by the Eternal Father, and with the knife of the Cross by the merciless Jews. Thus in Jesus Christ's circumcision did His true and holy humility, the high sublimity of His most holy name, show itself. His name was prefigured by the Holy Fathers, prophesied by the prophets, named by God on high, announced by the Angel, and exalted by the Apostles: this name of Jesus was holy and sweet in the mouth, gentle to the ears, and full of joy and gladness in the heart. It is He who frees us from the Devil's snares, keeps us from sin, and rescues us from Hell; if Jesus's name is so sweet, so gentle, so beneficial, and salvific, you can now truly sweeten, O Mary, the bitterness of your heart with it, and assuage the sorrow that you have felt in seeing the most delicate flesh of your Son cut, since you will carry with you to us that so very saving and precious blood of Jesus, composed of joy, universal salvation, and infinite mercy, who will always be praised and thanked throughout the centuries, without end. Amen.[88]

To the most chaste Virgin, Queen of all the kings of the World

Today, a new light (O Virgin, bright shining Star of God) appears in the East to be the trusted light of the great Kings. Who come to adore the immense and only King of Kings, your Father, Bridegroom, and Son. He who adores the air, the moon, and the sun, the earth and Heaven, and even Hell fears the voice and sound of His great eternal name. These [Kings]

87. Luke 2:21–39. According to Mosaic laws, the first male child was dedicated to God.

88. The circumcision and Simeon's prophecy were seen as the first of Mary's Seven Sorrows (see below, note 96). The circumcision and presentation are here conflated, cf. chapter 3, note 123.

bring incense, myrrh, and gold, as to God, to king, and to mortal man, from which, amongst so much evil, let there be abundant alleviation of your poverty. Therefore, brighten your beautiful eyes, beloved mother and daughter of God.

If all the Angels, with great jubilation and joy, could come from Heaven to earth to adore the great Son of God in His miraculous birth, how much more greatly should humanity humble itself, and go from one part of the earth to the other, to honor and adore (as it should) its God and Man with every sacrifice and reverence? Having so greatly humbled Himself on humanity's behalf, so that it might receive salvation and glory, it was truly right for the most high and divine God of all the heavens to be uniquely honored and adored by all the people and kings of the earth.

Whereupon the magnificent Monarch and great eternal Father made a star of extraordinary splendor appear in the eastern regions, in the air close to the earth, before the eyes of three Magi, who were so called because of the very great knowledge they had of natural things and of the orders and movements of the heavenly spheres, influences, and power of the stars.[89] These, having already learned from their early ancestors, as Balaam's prophecy had said, that the Star of Jacob would appear and the King of Israel be born, and that, by this Star, humanity had to journey to adore the above-mentioned King, on that account, each month they went up to the top of a certain mountain called Vettoriale, or Guide, and there promptly begged the Lord with great faith to show them the Star that Balaam had already prophesied to them.[90] On the day of the Lord's birth, the said Magi therefore met in that place to make their usual request. A star of wonderful splendor of extraordinary dimensions then appeared above their heads, on the top of which appeared a shining Cross, and a voice coming out of it said to them, "Go quickly to the land of Judea, where you will find that King, whom you wish to see." Whereupon, with many from their courts, they immediately started out on their journey on certain animals called dromedaries, which, because they are very fast when they run, by divine will

89. Matthew 2:1–12. The historical magi were astrologers of the Persian court, and priests of the Mithras cult that flourished in the Roman Empire in the early Christian period.

90. Balaam's prophecy occurs in Numbers 24:17: "I shall see him, but not now: I shall behold him, but not near. A star shall rise out of Jacob and a sceptre shall spring up from Israel." In the ancient Near East and in Greco-Roman societies stars were thought to be supernatural beings, identified with gods, and worshiped and placated according to the advice of astrologers, such as magi, a concept taken over into Christianity (Christ was the "bright and morning star" [Revelation 22:16]). The name of the mountain Vettoriale derives from the Latin verb *veho*, "to carry," and in its Italian and adjectival sense probably signifies "carrier," "traveler," or "guide"—the mountain being the place that carried and guided the Star.

they traveled in thirteen days from the East to Jerusalem, which is said to be situated in the middle of the entire earth. Arriving in Jerusalem, and not knowing precisely where the King of Heaven had been born, they first discovered where Herod and the high priests of the Temple lived. Then they asked them where the great King of Judea had been born, as they had seen in their region a Star that showed His birth, and said that they had seen this Star above Judea, where they had come to adore Him. In their request they were acknowledging that the King they sought was [both] man and God; man when they asked for the King, and God when they said they wished to adore Him.

On hearing these things, Herod became greatly disturbed, and with him also all the men of Jerusalem, for when two kings compete, both [their] peoples take opposing sides. Therefore, gathering together all his priests, he carefully asked them where the King of the Jews was to be born, to which they replied that he was to be born in Bethlehem, in the land of Judea. Then Herod called the Magi to him, and secretly asked them when they had seen the Star. This he did so that if they did not return to him, he knew what he had to do. And then, with humble and sweet words, he asked them, when they had found the Child, to come promptly and show him so that he could, like them, go and adore Him; he was pretending to be desirous of worshiping the One he greatly desired to kill.[91]

The Magi therefore wishing to go and seek the born King of Kings, the Star hid itself from them from the moment they entered Jerusalem, and nor did they see it again until they had left it. And this, it is said, came to pass through their preferring human help to the divine, seeking to know through humanity what divine light nevertheless was showing them. But they had no sooner left the city of Jerusalem than the Star appeared to them again, which led them and which they always followed until they saw it settle itself on the proper place where the Savior was. And they, seeing it and judging that the new King whom they sought had been born here in this place, rejoiced, but rejoiced even more greatly when, on entering His small and humble lodging, they saw that singular Star of the Virgin Mary, which guides the sailors of the sea of this world to the very safe port of the heavenly home.[92] Surrounded by rays of countless graces and singular virtues, adorned by gentle and holy words, she was accompanied by her dearest and only Son and by

91. Matthew 2:1–12. The three magi, or wise men (Greek, *magoi*), were the first Gentiles (or non-Jews) to believe in Christ. In the New Testament they were called sages. Tertullian (ca. 160–ca. 225) was the first to describe them as "kings." Origen (ca. 185–ca. 254) was the first to suggest that there were probably three magi as three gifts are mentioned.

92. For Mary as the "Star of the Sea," see note 11 above and the volume editor's introduction, 20.

Joseph her husband. Although they found them poor, and in a humble and mean abode, they nevertheless, by being truly full of true and firm faith that Jesus was the Son of God and of the Virgin Mary, kneeling humbly, adored Him as the King of Heaven. Opening their treasures, they offered Him very precious gifts: that is, gold, incense, and myrrh, through gold signifying the royal power of Jesus Christ, through incense that He was God on high, and through myrrh that the One to die a most bitter death for the world's salvation was also man.[93] Through the example of these three Magi, we too are invited to adore God made man who is to save us, and to offer Him the gold of precious charity, superior to all the other virtues in this world, the incense of gentle and holy meditation, and the myrrh of most bitter sorrow for having offended His lofty and divine Majesty. Doing this, let us also leave, in imitation of them, the first street of our errors, which leads to evil and murderous Herod, the great enemy of human nature, and let us return by another path of virtue to our heavenly home, in the way that the Magi returned to their country, both in earthly and in heavenly terms.

To the most obedient Virgin, Mother of God

Today, the most pure, divine Virgin leaves her dwelling and goes far away, now through mountains, now through lowlands, as a humble pilgrim; to purify herself, not being impure, under the ancient Law, given to others, and makes herself obedient to her great Father and omnipotent Son.

When Moses, the most faithful servant of the great God, proclaimed to the world the Law ordained by Him, that all women who had conceived by generation and given birth had to be purified, in observance of the Law, he showed and foretold that a woman, alone of her sex, would conceive without a seed and would give birth to a son. Nor could it be understood differently, even though it was impossible (according to human nature) for a woman to conceive without that means and give birth.[94]

93. Gold found as a precious metal in Egypt and Ophir was exported to Judah; its preciousness made it a gift worthy of Christ as king. In the Temple, frankincense symbolized the offering of prayer (Psalms 141:2; Luke 1:10). In the New Testament myrrh was also used as a narcotic and for embalming (John 19:39).

94. Matraini is a little confused here. Moses, as the primary leader of the Israelites from their exodus from Egypt, and mediator of the Law, dominates the Old Testament from Exodus to Deuteronomy. The purification laws are in Leviticus 12. Verse 2: "If a woman having received seed shall bear a man child, she shall be unclean seven days, according to the days of the separation of her flowers." Verse 4: "But she shall remain three and thirty days in the blood of her purification. She shall touch no holy thing: neither shall she enter into the sanctuary, until the days of her purification be fulfilled." When a girl was born the two periods were doubled. But Moses did not prophesy the Virgin birth; this was Luke's interpretation of Isaiah's prophecy in Isaiah 7:14.

And He wanted also likewise to show that such a woman would not be subject to observing the said Law as, in truth, it was the immaculate and most humble Virgin, who alone had conceived and given birth to the Son of God, by virtue of the Holy Spirit. Therefore, she was not held to observing the Law in the way that all the other women of those times were. Nevertheless, she, through humility, wished to make herself obedient to the ordained Law for other women and, accordingly, putting aside weariness and all discomfort, in Joseph's company she set off on the journey from Bethlehem to Jerusalem (a very long and rocky road) with her most beloved Son in her arms, to both present Him at the Temple and to purify herself following the customary practice of other women. Having heard of her arrival through mysterious and divine inspiration, Simeon, the holy priest, knew that he would see Jesus Christ before he died. He went into the Temple to see Him and, finding Him there, took Him in his arms and blessed Him. And knowing that He was God, he praised and thanked the eternal Father for deigning to send His only and beloved Son on earth. And then, wholly full of incredible sweetness and joy, he begged Him to allow him to rest in peace, saying, *Now thou dost dismiss thy servant, O Lord*,[95] then foretelling in the Virgin's presence the supreme glory of her blessed Son and the salvation of the world. She, even though greatly consoled by this, by hearing the hymn of praise to her Son, and of her by Simeon and by Anna the Prophetess who was present there, was nevertheless eventually overcome by extreme anguish on Simeon's prophesying to her again her Son's most bitter Passion and cruel and wretched death; and he added that for her He would be that very sharp knife that would pierce through her soul.[96] When the most pure Virgin at last offered her blessed Son, she also offered (not those rich gifts that rich women were bound to) but (as a poor young girl) two turtledoves, those chaste birds that symbolize the singular modesty and chastity of both herself and Joseph.[97] And if it truly seems to anyone that she would have

95. Luke 2:29: *Nunc dimittis servum tuum Domine*. The story of Simeon occurs in Luke 2:25–35. His canticle, now known as the *Nunc dimittis*, from the first words in the Latin, formed part of daily prayers from the fourth century.

96. Simeon's prophecy was the first of the Virgin's Seven Sorrows. The Seven Sorrows, according to the Roman Breviary (the liturgical book containing the Psalms, hymns, lessons, prayers, and so on, recited in the Divine Office of the Catholic Church), were: The Prophecy of Simeon, The Flight into Egypt, The Loss of the Holy Child, The Meeting with Our Lord on the Way to Calvary, The Standing at the Foot of the Cross, The Taking Down of Christ from the Cross, and The Burial. Anna was a devout elderly prophetess who greeted Jesus as the Messiah (Luke 2:36–38).

97. Luke 2:24: "And to offer a sacrifice, according as it is written in the law of the Lord, a pair of turtledoves or two young pigeons." When the requisite period of purification was over, the

been able to offer greater things through the very rich gifts that she had received from the three Magi of the East, we should nevertheless believe that she (as the Mother of Mercy she always was) had distributed them to other poor people, so that the prophecy that says, *She hath opened her hand to the needy, and stretched out her hands to the poor,* was fulfilled.[98] As she gave all she had to the poor, she earned sustenance for herself and for her Son a little at a time. The due offering therefore made, Jesus was redeemed with five silver coins, for all those who were of the Eleven Tribes of Judah paid the stated price with their firstborn while, on the contrary, the firstborn of the tribes of the Levites were exempt from this and, on reaching adulthood, always had to serve in the Lord's Temple.[99] Simeon then gave back her Son to the Virgin, and blessing Him, named Him with three names: Savior, Light, and Glory of the People of Israel. And then he, with the Virgin, Joseph, and Anna, made a solemn procession in honor of the Son of God, a procession that we continue to make on that day in memory of it, carrying a lit candle in our hands, which signifies the most pure humanity of Jesus Christ, and His soul, His divinity offered at the Temple. Thus the wax, created without any corruption (because when bees generate, they do not blend together), signifies the purest humanity of Jesus Christ and the white cotton wick, hidden within the wax, His purest soul enveloped in His most innocent flesh.[100] And the fire, or light, is a clear proof of the divinity of His most ardent love. Therefore, if we too wish to be purified and spotless before the countenance of God on high, we need to have purity of faith, good works, and our minds heeding the Lord in imitation of the immaculate and most pure Virgin, since carrying the lighted candle in our hands signifies how much she shows and teaches us.

---

woman was to offer a lamb, a "yearling," as a burnt offering and a young pigeon or turtledove as a sin offering. If too poor to offer a lamb (as is the case of Mary in Luke 2:24), a second young pigeon or a second turtledove might be substituted (Leviticus 12:6–8).

98. Proverbs 31:20: *Manum suam apparuit inopi, & palmas suas extendi ad pauperes.* According to the *Meditations*, "the child Jesus and also His mother received alms like poor people" (52). Medieval man turned to the protection of the Virgin Mary, or other saints, in times of disease and war, understood as the workings of divine judgment. The Virgin is shown as the Mother of Mercy when depicted in a cloak under which supplicants kneel. She was also given this title when she acted as an intercessor with Christ or God.

99. Joseph pays shekels to the priests, according to the custom, and the Virgin takes back the child Jesus. The Tribe of Judah was the most powerful of the twelve tribes of Israel. The Levites were priests in ancient Israel, believed to be descendants of the tribe of Levi. They were subordinate Temple officials who did not obtain full priesthood.

100. Matraini is alluding to the Feast of Candlemas, also known as the Feast of the Purification of the Virgin or Presentation of Christ in the Temple, held on February 2, according to the Latin rite.

To the loving Mother of the Son of God

Already, O Virgin, you are understanding the true prophecy of Anna and Simeon in your heart. Behold, you already have to fear and flee afar from wicked and cruel Herod, who strives to make away with the very life of your Son and your God, and His glorious infinity. Behold, from afar, already one hears the weeping of all the unhappy and grieving mothers of Bethlehem who see the innocents, their sons, all killed with swords, making a river of their own blood, whereupon each of them, bloodless, overwhelmed by grief, must fall.

Proud and iniquitous Herod, waiting for the three Magi to return to him (as he had specifically requested of them and they had promised him), to show him where this new King had been born, seeing that they were not returning to him, thought at first that they had been made fools of by the Star, and that through shame on this account, they had not wanted to return to him. Accordingly, he lost interest in seeking the Child and King of the Universe.

But hearing the fame of the new King being spread daily (for example, by the simple shepherds who had seen Him, and by the Magi, who had adored Him, and by Simeon and Anna, who had prophesied Him), he greatly feared and knew that it was not the Magi who had been mocked by the Star, but he by them. Then, driven by great rage and violent frenzy, through the dread he had of losing his kingdom and through anger at having been so misled by them, he decided to have all the male children killed who were in Bethlehem in Judea, up to the age of two, to achieve the death of the One whom he did not know.[101] But the supreme eternal Father, not allowing the plan to be effected, sent the Angel in a dream to Joseph to tell him to rise up and flee with the Virgin and her Son to Egypt, as Herod was seeking to kill Him. Thus awakened, Joseph went quickly to the Mother, telling her all that he had heard from the Angel. The Holy Virgin, hearing this, was overcome by extraordinary sorrow and so sad and afflicted and weeping ceaselessly, she took her sweet and dear little Son in her arms and fled in the night, through harsh and deserted places, with many travails and dangers, enduring the need to eat and sleep, and often fearful of violence and of robbers who might attack Him.[102]

At last, on her arrival in Egypt with her blessed Son and Joseph, all the idols fell to the ground and broke, following the predictions of the prophet

101. Matthew 2:13–18. Matraini's account closely follows the *Golden Legend* ("The Holy Innocents," 1:56–58).

102. Matthew 2:13–14; *Meditations*, 68.

Isaiah.[103] And when she entered the city of Hermopolis, it is said that a marvelously strong tree, called *persidis,* lowered itself with its branches down to the ground as a sign of reverence.[104] Meanwhile, fierce Herod, utterly incensed with enormous anger and frenzy over this, as he had been unable to remove the Lord of Lords (whom he strongly suspected and feared would overcome him) from the world by means of the Magi, had all the little boys of Judea from the age of two and under slaughtered, and even older, some say, believing that among so many, blessed Jesus was bound to be killed.

Now anyone who had heard, during that huge massacre, the sorrowful and wretched weeping, the saddest voices and loud shrieks of the piteous and afflicted mothers on seeing themselves robbed of their dear and loved sons through force of arms, and killed by means of the sword in their presence, would have to have the heart of some cruel tiger were it not to be broken through pity. News of this very horrendous and previously unheard-of incident reached the most holy Virgin's chaste ears in Egypt. Reflecting that it had all taken place because of her blessed Son, she wept bitterly and so greatly, thinking of the great destruction of Bethlehem, where she had been born and brought up, and where she had given birth to her beloved Son. For not even one of those little boys was still alive, among whom a just God, wishing to initiate revenge for such abominable and violent cruelty by so impious and wicked a tyrant, allowed one of Herod's sons, who had been given there to a wet nurse, to be killed among the others by his own executioners. Furthermore, [Herod] voluntarily had another three, still young ones, slaughtered and, after burdensome and long torments of mind and body caused by such unjust and evil persecutions of the Son of God, and of those innocent little boys, finally, as he was desperate, he wanted to kill himself.[105] Cruel and murderous Herod now dead, the Angel of the Lord

103. The fall of the idols during the flight to Egypt comes from Pseudo-Matthew (James, *Apocryphal New Testament,* 75). Cf. Isaiah 19:1: "Behold the Lord will ascend upon a swift cloud, and will enter into Egypt, and the idols of Egypt shall be moved at his presence, and the heart of Egypt shall melt in the midst thereof."

104. Hermopolis, or Huiusmopolis, or Heliopolis (Greek, "city of the sun") was a city in Egypt mentioned by Jeremiah in an oracle of doom directed against the Egyptians (Jeremiah 43:13). See entry "Heliopolis" by Donald B. Redford in *Anchor Bible Dictionary*, vol. 3 (New York: Doubleday, 1993), 122–23. According to the *Golden Legend* (1:57), and according to "Cassiodorus," the *persidis* tree cured "all sickness." Flavius Magnus Aurelius Cassiodorus Senator (ca. 485–ca. 583 [the last name was a surname, not a rank]) was a Roman writer, statesman, and monk, and wrote several histories.

105. Although Matraini follows the account of the massacre of the innocents in the *Golden Legend* (1:58–59), including the death of Herod's own son and his attempt to kill himself, the source of other details is unclear.

appeared to Joseph to inform him of his death, telling him that he should return to Israel. He therefore immediately returned with the Virgin Mary and her Son, not straight to Judea, as he had heard that one of Herod's sons called Archelaus still reigned there, but to the city of Nazareth, with incredible hardship and new discomfort.[106]

To those greatly desirous of true Wisdom

Whoever wishes to have high and true understanding with clear light within of the great eternal Lord, who today shows Himself to us as the little Child, following the steps of our guide, Mary and great Virgin, will find Him in the Temple among doctors, disputing and overcoming the older ones with all human experience.

The most wise Virgin always sought, in her active and contemplative life, her immortal and incomprehensible Creator, her soul wholly inflamed with divine love and shining with Truth's light, through every place and path, and she found Him in virginity, humility, obedience, poverty, and forbearance.[107] Therefore, through always being obedient and faithful, and an observer of all the laws, this most excellent Virgin went to Jerusalem with Joseph and Jesus Christ (then aged twelve), where they were to stay for seven days, since the time had come for the greatest rite of Easter, in which everyone, great and small, was obliged to go to the Temple in Jerusalem (there was no exception, other than grave illness).[108] When the visit was ended, they left to return to their home in Nazareth, and the Child Jesus remained in Jerusalem, a fact that they did not notice, as each of them thought that He was on the journey in the other's company. But then, not finding Him, they went with great anxiety to seek Him out among their relations and the people they knew, and were unable to find Him. The most long-suffering Virgin felt unimaginable sorrow over this, and was unable to eat, sleep, or rest, so that at last, driven by the loving wish to find Him, and not yielding to weariness or hardship, she set out with her husband Joseph to return to Jerusalem, where looking for him, they found Him in the Temple among the doctors, disputing with them. The doctors, who observed His marvelous knowledge at

106. Matthew 2:19–23. One of Herod's sons, Archelaus, inherited Judea, Samaria, and Idumea, but was banished to Greece by the emperor in 6 CE.

107. The active life is the cultivation of Christian virtues and devotion to Christian works, especially charity. The contemplative life revolves around meditation, prayer, and contemplation devoted to the idea of love of God. These were represented by Leah and Rachel, the wives of Jacob (Genesis 29:1–35), and Martha and Mary of Bethany (Luke 10:38–42).

108. Matraini calls the Jewish festival in honor of the exodus Easter. It is probable that the earliest Christian celebrations of Easter developed from the Passover rite.

such a tender age, and His acute replies to their very subtle questions, were amazed by everything they witnessed in His presence. Then, with great joy, the most holy Virgin found her so longed-for and loved Son again, after seeking Him with such perseverance.[109] If we, too, wish to find Him ourselves, let us follow the holy footsteps of the Virgin Mary, our guide and advocate, by the path of patience, and we will doubtless find Him within the temple of our hearts where He lives willingly through grace, and sweetly discuss lofty and divine things with Him.

To the most plenteous Fount of divine Grace

O Fount, nay great river, nay deep abyss of mercy, O great Virgin, who present at the happy nuptials and wedding feast, at the endless sea of grace made the water change into wine, I pray that with your joyful look, you turn a little to my needs also, and breathe into me so much grace from Him that being invited to His high nuptials, I may go there adorned in purple robes.

So great is the abundance of the water of mercy and grace that it spreads from the living fountain, or rather from the ample and very deep river of the Virgin Mary, which bathes and softens all the arid earth of our dry and sterile hearts, so long as we lack the supreme dew of divine grace through our sins.[110] As by means of the great river Jordan one passed through to the Promised Land, so we, too, through the Virgin Mary's prayers, pass into the Kingdom of Heaven. Thus with her great compassion and divine help, not only to those who call upon her but also very often before she is called, she helps us in all our needs with her grace and favor, as she did when she was invited with Jesus Christ and His Apostles to the wedding feast of Cana in Galilee, in the house of John the Evangelist (as it is piously believed). Being at the table, and seeing that the wine had run out halfway through the feast, since the guests were poor, on their behalf, and without being asked (to provide for their needs and so that they would not be embarrassed), she asked her most kind Son to provide enough wine, and obtained it, as Jesus, on hearing her entreaties, had servants fill six empty jars with water, and with His great power changed that water into very precious and perfect wine. So

109. Luke 2:41–52. The loss of Jesus in the Temple was regarded as the third of the Virgin's Seven Sorrows. The story showed Jesus manifesting for the first time his divine rather than earthly role.

110. A source of water, the fountain is symbolic of spiritual life and salvation and therefore an attribute of the Virgin Mary. The fountain of life is the source from which the rivers of Paradise flowed.

that all those who drank it were amazed and stupefied by its remarkable supernatural perfection.[111]

O most compassionate Virgin, always full of the most ardent wish for all our true and most perfect good, I pray to you, living fountain of every heavenly grace, to obtain for me the water of mercy from the infinite sea, your only Son, and, as I have at last reached the end of my long and exhausting journey, tired and thirsty, that I may taste some of His sweet and most gentle wine, which quenches the most burning thirst of worldly things, [and] that He fill my soul with divine sweetness. Lead me, I beg you, most abundant Queen of all the graces (despite my unworthiness), into the house, to the wedding feast of the King of Heaven, your Son. And dressed in that purple wedding garment, without which no one could ever enter, so that through your holy intercession I might taste the sweetness of the food of His heavenly and marvelous feast.[112] And as you are the Mother of Jesus Christ, I beg you, most merciful mediatrix between God and humankind, to lead my soul to its sacred wedding and ensure that it is always inseparably with Him, and that I keep faithfully the faith, so that it will never come to part from Him.

To the most sorrowful Virgin, Pattern of strength to all the martyrs and afflicted of this world

If that great joy was incalculable, which the Virgin felt at the great birth of the Son of eternal God, by whose side she is now glorious, what immense sorrow, what sea of tears, in eyes or heart, was then felt by any mortal who could see himself similarly gazing on a son wounded and broken; broken, wounded, and dead, does Mary see her Son, in her arms, wherefore through grief she swoons as her heart opens to her and torments her: the heavens darkened, the earth trembled, and only those unfaithful people without pity remained ungrateful to Him through envy and grief.

And there is no doubt that the nobler, more worthy, and more excellent something is, the more greatly (by the one who knows it) it is always loved and esteemed. And it is most certain that since acquiring what is greatly loved is the greatest joy and incomparable happiness, so also losing it or being de-

111. The marriage at Cana (John 2:1–11) was the occasion when Jesus performed his first miracle, prompted by his mother's request to supply the wine lacking at the wedding feast. Matraini refers to the popular belief that the feast took place in Saint John the Evangelist's house: this forms part of the legend that John was betrothed to Mary Magdalen before he was called by Jesus to follow him, something the *Golden Legend* denies (1:382).

112. Purple is traditionally the royal color, and the "purple wedding garment" in which Matraini asks to be robed refers to her entry into the marriage feast of the King of Heaven on her death.

prived of it is always extreme and unbearable sorrow. The very wise Virgin knew the supreme and divine object, God on high, and loved Him above all earthly and heavenly creatures, and in acquiring Him, which she did by conceiving Him and giving birth to Him, she had the greatest joy that any mortal creature could have. And thus, her most holy soul deprived of Him through cruel and most bitter Passion and death, she felt the most excessive and inexpressible sorrow that ever a mother or creature of this world could experience. O how bitter and countless her tears in the torments and death of her so beloved and innocent Son Jesus Christ, our Redeemer. O how loud were the shrieks and sorrowful the laments, seeing His beautiful face (which the Angels will want to gaze upon forever) so completely soiled with the spittle of the evil and ungrateful Jews, and His head, full of infinite wisdom, stabbed (alas) by sharpest thorns! The ears that used to hear the merited praises and sweetest singing of the angels now hear abominable and unjust words of sinners; the lips from which salvific and holy teachings full of truth used always to issue are now given vinegar and most bitter gall to drink; the hands that formed the heavens, separated the elements, created humankind in His divine image so as to be possessors of all His infinite goods, are now pierced by very sharp nails, and the feet, which used to tread upon the celestial spheres, are nailed to the wood of the Cross, with this wholly lacerated body, and this side opened by the pitiless lance.

O how much more greatly did her grave and bitter sorrow increase in the most sorrowful Virgin when she thought of the greatness of Him who was suffering so greatly, and of why He was suffering, which was for the sins of others, by whom He was so unjustly wronged and tormented by unheard-of and cruelest torments from those who had received great favors from Him. These were the things that, apart from what she saw, tormented her immeasurably. These were those knives that pierced (alas) her soul; these (alas) were those very sharp arrows that penetrated her unhappy heart to such an extent that if Jesus Christ's pain were measured, and His most bitter Passion, which could be compared to no other pain, so immense was that of the Virgin Mary, His most beloved Mother, that she, who in the guise of a strong column in prosperity and joys that God on high gave her, sank so deeply into the ground of humility that she was raised above the heavens by Him through glory.[113] She was so powerful in supporting the weight of her enormous adversities that she remained standing beside the holy Cross

113. The pillar or "strong column" was the religious symbol of spiritual strength and steadfastness (Revelation 3:12).

without ever wavering or doubting Jesus Christ's divinity, as did the Apostles and other friends.[114]

It is from her example that we unhappy sinners should learn to be always steady and constant in all our trials and adversities for the love of Jesus Christ, our Savior, without ever doubting His divine and perfect love, which He has marvelously shown us, and continually proves in so many ways and so often. We should ponder on what we should do to recompense for the so many extraordinary favors we have received from Him, since He, most innocent, sacrificed Himself to the Eternal Father in the fire of the most loving charity, on the altar of the Cross, to placate His Father's anger conceived through our sins. But what can we do to satisfy such an infinite debt we have to Him? Certainly, nothing other than (since through His great kindness He is satisfied with so little) offer Him our hearts as sacrifice in the fire of His sweet and most holy love, and with it purge all our sins lest we be consumed with them in Hell's fire.

To the most merciful Consoler of the afflicted

O Virgin, if your sorrow was greater than that of all others, in seeing your innocent Son die with so much grief for the faults, misfortunes, and iniquities of others, today you will have immense and infinite joy because He returns to immortal life with triumph and victory over the great enemy, whose gates of the lower kingdom of blind Hell He has broken down, where powerful and strong, He has bound him with great eternal grief. Behold Him, in how much lofty glory He shows Himself to your beautiful, holy eyes today, and in the Empyrean cloister, ascends a great deal higher than the clear and shining Sun, where you soon will be with Him, truly blessed, and made Empress of Heaven and earth.[115]

How joyful, how glad, and how incredibly happy should we imagine the blessed Virgin was when (risen from the dead) her Son Jesus Christ appeared to her? Truly, we ought to be sure that, since the object of her love was the supreme and infinite Good, the supreme and infinite Beauty, known to her (through divine grace) above all other creatures, and having by way of such love so great and immeasurable grief suffered in the cruelest and incomparable Passion of her Son, she should have as much joy and gladness and excel in every happiness as could ever be understood in the heart of any mortal creature whatsoever. And if the Evangelists did not write of the appearance that

114. Fortitude was one of the four cardinal virtues signifying endurance, courage, and strength.

115. The Empyrean, from the medieval Latin *empyreus*, derived from the Greek "in or on the fire" (*pyr*), is a place in highest heaven believed, according to ancient cosmologies, to be occupied by the element of fire. It is used as a name for the firmament, and in Christian literature is the dwelling place of God and the blessed.

Christ made to His Mother when He rose from the dead, this was because their purpose was to bear witness only to the Lord's Resurrection. And if it happened that the other women who saw Him risen from the dead were disbelieved, much less would the Mother have been believed, so that it did not seem appropriate to the Evangelists to bring in the Mother to bear witness to her Son, although it was most certain that Jesus Christ appeared first to His Mother before all the others, as she had loved Him more than the others had.[116] Therefore Christ appeared to His most unhappy Mother, and she felt incredible gladness and joy in seeing Him, seeing Him garbed in immortality, and knowing that He had broken down and shattered the gates of Hell, and there had bound and overcome the great enemy of human nature and made booty of all those mortal remains that pleased Him more, such as the Holy Fathers and other souls in Limbo.[117] Nor were the happy Virgin's jubilation and joy any less when she met Her glorious Son again on the Mount of Olives with His Apostles and saw Him rise into Heaven, surrounded by light beyond reach and infinite glory, telling them, "The time has come for me to return to Him who sent me."[118]

But what rejoicing and consolation, may we believe, were the Virgin's on seeing her triumphant Son open the gate of that blessed country, and lead those holy souls thither whom He had liberated from the dark prisons, to sit at the right hand of the Eternal Father! O what a rare and gentle sweetness she felt in her soul, seeing all the angels rejoice and celebrate in the coming of the victorious and triumphant King of Heaven, greatly exalting their King, her Son, for their own restoration and the reparation of humanity, whom they greatly love! The Apostles similarly rejoiced to see their dear

116. The appearance of Christ to his mother does not, as Matraini notes, occur in the gospels. The fact that he appeared first to Mary Magdalen and the other women was a source of puzzlement to commentators, and to make up for this seemingly unfilial behavior, they sought to fill in the lacunae. See the *Meditations* ("Of the Resurrection of the Lord and How He First Appeared to His Mother on the Sunday," 359–60). The argument that his mother loved him more than all others is a common one for the insistence that Christ first appeared to her after his resurrection, against all evidence to the contrary in the gospels. See James D. Breckenridge, "'Et prima vidit': The Iconography of the Appearance of Christ to His Mother," *Art Bulletin* 39, no. 1 (March 1957): 9–32.

117. In Latin theology, the souls of those who died before the coming of Christ remained in Limbo, the *limbus patrum*. Christ's coming opened the gates of Limbo for the Patriarchs. Whether or not Limbo existed is a matter of theological opinion on which the Church has made no definitive pronouncement; in 2007 the Vatican's International Theological Commission announced that the traditional view of Limbo reflected an "unduly restrictive view of salvation."

118. The accounts of the Ascension are in Matthew 28:16–20, Mark 16:19, Luke 24:36–53, and Acts 1:12. According to tradition, it took place on the Mount of Olives. The feast is celebrated on the sixth Thursday after Easter.

Master in such happy glory (although they would be deprived of His most gracious presence), and to see Him so highly exalted. But more than any other, the very pure Virgin rejoiced infinitely, thinking of how her powerful Son had brought a most happy end to His work for human redemption, which will not have been in vain for us if we, leaving our worldly concerns aside, climb the mountain of the living faith and hope of that blessed life by way of contemplation. Therefore let us lift our mental eyes (following the example of the lofty Mother of the Son of God) to Heaven, drawn by love of Christ, and urged by hope of eternal favors, for we shall find there our most safe repose and perpetual happiness.

Prayer to the Holy Spirit

O Holy Spirit, you who go everywhere, do you never breathe? Please breathe a sweet flame into the living nest of my phoenix [soul], so that little by little every mortal part of it may die by burning, and from its death could send forth a bird that, flying in the sky, aims towards Heaven. Behold, opening its wings, it seeks in its breast to make itself immortal.[119]

When the magnificent Monarch and King of the Universe sent to the world the gracious and most beautiful Virgin, chosen by Him above all the others to be Bride and Mother of His only born Son, He sent her dressed and adorned with the marvelous robe of the splendor of divine grace, accompanied by seven worthy and most honored young maidens. The first of these was named Prudence, where, as though gazing into a very clear mirror, she [i.e., the Virgin] saw how each of her works had to be governed properly, so that she had every perfect praise and full commendation from God and from the world. The second, called Justice, followed this one, by whom she gave to each as much as it was appropriate to give, whereby she gave all her love to God and honored Him above everything, obeying each of His laws given and observed by her good ancestors. Her third companion was called Temperance, who was so much more noble than the other virtues as the material form is worthier because, like the sun between the seven planets, she offered beauty and miraculous grace to all the others, so that through her the most excellent Virgin always appeared moderate and modest in every word and action while she was alive, being matched through her to that most worthy Tree of Life, which was placed in the earthly Paradise. The fourth, then, was called Fortitude, and she was always a most faithful friend to her,

119. In Christian symbolism the phoenix is usually applied to Christ, signifying his Resurrection. This legendary bird was believed to burn itself to ashes every five hundred years, and to rise again from them.

because she continually (without ever abandoning her) constantly accompanied her, in discomfort, in grief, and in long travails, and in her extreme sufferings, to the Cross and death of her only and beloved Son, bearing each of her great adversities with patience, until she then finally triumphed over the great enemy of human nature and entered victoriously into the supreme Kingdom of Heaven.[120]

The most worthy Virgin had these four beautiful virtues that concerned her fellow creatures on her left hand, and on her right three others concerning God only, of which one was Faith, which was so very powerful and strong in her that it supported the entire great spiritual edifice of God's glory since her holy soul was always illuminated with truth, taught and confirmed by the authority of the Holy Scriptures, given and dictated by the Holy Spirit. Through Faith, she always acted with the sole purpose of God's high glory, and fulfilled His most holy Laws with humility. Also, on her right hand, the glorious Virgin had that pleasing maiden called Hope, who kept her in constant expectation of the divine grace of eternal bliss, which is its sole cause, and not through our own merits. Hope made each of her grievous and unbearable sufferings and most bitter distress trifling to the holy Virgin, and made her keep her mind elevated in divine contemplation, without caring for worldly and transitory things, or death.

But more than all her other loved companions whom the most wise Virgin had on her right hand, she loved the one called Charity, without which nothing pleases God, and with which nothing displeases Him. Through her, she knew and loved God through pure intellect, beyond all earthly and heavenly creatures, and she joined inseparably to Him, entirely inflamed with His most holy love. She was that supreme virtue that gave nourishment and strength to all the others to live, weapons to combat all adversities and to triumphantly conquer in every battle; through her, the loving and holy Virgin became similar to gold, since she became ever nobler, worthier, and more perfect in the great fire of her torments. Charity was the one who finally led the Virgin into the fruitful and rich garden of the most worthy and holy works, and brought her the key with which she came to open the supreme gates of Heaven, where she entered the wedding feast of the great heavenly King, from whom she received the royal crown that adorned her head with immense and infinite glory.[121] She was then made Queen of Heaven by Him,

120. See above, note 26.

121. See note 26.

Empress of the World, most invincible warrior against the powerful enemy of humankind, Lady and Advocate of us wretched sinners.[122]

These aforementioned seven virtues, companions of the blessed Virgin, were those seven lighted lamps that showed her supreme and singular beauty before God's high throne. He therefore loved her above all His other creatures. Through His love, she was worthy that He not only concealed and impregnated her (in taking flesh from her) with the holy and divine Spirit, but also that (after His marvelous Ascension, on the day of Pentecost) she received the Holy Spirit, as well as all the other marvelous comforts she had obtained from Heaven, together with the other Apostles. Thus she came to feel invaluable happiness, greater than any other person, since He was the true Temple of the Holy Spirit, of whom, as it is said, she was earlier dignified and filled. This was that spirit who is called the good Holy Spirit, the upright principal Spirit of the Lord, gift of the highest spirit of charity, for whom the entire world has come to rejoice. So that when the blessed Queen of Heaven happened to be in Jerusalem, in the room where Christ had eaten the Paschal lamb with them, and while they were all praying, they heard at the hour of terce a sound like a huge wind, and in an instant several rays of fire in the form of tongues appeared above them. Thereupon, suddenly, they felt themselves set on fire with divine love, which prompted the Apostles to speak various languages, so that they were understood by all the different nations of this world, and believed by many, as they uttered words so burning with divine love that they inflamed those who listened to them. If we too therefore wish to receive the magnificent gifts of the Holy Spirit from the most liberal hand of God, together with the Queen of Paradise and all the other saints, let us seek and obtain, with every care and diligence, for the sake of His glory and of our salvation, to be wise, just, strong, and temperate, and to have Faith, Hope, and Charity. And thus this most holy fire will make us lightly rise to heavenly things and illuminate our souls, and banish the shadows of our errors and, through its power, convert us to God, making us die to worldly things and live to those heavenly and immortal. This is that gentle fire that purges us of all ugliness of sin and reduces humankind to ashes of humility, humility that will finally exalt it next to the highest throne of God on high.[123]

122. The title Queen of Heaven was given to the Virgin Mary in early Christian literature. It is also the title of the "Regina Coeli," the Latin Eastertide anthem to the Virgin, probably dating from the twelfth century. See the volume editor's introduction, 20.

123. Cf. Acts 2:1–41. Terce was one of the four Divine Offices recited at the first, third, sixth, and ninth hours. It was said at the third hour, representing the hour of the Crucifixion.

To the immortal and most blessed Virgin

Listen, virgin chaste soul of God, with what sweet words today your beloved divine Bridegroom calls you to Heaven. Come, He says, safe from the tempests, to what your heart desires, my dearly beloved, to my eternal divine resting place. Here is the supreme Sun, who shows you the high path of the Empyrean cloister. And the supreme choirs, wise, holy, and graceful, may they guide you by their sweetest songs. Rise therefore before your beautiful Sun, eternal, divine phoenix, with shining, pure, and chaste wings, to your Sun, to His brilliant and immortal aeons.

When the time had come for the purest Mother of the Son of God to loose herself from her bodily limbs and receive the prize and crown of infinite glory, her beloved and most sweet Son made it known to her through His usual Ambassador, the Archangel Gabriel, that she soon had to leave these our worldly miseries and ascend to Heaven, above all the choirs of angels, to enjoy the happiness prepared for her by her most loving Son. Hearing the longed-for news, the blessed Virgin thanked the supreme and merciful God for His divine grace and very humbly and joyfully prepared herself for her journey, receiving the most Holy Sacraments, to fulfill all the evangelical commandments and directions.[124] Among these is the teaching concerning being prepared and ready for death, something for which she felt no grief, nor did she fear devils, nor the sentence of judgment, since she knew that she had never sinned in any way. On the contrary, she even rejoiced, and felt remarkable happiness, as she was to be with Christ, her sweetest and beloved Son who, calling her, said to her, *Come from Libanus, my spouse, come from Libanus, come,* inviting her with such dear and sweet words to leave the world and rise up to His longed-for presence.[125] As she heard herself called so sweetly, she breathed her most holy Soul out of her body and felt great and incredible sweetness in the parting.

But before she expired, the Apostles, who had gone to different parts of the world to preach and convert the people to the gospel faith, miraculously and suddenly appeared there.[126] Therefore, on the blessed Virgin's last breath and to the great jubilation and joy of the entire heavenly court, the Apostles carried her with most solemn rites to bury her in a new sepulcher

124. Matraini refers to the preparations for death, which are, according to the Catholic Church, the sacraments of Penance, Last Communion, and Extreme Unction. She also refers to the apocryphal accounts of the Virgin's death. See the volume editor's introduction, 26–27.

125. Song of Songs 4:8: *Veni Sponsa, veni de Libano, veni.*

126. According to Mark 16:20, the apostles went out to preach after the Ascension. The story of their arrival from all the corners of the earth to be present at the Virgin's death first appears in Syriac writings.

with devout hymns and piteous tears, grieving that they would be deprived of her lovely presence, and rejoicing on the other hand that the Lord had transferred her from this perverse world to His most happy Kingdom, so that she might faithfully intercede there for us.

O most blessed Virgin Mother of the supreme and immortal God, who from this low valley of tears and wretchedness, and from the profound abyss of your humility has risen to that height above which no other creature could ever rise, and enjoys immense and eternal delights no greater than which could be desired, I beg you, among so much incomprehensible and priceless happiness, to remember this, your humble and faithful servant and, as becomes your burning charity, turn to look at her with the eye of your mercy, O most merciful and most powerful advocate of all those who apply to you devoutly, and obtain for me, I beg you, from your kind and omnipotent Son, the virtue of humility, of the living faith, and burning charity, with which I may obtain His divine grace, reminding Him of how I was created by Him, and redeemed with His most precious Blood; not so that His enemy might triumph over His beloved creature, but so that I should, through His merits and through yours, finally be made blessed.[127]

To the most blessed Virgin, and Mother of the Highest, sole Empress of the Universe

Today, marvelous, brilliant Dawn of the radiant heavens, surrounded on every side by angelic spirits, joyful she mounts the high spheres to the supreme Sun, who came forth from her virginal womb; she goes breathing the most fragrant perfumes. Today in Heaven, just like the most brilliant and most everlasting day that ever dawned, this day dawns in Heaven; and this day opens in Heaven for its beloved Bride, full of marvels and joy, and this day asks and says: "Who is this person, so beautiful and peerless, who ascends on high to the glorious Kingdom with so many high and worthy abundant crowns on her gilded and triumphal chariot?" But seeing her then placed by the highest King of the supreme, eternal, Empyrean sphere next to His sublime throne and with a splendid, lofty, and divine crown embellish her, above all other creatures, they [the angels] knew her to be the Empress of Heaven. Whence, full of joy, all the blessed spirits began a sweet song, praising their divine immense Sun, and His beloved Bride, with humble and eternal reverence, for both having brought about such a beautiful day.

After the blessed soul of the Virgin and Mother of the Son of God had left her incorruptible body, it pleased the high and divine Majesty that immediately after her death she should rise again and be assumed body and soul into the eternal and happy homeland. To which she went, victorious and triumphant

127. This prayer-like paragraph is based on *Salve Regina*, or Hail, Holy Queen, one of the earliest Marian antiphons dating from the end of the eleventh century.

over the most powerful enemies of the world, upon the chariot of the infinite multitude of angels, and clothed in the immense light of heavenly glory, and crowned with the most shining stars of singular virtues.[128] Pleasant and sweetest perfumes through good works and most holy examples breathed forth around her, and when she entered, the holy angels saw her so very marvelous and extraordinary beauty, and the exceeding triumph and glory with which she entered that most happy Kingdom, and how much light and splendor she spread all around her, that each, filled with wonder and marvel, inquired of the others what marvelous Woman this was, since she appeared to some of them, through her light, like the dawn, the moon, and the sun. Others, because of her great power, compared her to an army set in array;[129] yet others, marveling that she gave forth such an abundance of the sweetest scents, compared her with the vapor of most precious spices, and some others, noting the great abundance of delights and graces that she brought with her, never ceased to ask what an incomparable Woman this was, who rose from the desert above the sacred and celestial spheres with so much glory, since it was something quite extraordinary and new to them to see a pure creature rise above all the choirs of the angels and saints, and be placed on the right hand of the Son of God, and be crowned by Him with a rich and precious crown, and made Empress of the Universe.[130]

The reason for this had not yet been made known to all the angels by the incomprehensible abyss of divine Wisdom, but, at last, seeing her placed beside His high and sublime throne by their King, it was revealed to them by the higher angels that this most beautiful and triumphant Woman was the singular Virgin who had given birth to the Son of God. Thereupon, with great jubilation and joy, she was praised and magnified by all the blessed spirits as being most worthy and deserving of every praise and reverence, as they celebrated and sang around her, with every kind of harmony of sound and chanting, and thus she will always and endlessly be exalted. But while she has achieved the summit of all happiness and everlasting riches, and has been raised up in such everlasting glory and enjoys countless eternal joys, she does not forget our sorrows in this low valley of tears and unhappiness, so far from our heavenly home; on the contrary, she takes special care of us, especially when we live honestly, and confers on us many gifts through the

128. For the Virgin's Assumption, see the volume editor's introduction, 18, 26–27.

129. This is a gloss on the Song of Songs 6:3—"Thou art beautiful, O my love, sweet and comely as Jerusalem: terrible as an army set in array"—and presumably refers to Mary as the Church Militant. I am extremely grateful to Letizia Panizza for locating this reference.

130. Her coronation was the Virgin's final triumph, where she was crowned in heaven by her son. It is the subject of the fifth glorious Mystery of the Rosary.

kindness of her Son. Therefore we should seek to emulate her with every care and, as we need her help, we should turn to her for grace and mercy with every devoted affection and reverence, so that she may always be praised by us, and thanked, with her blessed Son, for ever and ever. Amen.

To the gracious Star, and most faithful Guide of all the sailors of the stormy sea of this world

Since you have reached your glorious end, Mother of God, beautiful Virgin, and made by the great Sun, the shining Star of our wandering and pilgrim souls, I beg that your divine eyes turn to your humble maidservant and see what a frightening tempest she finds herself in alone, and at the end of her life. Please, lead her from the shadows to your light, and from the rocks to your secure harbor, where, at last, you place her soul, weary and tired. Bring her aid, O my trusted leader, because my boat, barely alive, is almost entirely consumed and thus the afflicted spirit trembles and fails.

To the kind Reader

My thought dared too high an enterprise and glorious subject, in praising her who was mother of the great Son of the eternal Father: purest Virgin, of Heaven and without blemish. Too great my presumption to speak of something so high and noble, in so low a style. But duty pushed further my desire with so great a force that as much as I was able to put this labor into thought and practice, I gave it my all.

THE END

III
LUCREZIA MARINELLA'S *LIFE OF THE VIRGIN MARY, EMPRESS OF THE UNIVERSE*

EDITOR'S INTRODUCTION

Lucrezia Marinella was born in Venice in 1571, her father, Giovanni Marinella, a famous physician, writer, and philosopher from Modena, with links to the upper echelons of Venetian society. Of Marinella herself little was known until recently, other than that she was famous by 1604, the author of nine books by 1607 (the year of her marriage to Girolamo Vacca, another physician), and sister of Curzio Marinelli, yet another noted physician, humanist, and author. She was also the mother of two children, and the author of five further works, plus new editions of earlier ones, written between 1608 and 1648.[1] Her fame was celebrated during the seventeenth and eighteenth centuries. New documents have recently been discovered that

1. Major works: *La colomba sacra: Poema heroico di Lucrezia Marinella* (Venice: Gio. Battista Ciotti, 1595); *Vita del serafico, et glorioso San Francesco. Descritta in ottava rima* (Venice: Pietro Maria Bertano & Fratelli, 1597); *La nobiltà et eccellenza delle donne, coi difetti et mancamenti de gli uomini* (Venice: Gio. Battista Ciotti, 1600, 1610); *La vita di Maria Vergine Imperatrice dell'Universo descritta in prosa & in ottava rima* (Venice: Barezzo Barezzi, 1602, 1604, 1610, 1617); *Arcadia felice* (Venice: Gio. Battista Ciotti, 1605); *L'Enrico overo Bisantio acquistato* (Venice: Gherardo Imberti, 1635); *Essortationi alle donne et a gli 'altri* (Venice: Francesco Valvasense, 1645); *Arcadia felice*, ed. Françoise Lavocat (Florence: Accademia toscana di scienze e lettere, "La colombaria," 162, 1998); *The Nobility and Excellence of Women and the Defects and Vices of Men*, ed. and trans. by Anne Dunhill, introd. Letizia Panizza (Chicago: University of Chicago Press, 1999).

For further biography and bibliographical references, see Paola Malpezzi Price, "Lucrezia Marinella," in *Italian Women Writers: A Bio-bibliographical Sourcebook*, ed. Rinaldina Russell (Westport, CT: Greenwood Press, 1994), 234–42; Laura Benedetti, "Saintes et guerrières: L'héroisme féminine dans l'oeuvre de Lucrezia Marinella," in *Les femmes et l'Ecriture: L'amour profane et l'amour sacré*, ed. Claude Cazalé Bérard (Paris: Presses Universitaires de Paris, 2005), 93–109; Susan Haskins, "Vexatious Litigant, or the Case of Lucrezia Marinella? New Documents concerning Her Life (Part 1)," *Nouvelles de la république des lettres* (2006-1): 81–128; part 2, ibid. (2007-1/2): 203–30.

help to place Marinella in her social and literary milieu.[2] In 1605, in his introduction to readers of the *Arcadia felice*, the publisher Giovan Battista Ciotti refers to an accusation made against Marinella of not actually having written the *Vita di Maria Vergine*, first published in 1602, an accusation that was refuted on her behalf. Comparison of the 1602 and 1610 editions shows interesting discrepancies and additions made in the latter edition, which may have been prompted by the criticism.[3] Certainly the accusation rankled, and was reflected in Marinella's last major work, the *Essortationi*, published in 1645, when she was seventy-four. This, however, was not her final work: in 1647 and 1648 she was to publish spiritual writings on Saints Francis, Clare, and Giustina. Marinella died in Venice in 1653.

The Life of the Virgin Mary, Empress of the Universe was Lucrezia Marinella's third major work, and consists of her first sacred prose narrative, or *historia*, and an epic poem in *ottava rima* on the same subject, the two published under the collective title. First published in 1602, an enlarged ("molto ampliata") and revised edition was published in 1604, and reprinted in 1610 (the text here translated), with a further edition appearing in 1617 with new material, clearly showing its popularity. The first edition has an engraved title page and illustrations, which are included in this translation.[4] Dedicated to the Doge and Senate ("al serenissimo Prencipe et all'eccelsa Signoria"), the ruling body of patricians of Venice, Marinella signs herself their "most devoted subject and servant" ("di Vostra Serenità Divotiss. Suddita, & Serva"). With such a dedication she is celebrating the link between Venice, the city, "La Serenissima," and the Virgin Mary, "la serenissima Imperatrice dell'Universo." Her decision to write on the subject may have had *raisons d'état* as well as those of conventional piety and the upsurge in Marian devotion after the Counter-Reformation. Marinella moved in the circles of the ducal chancellery and of the famous Venetian Academy, and had acquaintances among the patriciate.[5] She was also to publish in 1635 *L'Enrico*,

2. See my article, "Vexatious Litigant."

3. These include an entirely new section about Mary Magdalen and visions of the Virgin towards the end of the *Vita*.

4. The engraved illustrations to the 1602 edition are of Joachim's Sacrifice in the Temple; the Angel Appearing to Joachim; the Meeting of Joachim and Anna; the Birth of the Virgin; the Presentation of the Virgin in the Temple; the Marriage of the Virgin; the Annunciation; the Nativity; the Adoration of the Magi; the Circumcision; the Flight into Egypt; the Massacre of the Innocents; Christ in the Temple; the Marriage at Cana; the Crucifixion; the Ascension; the Angel Giving the Virgin the Palm and Announcing Her Death; the Virgin Contemplating God on the Mount of Olives; the Dormition of the Virgin; the Carrying of the Virgin's Bier; and the Virgin's Assumption.

5. See Letizia Panizza's introduction to Marinella, *The Nobility and Excellence of Women and the Defects and Vices of Men*, ed. and trans. by Anne Dunhill (Chicago: University of Chicago Press, 1999), 9–11. See also my article, "Vexatious Litigant."

Figure 6. Portrait engraving of Lucrezia Marinella by Giacomo Piccini (1652), after a painting by Giovanni Battista Papa (1601). Biblioteca Correr, Venezia. Reproduced by kind permission of the Musei Civici Veneziani. The epigram by Alessandro Gatti quoted below Marinella's portrait reads: "Obstupscit, Musis astantibus, altus Apollo, / Versibus auditis, O Marinella tuis. / Hinc subito dixit; praesertim nomine Tassum, / Exuperat vates hec poetria meos. / Auratam tibi tunc Citharam donavit eandem, / Donavit radios tunc tibi quoque suos." ("Lofty Apollo is amazed in the presence of the Muses after listening to your verses, O Marinella. Hence he said at once, 'This poetess surpasses my bards, especially Tasso [the poet Torquato Tasso] by name.' He then gave you the same golden lyre and he also then gave you his rays.") The epigram first appeared in print on page 647 of the volume containing Marinella's poem *L'Enrico* (Venice, 1635). The inscription round the portrait reads "Lucretia Marinella annum agens XXII." At the time of the engraving in 1652, Marinella was in fact thirty rather than the twenty-two years of age she claimed.

overo Bisantio acquistato (*Enrico, or Byzantium Conquered*), another epic, this time in celebration of the Doge Enrico Dandolo, and again dedicated to the Venetian Senate.[6]

The Virgin Mary and Venice had long been associated in the city's partly legendary origins, and several of the city's foundations, both civic and ecclesiastical, were also legendarily dated to the feast of the Annunciation. Paintings, sculpture, and coats-of-arms showed Venice personified as the figures of Justice, *Dea Roma*, the Virgin, and Venus.[7] In what is not an uncommon trope, the painter Guariento painted a fresco of the Coronation of the Virgin to preside over the tribune wall of the Sala del Maggior Consiglio, or Council Chamber, in Venice, some time after 1365. Mary was thus seen as the protectress of the Serenissima in much the same way as Duccio's more famous *Maestà* (Italian, "majesty") of 1308–11 placed the government of Siena under Mary's protection.[8] During the sixteenth century the city was increasingly described in Marian terms such as "Star of the Sea," the imagery indebted to the dogma of the Immaculate Conception, and "Venetia Vergine," the virgin city that defends itself against enemies with its uncorrupted purity.[9] Such a rhetoric of political imagery is not unusual; it is a typical feature of Renaissance hyperbole. A further incentive to link and glorify the two was Venice's victory in 1571 over the Turks at the battle of Lepanto, due, it was claimed, to prayers said to the Virgin. This triumph was still much in Venetian minds many years later. Celio Magno, a patrician poet, secretary to the Senate and Council of Ten, and acquaintance of Lucrezia Marinella, and one among many who wrote on the subject, published a long panegyric in 1571, the *Triumph of Christ through the Victory over the Turks* (*Trionfo di Cristo, per la Vittoria contra Turchi*). Marinella's purposes may thus have been multifaceted: part conventional piety, part celebration of the city-state, and part public recognition for herself and financial gain.

The only author of the three to provide a "working method," Marinella outlines her "methodology" in her introduction to readers, "A' lettori." De-

6. This text is now available in translation: *Enrico, or Byzantium Conquered. Heroic Poem*, ed. and trans. by Maria Galli Stampino (Chicago: University of Chicago Press, 2009).

7. See David Rosand, "Venezia figurata: The Iconography of the Myth," in *Interpretazioni veneziane: Studi di storia dell'arte in onore di Michelangelo Muraro*, ed. Rosand (Venice: Arsenale editrice, 1984), 177.

8. Ibid., 180. Guariento's *Maestà* (ca. 1365), painted for the Hall of the Great Council in the ducal palace in Venice, was found under Tintoretto's fresco of *Paradise* (1587–90). It is now exhibited in the Sala dell'Armamento. Duccio's *Maestà* was painted for the high altar in Siena Cathedral. It was sawn in half and the panels separated during the sixteenth century.

9. Rosand, "Venezia figurata," 184–85.

spite criticisms against her grand style in writing ("la grandezza di questo modo di scrivere hora da me usato"), she would use it for the highest loftiness of eloquence ("il sommo dell'altezza dell'eloquenza"), with the authority of the most literary and famous writers, particularly that of Leontinus Gorgias, the Greek sophist and rhetorician (483–375 BCE), whose argumentation Aristotle had described as poetic diction ("il di lui ragionamento elocutione poetica"), as he used in prose all the "abundant ornaments and magnificent and rare words" usually used in poetry.[10] The purpose of such a style was to inspire in readers' souls wonder at the marvelous ("lo stupore della maraviglia"). Great, magnificent, or divine actions, surpassing those of humans, required grand and marvelous modes of expression, very different from those used in relating actions that were "small, humble, and base."[11] Further, a different style was required for actions of people who through the excellence of their natures exceeded men and heroes. Since both conditions were met in her subject, the Virgin Mary, the poetic diction and eloquence used by classical writers for pagan subjects were appropriate to her sublime subject. To this end, Marinella is to lard her narrative with all the poetic ornaments appropriate to the greatest actions and noblest persons, using rhetorical devices—"an abundance of epithets, hyperbole, description," and "repetition"—to render her lofty subject in the style appropriate to it. Marinella may well also have been influenced by her father's book on lexicography, *La prima [e seconda] parte della copia delle parole*, published in Venice in 1562, about the art of becoming a more copious and eloquent speaker.

Marinella's is an ambitious, literary, and extended work, containing—despite her claims to the contrary—liberal use of apocrypha in addition to the gospel narratives.[12] She has constructed a vast baroque edifice that, although possibly striking the modern reader as overwrought and overblown, accorded well with the spirit of her time: the new editions and reprints attest to its popularity. Concentrating on the miraculous and marvelous, Marinella creates fictional monologues and dialogues within scenes from the gospels or apocrypha, with long descriptive and highly visual passages (*ekphrasis*). These are elaborated upon to excite readers' imaginations and to prompt ap-

10. *La vita di Maria Vergine Imperatrice dell'Universo descritta in prosa & in ottava rima* (Venice: Barezzo Barezzi, 1610), fols. 4r–4v.

11. Ibid., fol. 6v.

12. Marinella also includes a "bibliography" (*Vita*, "Si conferma in questo capo con l'autorita de' Sacri Scrittori, ciò che in questi miei Libri si contiene," [A8]-[A12]), stating precisely her sources, but omits to mention her considerable debt to Pietro Aretino's *Vita de Maria Vergine*, first published in Venice by Marcolini in 1539 and reprinted several times subsequently, which itself made extensive use of apocryphal texts..

propriate emotions, a literary parallel to the role of contemporaneous visual arts, such as painting and sculpture, as part of the meditative process.

Marinella opens her Christian epic onto a landscape of the Holy Land, zooming in like a camera lens to focus on the humble place, Nazareth. Joachim and Anna, Mary's elderly parents, are introduced in a paean to marriage: they are tied together in its "holy bonds," with the "most tender love, which is to be sought in marriage" (129, 130). The theme of matrimony and its natural concomitant, the family, exemplified in the Holy Family, is a leitmotif throughout the *Life*, as part of the Church's post-Tridentine stress on the sacrament and on family ideology. Marinella's use of apocrypha is present from the outset, there to support Counter-Reformation Mariolatry, as does the image of the Virgin Immaculate on the half-moon that appears at the bottom of the title page of the 1602 edition (27). In keeping with her stated intent, Marinella then relates the story of the Virgin's conception, life, and death as a magnificent narrative replete with the miracles and marvels its heroine undergoes, a vehicle the purpose of which is to render the history in terms of Counter-Reformation Catholicism and to celebrate the Virgin and the dogma concerning her, such as her Immaculate Conception, the conception and birth of Jesus, Mary's perpetual virginity, and her assumption and coronation as the Queen of Heaven and Empress of the Universe.

From the outset, the narrative has a strong visual component, with its imaginative recreation of gospel and apocryphal scenes, as well as episodes invented by Marinella herself. Hyberbole is everywhere evident: Nature, effulgent and apocalyptic, reflects the actions of men and the miraculous. Aurora, the personified dawn, accompanies the Virgin's birth, and the birth of Redemption, lending a sense of magnificence to the scene. The wondrous Mary is the "newborn goddess" (143); as a young girl, she has spun-gold hair, which is fine and wavy, arched black brows over eyes of blue, and ruby lips. The western European Queen of Heaven, Mary is a Wisdom figure at an early age, able to unravel obscure biblical meanings (150).

Marinella's narrative would seem to be informed by the Christian art that she would probably have come across in her own life. She paints the scene for the reader: the tenderness shown between Joachim and Anna at the Golden Gate is depicted almost as a visual parallel to Giotto's fresco of the scene in the Arena Chapel in Padua (ca. 1308), where Anna caresses her husband's neck. Later Joachim sits "on a rock, dressed in clothes similar in color to ears of corn when the peasants softly play their pipes at harvest. His right hand [is] on his right leg and his left cheek [is] resting on the palm of his other hand, with his elbow on his left knee"—this might be taken directly from Giotto's scene of Joachim's dream (143). The angel tells the shepherds that they will recognize the house of Christ's birth from the golden streak emanating from it, something the modern reader would probably associate with Christmas card images but derives from medieval art. The Virgin's kneeling before the child, while Joseph awaits outside "swathed in his cloak," is another reference to medieval images. The magi genuflect before the Virgin and child, their "left hands to their breasts" and "the gifts in their right hands" (183), a description so precise that it would seem to reflect an actual depiction of the scene. Simeon's fantastical bejeweled cloak is similar to the description of the high priest's cloak in Exodus 28 of the Hebrew Bible, and appears in countless images of the Presentation (185–86). Equally, the vividness of the violence of the massacre of the innocents, rendering the *orrori* present to the reader, owes a debt to visual portrayals of the scene (194–96), as does the detail of Mary Magdalen's hair touching the feet of Christ on the cross (218).

Imaginative recreations of conventional Christian images and invented incidents lend a sense of verisimilitude to the narrative, as in Joseph's slightly stilted suggestion to Mary that they enter the hut ("I think, if you would like to, that it would be appropriate for us to take shelter under a roof," [173]), after their having tramped to Bethlehem through the wind and rain, which "struck their faces with pouring water, and did this so many times that [Mary] had to defend herself against it with her hands and then with her cloak." "The Lady of the Angels" reacts "cheerfully" and then follows "the upright man into a poor hovel," the language merging the sublime with the real (173).

That her readership was likely to have been in the main female is clear from Marinella's focus on female behavior and decorum and things of feminine interest throughout the work. Anna goes to meet Joachim "together with some respected women," as no "respectable" woman would be allowed out without a female companion (140); similarly, Mary, going to visit Elizabeth, takes "two elderly women," Anna's old servants, with her, presumably inherited on her mother's death, and possibly a mark of family continuity (168). As noted above, there is a strong emphasis on family. Despite the criticism by Church leaders of the stories of Joachim and Anna and of the infancy and death of the Virgin, these remained popular subjects in late sixteenth- and seventeenth-century art: Marinella's portrayal of their domestic lives, together with her scenes of the Holy Family, witness that popularity, their purpose to underline Catholic teaching about the Incarnation but also to stress family ideology, supported by the cults of Anna and Joseph. Mary, as a miraculous infant, unlike others who cry, never makes a noise (146). In a remarkable image Joachim finds pleasure "in laying out and heating the soft cloths and white swaddling clothes" to be wrapped around the Virgin, and, after the baby has been fed, "with a happy look, [he takes] the baby in his arms, amusing her with tender caresses and imprinting with a kiss on her cheeks the affection of his heart" (144, 145). Anna, dying, talks to her servant girls, apologizing if she has ever treated them badly (159).

The young girls who are Mary's companions at the Temple (which seems to serve as a kind of finishing school) are all of noble birth, but perform duties such as cleaning and polishing, which, as Marinella comments, "is still the case among us today," presumably referring to nuns' chores in churches (148). Punishable talkativeness is not part of the Virgin's makeup, but she has prudence, gentleness, charm, and modesty in abundance, all ideal requisites of young femaleness (149). Mary's frugality (148) derives from secular conduct books about household management (*economia*), as does her spare appetite. Family life in Egypt has the realistic adumbration of Joseph, as a foreigner, earning little; Mary therefore adds to the household economy by "practicing the virtues of embroidery and lace-making" (194). She is a model for all young women, especially wives and mothers.

Mary as a mother has natural anxieties over her son's activities, and they have long and sorrowful conversations in which he seeks to console her, alliteration and repetition stressing his sympathy: "Assuage the bitterness of your sorrows, the instruments of grief to my grieved breast, because by assuaging them, you will assuage part of that bitterness that distresses my soul for you." Jesus reminds Mary that her weeping is the paradoxical "cause of general joy" (210). The Virgin is given a more active role when she apostrophizes the crucifiers, a scene taken from medieval mystery plays, and based on the *Improperia*, as is the address to her as she stands by the cross contemplating her son (216–17). In Book Four, it is the Virgin who gives permission to the apostles and Mary Magdalen to leave for their travels (232–33), and she has visions of the Christian saints and martyrdoms to come, in a kind of prophetic knowledge of the future. (It will be noted that Marinella uses phrases such as "I believe," "I think," and "some writers relate" before recounting such incidents. While these do not appear in the first edition, their appearance in the second and subsequent editions denotes references to apocryphal material.)[13] The Virgin's last days are spent visiting the places where Christ had suffered, and in prayer, fasting, and meditation, the last three occupations posed as examples to Marinella's readers. Mary's "dormition," her bodily rise out of her tomb at Christ's bidding ("Rise, my Bride," [245]), is termed Mary's "resurrection" by Marinella, presumably to render it

13. See volume editor's introduction, note 47.

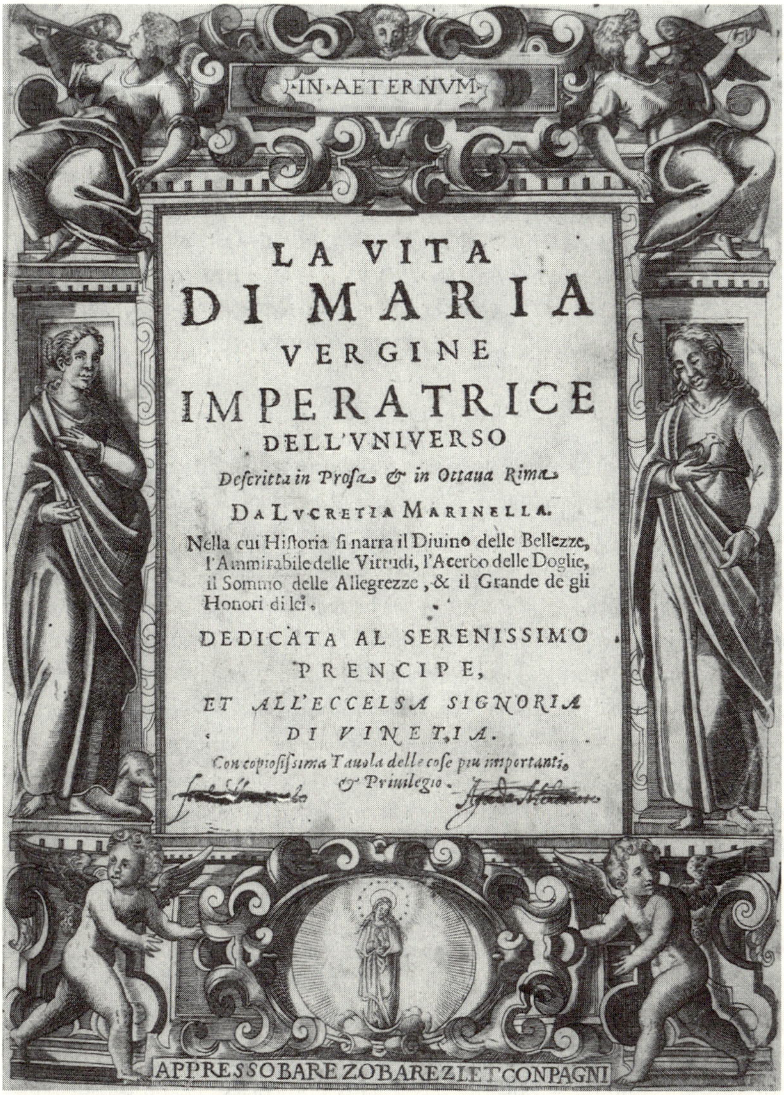

IN AETERNVM

LA VITA
DI MARIA
VERGINE
IMPERATRICE
DELL'VNIVERSO

Descritta in Prosa & in Ottaua Rima

DA LVCRETIA MARINELLA.

Nella cui Historia si narra il Diuino delle Bellezze, l'Ammirabile delle Virtudi, l'Acerbo delle Doglie, il Sommo delle Allegrezze, & il Grande de gli Honori di lei.

DEDICATA AL SERENISSIMO
PRENCIPE,
ET ALL'ECCELSA SIGNORIA
DI VINETIA.

Con copiosissima Tauola delle cose piu importanti, & Priuilegio.

APPRESSO BAREZO BAREZI ET CONPAGNI

Figure 7. Title page of the 1602 edition of *La vita di Maria Vergine Imperatrice dell'Universo descritta in prosa & in ottava rima da Lucretia Marinella.* Reproduced by kind permission of the Biblioteca Nazionale Centrale di Roma.

in glorious parallel to that of her son; her rise to heaven is called her "ascension," again, presumably, in parallel to Christ's, as a fitting end to the marvels and miracles of Marinella's Christian epic.

THE LIFE OF THE VIRGIN MARY, EMPRESS OF THE UNIVERSE, DESCRIBED IN PROSE AND OTTAVA RIMA, BY THE VERY ILLUSTRIOUS LADY LUCREZIA MARINELLA, AND NOW IN THIS THIRD EDITION, MUCH EXPANDED BY HER . . . DEDICATED TO THE MOST SERENE PRINCE AND TO THE MAGNIFICENT SIGNORIA OF VENICE. IN VENICE, 1610, PRINTED BY BAREZZO BAREZZI.

BOOK ONE

Summary: *In this first book are described the marvelous excellence of Joachim and Anna, Joachim's going to the Temple, from which he was expelled by the Priest with threatening words. Whence he went away into the loneliness of the countryside. Anna is afflicted in her very soul by her husband's departure. Joachim fervently requests children of the supreme Giver, who sends him an Angel, promising him the fulfillment of his wishes. Anna prays to the Lord for the same reason. The Angel comforts her. She then goes to find Joachim, and finds herself pregnant. Then her husband offers many gifts to the Temple. Mary is born, Queen of Heaven, and in that time laughter and jubilation are seen in all things with the greatest of joy. Joachim and Anna give thanks to God for their daughter, whom they offer at the Temple. What the virgins did who were in the Lord's great house is related. The virtues, wisdom, and beauties of Mary, who is persuaded by the Priests to be joined in marriage. Whereby she is for this reason beside herself with sorrow. God with His thundering voice commands that the male descendants of David come to the Temple. Then Joachim and Anna go to find Mary. The High Priest calls Joseph to him, in whose hands the dry rod flowers, and Mary is given to him as his bride, who returns with her parents to Nazareth. Joachim and Anna die, and Joseph makes his way to Nazareth to find the Virgin.*

Nazareth—of which scarcely the ruins are visible nowadays—lies in the center of that part of Galilee, the furthest tip of which is gracefully mirrored in the shining sea of Tiberias.[14] This poor place lacked those splendors that kings usually desired for their own palaces: but it was so abundant in Heaven's favor and divine treasure that many rulers, who defraud others' wills according to their own license, if they put aside ambition, swollen be-

14. Nazareth is in southern Galilee, about fifteen miles southwest of the Sea of Galilee, also called the Sea of Tiberias (John 6:1, 21:1). The Emperor Tiberius (ruled 14–37 CE) was the caesar during Jesus's ministry and Crucifixion.

neath the regal purple and the gold, would, reverently humble and humbly reverent, bow toward Nazareth.

Joachim and Anna united in Marriage. Joachim and Anna, of the priestly tribe of Aaron, lived in this happy part of the world, tied together in the venerable and holy bonds of matrimony, the happiest couple that the sun had ever seen, after its golden head had been drawn out of the void.[15] Anna's birth embellished Jerusalem and Joachim Nazareth's. Joachim's noble ancestors had withdrawn to such a place to flee their kings' wickedness. Pierced by the dart of suspicion, the kings feared that they would be stripped of their tyrannical empire, as Fame had given breath to as many trumpets as she had mouths [to blow them], and had unfurled the swiftness of her wings, bringing news of the coming of a new leader of the Jews, of the house of David. This had been foreseen and predicted from antiquity by the prophets. And, therefore, prompted by their usual monstrousness, the kings drove from Jerusalem all those who descended from the one who, tuning his mournful tones to the harmony of the lyre, and the sound of his sighs, asked pardon for his sins from Highest Clemency.[16] Joachim and Anna traced their origins from David who, having laid aside his ivy crown, adorned his brow with the royal diadem.[17] After David came Solomon, whose subtle wit was so shrewd that he saw the most hidden secrets in nature's breast. And further, in all he did marvelous greatness sprang forth with brightest splendor.[18]

Virtues of Joachim and Anna. These noble people were living in Nazareth,

15. The story of Joachim and Anna is entirely apocryphal and first appears in the second-century Book of James, or *Protevangelium* (see volume editor's introduction, 21–22). The story also appears in "The Birth of the Virgin," in Jacobus de Voragine, *The Golden Legend: Readings on the Saints*, 2 vols., trans. by William Granger Ryan (Princeton, NJ: Princeton University Press, 1993), 2:150–52. Aaron was the first of Israel's high priests and, according to Hebrew tradition, Moses' brother (Exodus 4:14). In Christian theology he is a type, or foreshadow or example, of Christ.

16. David (d. ca. 970 BCE) was the first king of the Judean dynasty (1 Samuel 16:1; Kings 2; 1 Chronicles 2ff. and 10–29). His repentance arose from his adultery with Bathsheba, the wife of Uriah the Hittite, whom he had watched bathing, lusted after, and seduced. After arranging for Uriah's death, he married Bathsheba (2 Samuel 2:27; 1 Kings 1:16). A poet (2 Samuel 1; he has been traditionally regarded as the author of the Psalms), he was also a player on the harp, for which he was summoned to the court of Saul (1 Samuel 16:14–23), where he ultimately became the king's armor-bearer.

17. This is a metaphor for David's assuming kingship in exchange for his literary and musical fame, David's ivy crown referring to his prowess as a poet. He became King of Judah on Saul's death and was celebrated by the Jews as their ideal king.

18. Solomon's father was David, his mother Bathsheba. Solomon reigned from ca. 962 to 922 BCE. Renowned for his wisdom (1 Kings 4:30), he carried out bureaucratic reforms and was much concerned with foreign relations. He fortified Jerusalem and built the first Temple.

enjoying the most tranquil calm and peace that anyone had ever experienced, and tasting all the greatest joys and worldly content, since they loved each other with that devoted and most tender love, which is to be sought in marriage. Thus obstinate wrath never disturbed their gentle breasts; they never stumbled on any occasion against the rashness of anger; nor did they allow themselves to be carried away by frenzied appetite (a likely event, once the controls of continence have burst), which seduces the pliant senses with worldly lasciviousness. They bore misfortunes with that steady forbearance that bridles ardent desires with its restraint in disasters, abstaining and sustaining: they observed with their innermost souls those precepts that divine law places on all those who wish to walk the path that leads to the heavenly city. Their pure modesty was a model for others as to how to moderate their own desires, and therefore these others became chaste and holy through looking at them. They loved (I believe) with the greatest tenderness of heart their neighbors regardless of social class, sex, and age; in fact their caring piety continually toiled in carrying out works that derive from the spirit of mercy, so that in being charitable to others it appeared to them that they were benefited by others. With joyful faces, they offered food to many in need, unprompted by complaints that came from needy mouths. And they were endowed with all that could be desired in excellent creatures, and without anything further, as they were noble in their behavior, graceful in their actions, happy in their intelligence, sincere in their souls, and ardently charitable in what they did, which sweetened their minds and softened their hearts. There were few of those days when they did not offer others help, wise advice, or tender words, or at least sympathy for afflictions, with compassionate tears, their breasts being true nests where they received the sorrows of those crushed by misfortune. No one, not even the worst of persons, with evil intentions—not to mention unkind words—dared to think of ruining the reputation of this blessed and happy couple because of these qualities. For this reason, they lived together with calm souls, the world's praise, and God's gifts, with such a flame of charity, with so much strength in their religious beliefs, and with such a zealous faith that they enjoyed in a certain way down here on earth what is enjoyed to perfection in Heaven.

Features and appearance of Anna and Joachim. For twenty years the sun had brought human beings the flowering and warmth of spring, and in its absence, equally often, the fearfulness and cold of winter, since these blessed people had been tied by the knot shaped by God's sweet hands in the joy of Paradise. Then that heat [of maturity], which burns the hand and the mind, began to grow cool through the ending of summer [old age]; never-

Figure 8. Engraving showing Joachim's Sacrifice in the Temple; the Angel Appearing to Joachim; the Meeting of Joachim and Anna; the Birth of the Virgin; the Presentation of the Virgin in the Temple; and the Marriage of the Virgin. From the 1602 edition of *La vita di Maria Vergine Imperatrice dell'Universo descritta in prosa & in ottava rima da Lucretia Marinella* (fol. 8v). Reproduced by kind permission of the Biblioteca Nazionale Centrale di Roma.

theless, Anna had the same serene brow, joyful manner, clear eye, and soft flesh that she had in the greenest April of her youth. Joachim had a liveliness in his face, accompanied by a certain kindly gravity, no greater than could be found in any other man, and the sincerity and loyalty of his heart were manifest in his eyes' movement and in his wide brow. It was said that in his deep-set eyes, his prominent brow, and great presence, he was not a jot dissimilar to Solomon's father.[19]

Nothing, therefore, troubled the calm of these modest persons who lived in their tranquility of soul and body, except the immense desire to receive from Heaven legitimate descendants, a desire that disturbed the holy peace in which, happier than all others, they dwelt. Thus they often prayed fervently to God's compassionate mercy that they might receive [this gift, i.e., a child], in praise and glory of His most high name, Jerusalem, which was celebrated in memory of the first humble dwellings or shelters made of branches, which the devout people of Israel had constructed in the wilds of the desert.[20] So wishing to request of the Ruler of Paradise the fulfillment of their desires, Joachim took a lamb, a pair of doves, and incense, to offer sacrifices and perfumes to the One who holds the perfection of immensity and infinity.

Joachim goes to the Temple. On arriving at God's great Temple, empty of every deformity of sin, Joachim fell to his knees on the hard earth, and with a heart full of religion, gentleness, and reverent humility, begged Him who from Heaven gazed with a kindly eye on the perfection and ardor of their souls, to grant to their ardent desire the sweetness of the fruit so wished by those who had placed their necks beneath the indissoluble yoke of matrimony. With a firm heart, he promised that whomever might be born of them would serve Him every day of his or her life in perpetual virginity.[21]

Joachim is chased from God's mansion. Then, blessing the greatness of His name and the magnitude of His works, Joachim wanted to offer the gifts he had brought on the sacred altar. Whereupon he heard the Minister of the

19. The description of Anna and Joachim follows the four ages of man—their births, youth, maturity, and old age are equated with the seasons of the year (spring, summer, autumn, and winter).

20. Exodus 5:1–23.

21. The story of Joachim's going to the Temple to pray for a child is of course apocryphal, but the purpose of the promise to dedicate that child to serve God "in perpetual virginity" is to underscore the Church's later dogma on the Virgin as "ever Virgin." In the Book of James, it is Anna who dedicates her child to God. See *The Apocryphal New Testament: Being the Apocryphal Gospels, Acts, Epistles, and Apocalypses*, ed. and trans. by M. R. James (Oxford: Clarendon Press, 1924), 40.

Temple, with a dark look and in a severe voice, criticize him for his natural defect, with the following or similar words:

> Do not encumber the holiness of our altars with your sacrifices, reckless man and one cursed by divine command, and do not desire to add your own unworthy gifts to the offerings of the just. Are you not ashamed that you are not adding to the Lord's people with an abundance of children, not to mention approaching the holy sacredness of this place, and mingling with family women and men? Remove your contemptible offerings from these altars, which are neither pleasing nor precious to Heaven.

Hearing himself insulted and humiliated before the people, instant shame inflamed Joachim's face, rather in the way that an extinguished piece of coal placed among flames is seen to revive and rekindle by the north wind's fiery breath, and for that reason, as sudden was the flush, so was the pallor, which was caused by the shame confined in his heart and which, yielding blood, spread its pale veils on his cheeks. And although scorn and shame, the first with sorrow, the other with the flames, offended and inflamed his breast and face almost immediately, nevertheless a certain bewilderment overtook him not unlike the feelings of a person who sees him or herself attacked in deathly violence by someone whom he had never harmed; or he was like an innocent man put unjustly into the darkness of a subterranean prison who, when he believes he has left it, hears the sentence of death against his life. And even though he was ashamed, sad, and terrified, his humility did not stop him from praising the Lord, who heard him from Heaven with His ear of compassionate mercy.

Joachim withdraws into the country. And thinking to himself that he wanted to make a new request of Heaven, with prayers and with fasting, for the longed-for gift, he left the great Temple of God, as it is likely, wholly engrossed in himself, his arms crossed and eyes lowered to the ground. And leaving his wife, country, friends, and relations, he went to the poverty of rustic hovels where, clad in shepherds' clothing, he looked after the flocks; his soul, like a wounded stag, pierced by the arrow tips of the priest's words, flooded every hour in invisible tears. There, with frequent fasting, he mortified his tender limbs, and spent not only the day in continuous prayer but also many hours of the night, while others are in bed, cherishing the warmth brought by their rest. Only a little hay did he gather around himself, when obstinate nature wanted part of the right belonging to rest and sleep from his eyes and limbs. He was continually sad and quite removed from the world's delights, which usually lighten souls that are swathed in mantles of melancholy. Beauty and joy, flaming within the bosom of roses, offered no delight to his eyes; nor did the bright truth that roams freely and joyfully through lily leaves; nor did the shoals of fish darting through the twisting paths of rivers even lighten the weight of his soul, the waters of these rivers shining and brilliant through their purity and freshness. His bitter anxieties were not diminished by the sound of shepherds' bagpipes, a bitterness that had fixed itself in his heart; nor did the birds, which disported themselves from myrtle tree to myrtle tree, and from beech tree to beech tree, with dulcet notes and graceful flight, brighten the dark and melancholy of his brow. His sorrows were scarcely assuaged by the simple sheep that lovingly gave milk to bleating lambs. On the contrary, the trees weighed down by fruit, the vine bearing the gentle weights of their own grapes, the green of the grass, the clarity of the air, the fountains' murmur, the height of the mountains, the pleasantness of the hills, and sunniness of the seashore, all equally exacerbated his own troubles when he thought of his own barrenness. So that his shepherd friends, who saw his pallor brought on by sorrow and abstinence, his eyes sunken into his head and almost hidden, his untended beard and rumpled hair, and withdrawal into the veils of melancholy, continued with their lives, were sorrowful and grew more so on account of his sorrow.[22]

Anna's lament. At this time Anna, the venerable lady, heard of the severe face, threatening words, and cruel voice with which the Minister of the Temple had reproached Joachim's barrenness and of how he had chased him from the Temple, the magnificent excellences of which were in great part their gifts. And how he was almost banished, reduced to the solitude of the country; thereupon, it is said, her face and breast were soaked with her tears, and falling senseless two or three times, it seemed that death had been victorious over her life. But as soon as she came to, she threw herself into sorrow's arms and began with the most sorrowful lamenting the most mournful plaints that any creature, pierced through by suffering, had ever uttered. This perhaps might have been her lament:

> How could it be that a priest of God, a just person, and one who is wholly charitable, wholly modest, and merciful, has expelled someone from the Temple with perpetual infamy, who neither betrayed God's commandments nor deviated from earthly laws? You see, O highest heavenly Power, that the early fruits of our fields, of our

22. The abundance of nature is contrasted with Joachim's barrenness.

> meadows, of our possessions, were always offered to You, not only with the readiness of our hands but also with all the sincerity and purity of our intentions. And with the diligence of all our affection we have tried to show ourselves to be what You desired us to be, souls worthy of You.

Then, as it seemed to sorrowful Anna that she had rebuked the Prime Mover for the righteous deeds they had done in His honor, she said,

> Forgive me Lord, forgive me, eternal Father, since these empty words of mine are dictated by passion's lips: nothing that Anna's husband, nor Joachim's wife ever did equaled the merit of one of the least graces that His divine hand pleased to bestow upon us. I know that all that comes from You brings with it a happy and joyful end. Therefore may the excess of passion flee from me, which usually burdens the soul with the mantle of flesh.

Anna said this as she pined, languishing in the way plants languish through the dryness of the hottest summer.

Prayer made by Joachim to have children. Anna's tears, sighs, and laments were reported to her sorrowing husband. Wherefore the perfect friend of God, already worn out by fasting and abstinence, added sorrow to his sorrows; he well knew Anna's merits and virtues, and the goodness of her judgment, and how she was almost perfect. Love, united with the merit of her gifts, made him therefore love her with all the fervor of that love that tender affections can draw from the innermost heart. However (some say), it came to pass that she melted like white snow when she gazed at the eye of that light, which is like the spirit and soul of the world. Beneath the terror of its great wings, blind Night had already forty times hidden from mankind's eyes the sights, colors, and charms of all those things with which the world is adorned, since the Priest, with hardened face and severe words, had banished Joachim from the golden Temple of the Lord who, seated in Heaven, roams above the wings of the winds.[23] Far from all pride, all vanities, wholly elevated toward God, Joachim knelt, and raising his eyes to Heaven's tran-

23. The night is described as blind because nothing can be seen in the dark; blindness is a metaphor for darkness, error, and ignorance. Similarly, blindfolding is a symbol of moral or spiritual blindness, hence the darkness of sin and ignorance. Personified, Night is sometimes shown standing in the lamplight with folded wings, head in hands, accompanied by two children, one white (Sleep), and the other black (Death). The symbolism of the number forty is derived from the forty days Christ spent in the wilderness (Mark 1:13; Matthew 4:2; Luke 4:2).

quility, and opening his arms, said from the depths of his soul these, or similar, words:

> Although, O Lord, the strength of my spirit is already exhausted beneath the weight of my heavy pains, nevertheless I dare to call out to You: as I have faith in the mercies of Your clemency, even though I am unworthy, and perhaps diminished in Your sight, darkened by the ugliness of my sins. But why do I say, "darkened," if I love You? You will always be mild not only with me, but with anyone who contemplates, with a mind freed from worldly tangles and with the burning desire of the repentant heart, the tranquil expression of Your marvelous countenance, from whose brow shine the rays of that glory that Your bounty bestows on each who desires to glorify himself in You. So You, O God, who casts out no one, nor is deaf to any prayers, but grants them with perfect love, listen to my prayers! Although I was conceived, born, and grew up in the mists of pride, in the darkness of sin, and in the rivers of vanity, if I offended You, O eternal Light, when my humble offerings were offered to the greatness of Your name on the pure altar, I feel wounded to the quick by the arrows of repentance, and beseech peace and forgiveness from You. But if Anna and Joachim have ever offered prayers, sacrifices, or incense, which have been granted by and received from You, I beg and beseech you, neither through the merit of our prayers nor of our gifts, because I know that they are worth little, but only through the grace of Your holy will, to deign to grant the desired gift of our burning entreaties, which when we have obtained it, will be dedicated to You with the chastity and modesty of its body, until it pleases You to undo with your hands its reasons for living.

So spoke the noble man, the honor of revered old age, flooding with tears that flowed from his heart's veins not only his cheeks but also the grasses that rose from the earth. As he finished speaking, he heard Heaven murmur, and the murmur was mixed with flashes of lightning, and with some terrors that struck no fear at all; it flashed swiftly and often, and it seemed that every time the thunder burst, a bolt of lightning would be delivered in the splitting of the clouds. Then the mists that roamed over the fields of the sky, struck by the light of the eternal fire, were changed into the color of gold; and, behold, a Messenger of the celestial mysteries came out of the heavenly gates, in the form of a falling star, from the serenity of the night, into the earth's womb, and descended, leaving in his wake the air streaked with rays of shining virtue that flowed from his heavenly countenance. The Angel's speedy flight stopped on the mountain top where Joachim's simple flock was grazing. The blowing breeze calmed down entirely, and took comfort in pressing the delicate garment swathing his limbs, purer than innocence itself; at the same time, it made his curly locks flutter around his head, surpassing the sun's rays in splendor. His alabaster face seemed sprinkled with the brilliant red of roses, and his eyes flamed like diamonds struck by the light of day. Stupefied and frightened by so much splendor, Joachim was unable to bear the sparkle and rays that came from the angelic creature; and in his bewilderment he heard, in similar harmony, God's comforting words from the lips of the ordained Messenger:

> Joachim, that friend of ours from whom the happiness of every good thing comes, sends me to you to announce the joyful news for so many years desired and hoped for on earth and in Heaven. Therefore rejoice and be glad because your prayers have risen on wings to the bosom of the Father of the Angels, on wings inflamed with burning love; He receives them as the loving father receives the daughters he so loves. Now, chase from your brow, eyes, and soul the sadness, tears, and sorrows and receive in their place tranquility, calm, and joy. God was very pleased with the patience with which you suffered the Minister of His holy Temple, when He gave you exile with the trumpet of reproof. And He approved of your being rebuked for the defect of barrenness, so that your virtue would be made more perfect through sorrow. He did not avenge Himself on nature's failings, nor does He regard as mistakes nature's limitations.[24] Now, after the course of so many years, He will enrich you with a daughter, in such an advanced age, white-haired and impotent, by working His miraculous power. This daughter was in His presence before He began to create all things with the fruitfulness and power of His words.[25] All those excellent things and all those graces that nature and heaven can cause with the greatest of their powers will shine forth in her beauty. You will call her by this venerable and admirable name of Mary.

The blessed spirit bowed his head and knelt, pronouncing the great name. And then he added:

24. God's pleasure at Joachim's behavior in adversity evokes Matthew 3:17: "This is my beloved Son, in whom I am well pleased."

25. This refers to God's omniscience and prescience about the Fall. The Virgin was part of the divine plan, preordained.

> The holy womb of happy Anna will be filled with the virtue of the Holy Spirit, and she will be born as one born for the highest pomp of Heaven, and day and night to the utmost of her powers will serve the King of all. To reward the greatness of her merits, God will clothe the inscrutable eminence of His only Son in her pure and chaste womb with the fragility of your humanity. Rewarding the world, He will heal the wounds, the deadly poison of which draws the souls of mortals into the abyss. She will be praised, revered, feared, and loved by God, by mankind, by the devils, and by angels. And as a sign of this, you will meet your sorrowful and faithful wife, mournful because of the lateness of your return, on the way to the home of your fathers.[26]

When he had said this, he disappeared, like a candle extinguished by the impetuous breath of wind, leaving behind him the perfume that the delightful slopes of Paradise perpetually breathe forth.

Joyful Joachim. The perfect man remained (as one might imagine) with his soul full of incomprehensible joy at the unhoped, but longed-for, news. And he was so amazed, confused, and trembling that he could scarcely see things nearby that surrounded him, for he was like someone who stares into the sun's face and seems to see that Night, turning its wheels, fills everything with darkness and fear.[27] As soon as he came to himself, he gave the utmost thanks to the Giver of all graces. Unable to contain in his breast the joy of such great news, the waters of his joyful sweetness poured out through his brow, mouth, and countenance. In the calm of his brow, tranquility knew itself and the peace in his soul. Then he joined his friends and shepherd companions who marveled at his changed appearance, and with kindly humanity he revealed to them the beginning and end of his sufferings and of his joys not without the sorrow and joy of the dwellers of the countryside.

Anna sorrowing because of Joachim's departure. Anna prays to the Lord to have children. God sends the Angel from Heaven to Anna. At that time Anna, sorrowing in her lamentations, which had already made their imprints in her breast, sadly turned her steps through the lovely greenery of her garden; and while there she thought of the abundant fertility of the insensitive plants and her own infertility and, shedding the most abundant tears from her eyes, and kneeling on the ground, took up the pose that sorrow taught her, and struck Heaven with words like these:

26. This passage is a paraphrase and adumbration of the angel's annunciation to the Virgin Mary in Luke 1:28–38.

27. Night was part of the revolving heavens of the universe.

> Although You, O eternal Creator, are in supreme glory, and I am in the midst of sin, yet I dare call out to You so that You hear me, name You so that You answer me, and pray to You so that You grant me. And knowing that as sweet as it is to You to listen to the voices of those who pray to You with repentant hearts in this life full of death, so it is important to You to hear the thanks that souls render You who have already risen to the peak of bliss—I beg You through the sincere hope that Joachim and Anna have in Your mercy, to wish to give to our age, which is hastening toward its decline, that so longed-for pledge that our souls wish for. And forgive, O Lord, forgive the tiresomeness of the requests that we constantly make, since, as God, You allow the steadfast faith that people have in You to compel the goodness of Your mercy. And I know very well that if the privilege of being Your creatures is removed, we are nothing.

That most excellent woman Anna wrenched these words from the depths of her heart, not unlike the raging tempest wrenches a tree root from the grasping earth. Then God, who looks down tenderly on the contrite heart, immediately despatched one of his winged messengers to comfort her. At once, as a flash of lightning, the incorruptible spirit alighted, and without delay, from the immeasurable height of Heaven. He came to rest above the garden, the ethereal body he had assumed hovering and above his own wings; he flashed and blazed through his golden locks and crimson cheeks; and staying still among his lights like a burning coal among its flames, I believe, he said with the harmony of that voice that blessed souls hear from God's lips:

> Great Lady, Lady of celebrated virtue, honor, and pride of little Nazareth, the One to whose power everyone bows down has sent me to you, the saving force, and the joy of His words sounds through mine, to reveal to you how will come forth from your most holy womb that fortunate tree, which among the purity and whiteness of its holy roots will receive the spirit of God, as if in its own nest. Then the one who is the salvation of the incurable and inconsolable world will be born of you. She will have in her breast all the excellence and perfection of those virtues that make humankind happy on earth and holy and blessed in Heaven. Therefore not only will the kings and first rulers of the world bow down before the one who is first Empress of Heaven, but temples, altars, burnt incense, and weighty prayers will be consecrated to her. Operating the wonders of that power God granted

> her from the beginning, she will help and support the sick, the poor, and those falling into ruinous misfortune. Evil spirits will flee from the sound of her powerful words, as shadows flee at the appearance of light. And thus the amazed world will consecrate chaste virgins to the glorious memory of the immortal Lady in wonder at her marvels, and she will live most humbly among such greatness. Wherefore the heavenly Kingdom will rejoice, seeing her crowned with all her honored joys and not become lofty in any way. Her name will be Mary, a marvelous name, meaning a star lighting the shadows of perpetual death. She will soothe God's angry brow and receive from Him all those graces that He has poured upon all mortal creatures to make them perfect. Rise then and turn your hasty steps toward the rustic dwellings, and you will meet righteous Joachim midway, your husband, who is coming joyfully for the same reason as your joy, with the certain intention of finding you, halfway along the road.[28]

Having said this, he vanished from her sight, like a shining star that vanishes behind fog or damp mists that rise from the earth.

The noble lady, dazzled by the light of the supreme Messenger, was amazed and terrified in her soul, and, while he directed his flight to Heaven, she followed him, as it is believed, with her voice, saying, "Blessed spirit, relate in the Creator's presence how His handmaid's humility is prepared to be at His disposal with ready obedience."[29] Having said this, she thanked the One who created all from nothing; and with purity of mind and with faith and hope, she rose from the ground. At the sound of such joyful news, her radiant face appeared like a sun, a sun that chased away the veils of mist from all around, which had prevented it from showing the beauty that burned in its rays. She had scarcely arranged her veils around her head, and tidied her clothes, which were in disarray around her, when she immediately set off by the path shown to her by the citizen of Heaven, together with some respected women who left their houses still dazzled by the light of the miracle. At that moment, her love and will, consumed in the desire to see her beloved husband, became the spurs that not only added vigor to the diminished strength of slow old age, but also made her run as if in early youth.

Anna goes to find Joachim. She had not gone far when she saw Joachim, father worthy of reverence. Then turning to her women, she said, "Here is my dear husband, as God's Messenger told me." In the same way, he from the

28. The angel's speech is again based on Gabriel's greeting to the Virgin in Luke 1:28–38.

29. Anna's reply is a paraphrase of Luke 1:38.

other side said to the shepherds in a joyful voice: "Here is Anna, my sweet wife, given to me by Heaven."

Anna greets Joachim and he her. As Joachim to Anna and Anna to Joachim drew closer, immense bliss and tender joy drove their feelings and the soul of their spirits in such a way that their hearts and tongues trembled. But Joachim's words, which Anna wanted to utter, and Anna's voice, which Joachim wanted to shape, became entangled in such a way that the two were tongue-tied; they appeared like little children beginning to unravel the first sounds of their wet nurse or father: but their arms with affectionate embraces replaced affectionate words. Loving tears streamed down the faces of the happily reunited pair, while their faces and breasts brought close together gave vent to their yearnings. The shepherds and women present at the righteousness of such tender greetings showed the joy of their souls with tears poured out by sincerity and true love.[30]

Anna's conception. After this, the blessed couple went to Nazareth to await the high promise with a gladness no longer experienced. The Mother of God was thus conceived by righteous Joachim and happy Anna far in every way from any desire for pleasure, and with all the innocence and purity of their souls and bodies, and with the grace therefore of the One who lights the stars with joyful light.[31] Thus she whose incorruptible and immaculate body would rise above the stars and have the crown above the angels and devils was conceived in Anna's most holy womb. Once her glorious soul was infused into her body, all the benign influences rained their merits upon her, and the ornaments of their excellences, and all the sweetness of their good gifts; and all the virtues descended from above that had never been gathered in the tainted breasts of humankind, assembling in her breast like simple birds in their own nests. At the same time the great Father turned His beneficent eyes from Heaven toward His created daughter and, from the depth of His intellect, spread into her blessed soul the sources of wisdom.[32]

Anna is pregnant. Clear signs of pregnancy appeared in the very great

30. This scene is traditionally known as the Meeting at the Golden Gate. It first occurs in the Book of James (see James, *Apocryphal New Testament*, 40).

31. This passage concerns the doctrine of the Immaculate Conception, the conception of the Virgin Mary in her mother Anna's womb. For Mary to have been "kept free from all stain of original sin" (Bull "Ineffabilis Deus" of Pius IX, December 8, 1954), it was necessary for her, as the Mother of God, to have been created without stain of sin. She was thus conceived by Anna without passion ("far in every way from any desire for pleasure"), ergo without sin, and given birth to painlessly, as the Second or New Eve, whereas God's punishment to the first Eve, for the Fall, had been "travail and labor" (Genesis 3:16).

32. Saint Ambrose (d. 397) was the first to propose the Virgin Mary as the model for all virtues (see volume editor's introduction, 17).

Lady, the honor of her age. The cry spread from ear to ear, from region to region, town to city, of the news in which all rejoiced, as if in their own joy.

Joachim makes many gifts to the Temple through joy at Anna's pregnancy. Joachim made many sacrifices for so many graces to the One who, being the perfection of all, embraced all. And going to God's great Temple in Jerusalem, he offered incense, lambs, calves, doves, salt, flour, and oils on the altar, and all those gifts devout people were accustomed to bring in thanks to the Lord; and he praised within his soul the goodness of God who is always ready with mercy, as he was unable to do it in words since joy made him tongue-tied with the nooses of its sweetness. When he had finished making his offerings, he returned to the usual dwelling, rejoicing in God's grace together with Anna. At that time they seemed to be souls surrounded by bliss and glory rather than human beings.

Birth of Mary the Virgin. Aurora, already appearing in the window to the East, let fall from her breast the most beautiful, fresh, and sweet roses she had ever gathered in the heavenly gardens, as Anna, gazing with her lovely eyes at the roads to Paradise, and absorbed with certain joy, worshiped the Lord.[33] Having finished her discourse with the Lord, she felt a movement in her womb that she had not felt before, by which she understood that the longed-for moment of birth was drawing near. So she lay down modestly on her holy and chaste marriage bed. Concentrating on divine things, she was so exalted in contemplation that she neither heard her women's conversation nor any sound that could be made, however great. And behold, the rose, brought forth with little pain by her mother Anna, peeps out from the maternal shell, fragrant in her fine features. Behold the blessed little Angel who, coming out of the holy womb, made the world worthy of itself. Behold the great Lady, a little baby girl who gazes at the world full of sorrow with the eyes of her merciful goodness.

Joy at the birth of Mary. Then, it may be truly believed, cloudbursts of lilies, privets, and violets, whiter than the snow's whiteness and the shine of pearls, came down from the heavenly regions.[34] The entire bedroom must have been full of the sweet fragrance given off by the variety of flowers gathered by angels in the heavenly gardens. The stirring of feathers and beating of wings made by the spirits of Paradise through their mansion must

33. In Greek mythology, Aurora is the goddess of the dawn, often referred to as "rosy-fingered" by Homer.

34. These flowers and plants are all symbols of the Virgin, because of their whiteness and purity. A privet is a semi-evergreen shrub of the olive family, with snow-white flowers and black berries; the violet was the Christian symbol of humility, and appears in images of the Christ child, and the Virgin and child. My thanks to Paul Taylor for this information.

have been heard by the lucky and amazed servant women, so that they must have become like people in the presence of miracles.[35] The sparkling stars spread sparks of fire and gold from the tips of their rays and, gathered in joy, awaited the happy day when they would crown Mary's divine and superhuman beauty with the intensity of their splendors. At the same time the fixed stars traveled (as I should like to imagine them) through the sky, and some planets put themselves in the places of the fixed lights. Then, more than usually joyful, with cries exulting in the bliss of so much joy, the angels before the throne of the heights of the divine Majesty praised the newborn goddess, and singing, tuned their voices to the sound of the holy lyres fingered by the heavenly sirens. The sun doubled its light, and was seen surrounded by such intense rays that, charmed by its own beauty, it rose higher than its usual height along its normal orbit. Snakes, having put aside their natural poison, played among the green of the grasses and the variety of flowers without wounding the foot of the incautious shepherdess. The spring winds released their warm breaths with loving sweetness and went lightly tasting the charming scent given off by the roses and lilies. The birds dancing from branch to branch joyfully honored the great birth of the Virgin with the harmony of their songs. The sky itself was adorned with the most shining splendors: the air was tranquil and at its most peaceful; the waters had lost their muddiness and seemed like flowing crystals; the earth was clothed in the delightful cloak of spring, and therefore all rejoiced.

Joachim thinks of God's power. At this time, according to some, Anna's husband sat on a rock, dressed in clothes similar in color to ears of corn when the peasants softly play their pipes at harvest. His right hand was on his right leg and his left cheek was resting on the palm of his other hand, with his elbow on his left knee. He was wondering to himself about the kindness, providence, glory, and goodness of God. And it came to pass that he was lulled in divine contemplation despite the news that was becoming apparent in everything, and his contemplating heart awoke to look at such miracles. As he gazed at the splendor of Heaven, the brightness of the air, the purity of the waters, and the joy of the earth, he saw an Angel coming from the right, dressed in white vestments similar to the whiteness of the dawn, or to that of lily petals as they gather the riches of the pearls that Aurora's lavish hand spills on them. His face was brighter than the sun's. He said to Joachim: "Why do you not now direct hasty steps to your home, upright man, since she who Heaven promised has been born to Anna?" Having said this, he disappeared from Joachim's sight. Amazed, Joachim rose to his feet and set off

35. See the introduction to this chapter for Marinella's use of pictorial imagery (124–25).

to find her who with similar thoughts, and similar wishes, and purposes, had been united to him by the yoke of matrimony. The nearer he came to his house, so much greater miracles made themselves evident.

When he entered the house, which was more like the sun's home, or Aurora's bedchamber, as it was decked with flowers and flashes of light, and scented and lit, he stopped in the doorway with a gesture of amazement, put his hand once and then twice to his eyes, his weak sight unable to bear the strength of the heavenly rays. Finally, having reassured himself somewhat, he saw Anna, the venerable matron, lying among feather cushions, surrounded by the beauty of lilies and jasmine, with a divine rather than human majesty, and beside her the newborn goddess. Confused by the sight of the new miracles, and already certain of his happiness, the righteous man went toward the bed, and as he drew nearer, paternal tenderness filled his joyful heart and made tears of joy fall from his eyes over his wrinkled cheeks, his white beard, and his clothes. Then Anna, whose mind until that moment had been in Heaven, where she saw her daughter, to whom she knew she had given birth, seated in the height of the Thrones, adored and revered queen of blessed souls, was dazzled by bliss in her return to herself, and heard Joachim's voice, saying, "Anna, is this your daughter or the Angel of God? [36] Since she has brought such beauty from Heaven I dare not gaze at her wonderful appearance." She said, replying, "This is the daughter of God, to whom I have given birth with light exertion and pain."[37]

Joachim thanks God for having given him his daughter. Then Joachim, falling to his knees, raised his eyes, full of tears, to the heavenly regions, and clasping his hands together and holding them outwards, spoke such words as these:

> O Mover of Heaven, O cause of causes, of whose infinite and immense power, man, who is small and finite, can establish neither the end nor the measure, we give You those thanks that may be given to You from the lips of humankind; since You have made us worthy not only of having a child, but have also created her from whose pure virginity will come forth the One who will be the salvation of His people, we, Your servants, therefore give and consecrate to Your great name, with the souls of our spirits, the daughter whom You have been pleased to give us.

36. By "Thrones," Marinella may be indicating the third order of angels as described by Dionysius the Pseudo-Areopagite in his *Celestial Hierarchies*.

37. Anna's giving birth virtually painlessly to the Virgin Mary prefigures the painlessness of the Virgin's giving birth to Jesus.

On saying this, he bowed to Heaven and was silent.

Anna gives thanks to the Lord for her daughter. Similarly, Anna, lifting her face, full of gentleness, to the heavenly house, and with her right hand on her breast, and her left arm and hand held out, said in a low voice:

> O eternal King, to whom the impossible is easy, I praise, adore, and thank Your power, Your deity, and Your love, since at the end of our days, it has pleased You to enrich our poor barrenness with a creature to whom the angels bow, full of wonder at her beauty and her virtues, and to whom not only statues will be erected, incense burned, and vows consecrated, but also hearts, burning with zeal, be dedicated to chastity. The daughter You have given us, we dedicate to perpetual chastity, with the sincerity of our hearts; and unable to utter Your name in words, to thank You for such a gift, I will become silent, as Your immense favors are miraculous. So that You are more praised with the voice of our silence than with words.[38]

Joachim and Anna contemplate Mary's beauties. Then Joachim took the wonderful baby girl in his arms and presented her to his wife Anna, and when they had blessed her, they began to contemplate her with wonder in their souls. First they gazed at her hair, which, most soft and curly, shone in its bright blondness; marveling, they saw coming from her brow the rays of that divinity with which God had adorned her before time, and which encircled her golden hair almost like a royal tiara. It seemed to them that they could see coming from her bright eyes flashes of salvation and peace: perfumes other than ambrosial issued from her beautiful mouth, her lips shining like the brightness and brilliance thought to be in cherubim wings. Her cheeks trembled in the tenderness of milk and blood. The whole of her glorious body was a composition of ivory, which breathed, on which nature had sprinkled the rosiness of Aurora's cheeks. They could not have enough of looking upon that divine face, whose salvation-giving demeanor nourished their hopes, so that they experienced the joy of a person who sees his or her desire united to supreme joy. Elderly Joachim seemed to become younger in the pleasure that he took in laying out and heating the soft cloths and white swaddling clothes that maternal prudence turned and wrapped around her.

38. Anna confirms her daughter's dedication by her parents to perpetual virginity (see above, note 21). Reference to Mary's vow of perpetual virginity is to be found in the Gospel of Pseudo-Matthew, the locus of this concept, and is not stated in Luke nor in either of the two other synoptic Gospels. See James, *Apocryphal New Testament,* 73.

Anna, baring her bosom, offered her the milk's sweetness, which gushed from the sources of her breast. When she had given her the white liquid that arose in her breast, Joachim, as I seem to see, with a happy look, took the baby in his arms, amusing her with tender caresses and imprinting with a kiss on her cheeks the affection of his heart. She never turned her parents' love into anxiety through her tears since, if she sometimes cried, they saw her eyes and cheeks wet without hearing the weak, sorrowful laments that other babies made.[39]

Mary grows up. The glorious young girl grew, like a gentle plant grows in the softness of the earth, while in her favor the light wind, sun, and dawn, with their loveliness, strength, and dewdrops, cherished, warmed, and refreshed her. She reached the age of five, and in her behavior, actions, manners, words, and in her laugh showed the manners, beauty, and knowledge of the angels. Her own parents, therefore, amazed at such a sight, always listened to her, gazed at her, and touched her with respectful humility, recognizing the excellences in her manners that shone in her like the multitude of buds comprised in the circle of a rosebush, about to open. It is impossible to think of, even describe, the purity and refinement of her body through which her soul showed its light in the way the moon, veiled by the whiteness of a fine cloud, is revealed; and despite her youth, she fasted often, and was always praying or discussing holy matters.

Virgins who were in Solomon's Temple to serve God. At that time Father Joachim and Anna, venerating, resolved to offer God the gift already promised to Him with the sincerity of their love, even though they felt their souls leave their breasts when they thought of being deprived of her. However, as servants of the One who governs all with His intellect, they arranged a great and honored display and many sacrifices in Solomon's great Temple. They first called all the priestly company together to make offerings in the holy monastery where the virgins, their Queen, were, who lived there, placed by their parents or relations until the time came to join them in marriage. The young girls were all from illustrious lineage, of noble blood, all daughters of princes, high lords, and lordships who competed to put their daughters there, so that they were made fully learned in religion, in the divine cult, and in the knowledge of the Holy Scriptures. Therefore there was great honor

39. This domestic scene is derived from contemporary images of the birth of the Virgin, but with Marinella's own interpolation of Joachim's presence. Anna is usually shown lying in bed, while nurses wash and swaddle Mary; this is followed by Joachim's entry, having been in another room waiting. Marinella's scene is intimately described and extremely unusual in having Joachim laying out and heating the swaddling clothes and observing Anna's breast-feeding of Mary.

and glorification to any man who might receive one of these young girls as his wife.[40]

Mary is offered by her parents to God. Led by her parents to God's great mansion, and accompanied by all the tribe of Judah, Mary was seen by Zaccharias, who understood in the gentleness of her manner the blessed and venerable condition for which she would be renowned in a holy way. Then, in high solemnity, the wonderful creature was offered by them to the King of eternal understanding. The various hymns had already begun, and the high altar was lit up by abundant lights. Then a golden ball, similar to the sun, appeared on high (as some writers relate), above the head of the dedicated Virgin, and, as when the sun hides the unbearable light of its rays among a few clouds, the ball, bursting into many flames, and the flames into many sparks, brought a marvelous splendor into the holy mansion.[41] Those who saw the heavenly light were amazed. After the prayers and sacrifices had ended, she, who is His sole glory, rose to her feet, and turning her tranquil and humble holy eyes two or three times toward the dense throng of people, and then, like a person who first thinks of the meaning of words and then speaks, remained a little silent in thought, and then breaking the silence, made her soul's intention heard by the people around. First opening her gracious lips in a most majestic way, she gave thanks to God who had made a sign to her that she was pleasing to Him. And in a manner only used by her here on earth, and perhaps by the angels in Heaven, she bowed to the high priests, the priests, the large gathering of families and friends, and holding out her merciful arms with tender love, wordlessly embraced the just Father and perfect Mother. For that reason, love, which she was bringing them, took possession of their souls in such a way that it was impossible not to kiss them and bless them with her soul's emotions and gestures of her hands. The parents, taken by an excess of love for their daughter, were unable to talk or scarcely move, seeming more like statues than living persons. Then moving her tiny feet, and going up the great staircase, Mary entered the humble place where the young girls lived, to serve the One who is alone the beauty of all beauties.[42]

40. The source for the Virgin's life in the Temple is the Book of James (James, *Apocryphal New Testament,* 41–43), and details are further elaborated in the Gospel of Pseudo-Matthew (ibid., 73–74). The story is also related in the *Golden Legend,* 2:152–53. Young Jewish girls were not, however, allowed into the inner Temple, nor dedicated to it, as had happened in pagan times.

41. The writers of the apocryphal texts were clearly Greek, or from a milieu in which vestal virgins were part of the late classical temple.

42. The image of the tiny Virgin walking up the Temple steps occurs in almost every cycle of her life, and is known as the Presentation of the Virgin in the Temple. It first occurs in the Gospel of Pseudo-Matthew (James, *Apocryphal New Testament,* 73).

Joachim and Anna return to Nazareth. On returning to their home in Nazareth, Joachim and Anna, their brows, where serenity and joy of peaceful souls were once gathered, and were now surrounded by gloomy darkness, spoke little, as may be believed; they scarcely smiled and were like parents whose children, the hope and amusement of their old age, have been torn from their arms by death. Their daughter's worthy words, gentle laughs, chaste kisses, and dear embraces were always present in their minds. And thus they had fixed their minds on her, so that wherever they looked they saw her before them, and often when sleep with its pleasures lulled the unease of their minds, they saw her seated with divine majesty in God's wonderful Temple, crowned by the other virgins like the sun surrounded by stars or a rose encircled by flowers of lesser worth; the virgins not only honored her as something superhuman but, with devoted gentleness, adored her. Awakened, [the parents] were consoled by visions and memories of her.

It is said that every day, at the hour of feasting, or at *none*, the Angel of God, surrounded by light, brought Mary food cooked by angels with the heat of that fire with which the purity of blessed souls burns.[43] This should not seem extraordinary to anyone, as God's greatest mercy did the same for Daniel, Elijah, and many fathers living in solitude in the deserts; sometimes, even, the food was doubled for them when they had to include their pilgrims. Therefore it should seem to us as something most appropriate that everyday things necessary to the frugality of her holy way of living were brought to her with the wonder, fear, and reverence of the surrounding virgins, to her in whom all the virtues and excellences of Heaven were united, and who was full of the divine spirit and chosen by the One who moves all for the Mother of His only Son.[44]

What the young Girls did in the Temple. These young girls proceeded in turns to carry out the duties given them by the holy priests (and this is still the case amongst us today).[45] At dawn they entered the Lord's golden Temple, singing

43. *None* (Latin, *nona*) is the third of the daytime canonical hours of prayer, appointed for the ninth hour (three p.m.). The Desert Fathers were said to have heavenly food brought to them by angels; we thus see images of Saints Jerome and Mary Magdalen being fed by angels.

44. The legendary figure of Daniel, renowned for his wisdom and piety, appears in Ezekiel 14:14 and 28:3. The Book of Daniel, which was traditionally ascribed to him, contains the popular stories of the Burning Fiery Furnace, Belshazzar's Feast, and the Lions' Den (Daniel 6:16–24), where Daniel in the den is brought food by an angel and is protected by the angel from the lions. Elijah was the most famous of the so-called ecstatic prophets of the ninth century BCE. His overcoming of Jezebel is told in 1 Kings 18:38; he is named in the New Testament (Matthew 17:10–13).

45. As noted above (note 40), young Jewish girls were not brought and left in the Temple; Marinella may be describing the activities of young novices in the Church.

psalms, some putting candles into the golden candelabra, which they whitened through the whiteness of the wax; others made the tiles shine, which had been darkened by the frequent footsteps of others; some decorated the holy altars with splendid church hangings; others placed gilded vases on them. The great Temple embellished and cleaned, words and hearts then turned to God. At terce some went to eat, food without which our lives could not be maintained, and some others remained to take care of the divine rituals.[46] When they were refreshed, they returned. Then those who had stayed went to eat food that, to them, was a magnificent and royal preparation. They made lace from feasting to none, decorating the great cloaks and stiff golden vestments with pearls for the high priests and for the holy altars. Afterward they read the Holy Scriptures.

Mary's virtues. In the holiness of such a place, Mary went in her youthful state with so mature a step that paternal hopes could not have asked for more. The light of her merits already not only lit the earth but Heaven; she was already known for her excellent nature and divine soul as queen of those virtues that are usually desired but not found in a person who is supremely happy, as everything she did was done with the greatest of prudence, foresight, and providence. There has never been, nor will there be anyone, after Adam gazed at the world's marvels, who with a greater sense of justice gave to each what was appropriate. With her strength of soul, she was always ready to thwart frightening encounters, and to not deviate from that good that is modesty, the cause of all good, which she harbored in the center of her heart, as if in its own nest. She ate sparingly, and only as much food as was humanly necessary. The firmness of hope, the inviolability of faith, and the fervor of charity were found at their most perfect and in their own essence in her.[47] She therefore passionately loved God and those nearest with a tender love. Some other virtues accompanied and honored these, her highest gifts, deriving from them, such as her unswerving fortitude in unfortunate circumstances. Her patience was unyielding: she was most humble and full of peaceful fidelity. Swollen pride, punishable talkativeness, impetuous rage, and tenacity of greed were all far removed from her.[48] The same gentleness, charm, and modesty were in both her actions and her deeds. She did pious

46. Terce (Latin, *tertia*) was the first of the daytime canonical hours of prayer, appointed for the third hour of the day (around nine a.m.). The name given to the office appointed for that hour also commemorates the hour of Christ's crucifixion.

47. The Virgin exemplifies the theological virtues, faith, hope, and charity. She is also the model of moral virtues such as prudence, foresight, providence, and frugality.

48. Pride, vanity, garrulousness, rage, and greed are vices usually associated with the female sex in sermons and literature describing female conduct.

works that surpassed that same piety. No one could ever say that she had obscured truth's serenity with the shadow of untruth. Therefore one could compare the sight and the reputation, which originated from and was caused by this illustrious daughter illuminated by divine grace, with that delicate display and agreeable scent that originates from the brilliant lily in the field, where it takes its lively whiteness to nature's glory.

Mary's wisdom. The most serene Lady had the greatest abundance of divine grace and of all the kinds of virtue and manners that could be found in human actions, manners, and virtues, because in creating her God poured into her as much good and beauty as the power of His right hand was able. Therefore she was perfect in will, election, free will, and judgment.[49] The purity that burns in a cherubim burned in her heart, and founts of eternal wisdom sprang from her soul. However, the virgins, priests, and high priests were all overcome by wonder on hearing her interpretations of the obscure meanings of the Holy Scriptures and the way she sweetly unlocked confused interpretations in the arcane subjects, arching her brows and pursing her lips together. The listening girls understood with thoughtful reasoning the least part of the marvels that she told them, but in the process of time they easily understood (thanks to her) with their souls' apprehension the beauties of the meanings, by the powers of which is sustained the most wonderful body of the great Bible. Similarly she showed them the way that anyone had to go who wished to please God, who made all perfect, and which things they had to avoid, such as mortal sin; and how they should spend the days of their lives thinking of God and for God, and showed how our lives are like the day, which in a few hours comes to its end, encouraging them to put all their hopes and love in the Giver of all good. And with many words, but few in respect of the greatness of the mysteries, which are hidden, she directed, strengthened, and invited the passionate minds of the young girls to Heaven. Her discourses benefited their souls in the way that grass scorched by the sun feels when it absorbs rain.[50]

Mary wishes to serve the woman who will be chosen by God as Mother of His Son. Her divine intellect was in a way endowed with the knowledge of the Holy Scriptures, so that her mind's eye bore the light of the splendors to which the tongues and pens of God's scribes had access in dark prophetic passages.

49. Election (Greek, *eklogi*, "choice") is an act of the Divine Will.

50. Mary's wisdom and her life in the Temple are related in the *Meditations*. See Pseudo-Bonaventure, or Giovanni de Caulibus, *Meditations on the Life of Christ: An Illustrated Manuscript of the Fourteenth Century. Paris, Bibliothèque nationale, Ms. Ital. 115*, trans. by Isa Ragusa, ed. Isa Ragusa and Rosalie B. Green (Princeton, NJ: Princeton University Press, 1961), 10–14.

Among the obscure readings that very often exercised the mind, the holy Virgin read the words of Isaiah the prophet, from which it was understood that the Savior of the world was to be born of a woman, both virgin and chaste.[51] However, as she wished to see or to serve the woman chosen by God for so great a dignity, she let fall a teardrop from her beautiful eyes, and fixing her eyes on Heaven's serenity, her palms resting on her virginal breast, she spoke meekly in this fashion: "Lord, whose bounty anticipates our requests, may it overcome my so great lowliness and unworthiness to make me worthy of being one of the maidservants of that blessed maiden from whose pure virginity the salvation of lost humanity is to come. But if my request is reckless and my wish too lofty, allow me to kiss the earth where the happy lady places her foot; forgive the simplicity that loosens my tongue, as I am perhaps asking something impossible and unbecoming." Then, penitent for having spoken too passionately to God, she grew shy, sorrowful, and ashamed: Aurora's tears spilt into the centers of roses are not as beautiful as the dew love dropped, mixed with fear, from her eyes.

Heavenly dove that comforts Mary. They say that while her eyes were on Heaven, she saw coming, and did not know from where, a dove, fluttering its silver wings through the joyful air, bringing light to the sun's crown and sweetly surrounding her splendid head. It said, in a voice more divine than human: "O Virgin, Heaven has chosen you for the highest honor." Then he flashed a ray toward her, filling her with joy and with new comfort, adding that, in the future, he hoped to serve her, the one whom the angels had to obey. And, more fervently than ever, she thanked her Creator for the grace He deigned to grant her.[52]

As time swiftly passed, it brought those days when the group of honored virgins was led in solemn ritual to the sacrament joining two lives, two souls, and two wishes within the same knot. Every day a virgin left the Temple married to this one or that. As anyone might imagine, prayers and sacrifices were made to God and to priests by this young man and that one, asking for Mary as his bride. Amazed by the excellence of her most beautiful soul, housed in the most beautiful body that nature ever created, they wished to do nothing without a sign from God, because they knew her divine soul and miraculous beauty were things made by Him and for Him.

51. Isaiah 7:14: "Therefore the Lord himself shall give you a sign. Behold a virgin shall conceive and bear a son: and his name shall be called Emmanuel." This passage serves to stress Mary's humility in that it never occurred to her that it might be she who would become the Mother of God.

52. Cf. Luke 1:28–38.

Beauty of Anna's daughter. It is impossible to depict in thought, imagine with the intellect, or describe in writing the least part of the sublime beauty with which she was adorned: the world justly revered her, and Heaven loved her, for she was peerless. And not only did she supersede the beauty of all human creatures, but even that of all the heavenly angels. Her hair, fine and wavy, as can be truly believed, was hidden beneath a delicate veil, and was spun of gold far brighter than the sun. The arches of her eyebrows, darting arrows of divine love into the breasts of angels, were blacker and more glistening than ebony. Her modest, gentle eyes spread rays of grace and salvation: her sweet glances prompted chaste desires and holy wishes in others' breasts. The pink of roses and the white of lilies paled in comparison with her cheeks. Her lips could equal rubies had they been quarried in Heaven: even when polished, the highest grade of white ivory never reached the delicate glow of her limbs, supported by life's breath, by the power of her senses and strength of mind. And in her every aspect was a touch of the ineffable, which, being ineffable, cannot be put into words. All that remains is wonder at the miracle, and the miracle of wonder. Her divine beauty was bestowed by nature and by Heaven, not simulated by art, and appeared adorned with all those delights that the heavenly treasure chests almost hoard in their breasts. The heavens were therefore astonished by her excellences and gazed at her with joy and love and coveted her as their own.

The Virgin's clothes. She shone, not among the purples and golds beneath which the swollen vanities of women are concealed, but among the whiteness and simplicity of a pure, plain single robe, a decoration of the soul's ostentation; and the beautiful adornments admired in her seemed to challenge her natural lowliness. Nonetheless, in the purity of such a garment, she appeared almost an angel, shining in the whiteness of his heavenly tunic. Anyone worthy of seeing the joyousness of her actions was amazed by her gracious manners and happy ways. The favor Heaven had poured abundantly into her was revealed in her every movement.

The priests attempt to persuade Mary to marry. Confused by her decision,[53] the holy ministers of the Temple were moved by the awe that divine virtues and the splendor of beauty prompted in others' minds, which they saw in Our Lady's countenance. Assembling together, they decided to persuade her in humble words to do what God had commanded and instituted through the mouths of His holy prophets.[54] Having agreed upon this, they went into her

53. This refers to the apocryphal dedication of Mary to God by her parents. See note 38.

54. God's injunction to his creation ("in his own image . . . male and female created he them") to "be fruitful and multiply" is found in Genesis 1:28.

presence, and the one who, by reason of goodness, authority, and honor preceded the rest, said, in such words, which is a pious thing to believe:

> You must know, O Mary, that the time has already come for you to be chosen as his wife by a man worthy of you, even though we believe that there is no one in this world worthy of you, as we know very well that you are not this world's creature but Heaven's. God's law imposes and commands this. Therefore, prudent maiden, honor His commandments to join yourself in the holy knot of matrimony, with whomever His merciful providence grants you.

Through the simple chastity of her soul, there had never been cheeks sprinkled with such girlish shame (as might be imagined) as the chaste blush that colored Mary's cheeks. She was like someone who is denied what she long wished for and loved, as she had firmly thought of spending those days that God's mercy allowed her in carrying out divine works with perpetual virginity. However, disturbed by these words, she raised her face, sprinkled with tears of modesty, fixed on him the two living stars, gathered together her sighs and released them. Then her voice broke through with audible gravity:

> See, O Maker of what is visible and invisible, into what sorrow the strength of Your Law has put one who believed in keeping her chastity dedicated to You, not only by me, but by my parents, not only after my birth but before my conception. So please reply for her, O bright Guardian of the stars, reply, she begs You, not wanting the Law that came from Your prophets' trumpets to cancel the purity, firmness, and modesty of the heart I consecrated to You.[55]

The high priests were overcome on seeing her humility and hearing her chaste intentions. Confused by the light of her divine virtues, they went to the great Temple to beg the One who is the highest power in all things to obtain advice from Heaven appropriate for settling the matter in an honorable way. Then, kneeling with palms joined together, their minds far from fleeting vanities, they begged the One who possesses all to take care of Mary, who was more worthy of Him than anyone else who had come into the world.

The Virgin is sorrowful. When the priests had left, the Virgin wore herself

55. An apocryphal scene, again to emphasize the Virgin's perpetual virginity.

out in laments, and with anxious thoughts assailing her, began to pray to her Creator and God that He would wish to find an answer for her sorrows.

The Angel consoles Mary. While her grief was pouring tears from her eyes, behold, there was one of those spirits worthy of hearing and of carrying out God's commandments. Standing within the light that emanated from his purely spiritual body, like a sun among its rays, he said:

> Mary, in whose sacred breast holy modesty is seated like pure soul in most purified body, turn your anguish into joy and by your obedience accept the chaste man, the just old man, whom God has already destined to your chaste self. He is all religion, all mercy, all humility, all charity, all goodness, and all faith: virtues for which he is loved by God just as much as he is admired by the world. Accordingly, you will not reject the chaste old man, who will be companion, servant, and guide to you in your goodness, needs, and journeys, and, keeping the vow, you will obey the commandments of the Law.

To the Virgin's troubles, these words were like the tranquil air that calms the stormy waves of the angry sea.[56]

When the dawn of the following morning appeared at the balcony of the East dressed in purple and gold, and the sun had not yet risen to dry the hoar frost on the flower petals, the high priests, surrounded by their usual rituals, worshiped the Lord with heartfelt purpose and passionate fervor.[57]

The divine voice commands the descendants of David to come to the Temple. At that moment, when torches shone and incense made the sweetness of its perfume smell, and when the people communed with the spirit in holy ceremonies and sacred rites, the sky was seen to flash with lightning, as holy men have written, and flashing, to say:

> Upright men, you who do not wander from God's ways, order all those males of the royal house of David, except children and those subject to the yoke of matrimony, to make themselves be seen in this great Temple, holding a small staff in their right hands. And to the one whose withered staff becomes clothed in the beauty of flowers through miraculous will, give Mary as wife, which thus pleases

56. A paraphrase of the justifications for Mary's marriage to Joseph that appear in the *Golden Legend* (1:197).

57. This elaborate description of the dawn is part of the poetic prose that Marinella adopts for her epic narrative.

the One whose powerful hand, hurling harmful lightning, strikes the swollen pride that reigns in the rulers of conceited nations.

At these words, at the sound of the voice, at the wondrous news announced in the holy Temple by the heavenly Messenger, the people were diligent in their holy offices, like those who hear something entirely remote from their expectations. When they heard the divine command, the Temple priests, joyful that the King of Heaven had replied to their requests, cutting short every delay, called all the descendants of the great and distinguished line of the one who, from being a shepherd of his flock, became leader of the Jewish people.[58] The message was spread so that every ear heard its reverberation. Then the golden house of the Lord was immediately full of the illustrious line of Judah, like a swollen river that, thanks to its fury, breaks its banks, submerging the countryside. Each naturally entertained a slight hope that the Lord's will would choose him as consort of the glorious Virgin. Do not think that amongst so many there would be anyone who would pass into the spheres of dishonorable lust with licentious thoughts since, I say, not only in seeing her but in thinking of her, minds became havens of holy chastity!

Joachim and Anna come to find Mary. At the same time Fame with its clamor proclaimed the wonderful betrothal of the miraculous daughter of Joachim and Anna. On hearing this, and filled with incomparable joy, they arrived at the holy hospice, home of virginal purity, hastening their slow and dull feet. Her dear parents arrived precisely when the glorious maiden had been consoled by the Angel. Filled with the loving tenderness they bore her, they could not prevent their hands from trembling, their faces turning pale, and their eyes overflowing with loving tears. After repeated embraces and kisses from parents to daughter and from daughter to parents, and after some words full of warm affection and fatherly love, Joachim went to the Temple to see who it was, so pleasing to Heaven, whose hands were to support the greatness of such a miracle.

The high priests and other priests, adorned and clothed in garments usually worn for ceremonies, stood around the sacrifice among the lamps and perfumes of the sacred incense. Kneeling with withered staffs in their hands, the noble young men from the house of Judah, empty of all lascivious desire, prayed to God that the generosity of His mercy would grant them the great favor of obtaining the Virgin as their bride. The crowds of people who had come to see the result of such an event had taken up all the empty places in the Temple. However, Joachim, weighed down by his years, as may

58. This circumlocution alludes to David.

well be believed, sat down in a place declined by the people, and while he was there prayed and waited, praying and waiting for the miracle in which white flowers would blossom on the infertile staff.

The High Priest calls Joseph to him. Then Joachim heard the great High Priest's voice call Joseph: "O, Joseph of Bethlehem, the supreme Maker reveals you to my eyes. Come to me, righteous man, as God commands you." And beckoning to him, he made all the multitude's eyes turn to him. At the sound of the sacred High Priest's voice Joseph was bewildered and disturbed, no differently from anyone who sees himself raised to a lofty rank, the height of which he dreads. Turning his eyes to the man from Bethlehem, Joachim knew by his calm appearance that simple goodness was innate to his disposition. Then rising to his feet, and walking through the assembled people, Joseph knelt before the High Priest and told him how his vow of virginity and the chastity of old age distinguished him from the others, and that he had hidden the withered wood beneath the cloak that covered him.[59] It seemed to him that he had thus obeyed God, since he had come to where he had been called and, at his age, he had sat down in a suitable place. Revealing the staff to obey the Priest, he held it between his clasped hands and, as he was praying, did not hear the great Priest praise his holy intention with lofty words.

The withered staff flowers for Joseph. Behold, in less time, as many can verify, than I can relate, the infertile wood became clothed in the whiteness of the most beautiful, delightful, and scented flowers that had ever smelt sweetly or had been seen. God's house was then filled with their sweetness. The people watching the scene, seeing the flowers turn white in the hands of an old man who was nearing his last days, expressed the wonder in their souls.[60]

Joachim was somewhat stupefied on seeing the miracle take place in the old man's trembling hands. But then thinking of the truth that God had told him through the words of His blessed Messenger, such as Mary's pure virginity producing heavenly fruit through divine power, he praised and thanked the Creator of the world.[61] Suddenly, he rose to his feet, going to his daughter and to Anna, who were awaiting the outcome of God's will. Then the High Priest and the holy priests called the Virgin to the Temple. Praising

59. In the Book of James, Joseph's excuse not to marry the Virgin is that he is too old for her, already has sons, and does not wish to become a laughingstock (James, *Apocryphal New Testament,* 42). See also volume editor's introduction, 22.

60. The story of Joseph and the flowering rod first appeared in the Book of James (James, *Apocryphal New Testament,* 42). Marinella emphasizes an aged Joseph to reinforce the concept of the Virgin's purity.

61. Cf. Matthew 1:18–25.

God's name and His works, and with reverent humility in her simple native grace, she entered the Temple between Joachim and Anna. The marvelous countenance of God's daughter as she appeared to the assembled people was far more beautiful than even Aurora who, when the skies are clearest, shows off the gold, lilies, and roses of her hair, breast, and cheeks from the eastern balcony.

The High Priest's conversation with Mary and Joseph. On her arrival in the High Priest's presence, and placing her tender knees on the firm ground, the Virgin raised her eyes and mind to Heaven. And in solemn voice, the Priest intoned the following words: "It pleases the Lord, who restrains and drives the stillness and wandering of the moving and fixed stars, that Mary and Joseph be united together under that yoke, the sweet power of which makes two bodies live within one single spirit and one single wish." Hearing such words, the modest young girl shamefacedly lowered her eyes and let the shame be seen burning in her face, painted in its crimson hues. Then, raising her eyes again to Heaven, she said in her sweet voice words like these: "My will is ready, O Creator of all. I accept the husband that Your will and miracle offer me." Then turning with those eyes that calm the sea's stormy pride toward Joseph, who was astonished, she said, "I will be to you, who are chaste, whatever it pleases God, who has chosen you as my husband."

Betrothal of the Virgin. It seems to me that he reverently said to her, "He is pleased (for so He has shown to my soul) that I should be your husband in name, father in years, servant in obeying you, and companion in goodness."[62] Having said this, the aged saint placed on her holy finger the blessed ring, the sign of peace and faith.

At the end of the magnificent betrothal, and after the greetings and praises given by Joseph to Joachim and Anna, and by Anna and Joachim to Joseph, Joseph returned to Bethlehem to arrange the chaste wedding. Having bowed to the High Priest and priests, and bidding farewell to the virgins, the Virgin departed with her dear parents, leaving there the sense of loss, a widowhood of sorts, that remains to those children whose father goes off to travel along unknown paths. The young girls, used to chasing after the flowers of the words she uttered, consoled themselves in her absence, feeling bereft of either soul or spirit. It is said, when they saw the Temple deprived of her services and of her look and of her prayers of praise, that in perpetual memory of her merits the sorrowful priests placed in the spot where holy relics were kept the dried staffs held in the hands of the descendants of David

62. The emphasis on Joseph's chastity and age is again to strengthen the impossibility of the Virgin and Joseph having sexual relations.

who, with repentance of soul, tears of eyes, and the sound of his lyre, had made contrite, had bathed, and had mellowed the boldness of his heart, with his tears flowing from his eyes, and sweetened the bitterness of his soul.[63]

The Virgin returns to Nazareth with her parents. When the noble maiden returned to Nazareth, there was no one so ill or so weak who, hastening the languidness and weakness of his or her feet, did not run to look at the grace and splendor that came from her venerable beauty. Among themselves, they said, "What light, what marvel is this who comes to lighten the shadows that keep our minds drowsy?" Nor did anyone fail to display with their bows and words of honor the reverence her virtues created in their breasts. For that reason, her parents were enjoying being gathered in the arms of contentment and happiness. Having reached the last days of their old age, already tired and trembling, they bent their shoulders beneath their weight of years, and their vital spirits, gnawed by time, were losing their vigor, and the strength of each of their senses had almost lost its own power. They were waiting from moment to moment for death's coldness to destroy that little warmth that life administered to the heart. When they saw and knew the one who would give birth to our salvation, seeing and realizing how useless the nourishment and sweetness of consolation were in keeping them alive, and feeling their extremities become chilled from death's ice, and their feeble and scarcely heard words, Mary was stung by natural charity itself, the compassion of which never loses its gifts. And she allowed herself to be overcome by warm emotions, which create love towards those tied by blood and, yielding to grief, to her age, and nature, she began to weep and lament in such a dear way and with such graceful gestures that it would have softened the hardness of diamonds, let alone human hearts. Not since Eve, our mother, shed the first tears, have other eyes dearer, more beautiful, or gentler, ever wept.[64] Her tears (which, almost a living source of water, sprang from the two clear stars) watered the pale violet of her cheeks where roses were transformed (thanks to the trouble that tormented her breast), and between the sighs and sobs were interspersed some extraordinary cries of woe with such a pitiful sound that it is believed that some spirits in Paradise—as I am imagining in my mind—did not refuse to descend from Heaven to console her.

Joachim and Anna near to death. As they felt their lives reach the last step of their joint voyage, and wholly loving and intent on God, Anna and Joachim

63. For David and his repentance, see above, note 16.

64. The tears of Eve are often referred to. According to the common interpretation of Genesis 1, she would naturally weep for having instigated, as understood by biblical commentators, the Fall and its consequences, travail and pain in childbirth.

called the sorrowing Virgin to them. And as the most excellent old couple became aware of her weeping and laments, one took her by the right hand and the other by the left, and overcome by paternal and maternal love, they were silent, looking at her, and silently wept, and weeping resembled the shadows of afflictions and the images of suffering. Then, finally, Anna, overcoming with love and will power her weakness of tongue, and embracing and kissing her dear daughter, said, as it may be imagined:

> Soul of our hopes, pledge given us by Heaven, do not upset your serene countenance with mists of sorrow and clouds of tears. Do you not know that you understand the most hidden secrets in God's breast, that all humankind, produced by nature, is destined from birth to the frightening tomb? Sorrow, which grieves our hearts, is only on your account, because leaving you afflicts us too much. Through your merits, the Lord has made us worthy of seeing His heavenly visions, and of hearing the most hidden mysteries that have ever had a place in His high intelligence. And although death is the awful end to every creature, nevertheless, having faith in heavenly help and in the ringing cries of your prayers, we know that now, becoming silent, they are crying out on our behalf in God's presence, and we are comforted and willingly go on the path by which He calls us. Therefore may our spirits, comforting you, drive away the suffering that saddens you so that our peace may not be disturbed. And please commend us to Him in your prayers, who reigns over all.

When she had said this, she called the small number of servant girls in her service, in a voice hardly audible, and said to them, "Daughters and sisters, if I have been arrogant out of pride as your mistress in my actions or my speech, or scorned, offended, and humiliated your humility, ears, and condition, I beg you to put aside every aversion and every memory of injury and, excusing our fragility, to forgive me." Here the grand old lady grew silent, and holding Mary with one hand and placing the other on her breast, looked at her intently. The faithful servants were unable to reply to her without weeping and sobbing, as the affection they bore her filled their hearts' veins in such a way that it only allowed them to express it in weeping.

Death of Joachim and Anna. Joachim, turning to the Virgin, and opening his already cold and pale lips with strong emotion, in all likelihood said:

> Daughter, soul of our souls, by dying we are returning this body to the earth from which it took its being through the debt of nature. And,

> as we are dying in your presence, we would say that the condition of our death is happy. Closing our eyes to the light of day, we shall sleep that great, long, and deep sleep of death in the sepulcher, until the angelic trumpet sounds to awaken our mortal bodies. We are going on that difficult journey that nature detests, willingly and with readiness of heart, since we love God and, loving Him, we want Him, and wanting Him we hope, and hoping for Him we will rejoice in Him, if this pleases Him. But, adornment of our honors, as the little light that remains to my eyes is already darkening, I feel I lack my usual strength. I am dying.

"However, we beg you to never forget," he wanted to say, "our love," but was unable to. Then he attempted two or three times to put his arms around the grieving Virgin's neck, and would have done so if the weakness and trembling that enfeebled his arms, making them collapse, had allowed him. The tenderness of such words pierced Mary's kind heart in such a way that tears that she was trying to hold back out of a sense of prudence poured from her eyes. And as she embraced and kissed her already cold father and her chilled mother, with her silence she represented silence itself, since her sorrow would not allow her to say a word. According to some, and it is quite likely, she saw coming from their mouths two very bright flames, almost two stars, arranged in their most joyful and most brightly shining guise.[65] Drawing nearer to each other, they fused together two rays that derived from their beauties. At such a sight, between joy and sorrow, the sorrowful young girl, kneeling and raising her arms and hands up high, said:

> Go, glorious souls, to the seats that the One who is alone mercy has prepared for you. And as you were united in a holy bond on earth, may you enjoy happiness together among the holiness of the blessed Fathers. You may be certain that I shall always commend you to Him in the prayers and words that my soul directs toward God. And you will have those honors that are due to you from me, since I know very well the origins of this soul and these limbs come first from God's supreme hand, and then from you. Your virtues, goodness, and compassion, blessed souls, merited that the King of Heaven showed you the holiness of His visions and revealed His hidden secrets to your eyes and minds; and, after a long and happy period of years together spent

65. This scene is drawn from Aretino's *Vita di Maria Vergine* (ff. 52r–53r).

with love, He called your souls, embellished with the same splendor, to eternal rest at the same time and at the same moment.

Then, with honorable funeral ceremonies, the most serene Lady had the sacred bodies of her great parents closed up in the marble tombs of her illustrious forebears.[66]

Joseph learns how the Virgin's parents went to eternal rest. While Joseph, the nobleman of Bethlehem, was taking care of the arrangements for the holy wedding, he heard from one of Mary's messengers how just Joachim, his father-in-law, and perfect Anna, his mother-in-law, had on the same day and at the same time returned their souls to the One who had created them. Then, overcome by such sorrow, he was unable to stop the streams of tears overflowing their banks and drenching his face. Leaving his own region in haste, having charged some of his affairs to his friends, he went with the messenger to Nazareth. On the way, the latter told Joseph about the great actions, magnificent works, and his parents-in-law's holy words. I believe that while he listened to these words, Joseph often looked toward Heaven.

Joseph reaches the Virgin. On arriving in Nazareth, he grieved with Mary, as so great a loss required. And he comforted her little as he was well aware that she did not need comforting since she had been born to calm others' sorrows. Hearing her parents' dear names mentioned, she could not check her tears, which drenched her face and breast, but soon dried them so as not to trouble the souls of her beloved dead people.[67] That same reverence and honor that she had brought to her father Joachim, she brought to Joseph, who, tired and wearied by the journey and his age, rested and took that nourishment that sustains our mortal bodies in life. O, how many times while he was eating, thinking of the virtues of the dead holy people, almost as though he had forgotten what abstinence required of his body, did he have to stop with his mouth full, and sighing, raise his brows, and bless them silently, or in a loud voice, and return to the almost forgotten food, thinking himself happy only for having known them. The Virgin, as the one born to

66. The genealogy of Christ from Abraham to Joseph begins Saint Matthew's Gospel (1:1–16), and we also learn that Joseph is of the house of David in Luke 1:27. Nothing is known, however, of Mary's lineage until in the Book of James it is stated that her father Joachim is "extremely rich" (James, *Apocryphal New Testament,* 39); in the Pseudo-Matthew, Joachim is of the tribe of Judah, wealthy, and marries Anna, daughter of Ysachar (ibid., 73).

67. This would seem to contradict the previous sentence, which describes Mary as not requiring comforting!

relieve the poor, gave away many of the few possessions she had inherited. Her holy mind was always absorbed in divine contemplation, her chaste hands in holy almsgiving, and her charming mouth in divine prayer.

BOOK TWO

Summary: *This second book relates how the One who is the utmost perfection decides to send His Son to the lowly earth for the salvation of all. He tells Gabriel to announce the Incarnation of Christ to Mary. She thanks the supreme Creator. Then she goes to Elizabeth and extols the greatness of the Lord's works. After she has stayed there for three months, she returns to Nazareth. Joseph comes to find the Virgin, and his serene expression is disturbed by [the news of] her pregnancy. The Angel reassures him about the chastity of her soul and body. Caesar Augustus has the people subject to his great majesty register themselves. Mary and Joseph go to Bethlehem, where our Redeemer is born. Then countless miracles appear throughout the world. An Angel signals the great birth of Jesus to shepherds, who go to adore Him. The Star appears in the East, and the Magi, following its brightness, come to Bethlehem to adore Jesus and offer Him gifts. Mary goes to Jerusalem, to the golden Temple of God, to have her Son circumcised. The beauties of the Temple of Solomon are described. Anna the Prophetess tells the people that Jesus is the true Messiah. Distressed by Simeon's words, the Virgin returns to Bethlehem and then to Nazareth. The Angel appears to Joseph, and advises him to take Jesus and Mary to Egypt. Then in the deep silence of the night, they leave Nazareth, obedient to the Angel's commands.*

God decides to send His only Son to earth. The Creator of all, surrounded by the vermilion splendor of cherubim and seraphim and seated on the throne of His glory, trod the heads of time, nature, and circumstance beneath His sacred soles. Being as far away from the heaven that is nearest us as Heaven is from hell, no less did He listen to the sorrowful sound sent to Him by the misfortunes of the human race than He heard its sighs and saw its tears.

Then, turning the salvation of His blessed eyes through the wide spaces of the great celestial palace, He saw that an almost infinite number of thrones were empty, as the pride of the infernal angels fell:[68] and lowering His gentle gaze, and penetrating into the innermost parts of the world He had created, He saw with His sorrowful mercy, so tender to our injuries, the common enemy who, in his proud nature, rode on his chariots and beneath his own banners, leading countless victims stolen from Heaven into the abyss with the claws of his wickedness. He knew how the goodness of the good longed to see the unfortunate souls, now unhappily fallen into the devil's

68. The fall of the angels is referred to in Luke 10:18; Matthew 25:41; 2 Corinthians 12:7.

Figure 9. Engraving showing the Annunciation; the Visitation; the Nativity; the Adoration of the Magi; the Circumcision; and the Flight into Egypt. From the 1602 edition of *La vita di Maria Vergine Imperatrice dell'Universo descritta in prosa & in ottava rima da Lucretia Marinella* (fol. 23v). Reproduced by kind permission of the Biblioteca Nazionale Centrale di Roma.

web, rise through the Messiah's coming, something that had been foretold. He heard the sighs and saw the tears that the blessed fathers spilled in the darkness of Limbo.[69]

Then He rekindled the fire of His mercy and love, which the Stygian waters of our sins continuously maintained, and while it was reviving, extinct, He said, "Behold, the moment we have been waiting for has arrived when I shall dry the dew of the tears that continuously falls on the flowers of their hopes by sending the heat and light of that Sun that restores light to the heavenly spaces, from the highest mountain-top of Heaven."[70] As He said this, the heavens trembled through reverence, and Nature, shrunk into herself, showed Him her generosity, by now tired of nourishing the people who were being drawn into the eternal abyss by inimical evil. At the same time the Virgin was praying and, glad in His continual joy, He welcomed the innocence, purity, and fervor of her prayers. Then, with a marvelous appearance and serene brow, He turned His gaze, whereupon the storms in the air and sea were calmed. He fixed it on her, and having gazed at the purity of her life, calmness of her will, and righteousness of her deeds, raised the eyes that delighted Paradise, showing His desire to speak. The harmony of the divine lyres, the motionless instability of the heavens, the voices, and the angelic wings thus turned into the stillness of silence. And He motioned to Gabriel, the prince of an angelic hierarchy, to come to Him, who immediately and reverently appeared in the great presence. With His voice made of the purity and simplicity of His divinity, and tuned by a gravity of sound, which was partly understood by the angels, God said something like this to Gabriel:

> *God talks to Gabriel.* Leader and honor of your choir, tell her what I will say to you, she whom I have chosen beyond all the creatures of the world, Mother of my only begotten Son. Now, leaving our Kingdom, you will go down to Judea, the region between Phoenicia and the River Jordan, the noblest of all rivers as it will be worthy of washing

69. In Latin theology, the souls of those who died before the coming of Christ remained in Limbo, the *limbus patrum*. Christ's coming opened the gates of Limbo for the Patriarchs. Whether or not Limbo existed is a matter of theological opinion on which the Church has made no definitive pronouncement; in 2007 the Vatican's International Theological Commission announced that the traditional view of Limbo reflected an "unduly restrictive view of salvation."

70. The Styx was the mythical dark, gloomy river in Hades, over which Charon ferried the souls of the dead.

> the pure humanity of my only Son.[71] You will end your flight in Nazareth, and so that you do not err in carrying such a message, you will recognize the chosen Virgin's house by a light that, coming out of its roof, will reach the sky, almost a golden streak. In my name, you will tell her that I wish the divine person of my Son, clothed in the garb of humanity with the might of my spirit, to be in her chaste womb.

Here He was silent, the One who gave sweetness to the heavenly harmonies.

The lily Gabriel carries. Gabriel, joyful at seeing himself raised to such a dignity, bowing his head and kneeling with great humility, flew faster than the flight of the mind into one of the gardens of Heaven and picked a lily still full of the sweetness of the dawn-spilt dew, which appears to angels, no other whiteness daring to compare with their measureless whiteness. When he appeared, Heaven opened, and the music of its spheres was heard on earth and rippled in circles like those that form in a tranquil lake when something heavy is thrown in. He dazzled the sun with the flashing light that came out of his hair and wings; and, continuing the journey, he arrived in Nazareth, and blessing it, praised it above the haughtiness of the most magnificent cities. Then he came to a halt on a temple top and, looking around, he recognized the Virgin's house by the brightness of the flame that, emanating from the purity it contained, joined Heaven. And praising the flame, he blessed the precious gem that dwelt within her breast. Then with his wings raised slightly, and beating them somewhat, like a dove that desires to begin its flight, he spread them toward her happy house. The stones and mortar gave way to the power of the Angel's piercing ray.

Gabriel announces to Mary the incarnation of Christ. On going in, he found the Virgin whose mind was raised beyond the things of this world; she was praying to God that He would send His only Son to earth to save all humankind. The Angel filled the entire holy house with light and perfumes, which, compared with the sweetness that came forth from Mary's virginal purity, lost as much of their sweetness as violets do in places where roses flame. He bowed to her gently and reverently and, amazed by her beauty, adored her. Then he said, in a voice used only by angels:

> Hail, Queen of Heaven, whose virtue and beauties have inflamed the heart of the One to whose power all the heavenly and human pow-

71. This refers to Christ's baptism in the River Jordan by John the Baptist (Matthew 3:13–17; Mark 1:9–11; Luke 3:21–22).

> ers yield. In you, you have the supreme abundance of graces. Therefore you are blessed and blissful beyond all the blessed and blissful. The Lord who, with paternal loving eye, watches you from the heavenly spaces, wishes you to conceive, give birth, and give sustenance to the One who will heal sick souls and those in danger of falling into the Abyss.

Bewildered by such a sight and such a message, and entirely bound up in her humility, and unsure about these praises, the Virgin's face paled. But then fear yielding to modesty, she blushed deeply pink, similar to Aurora when the wind, jealous of her face, hides it with the flame-colored veil. Seeing her gathered in her beautiful decorum, silent, fearful, and thoughtful, the heavenly Messenger said:

> Do not be frightened, Mary, Star first seen in the sky before being seen on earth, because the virtue and grace of which you are full, by killing death will draw life from the tomb, life that until now has lain extinct, through your giving birth to Jesus, Savior of the world. He will be called Son of most high God, whose kingdom, as it is eternal, will never end.

With these words he made known the intention of his soul. And, while the blush that inflamed the angels lit her face, she opened her beautiful lips and said, "How can your words ever be true, as I know not man?" And he said, "The power of God's spirit will come down upon you, so that your soul becomes surer of the truth of such a conception. Behold Elizabeth who, in the final years of her old age, has conceived a son, and this is the sixth month of her pregnancy. Thus you may know that God's power is infinite, and also infinite are the marvels of His works."[72]

Mary's reply to the Angel. And showing the gentleness of her meekness and turning her [bodily] eyes, but even more so her spiritual eyes, toward Heaven, she said, it is thought, the following words: "Behold, O omnipotent Father, the lowliness and unworthiness of Your maidservant, who obediently and humbly accepts the truth hidden in the light of the words of Your holy Messenger, and offers You not only her womb and breast, but also her soul and heart." Then a flash of that Sun, which had never set in the humble little room, was seen. Behold the glorious Lady surrounded by rays of immortal

72. Gabriel's salutation here is based on his greeting in Luke 1:28–33, and on the prayer Hail Mary, which is also based on the passage in Luke.

fire! Behold the uncreated Word, which, passing through the purity of the virginal cloister with its immense power, rests in it, like a dove in its nest![73] God's spirit took up residence in her heart and, burning with His love, penetrated lightly through all the inner parts and bones of the happy young girl. The emotions of so much love rendered marvelous things in her, while the person who was full of divinity assumed humanity's body, and Nature, overwhelmed and absorbed by God, truly experienced things never experienced before. As God's power was enclosed in Mary, alight, it began to make her shine, like a star shining in the darkness of night. Leaving behind the lowest part of the world, Gabriel, the Messenger of divine mysteries, unfurling his wings, lifted himself from the earth, and Mary followed him, saying silently, "You, Messenger of God's will, tell Him of my humble obedience." On his arrival in the most serene parts of Heaven, the Angel rejoiced in describing the rare excellences of his Queen to the great Leader.

The Virgin thanks God. The glorious Lady remained marveling, unable to find words worthy of thanking the highest Power, whose incomprehensible kindness had not only chosen her but made her Mother of His Son. Attributing the reward of so much favor to God's highest judgment, she said, all gentleness and love, "Lord, to whose power all created things obey, I praise the greatness of Your great works with the purity of my mind; and because my spirit, dazzled by the light of Your miracles, cannot thank You with such great thanks as it is scarcely worthy of it, confused, it is silent, and bows to You with all humility." As she rose from her prayers, the simple words of which, similar to the purity of her heart, restrained God's just anger against us, Mary appeared full of new beauty, full of such excellent qualities that with a mere glance she performed miracles in others' breasts. Wherever the majesty of her countenance appeared, it drove from others' hearts the sorrows that clouded their serenity of mind. If she sometimes showed a smile, she did not show it for her own delight, but for the sorrowful who were made joyous through her joy. And although she saw herself raised above every loftiness that God's merciful hand could give, she was full of such humility that the meekness of lambs would have appeared as pride in comparison to her.

Mary goes to Elizabeth. As she had heard from the lofty Messenger that Elizabeth had reached the sixth month of her pregnancy, the royal young girl, full of the sweetness of joy, arranged to go into the mountainous wilds of Jerusalem, where Zaccharias lived, to see her.[74] She accordingly set out

73. The "uncreated Word" is the Godhead.

74. Luke 1:36–37.

on the journey with righteous Joseph and two elderly women who had been in Anna's service. Many holy men relate that because of the light that came from the divinity of Mary's soul, her admirable presence caused not only the treetops and mountaintops to bow down, but also the sun, seeing the Temple of the one that gave it light, to reverently incline its golden rays;[75] the flowing rivers stopped their progress and marveled at her, greeting her with the intricate murmur of their waves; and each mountain, though barren, clad its measureless ridge with the greenness of grass and lovely flowers; there was no bird so wild and shy whose nature did not know that its Maker dwelt sweetly with all the light of His heavenly virtue in Mary's wondrous sanctuary.

Mary soon arrived at the house of Zaccharias's venerable wife who, as she had heard that she was coming, overwhelmed at what she owed so great a young girl for her visit, went to meet her, her face the color of a person who, dazzled in a king's presence, is confused by the reverence that he owes to the other's greatness. In her, however, it was the ardor of all those joys and of all the gladness that could be seen in the brow, eyes, and lips of a person in the depths of happiness and, opening her arms in the way that a maidservant might, she said, "So that I do not offend the humility of your gentleness, I have not thrown myself at your feet, as I should do to the Mother of the Savior."[76]

As Mary opened her sweet mouth and let the greeting go forth from it, the child who was lying in the womb of the old matron, rejoiced; kneeling in the humble space in which he was enclosed, he adored the Lord with the silent voices of his soul.

Words of Elizabeth to the Virgin. Then great Elizabeth, consumed with flames of the divine spirit, cried out:

> O blessed and glorious among the most glorious and blessed women whom Mother Nature will bear or has ever been born. Blessed and sublime is the eternal fruit that dwells in the purity of your womb. How am I worthy, what grace is mine, that the Queen of Heaven deigns to adorn our poor hovel with her sublime presence? The liv-

75. In the story of the flight into Egypt, a tree bends down to the ground to adore Christ (*Golden Legend*, 1:57).

76. Although the Virgin is usually credited with saying the Magnificat, where she refers to herself as handmaiden, here it is Elizabeth who sees herself as of inferior status, because she recognizes the Virgin as the Mother of God (Luke 1:48).

ing babe in my womb has recognized the rays of his Creator with his mind's eye. Whence he has bowed and adored Him.[77]

Mary magnifies the Lord. And with the grace of her holy tongue, the Virgin spoke thus:

> The soul of my soul, with the loftiness of its voices unheard by the senses, magnifies the One whose sublime loftiness does not contain what is lofty, His abundant generosity does not comprehend what is wide, and His deepest profundity does not understand what is profound. My spirit, full of the most humble of humilities, reflecting on His joy, rejoices as the heart of a simple and loving child does in its father's loved face; for He deigns to turn the eyes of His compassionate mercy toward the maidservant with His favors, and toward the handmaid with His mercy. Therefore I shall be raised to such a height that all will call me blessed and happy, until God strikes with the strength of His fury through supernatural power since He has performed in me the great and marvelous of His great and marvelous miracles, as He is the Power above all powers. And the pities of His mercy will flow with the years in the hearts, minds, and intellects of whoever will know how to fear and love Him. By removing regal pride from the seats of swollen ostentation through the power of His unconquered arm, not only will crushed humility be raised, but it will be raised even above the steps of Heaven. Thus loading the lowliness of poverty with the sweetness of glory, He will deprive those who enjoy an excess of riches, possessions, and their longed-for comforts. Behold Israel who, remembering divine mercy, has received His Son, assuring our fathers Abraham and his descendants of the infallibility of His promises.[78]

With what sound of words did the most serene Virgin express these praises, with what humility of bearing and fervor of heart, that the One will know who can imagine with what fire of love, what sweetness of harmony, and what humility of awe the inflamed cherubim sing the inexpressible and infinity of His greatness.

Meeting of Zaccharias and Joseph. After she had rejoiced with Elizabeth over the barrenness that had changed into fruitfulness, Joseph and dumb

77. Luke 1:41–45.

78. Luke 1:46–55. See the Magnificat for the sense of this passage (appendix).

Zaccharias embraced each other with loving brotherliness and kissed each other.[79] Then the righteous men, venerable through age (as may be imagined) and through illustrious nobility, sat down together.[80] One with signs and the other with words revealed the miracles that operated through God's power. One with his raised brow made known by raising his hands the wonder in his heart, while the other did so through spoken words. After she had rejoiced with her dear kinswoman over the gift she had received from the eternal King, the Lady of Heaven wanted to stay with her for a period of three months. Understanding this, Joseph, however, took leave of Zaccharias, the noble Elizabeth, and the Bride of God, and returned to Bethlehem, spending the time decided upon for the Virgin's return to Nazareth in prayer and in his trade.[81]

Mary returns to Nazareth. Who could describe the calm sweetness, holy comfort, and joy fulfilled that the happy cousins, full of the Holy Ghost, tasted together? Surely no one. Only she, whoever she might be, could show it to us in Paradise. Their pure discussions, passionate prayers, and charitable works were now always directed to God and done for God. Three months had passed (since the sun had been housed in three of those signs that adorn the zodiac) since the Virgin had come to Elizabeth.[82] She therefore took leave of her, and returned home, accompanied by some women, whom age and blood had made noble and venerable.

Birth of John the Baptist. After the Mother of our Salvation had left, Zaccharias's wife brought forth the forerunner of Christ. He came to the world the citizen of solitude, the trumpet that preached the virtue, name, and actions of the Son of the Highest. Then the nooses that had restrained Zac-

79. An angel announces to Zaccharias (Luke 1:5–80), the father of John the Baptist, that Elizabeth will give birth to a son. When Zaccharias asks for a sign as confirmation of this, he is struck dumb (v. 20). His speech returns to him when his son is born (v. 64).

80. Although Joseph is described as a carpenter (Mark 6:3), and Jesus as the son of a carpenter (Matthew 13:55), he has a building trade by the time he appears in the Book of James (James, *Apocryphal New Testament,* 42). In Luke and Matthew the evangelists establish Joseph's noble bloodline, tracing him back to Abraham and David, but Marinella's description has more to do with the medieval view that holiness was akin to high rank.

81. The Virgin Mary was given the title of "Bride of God" after early Christian allegories in which the Bride, or the Shulamite, of the love poems known as the Song of Songs became identified with her. This idea was much amplified in the twelfth century by Saint Bernard of Clairvaux, and became central to much of the imagery concerning the Virgin. See volume editor's introduction, 28.

82. The signs of the zodiac are the twelve equal parts into which the celestial sphere was divided, through one of which the sun passes in a month, and which are named after the twelve constellations (Aries, Taurus, Gemini, Cancer, Leo, Virgo, Libra, Scorpio, Sagittarius, Capricorn, Aquarius, and Pisces).

charias's tongue with their strength loosened. Full of wonder, he praised God's bounty, which is all, for all, and in all, to the surprise of those who had known him speechless.

Joseph comes to find the Bride. When chaste Joseph heard how the blessed Bride, with the gift of Heaven's ineffable kindness, had returned to Nazareth, without a moment's hesitation he decided to go and find her, to pay his respects to her, look at her, and venerate her, as something sacred and belonging to God. Equipping himself hastily with some of his labors, he went to the Virgin.[83]

Joseph suspicious of Mary's pregnancy. On his arrival, and noticing that she was pregnant, he was perturbed, his face like a cloudless sky disturbed when ravaged by clouds. Then, as we read, his eyes dimmed, and pale-faced, with a bitter mouth, head bowed, and with a breast buffeted by all the contradictory thoughts, he withdrew into a small room, which he had made privy to his anguish, and in his sighs, gestures of his hands, and movement of his eyes seemed the specter of grief.[84] "How could it be," he said, "that she whose holy honesty God's powers delighted in, knows the stain of vice? Perhaps my advanced age should have brought with it some of that sane judgment that was in me? And, yet, I cannot distinguish truth from falsehood. If this is a miracle of God, it is not reasonable for me to have these doubts, because it is impossible for her to cast lascivious looks, let alone take delight in her beauties." Another thought awakened in him, destroying his tranquility with its unease, which had been prompted by the earlier one, and he thus reasoned mentally with tears in his eyes. "It is indeed true that she is pregnant, as the eye does not deceive itself about what it sees." Then shame wounded his heart no less than it inflamed his face. Finally, he decided to leave without letting her know, the one whose whiteness of virginity Heaven admired. While his soul grieved between the tempests of varying thoughts, sleep with the sweetness of his rest sweetened the bitterness of sleeplessness.

The Angel appears to Joseph. Scarcely had the suspicious, aged Joseph closed his eyes in pleasurable sleep than a heavenly Messenger, adorned with lightning and gentleness, revealed himself to his mind's eyes, and said joyfully, in the following, or similar, words:

83. John the Baptist was known as the "forerunner of Christ," as his miraculous birth, being born to two elderly parents, heralded that of Christ; he was regarded as prophetic and as a missionary (Luke 1:57ff.). The word "venerate" is used here as it is the technical term for the type of homage specifically due to the Virgin (Greek, *hyperdulia*), rather than worship (Greek, *latria*), which is reserved for God.

84. Matthew 1:18ff. It is not clear who was the source for Marinella's assertion "as we read."

> Calm your heart's expression, O servant of God, because Mary's pregnancy is not the result of earthly evil, but through the power of the Holy Ghost. The One who will be born to her will be called the only Son of the Creator, and His name will be Jesus, that is, Savior, since He descended into Mary's virginal womb to save humankind.[85] And what she was before she conceived she is still, and shall be after the birth, ever Virgin, ever innocent, ever pure. And since you are chaste, Heaven has chosen you to be the faithful guardian of the chaste Lady.[86]

When he had said this, he hid his beautiful face between his flames and vanished. Awakened, Joseph saw a little light and smelled the sweetness that the blessed Messenger had left behind him, and was as happy as it was possible to imagine, but sorrowful for having thought, incorrectly, that she, the embodiment of chastity, could be unchaste. To make amends for his error, he threw himself at the Virgin's feet, full of true humility, asking her pardon for the madness of his thoughts. She was very saddened by the reverence made to her by Joseph, whom she honored as her father.[87]

Augustus's order. At that time, Caesar Augustus, ruler of countless peoples and measureless seas, spurred by pride, which in its own way burns continually in the desire for immortality, wanted to know the number of people subject to the power of his majesty (which would be as easy to do as to count the drops of rain Heaven spilled when clouds of tears have obscured our eyes). As all were called to the place where the subjects of the great Roman Empire were to pay money and register their names, Mary and Joseph, as upright persons, and full of humility, left Nazareth and went to Bethlehem to make known their names and pay their dues to the great leader of the peoples. Full of divine virtue, Mary appeared to go there, not where the order called her, but to wherever the will that moves all took her. She walked with her breast and heart full of happy gaiety, the rays of which, coming out of her eyes (light of Paradise), lit up the thick air, which was troubled by a brief shower.[88] As the wind blew, as one might imagine in such a season, it

85. Cf. Matthew 1:1–24.

86. Marinella stresses Catholic teaching about Mary's virginal purity and freedom from original sin, from her conception by Anna (the doctrine of the Immaculate Conception) to her own conception of Christ.

87. Marinella emphasizes again the chaste relationship between the Virgin and Saint Joseph, and also Joseph's age.

88. In medieval optics it was believed that rays came out of people's eyes to illumine the object of their vision rather than light being the source.

struck their faces with pouring water, and did this so many times that she had to defend herself against it with her hands and then with her cloak. And although it then seemed that the south wind dominated the air, the north wind warring with it made its biting freshness felt, its unbearable cold freezing Joseph's hands and feet in such a way that he was scarcely able to move a step, and his hands, which had almost lost feeling, were unable to feel the stick that supported the weight of his years. Similarly, the Holy Virgin, feeling frozen, was unable to bear the discomfort brought by the angry gusts blown by the furious north wind, and because the night was embracing with its gloomy wings the darkness of the clouds that surrounded Heaven.

"Since night is concealing the brightness of day with its blackness,"said the man of Bethlehem to the sovereign Maid, "I think, if you would like to, that it would be appropriate for us to take shelter under a roof, since it is too late to enter Bethlehem, which must be full of traveling people, and we did not find a way of being able to stay with our families." On hearing this, the Lady of the Angels, full of her humility, went cheerfully with the upright man into a poor hovel, or little hut, the shelter for animals belonging to some shepherds.

The place where Christ was born. It was the place, as it is written, beneath the lowliness of which they retired, the ruin of a building, the ancientness of which had been thrown to the ground by Joseph's weak arm, as some pieces of broken columns and some walls bore witness. Ivy and thorns, in their arrogance, had taken over others' rights. Part of the building was still upright, thanks to the shepherds' care, and was covered by reeds set up rustically with leaves and roots. These were held up above some beams, weakened through rain and age. The door, which had fallen by the entrance, was of entwined willow-tree twigs. Here, praising eternal wisdom for the place, Joseph blew on his frozen hands to warm them up and, swathed in his cloak and overcome by tiredness from the journey, he settled himself on a little dry hay.

Her clothes and hair damp and soaked with rain, the holy Virgin felt an unbearable cold. Nevertheless, she overcame her distress with her strength of endurance, and with the fire of love that burned in her breast. And although this happy and blessed couple had none of the things necessary for creature comfort, still, their hearts fixed on God, the source of every good, they rejoiced and did not feel the extremes of misery in which they found themselves. Behold, the hour waited for, longed for, and hoped for drew nearer. Then the air, which until now had been darkened by clouds, made damp by the forces of the south wind and cold by the north wind's blasts, their penetrating natures going straight to their innards, abated (as it may be imagined) in the tranquility and serenity in which summer was welcomed, and in the warmth of spring. The earth that, almost greedy of its beauties, had held them hidden within its breast, became lavish with its treasures, scattering them with full hands. The short wild grass, which covered the humble hut, yielded roses and lilies that breathed scents other than those that happy Arabia gives us.[89]

Signs of the birth of Christ. Full of wonder, therefore, Joseph raised his eyes on high as people in wonderment do. And he saw Heaven embellished with stars, which scattered golden sparks and gilded fire flames. He saw the moon, its whiteness superior to the purest white seen in pearls newly taken from their white havens. He heard the sweetnesses of the harmony made by the spheres as they gyrated the lightness and denseness of their bodies. He saw the dances that the stars in a masterly way joyfully led through the open shores of Heaven. Then he rejoiced no more than if he had been taken to Paradise, and seemed like a man almost lifeless.[90]

Birth of Christ. At the same time Mary tasted the height of happiness and sweetness enjoyed above the spheres. However, her soul, full and surrounded by every good thing, shed tears that poured the tenderness of divine love from her eyes; and, wholly elevated to God, she gazed at Him with her eyes, praised Him with her mouth, and adored Him with her humility. But, behold, Heaven, which, murmuring, flashes, and flashing, thunders.[91] Behold the black of night, which, clothed in heavenly splendor, shines more than the day; seas flow; rivers stop their flow; and, foreseeing the damage they might do, abysses tremble. In the knowledge that they were unworthy of being worshiped, statues of false gods threw themselves to the ground, broken. Joseph's spirit had ascended into God's bosom with the wings of its goodness, and there it gazed, marveling, at the greatness and the marvelous made by eternal providence through the miraculous birth of His most holy only Son. Joseph saw with his mind's eye the great joy with which the souls of the angelic spirits gazed from Heaven at the miraculously born Child and how, opening their gracious lips, they intoned with sweet harmonious voices

89. Arabia Felix (Latin, "happy, prosperous") was the ancient Roman name given to the southern part of the Arabian peninsula, often identified with the Yemen. The name Yemen is believed to have derived from a Greek translation of the Arabic name, *al-yaman*, which also has the meaning "fortunate" or "blessed," which may also refer to the growing of spices in the area.

90. The metaphor of life as a sea journey toward its haven, "the shores of Heaven," is alluded to here.

91. This passage suggests the Virgin's prescience—at Christ's birth she sees his death, foreshadowed through the reference to heaven's thunder and lightning (Luke 23:44–45; Matthew 27:51–52; Revelation 4:5, 11:10).

before the throne of God, which was decked with cherubim. Then he saw the bands of angels who, leaving the celestial Kingdom, descended to earth, some of whom with the slender bodies they assumed, concealing the happy hut, others embellishing the air with the beauty that came from their beauties. Then he saw a flash from the eternal Deity that, attacking the air with a terrifying flame, came towards the happy region where Jesus was born, to whose splendor, it seemed to him, the world was inclining its head. However, his soul, frightened and confused, returned to the normal function of his body. The righteous man, awakened and unable to bear with his mortal eyes what he had seen with his mind's eye, had to close them again, since a cloud, shining more than the sun, and surrounding the Virgin, confused him in such a way that he seemed to be someone lost in the pleasures of sleep; then, honored with grace from above, he was able to gaze at the inflamed faces of the divine birds. He saw their faces of a fiery crimson similar to fire and of fire similar to crimson, and their hair and clothes caught by the breezes, and the dear gusts of the west wind, masters of the winter, played with the heavenly ornaments of the blessed spirits.

Joseph sees the birth of Jesus. Then, stupefied, he saw and gazed in wonder at the Son of the eternal Father placing Himself on the hay, between the ox and simple ass, a Child whose face seemed a flash of lightning that burned with all the light and fire of divine glory. Which is why (I think) he let drop from his hands the stick that had fallen there, while his mind had been enjoying the beauties of Heaven and, wholly burning in hope, with his heart full of faith, and almost free of his bodily ties, he pondered on God's will, seeing the One who opens Heaven's floodgates, who drowns the earth's face with water, who shakes the mountains' firmness, and who clothes the night with its starry mantle. And the One who decks all, and clothes all, being born in the lowliness and unworthiness of such a place, was wrapped only in those few veils that the tender Mother had removed from her head. He saw the splendor of the light that came from the great Child strike her hair and make it shine more than the living sun. Then on his knees, he adored Him with the voices of his heart and silence of his lips. The Virgin Mother, full of venerable majesty, was similarly kneeling before the Son to whom she had given birth, with the reverence of a daughter, love of a bride, and humility of a servant.[92] Gazing at Him, she recognized in Him the divinity in which souls, thanks to His mercy, had to cloak themselves.

92. Paintings of the birth of Christ often show Mary kneeling on the ground before the Christ child. See volume editor's introduction, 125.

Mary renders thanks to God. Whereupon, happy with incomprehensible gladness, which was overflowing in her breast, which was flooded with joy, and which came from her soul and heart, she said something like this:

> What words, O King of Heaven, shall my spirit and lips form to give You the greatest thanks that will be worthy of the immeasurable favor given to my lowliness by Your sublimity? Your goodness wished me to conceive and give birth to You. And then, You deigned, O eternal Mind, that my eyes (O happy eyes) could see Your light. These are all the effects of Your clemency, love, mercy, and kindness, although I, Your servant, do not merit them.

Not far from that place where our Salvation was born was a tower called Ader, in which shepherds, just and righteous men, were staying.[93] They grazed the flocks of the nearest townspeople, enjoying rustic lowliness in their poverty, and rarely accepting the harmful acquisition of gold. God, who always loves those who are humble and simple in the pastoral life more than the haughtiness and pride of royal living, desired His angels to announce to them the miraculous birth of the great eternal Leader.[94] In the night's deep silence, the shepherds discussed among themselves God's power and mercy rather than the shepherd's cares or innocent lambs, like people learned in divine matters, with cheerful minds and gay faces and hearts impossible to describe. And while their hearts fed on the pleasure of that certain something, the graces of which transported them almost beyond the stars, a Messenger from the heavenly court arrived, flashing through the sweet fire of his face and shining hair, which, curly and quivering, appeared to tumble out of place, his cheeks trembling in the fresh milky whiteness and vermilion of which they seemed to be made. With the splendor of his brightness, he encircled their rough natures. Stricken with cold fear by such a light, they fell with faces down, confused and overcome by the flashing brightness that blinded them.

The Angel announces Jesus's birth to the Shepherds. The Angel spoke kindly to them:

93. Marinella seems to have taken the name Ader from a site in ancient Moab on the Transjordanian Plateau (Ader, Khirbet), around seven kilometers northeast of the modern city of Kerak, Jordan. Although it was occupied during the Iron Age II, its city wall was constructed in the second and third centuries CE. It had a tower on the north city wall of the late Roman period, which was repaired in the Byzantine period.

94. Cf. John 10:11: "I am the good shepherd."

> Men faithful and loved by God, the rays bring you no terror. Deriving from our faces, they touch your eyes since they are lights of joy and not shadows of fear. I am the Messenger of that eternal joy, the joy that fills not only Heaven, the earth, and the sea, but passing through to Limbo, makes the blessed Fathers joyful, freed from the weight of earthly flesh. Rejoice, as the One who is supreme Wisdom has preferred your lowliness to the loftiness of kings, and calls you first to see the holy presence of His only Son. To find Him you will go to Bethlehem, village of the one who, with the help of the catapult, gained the Kingdom.[95] There you will see Him wrapped in the fine veils of His Virgin Mother, and placed on the hay. And this will be witness to the truth that comes from me.[96]

At these words the shepherds were frightened and confused, with their heads bowed to the ground. Having delivered his message and risen into the air, the blessed spirit joined an infinite multitude of ardent and heavenly sprites. The happy men heard them sing the glories of God's endless power, saying, "Glory to the great and immense name of the One who is the greatest power in Heaven, and peace be on earth to all men who believe in Him."[97] Not only did the angelic words feed the hearts and souls of the pastoral company with their sweetness, but they were also the living food that invigorated the hearts and souls of each living person.

After the Angel had vanished, the fortunate guardians of the flock, in wondering chorus must have said, "O what a very great marvel! The Lord must surely be among His people." As they were saying this, they hastened, rising from the saddlebag on which they had rested their tired limbs. And with some blades of straw and hay in their unkempt beards and wild hair, they dressed themselves in the kind of clothes that they normally wore for the most important rituals. Some had hats of wolves' skins, some of plaited straw; one took a wicker basket full of flowers, and another full of milk curds; yet another took jars full of milk and wild honeycomb. One person brought a pure white lamb around his neck, holding its fore-hooves with his right

95. The angel appears to the shepherds in Luke (2:9–18). Bethlehem is "the city of David" (Luke 2:11), who gained the kingdom of Heaven with his sling (1 Samuel 17:40): "So David prevailed over the Philistine with a sling and with a stone, and smote the Philistine, and slew him" (v. 50).

96. Luke 2:8–13.

97. Luke 2:14: "Glory to God in the highest. And on earth peace among men in whom he is well pleased."

hand, and its hind regions with his left. Then they started out on their journey with sticks in their hands, followed by the faithful watchfulness of their dogs, which, with heads held high and wagging tails, showed themselves to be part of the general joy. The shepherds walked along, thinking in great silence of the things they had seen and heard, and none dared open his mouth or form words. Then raising their eyes, they recognized the holy place by the light that, issuing from Christ's divinity, came forth from the roof tiles of the poorly built dwelling, its brightness forming almost a cloud of gold round the sacred stable. Doubling the speed of their steps, their breasts filled with the love and joy that blessed souls have in Paradise, they drew nearer and venerated it with heartfelt voices and on bent knees. Entering, they saw (O wonderful sight) God made man to make us gods and, gazing on Him with humble eyes, they recognized Him swathed in His Mother's veils. They recognized her by the brightness that encircled her, as if a heavenly and blessed soul. Having venerated her, they gazed at Jesus and, gazing at Him, trembled with fear at His great majesty and promptly fell to their knees.

The Shepherds adore Christ. Since they were full of great humility, perfect love, and total faith, they bowed to Him as their Lord, they loved Him as the Father, and they professed their belief in Him as God. Then, all of them, almost simultaneously, said the following, or similar, words:

> How should we praise, with our unworthy words, the greatness of Your name, which the angels, lit with Your light, silently adore with admiration? With the souls of all the spirits, we thank Your immense goodness, which has deigned to call us first before Your venerable presence. We, Your servants, therefore, will become trumpets heralding Your miraculous birth.

Having said this, they were silent, knowing that still tongues and silent hearts were enough to praise Him. Then penitent, and believing, they adored the great Mother of the Redeemer and presented her with the woodland gifts: milk, milk curds, flowers, and lambs. Blessing them, she received the humble offerings, and Joseph put them aside. Full of wonderment and dazzled by the heavenly light, the shepherds left, having made obeisance to the reverent old age of the patrician of Bethlehem. They went, making known the birth of the longed-for Salvation to the amazement of those who heard them.

Miracles that take place during Christ's Nativity. Apart from the shepherds, Christ's great coming showed to the world the incredible ruin of the most famous temple, which was dedicated to peace. Apollo's oracle had said this would remain whole until a virgin miraculously delivered to the world a heavenly son, something that appeared impossible to everyone. Therefore the following words were inscribed in gold letters above the temple door: *Templum pacis in aeternum* ("the Temple of Peace in eternity"). But to the shame of such a title, the temple fell crashing, from its top to its foundations, during the same night the glorious Virgin showed the World, clothed in human flesh, the One who clothes souls in light.[98] At the same time those spirits that, hidden in trees and in statues, are adored, giving answers and deceiving others' simplicity, fled headlong from the world, frightening the infernal leaders by the suddenness of their flights.[99] The vineyards of Engedi, which produce balsam in the night that gives birth to the day, which relights our blindness, miraculously showed the delightful beauty of their scented flowers.[100] In Rome a fountain of water, brilliant in its freshness and limpidity, changed into oil and flowed all night and all day into the Tiber, showing that God's bounty, which was united in Heaven, was spread on earth with liberal abundance.[101] On the day following this happy night, a shining light, similar to a golden eye, was seen in the pure serenity of Heaven, an eye in the middle of which appeared a lady of venerable majesty who held a little baby in her arms out of whom came a light that hid the sun. So the Sibyl, relating this to Caesar, said, "O ruler of the kingdoms, whose swollen pride reveres no one, now having discarded it, adore the Child I am showing you on the neck of His Virgin Mother, since He will overcome you in power, rule, and eminence, being your Creator and Benefactor."[102]

Magi. While the perfect shepherds spread Christ's miraculous birth in loud voices, there were in the East three Arab Kings who were descendants of the great prophet Balaam. These were wise men, expert in the science of the stars and full of the mercy of goodness and fear of God.[103] As righ-

98. The story of the Ara Pacis, or Temple of Peace, and Apollo's oracle is related in the *Golden Legend* (1:40–41).

99. Christ's birth was said to lead to the destruction of false idols and prophets.

100. Engedi is on the western shore of the Dead Sea. Vines and palms were once cultivated on the plateau 2,000 feet above the sea, which is now among the wildest and most desolate places in Palestine. See the *Golden Legend,* 1:41.

101. This legendary incident is related in the *Golden Legend*, 1:40.

102. Ibid. This episode forms part of the attempt to link the pagan past, symbolized by Augustus, with the Christian era, symbolized by the Virgin Mary. The emperor consulted the Tiburtine sibyl about Christ's birthday as the Senate wished to elect him a god since he had brought peace to the world, but the sibyl told him that a king had been born that day who would be more powerful than him, and Augustus accordingly refused his deification.

103. Matthew 2:1–18. The three magi, or wise men (Greek, *magoi*), were the first Gentiles (or non-Jews) to believe in Christ. In the New Testament they were called sages. Tertullian (ca.

teous men, they grieved over the sorrows of their neighbors and rejoiced in their happiness. Aversion to anger did not lead their hearts to sudden rage; neither hate nor deception was nourished in their breasts, but rather justice and love; they always harbored within them the union of harmony, compassion of mercy, wisdom of prudence, and the simplicity of goodness they had in their hearts, as in their own dwellings. Every year, moved by the words that Balaam's prophetic spirit had left them, which said that when Jacob's star rose, the Virgin would give birth to universal redemption, they went up on top of a mountain, fasting and praying to the One to whom all is possible, that He might wish to show them the rays of the Star foretold by Balaam, their father.[104] And they dwelt so long there that the sun hid its beauty three times from mortal eyes and, jealous of their beauty, made the stars' faces disappear with its light.[105] Many years had passed since they had prayed to God that He would show the Star to them. At the moment when our Salvation was born, they found themselves (O happy occasion) on top of the mountain, fasting and making offerings to the heavenly King so that He might show them the dazzling sight of the Star that had been prophesied.

The Star appears to the Magi. Behold the long-awaited, which appeared to them, and as it was between the height of Heaven and the lowness of the earth, and shining with extraordinary light, it hurt their eyes. Within the Star, as someone has written, was the figure of a little boy holding a cross, shining brighter than the sun, above his head.[106] And while it was flashing in the righteous Ethiopians' eyes, they heard a murmur, as if of a great deal of water, the distinct sound of which said in words, "Friends of the prince of heavenly warriors, quickly leave the eastern kingdoms and go to the city of Judah in which the great King, great God, and great Lord whom you longed

---

160–ca. 225) described them as "kings," and Origen (ca. 185–ca. 254) was the first to say that there were probably three magi as three gifts are mentioned. Marinella follows the later tradition of the wise men being kings, and she is clearly aware that they were probably astrologers. Their acknowledgment of Jesus as Messiah is the evangelist's way of showing the submission of magical arts and superstition to God. The names given to them, Caspar, Melchior, and Balthazar, are a later tradition. See also chapter 2, note 89.

104. Balaam was a non-Israelite prophet who appears in the Book of Numbers (22–24). His most famous prophecy was "I shall see him, but not now: I shall behold him, but not near. A star shall rise out of Jacob and a sceptre shall spring up from Israel" (24:17), which was probably the source for the account of the star followed by the magi (Matthew 2:1–12). See also chapter 2, note 90.

105. This refers to Christ's resurrection ("He rose again on the third day").

106. In the *Golden Legend*, the star has the "shape of a most beautiful boy over whose head a cross shone brilliantly" (1:40).

for has been born."[107] The excellent Kings were dazzled, uncertain, and astonished by the lightning, sound, words, and beautiful appearance of the Star. Then returning to their earlier state, they praised with their souls and bodies the One who is the greatest Good. And straightening their knees, which were bent for prayer, and making reverence to Heaven, they returned to their royal dwellings with a joy that, unable to confine itself within the bounds of their hearts, poured out of their eyes, lips, and brows.

Departure from the East of the Magi. The three Wise Men prepared themselves for the long journey in the shortest time, taking with them their precious gold, perfumed myrrh, and manly incense, gifts as worthy as was humanly possible. Then they set off, decked in their exotic garb, towards the regions shown to them by the heavenly voice, leaving the Persian and Chaldean countries, and the region watered by the River Saba, accompanied by a royal multitude of people, horses, and dromedaries.[108] They followed the Star, which reflected in their own eyes, shining before them, and which showed its magnificence with great display, leaving a long golden streak behind it. People left their dwellings to see with what embellishment of rays, circle of lights, or with what flashing sparks the Star progressed between earth and Heaven, the lamp lit by God's command for the glory of His only begotten Son. And they saw the splendor of gold and jewels that adorned the black Kings with royal dignity. They were amazed as they gazed at the variety of clothes and grandeur of those who always kept their eyes fixed on the heavenly Light and the eyes of their souls fixed on the face of God. Many write that they went with greater speed than clouds go through open fields of the air, pushed by furious blasts of wind.

The Magi, on arrival in Jerusalem. On their arrival in Jerusalem they asked where Christ, the Shepherd of the Jewish people, had been born, because (they said), "We have come to adore Him, as a light from His Star was shown to us in the East." Having heard this, Herod called all the priests and doctors to a council, all of whom were subject to his power, and asked them where Christ, the Son of God, was to be born. They replied [that he would be born] in Bethlehem in Judea, as the prophesying spirit had left Micah's truth written, whose words they were: "And you, Bethlehem, land of Judah,

107. Marinella here describes the wise men as "righteous Ethiopians"; below they are described as "wise Ethiopians" (184). From 715 to 656 BCE Ethiopian kings reigned in Egypt. They were also allies of Hezekiah of Judah (Isaiah 18:1–2, 20:1–6). References to the Ethiopians in the prophets (Jeremiah 13:23; Amos 9:7) show that they were well known in Israel and Judah.

108. Saba was the name of a state in the ancient Yemen. There was also a tribe, the Sabei, mentioned by classical writers from the third century BCE whose land, "Arabia Felix," was fabulously rich. Whether there was in fact a river is not known.

you are not least among the princes of Judah, since the leader who will rule His people with mercy will be born in your happy breast."[109] At these words Herod, bewildered, like the tyrant who hears the shout of the conspirators holding a sword over his head, concealing his pain with courteous appearance and splendid invitation, had the rulers of those kingdoms who, coming from the East where the day is born, are of the color of night, brought to him.[110] And he wanted to hear from them how, when, and where the Star, their guide, had appeared, and how it was showing with its light the birth of such a great leader. With sincere hearts the Kings related all to him, and he, hiding the impiety of his heart under a peaceful appearance, begged them to seek the glorious Child carefully, and when they had found Him, to make known to him, if it were not irksome, where He was, as he wished to adore Him and profess Him true God and true Messiah.

Arrival of the Magi in Bethlehem. Hurrying hastily, the illustrious heroes arrived in Bethlehem, and saw the Star again, which appeared to them when they entered Jerusalem, halting its pure and saving rays over the poor hovel inhabited by God. Seeing it stop, the happy Kings understood that this was the place where the One had been born whose infinite power shakes the mountains' firmness, stops the winds' furious course, and quells the pride that agitates tempestuous thoughts in the sea of our minds. Then they became silent (as we are obliged to believe),[111] and shaking and overcome by a reverent and pious joy and delight, tears trickled from their eyes, which tender love drew from the depths of their hearts. On drawing near to the glorious hut, the Wise Men dismounted and took the gifts they had brought from their distant countries. Entering with simple and devout hearts and reverence, they saw the great Child, and their faces quickly became the color of the face that a person in a king's presence goes when he is terrified and confused by the respect carried by eminent majesty, and trembling speaks and speaking trembles. And then they knelt at the Child's feet. The sudden and unexpected arrival of the foreign Kings made Joseph's few hairs stand on end, peeping out, white-haired, around his bald head; and, full of wonder, completely shrunk within himself, he looked on and was silent. Then the Wise Men gazed, amazed at the humility of the King of Kings who, lying in the lap of the Virgin Mother, embraced her neck with His tender arms, and

109. Matthew 2:1ff. Micah was one of the minor prophets of the Old Testament. His prophecy (Micah 5:2) is interpreted by Matthew (2:6) as a prediction of the Messiah being born in Bethlehem.

110. Matthew 2:1–8.

111. Matthew 2:9ff. It is not clear why Marinella feels that the faithful are obliged to believe this, since her adumbration of the magi's story is merely derived from popular piety.

sucked the sweetness of the milk from her breasts, like Nature's joys in her ivory-like bosom. Reflecting to themselves on His infinite power, they saw the despicable poverty and rough clothes that covered Him. Then almost beside themselves, they put their left hands to their breasts with a humility no longer seen and held the gifts in their right hands, standing with bowed heads as a sign of humble and gentle hearts, resembling flower heads collapsed on their stalks through an excess of dew shed on their bosoms by the night's damp hand.

The Discourse of the Magi with Jesus. Then in unison and in the following words, they announced the secret of their hearts:

> O eternal leader, whose power passes the summit of all boundless power, look on us, Your humble servants, with a merciful eye. Having already left the swollenness of pride of the Eastern kingdoms, we have come at the first sign that the light of Your will made to us, to contemplate salvation in Your serene face, which the infirm world has been awaiting anxiously for so many years. But how shall we look upon that sun of divinity, which gently resides in Your tranquil brow, since our humanity is incapable of seeing Your divinity and can only look at it thanks to Your kindness, which has given us a heavenly guide for such a long journey.
>
> *Gifts of the Magi.*
> And since You have been so pleased to raise our unworthiness, do not scorn, Prime Mover and supreme God, to receive the offerings that we have brought from our kingdoms. Behold, we offer You manly incense, as You are God; we present You with precious gold, as You are King, and we offer You incorruptible myrrh, as you are Man.[112] With such gifts, receive our hearts, burning with the fire of great zeal; and may it please You that the memory of such gifts lasts until Heaven nourishes its stars, and the sea the earth; and we beg You with all the strength of our hearts to remember us when we reach our final days and last hours of this life. When we have arrived in the realms You have given us, in works, thoughts, and words becoming the best, we will keep ourselves

112. Gold, as a precious metal found in Egypt and Ophir, was exported to Judah; its preciousness made it a gift worthy of Christ as King. In the Temple, frankincense symbolized the offering of prayer (Psalm 141:2; Luke 1:10). In the New Testament myrrh was used as a narcotic and for embalming (John 19:39). According to later tradition, it symbolized grief or mourning, which is what Marinella alludes to here, Christ as man rather than God. See also the symbolism of offerings in the following paragraph.

in Your love, the provider of those joys enjoyed by those who glory in being Your servants.

Thus the noble pilgrims spoke with their tongues and even more with their hearts. Then Caspar (as I seem to see), with his left hand on his breast and his fingers quite spread out, offered the sacred incense to the glorious little Boy. With his knee on the ground, and his left hand on his left thigh, Baldassar offered Him the pure gold. And Melchior, totally humble, presented him with the scented myrrh.[113] The three gifts signified His precious divinity, most holy soul, and incorruptible flesh. In a divine manner, the blessed Mother accepted the gifts presented and, with a gracious smile, the eternal Son raised His tiny right hand and blessed the happy Kings. With this benediction, they turned their words and praises to the holy Virgin, exalting the excellences and marvels they saw in her. Full of her most humble humility, her face became the color of rose petals at the beginning of day, showing them that what they saw in her that was superhuman and noble was a gift neither of her nature nor intellect, but only a gift from Heaven. The wise Ethiopians were confused by the superior being of the glorious Child and by the pious loving Mother and their extreme humility. Then, reverently, they took their leave of them, and similarly of old Joseph, and left the place where they had honored Jesus, with the firm intention of going to find Herod, so that he might come and adore Him. But in the night while they were between sleeping and waking, thinking of the glorious sight of God, a miraculous light appeared to them in which was one of the spirits of Paradise, who told them to return by another way to their kingdoms and not to go to Herod as they had promised him.

Return of the Magi to the East. Obeying, they returned by another route to the East, entirely obedient to the love of the One who created all from nothing.[114] And, with a change of heart, they restricted themselves to a humble way of life; they then led holy and blameless lives and made the peoples subject to their majesty do the same.

God, who gives laws to the heavens through the lips of that great Moses who in the dark cloud spoke to God face to face, commanded that every woman who had, like a fruitful vine, brought a male child into the world, should present herself in the Temple after forty days. If she had plenty of

113. The precise descriptions in this passage of the way Caspar and Melchior are kneeling derive from Marinella's knowledge of conventional Adoration imagery. See volume editor's introduction, 125.

114. Matthew 2:12.

harmful riches, she was to offer a lamb to the sacred Temple, but if not, through fate's fickleness, she was obliged to offer a pair of doves or turtle-doves. However, Mary, seeing that the due time was past, said to Joseph in her angelic sounding voice, "As Moses' trumpet announcing God's truth commands that women who have been worthy of giving birth to sons should go to the Temple in Jerusalem after forty days, following the usual and ancient custom, I should like us to go there." And he replied, "I am prepared to follow you there, where Heaven's desire and the virtue of your will leads us."[115]

Mary goes to the Temple in Jerusalem. Having gathered his relatives together, Joseph started off with them behind the Virgin's holy footprints. It is written that she was dressed in a garment similar in color to a strip of what cloaks Heaven, over which she wore a purple mantle.[116] She traveled with her little Child (joy of Paradise) on her left arm, resting against her breast with such majesty in His countenance, with so much divine light, that His gestures or movements were incomparable in relation to those of a human creature, but more akin to a spirit surrounded in glory and blessedness. The fixed stars seen at Heaven's windows, charmed by her gracious beauty, spread sparks of holy and heavenly fire. The wandering stars, united in various groups, followed her. Whereupon the air, cleared by their movements, and by Jesus's light and the Virgin's, rejoiced. All who were watching remembered their tremendous astonishment and joy of the wonder.

Simeon sees Jesus. They were not very far from the Temple when Simeon appeared before them, standing at its threshold. Simeon was the interpreter of Nature's Ruler who, full of God's spirit, had foreseen, waited for, and wished for His coming.[117] His great beard, almost covering the width of his breast, shone more and was whiter than silver, and added grandeur and majesty to the gravity and authority of his appearance. His venerable clothes were as follows: first, he wore a tunic, its whiteness whiter than snow, over

115. Luke 2:22ff.

116. The Virgin is usually depicted in art dressed in blue and white, or blue and red, the color blue being symbolic of the sky or heaven, or sea, and the Virgin's own color. There also was an economic reason for the color, since blue was an expensive pigment made from crushed lapis lazuli, which came from Afghanistan; this, together with gold, made the color appropriate to Mary's role as Queen of Heaven. She also sometimes wears a purple cloak, symbolizing the royal descent attributed to her, and again her status as Queen of Heaven.

117. Luke 2:25–35. From the fourteenth century Simeon is usually identified with the high priest of the Temple ("interpreter of Nature's Ruler"), and in visual representations shown wearing heavily ornamented liturgical vestments. The description derives from that in the ritual requirements as ordered by Moses for Aaron and the priests in Exodus 28:1–43. See also Exodus 39:1–31.

which was a short robe, embroidered with pomegranates and lilies of the valley imitating thunder and flashes of lightning.[118] Over this was the great cloak, stiff with gold and weighed down with jewels, with a border around it decorated with various figures of such subtle artistry that they appeared to breathe and move. The figure of History, which was on the right side, showed as the Angel of the Lord commanded the great patriarch Abraham to offer his only son (the joy of his old age) in sacrifice to the One who gave Law to all. Then the obedient father, his face drawn by death's brush, and cheeks bathed in sorrowful tears, was seen to have bound the innocence of his hope on the altar, where it appeared that the tender, pale child, almost lifeless, awaited the harmful blow to remove the remaining warmth from within. And it was seen how Abraham raised his arm to kill him, and the Angel held it from him, so that his pure innocence was not struck. And similarly how a lamb came willingly to offer itself as a sacrifice to God.[119] On the left side was shown how the envy of brothers with evil intentions had enclosed righteous Joseph in the well, and how Reuben's pity was the reason for dragging him out and selling him to the Egyptians; how the chastity of his upright spirit distressed him in prison; how, adorned on one side with the Pharaoh's power, he was adored by his brothers; and, finally, how perfect Israel, overcome by age and by excessive joy, closed his eyes to eternal rest before his found again son, Joseph.[120]

118. The pomegranate is the Christian symbol of the Resurrection, deriving from its association with the classical story of Proserpine who returned every spring to regenerate the earth. It is also a symbol of chastity, as in the case of the Virgin Mary, who is sometimes shown sitting beneath a pomegranate tree. The lily of the valley is an attribute of the Virgin, to signify Advent, and derived from the name of the Shulamite, or Bride, in the Song of Songs, with whom the Virgin was linked in Christian exegesis ("I am the flower of the field, and the lily of the valleys" [Song of Songs, 2:1]).

119. The story of Abraham and Isaac appears in Genesis 22:2–14. Abraham's willingness to sacrifice his son made him a model of perfect obedience to God's will, and came to prefigure Christ's death, the Lamb that offers "itself as a sacrifice to God." See also note 189 below.

120. This passage refers to the story of Joseph, the favorite son of Jacob (Genesis 37:1ff.) and Rachel, as well as to Reuben, the firstborn of Jacob and Leah (Genesis 35:23, 49:3–4). Joseph's envious brothers try to kill him, but he is saved by his half-brother Reuben, and cast into the well alive (Genesis 37:21ff.). Through another brother, Judah, he is sold to the Egyptian Potiphar. Potiphar's wife tries to seduce Joseph (39:7ff.); in retaliation for his rejection she accuses him of trying to seduce her, and he is imprisoned. In prison his ability to interpret dreams brings him to Pharaoh's notice (40:1–14); he interprets Pharaoh's dream as foretelling seven years of plenty and seven years of famine, and is charged with preparing for the famine years (41:1ff.). In the Middle Ages, many of the episodes in Joseph's life were seen as prefigurations of Christ's life. For example, the famine episode foreshadows Christ's feeding of the multitude with loaves and fishes in the desert. Joseph's family is reunited through repentance; Jacob, believing that

Simeon talks to Jesus. Wrapped in his mantle, Simeon, trembling and awestruck in his Maker's presence, and full of wonder and joy, appeared like a spirit at the gates of Paradise. His weak knees falling to the ground, his old cheeks watered with tears of joy, with a palpitating heart he said:

> O aim of my long desire, O my Lord, O my Creator, do You come here indeed according to the truth of Your promises to comfort my soul and heart with Your divinity veiled in human form? But who has ever doubted mistakenly, when truth itself has promised it with its infallibility? Spurred by ardent desire to see You, I often used to say, when will You come? When will You show yourself to the world? Could I live so long that I might be able to bring the happiness of such a great announcement to the blessed Fathers who await Your coming? My eyes will never see You, as they will soon be blinded by the veil of their weakness. You promised me that I would see You before death jolts its death-carrying sting into my breast. Now I recognize You, and I see You in the chaste arms of the Virgin Mother. Therefore I await nothing else, only that You allow me to leave here in peace. In peace, I say, because I see peace, and hope in peace and eternal rest.[121]

Saying this, he worshiped Him. The pleasure he had in having to leave the world with such a joyful message made the sweetness of new tears flow from his eyes.

Anna tells the people that the Son of Mary is the true Messiah. At the same time Christ was seen by Anna, daughter of Phanuel of the ancient tribe of Asher. Full of the spirit of God, like a new sibyl, and prophesying, she awaited the redemption of Israel. She had wreathed her head and chin in white veils, and the rest of her body was cloaked in draperies of widow-like darkness. She had lived for seven years with her husband and eighty in God's golden Temple, spending her days in His service. Fasting, flagellation, and prayers were the objects of her hunger, flesh, and mind. Her wrinkled face and trembling steps personified ancientness gathered in those draperies. Then the spirit of truth within her changed her internal spirits governing the breath of life.

Joseph is dead, having been shown his bloodstained "coat of many colors" (37:3), is reunited with his favorite son, as God is with Christ.

121. Marinella has based Simeon's prayer on Luke, chap. 2:25ff. It ends with Simeon's request for eternal rest, "Now thou dost dismiss thy servant, O Lord, according to thy word, in peace" (v. 29). Simeon's canticle, now known as the *Nunc dimittis*, from the first words in the Latin, formed part of daily prayers from the fourth century.

With a terrifying voice, raving speech, flaming eyes and face, and with restless breathing and strange movements, she made known the Son of God, the true God and true Messiah, to those around.[122]

Simeon circumcises Jesus. As she was announcing Jesus to be the supreme Creator, Simeon rose to his feet with effort, having worshiped Jesus. And, as he had been directed, with a heart full of loyalty, he took the great God in his trembling hands and gazing at Him with eyes of love, said:

> Now You, sweet Lord, let Your servant leave in peace the ugliness of sin, of which the world is full, as You promised me in the abundance of Your goodness. Because I have seen that Light that gives light not only to the darkness of my eyes, but going into the darkness of sin will make it light, which You resolved to send in the beginning, so that the foolish ignorance of the people will know Your truth, and so that they might (the veil ripped from their blindness) rise with the wings of Your glory to the seats that pride of presumption made the angels leave empty.[123]

Here he was silent, and then offering Him to the tender Mother, with his wrinkled cheeks bathed in tears of joy, said, with a speech of frightening import, "Behold, Lady, a sword of bitter sorrow will pass through your heart."[124]

The Virgin's sorrow at Simeon's words. On hearing this from the great old man, it immediately seemed to the venerated Mother that the fear of danger hanging over her Son pierced her heart with icy hands. Then having dispelled every joy from her breast, as calm waters are dispelled by the winds' fury, and withdrawn into herself, she thought of her sorrow and weeping of which He would be the cause. Nor could she ever return to the clemency of

122. Luke 2:36–38. The tribe of Asher (v. 36), although one of the Ten Tribes of the Dispersion, was still represented in Palestine. Anna's age is a little unclear: she was either a widow of eighty-four years of age (Authorized Version), or more probably about 105 (Revised Version), as seven years of married life followed by eighty-four years of widowhood would make her that age.

123. Luke 2:29–32. Although Marinella gives the heading "Simeon circumcises Jesus" to this section, she is in fact incorrect, as the scene is that of the Presentation of Jesus in the Temple.

124. According to the former Roman Breviary, Simeon's prophecy was the first of Mary's Seven Sorrows. The Roman Breviary was the liturgical book containing the Psalms, hymns, lessons, and prayers recited in the Divine Office of the Catholic Church. The six other Sorrows of the Virgin were The Flight into Egypt, The Loss of the Holy Child, The Meeting with Our Lord on the Way to Calvary, The Standing at the Foot of the Cross, The Taking Down of Christ from the Cross, and The Burial.

joy, if her Son (as it was thought), unable to bear her pain to begin so early, falling on her breast with endearments, sweet kisses, and the gentleness of a small smile, did not chase sorrow from her breast.

Beauty of the Temple of Solomon. The most chaste turtledoves, as some relate, were offered by holy Joseph on the altar, with the gold, incense, and myrrh that the Magi had given the child Jesus.[125] Simeon arranged them all as if they had been sacred relics. While the Virgin spoke with her Son of the sorrow that she did not understand that He was to give her, Joseph walked around, gazing at God's Temple, which was excellent for its marble, precious for its gold, perfumed by cedarwood, and a marvel in its architecture. There were two great cherubim made of purest gold, which almost entirely covered the view of the holy house with their huge wings. These symbolized the hugeness of God's mercy and the loving compassion with which He encircled the miseries of all humanity. Then Joseph turned his eyes to the *Sancta sanctorum*, the Holy of Holies, the chamber of the King of Heaven, decorated with metal plates, the nature of which impoverishes the wealth of greedy men, its top encircled by a grapevine with widespread shoots, weighed down by its golden grapes, which signified the life of the people watched over by God. The shoots and roots symbolized the years that men lived, troubled by various misfortunes, and the vine leaves the hopes placed in God, which make us taste the fruits covered by them. Joseph gazed at the censer, weighed down by its own silver, and the great candelabrum that, extending seven arms, signified seven planets.[126] In wonder, he gazed at the table, which was admirable as much through artistic endeavor as for the excellence of its material. He saw the veil of Babylon, of cochineal, purple, sea silk, and hyacinth, colors that signified the image of things created: cochineal imitated fire, purple the sea, sea silk the earth, and hyacinth the air.[127] After he had gazed in admiration at God's marvelous Temple, he returned to the Virgin who, between joy and sorrow, was troubled, and rejoiced.

Return of the Virgin to Bethlehem. On leaving the Temple, the heavenly Lady returned to Bethlehem to Joseph's home. There they met, after her relatives had accompanied her to the dwelling, where they took leave of her, graciously, and full of kindness, confused by the things they had heard from the

125. Luke 2:24. A "pair of turtledoves, or two young pigeons" were required sacrifices at the Temple on the birth of a male child; Marinella has embellished the gift giving with the addition of gold, frankincense, and myrrh.

126. This is the *menorah*, the seven-branched candelabrum of the wilderness tabernacle and temples of Jerusalem.

127. Sea silk (Italian, *bisso*; Greek, *bussos*) was an exceptionally fine material made from filaments excreted by a variety of molluscs.

prophet and from Anna's shrill voice. They were people full of hope and fear, of hope because they knew that general salvation was near, of fear through the words that righteous Simeon had spoken to Mary. The venerated Virgin, full of her usual kindness, and watching her Son with piteous eyes, said:

> If it is permitted to ask, as a special gift, the mercy of Your sweet goodness, that all these sad misfortunes pour on me, which, with Your will, must strike You, I pray, in thanks to the clemency of Your mercy, that You deign to hurt not only my sinews and bones, but also my spirit and heart with every kind of passion. If I receive this from You, I will feel myself Your grateful servant and Mother.

On saying this, some drops of tender and loving tears dripped from Anna's dear daughter's beautiful eyes. And gazing at Him, and thinking of Him, she seemed to see Him now stricken by unknown sorrow, now joyful, surrounded by immortality and divinity. Then He appeared as a rose, quite joyful and laughing in the beauty of its greatest beauty, then a violet shrunk in the extremes of its pallor, afflicted by the night cold. But she rejoiced and sorrowed, and rejoicing and sorrowing she consoled herself in Christ's power and began to exercise her invincible virtue of fortitude.[128]

Death of Simeon. Shortly afterward, Simeon died, bent by his years and feeling unwell, but full of goodness and joyful that he had been worthy of seeing the world's Salvation garbed in our human fragility. He died like a simple babe in arms who, because he had come (as is credible) among righteous spirits, among perfect kings and famous prophets, showed them that he had not only seen, but adored, and held in his arms the Son of God.

Sayings of the Prophets who were in Limbo after the arrival of Simeon's soul. Full of incomparable joy at such an announcement of salvation, these prophets again took up the trumpets of truth with joyful voices, and with the force of their usual breath, all together they sounded the prophecy of the born God, the born King, and the born Man with proud words. Isaiah said, "The words were true that God said with my tongue, which are: 'Behold the Virgin, who has given birth to the Child Emmanuel, and Bethlehem has become great among the lands of Judah; because the leader who will rule the people with mercy has been born of her.'"[129] The one who with the trumpet's strength changed the pastoral rod into a regal scepter, repeating God's words, said,

128. Fortitude is one of Mary's virtues.

129. Cf. Isaiah 7:14. This is Marinella's interpretation of Isaiah's prophecy, which does not refer to Bethlehem.

"I have placed the fruit of my womb on your throne."[130] Jacob added, "The greatness of the scepter shall not be taken away, as he has been born who will save the lost generations with the power of his virtues,"[131] and similarly Daniel and Micah renewed their ancient prophecies.[132]

The Virgin goes with Jesus to Nazareth. After the Queen of the Angels had stayed several days in Bethlehem, she went with her Son and Joseph to Nazareth. There holy Jesus grew in years, grace, and beauty, but not of course in divinity since, as much in His birth as in His perfect state, He was always supreme, always great, and always greatest. His eyes shone with luminous clarity; His flesh glistened with soft delicacy on His limbs. The holy Mother had no effort, hindrance, or problem in looking after Him. The linen (a likely thing) and clothes, which covered and wound round His miraculous body, gave off a perfume that smelt sweeter than the happy Orient. He did not trouble His Mother by weeping nor did He worry her with tiresome cries; but if His soul was pure, the glorious Child's body was equally so, and white and stainless. The Bride of the Eternal Father often turned her clear, lucid gaze to the gracious light of her Creator's eyes and, contemplating Him steadily, with lofty voices that came from her heart, begged His forgiveness that her unworthiness dared to touch Him. And it came to pass that the Queen of Heaven was known, sung, and glorified by the blessed souls. She did not, however, feel any pride or experience any arrogance, but in her simple humility, with the sweetness of her rosy lips, continually praised and prayed to her Maker and Creator to have mercy on the miseries of humankind. Similarly, Joseph was never slow to exalt God's great works with his ready affections.

The Angel appears to Joseph. Almost two years had passed since the world's Salvation gathered the splendor of His rays beneath humanity's garments and showed Himself to mortal eyes. Night had already spread its mantle and made the stars appear at Heaven's gates when Joseph, withdrawn into his poor little room, prayed and gave thanks to God for having chosen him to be father in name of Jesus's greatness and guardian of the pure virginity of the glorious Virgin. After he had sent countless prayers to his Lord with his soul's affection, sleep's slowness spread in his eyes. Then his eyelids, growing heavy, veiled their light, allowing themselves to be swamped by the sweetness of repose. Soon his senses, intoxicated by its allurements, enjoyed their relief. Behold, before his mind's eyes, ever awake, a wonderful light

130. David.

131. Genesis 49:10.

132. Daniel 7:13–14; Micah 1:1ff.

presented itself, within which was a young man of the age between early youth and the end of boyhood. His face shone like the sun's: his robes were as white as snow that has never floated down from the sky. The brightness that came from him dazzled Joseph's mental eyes. His hair enveloped him like a golden circle, beside which the sun's face would have lost its splendid beauty. Releasing the sweetness of his voice with that charm that loosened it in Heaven in praise of the One who had created him, he said, in words such as these:

> Father, more just, loyal, and constant than anyone we see from Heaven's heights, God, who gave you the spirit of life, commands you to rise from your rest (do not be afraid of the darkness of night) and to lead the Virgin Mother (Nature's ornament) and the baby Jesus, joy of Paradise, into Egypt, as Herod, with his heart swollen with the poison of evil seeks to kill Him. Flee, flee, immediately, as I tell you that until you are in the secrecy of such a place, you will hear the sorrowful groans that maternal piteousness sends to Heaven's purity. Not even the terrible sound that the Nile makes will protect you from it.[133]

On saying this, he hid himself in the center of his light and vanished.

Mary's fear. Then the sleep that sweetly bound up Joseph's alertness loosened its knots. Soon, opening his eyes, he gazed at the angelic light, which was still shining in the narrow space of his cell. Rising from his bed, he hid the shame of naked flesh with the chastity of clothes, and hurrying his hurrying, ran to tell the Virgin of God's secret.[134] Immediately on hearing it, and overcome by anguish (as might be imagined), the color usual to petals of a fresh lily was visible in the Virgin's face. The Virgin already seemed to hear the sound of the enemy sword.[135] It appeared to her that she already saw it above the head or in the breast of the little Jesus, her hope. All delay in staying removed, she left her bed, and had scarcely dressed herself in her usual clothes before taking her dear Son in her arms with the kind of tremor of a person attacked by bitter cold, and with effort, as she was impeded by her trembling hands, she dressed Him in His customary garments. Although she wished to lament for the privations that she would have to experience during

133. Cf. Matthew 2:13.

134. The "shame of nakedness and chastity of clothes" derives from the story in Genesis when the previously naked (and chaste) Adam and Eve (3:7) discover their nakedness (and therefore shame): "And the eyes of them both were opened: and when they perceived themselves to be naked, they sewed together fig leaves, and made themselves aprons."

135. This refers to Simeon's prophecy, above.

such a long exile, she was unable to speak, as fear had made her tongue-tied. Then finally, in a trembling voice, she formed some words that came from her heart, as sad and sorrowful as the source whence they took their origins. When she had finished dressing Him, she kissed His cheeks, which were lit by the zealous fire that burned in His breast for our salvation. Turning His serene eyes to His Mother's, He shone with new beauties. Then the Virgin recovered her serenity somewhat, the darkness clearing from her brow, and put Him back to sleep. With the greatest possible speed, she gathered together several things without which life is difficult to maintain, making her home echo with her sighs.

While the glorious Lady lamented, sighing, Joseph, his breast stricken by the continual storm of sorrow, covered a donkey's back with some poor garments. The young ass (a little donkey), an animal almost capable of reason, waited for its sacred burden.[136] Having saddled it, Joseph took the faithful stick that was strong enough to hold up the weight of his life and put several bags over his shoulders, which hung down both in front of and behind him; they contained the few things that Mary had been able to hastily gather together.

Mary's journey into Egypt and its discomforts. Having taken her beloved treasure in her arms, she mounted the little donkey, which was led by Joseph's care. When the most serene Virgin saw the night's darkness and thought of the length and difficulty of the journey, she was bewildered and trembling, and felt more cruelly than ever the stabs of sorrow that pierced her as deeply as her heart of hearts and the soul of her soul. It seemed to her that she always saw the ministers of the royal cruelty who had uprooted her comfort from her breast.[137] So, at every little movement of a leaf or bird, at every little tread, fear produced its greatest chills in her. Then she trembled like a delicate reed in the puff of the southeast wind. And weeping, she lamented in a sound so beautiful that it softened the hardness of nearby unfeeling stones. Pale and weeping, she traveled with the greatest speed possible in the depth of the silent night, without help and without all those good things that fortune usually gives anyone less worthy, through rocky and unknown routes, which were very often muddy and slippery. Often overcome by tiredness and hunger, the animal, as one can imagine, on which she put her sacred weight, fell beneath her. And during the journey, old Joseph, troubled by its length, his age, and by the need for things necessary to

136. Praises of the ass are common in Renaissance literature. It is a symbol for humility—this is why it "kneels," is obedient, and is willing to perform everyday tasks that others will not do.

137. That is, Herod's men.

the human body, was sometimes unable to follow her. Whereupon, troubled by so many adversities, she praised her Creator. Besides this, she was wearied first by the rain, then the heat of the sun with its humidity and then the excessive heat. The holy persons traveled toward Egypt all night and all day, rarely taking a rest, and, after many dangers, tears, sighs, and much weeping, sleeplessness, and discomfort, they heard the furious roar made by the Nile coming down from on high.

The arrival of Mary in Egypt. Then the royal young girl became serene again, removing the gloomy clouds of her troubles that darkened her brow, knowing that her little Jesus would be safe in such a place. They lived there without those riches that impoverish their possessor in the humility of a little house, in which they endured not only excessive heat and cold but also lack of food. But the bitterness of roots and herbs was often sweet food to them, and the clarity and purity of a crystal stream were sweet nectar. Often they ate only bread cooked in the pure fires of Heaven.[138] The Virgin was always patient and strong in the face of the blows that rained on her above and beyond the trials and adverse afflictions. With the integrity of his craft, Joseph obtained a little of the food our nature needs for its preservation. As he was a foreigner he earned little. However, in great poverty they survived. The Virgin, too, whom Heaven elected as its queen, was in the straits of necessity, but by practicing the virtues of embroidery and lace-making, which she knew how to do very well, she made their great poverty a little less burdensome.[139]

Death of the Innocents. Herod, thinking that he had been laughed at and scorned by the great rulers of the eastern realms, and remembering the truth of the ancient prophecies, and afraid that the scepter of the Child who had been born King of the Jews had not been taken, enraged and poisoned with a tyrannous mind, decided to avoid this impending danger by showing his people an example of cruelty beyond any terrible belief. And it was not long before his pride gave way to rage and, his anger bursting from his lips, he ordered his ministers to put to death all the male children in Bethlehem and in the surrounding area. On hearing this, his followers, who constantly thought in terms of the wickedness of the most evil actions, were

138. This refers to manna, the food miraculously provided for the Israelites on their pilgrimage through the wilderness from Egypt to the Holy Land (Exodus 16).

139. This charming little vignette shows Mary taking up the ladylike pastimes of "embroidery and lace-making," as depicted in medieval and later images of her. The *Meditations* relate that Mary employs the spindle and needle to eke out a frugal living (68, 75–76), but never doing fancy work, while Joseph practices his carpentry (76). Delightful illustrations accompany the narrative (plates 62 and 63).

pleased. But Heaven, to prevent evil from prevailing over innocence, disturbed the calm and clarity of its appearance. Soon the wicked men began the unheard-of cruelty. Behold (as many have written), the sound and flash of swords are now heard and seen by the earth's sorrow; behold the shrieks are heard, which spread to Heaven the wretched anguish moving in the mothers' breasts. Then a tremor, a pallor, and a sorrow were born in them that was no different from the tremor, pallor, and sorrow that is the manifestation of death in other faces. Growing offspring were torn from arms, breasts, and laps with violent ferocity. Breasts, cradles, roads, houses, beds, and squares were seen full of blood, and limbs were cut away from the innocence of delicate bodies. Here a young girl, who saw her son torn from her arms, whom she loved more than her own life (like a gentle plant plucked from the earth in which it took on life and nourishment), taken by his feet, and the sword given to the tender neck, his head and remains thrown to the ground. Another woman saw her two little boys torn from her arms, and, with bestial evil, the heads of the poor brothers hit together so much that the one killed the other. Some children were thrown into wells, others into fire, and the tender heads of not a few were trampled on by the savage heels of the wild, cruel people.

But listen to something strange (as it seems to me): while a beautiful little boy, similar in appearance to an angel, was gurgling, a child in his mother's lap, and in whose breast moved simplicity and innocence, who received kisses from his mother and returned them, he received a sword blow in his stomach from one of the villains so that the milk that she had given him only a little time before leapt out of the child's mouth into his mother's. Elsewhere, a young woman with a very noble and graceful appearance, adorned with a beauty almost divine, set out with her little boy, her only one, in her arms, perhaps wishing to go to the Temple to thank the Creator of all who had given her such a dear and welcome token. Behold, someone came upon her whose reward for wickedness showed in his face. Missing an eye, and with scars on his cheeks, brow, and nose, which his limited nature had known how to obtain, he had also lost his ears through punishment. Seeing the lady, who showed in her eyes and brow the joy in her heart for her son, whom she was carrying around her neck, he rushed at her with the frenzy and rage with which the wolf goes towards lambs and tore him from her arms. Stupefied by this sudden attack, and even though she had no hope for her child's well-being, she still tried to restore the spirit of his soul with the tears of her sorrow and the charm of her prayers. It was all in vain, however, because the wicked man, having slit open the child's breast from its throat to its stomach, showed her beloved son's still beating heart to his weeping mother, and then tearing it out of the breast, threw it far away from him. Then, laughing, with his foot he thrust the body into a deep ditch. Another man, no less wicked than this one, had ripped two little boys from the arms of their pitiful mother who, weeping and lamenting, was like an afflicted little swallow whose dear offspring have flown, and begged him to return her hopes to her. The cruel man, making his cruelty more cruel, took the innocent children by their feet and struck them on the head so hard, and also on the unhappy mother's back, that he killed them, while she herself remained scarcely alive.[140]

Herod's joy at the death of the Innocents. Anyone who could tell of the various, all really dreadful, guises in which death appeared in the unhappy city, and in all the neighboring areas of Bethlehem, would recount again life's woes and death's tears. Each can estimate on his own account how much blood was shed, as 140,000 children were killed through the wrathful king's wickedness. Then, everywhere, the tearful sound of laments and shrieks was heard, made by the unhappy mothers who often raised their eyes to Heaven's serenity to see if the One who moved all appeared on the balcony of Paradise to pour His compassion on their miseries. But what reward, O blessed souls, does Christ prepare for you, since you are the first deaths for Him who is killed for you? May your fathers and mothers rejoice with you, because if their eyes are deprived of the sight of you who were their lights, now laughing and joyful you shine before God. Herod, seeing every place entirely full of mutilated and torn limbs, blood running and oozing in every part, and hearing the groans and sighs, seeing the fathers and mothers wrapped in clothes that showed their mourning spirits, and believing that among the dead bodies was that of the One who had been born King of the Jews, rejoiced, like a man who rejoices knowing that the excellences of his unique virtues have saved a city from falling into the hands of proud enemies.

BOOK THREE

Summary: *Herod has the Innocents slaughtered, and rejoices with the greatest of joy in their deaths. Joseph leads Mary and Jesus to their home, then goes with them to Jerusalem for the feast in the holy Temple, where Mary loses her Son, who is finally found by her among the doctors, and who returns with her to Nazareth. Joseph dies, comforted by the Virgin and Jesus, who then goes away into the solitude of the desert, where John was, by whom He is*

140. The story of the massacre of the innocents is told in Matthew 2:13–18. This account is Marinella's own gloss on the story.

Figure 10. Engraving showing the Massacre of the Innocents; Christ among the Doctors; the Marriage Feast at Cana; the Crucifixion; and the Ascension. From the 1602 edition of *La vita di Maria Vergine Imperatrice dell'Universo descritta in prosa & in ottava rima da Lucretia Marinella* (fol. 46v). Reproduced by kind permission of the Biblioteca Nazionale Centrale di Roma.

baptized, and fasts for forty days. He then accompanies His Mother to celebrate the wedding feast of Cana in Galilee, where He transforms the tastelessness of water into the taste of wine. Beyond that, various miracles performed by Him are related, and the conversion of the Magdalen. Mary sees Jesus taken by enemies. Then, overcome by extreme sorrow, she faints. She then sees Him tortured, dead, and placed in the sepulcher. He appears to her. She goes up to the Mount of Olives with the apostles to see the ascension of her Son, and having witnessed it, returns to her modest dwelling.[141]

Seven times already had spring shown its garments embroidered by flowers and, equally, summer had revealed its rich brow crowned by golden corn ears to Heaven, singing their happy abundances, since the Virgin, Jesus, and Joseph had left Judea, when the One who, knowing all, governs all, and with the greatest providence provides for all, wanted Joseph to understand that he should lead Mary with Jesus back to their own country. He therefore called to him one of his messengers and made him know His desire. The Messenger, having heard what the Lord wanted to command him, reverently bowed his beautiful head and made himself available to execute whatever was required of him by the heavenly Leader.

In a dream, the Angel tells Joseph, who was sleeping, to lead Mary and Jesus back to their country. At this time, as Night, in its dark mantle, had invited people to the calm of repose, Joseph, overcome by the tiredness of what he was doing and by his age, laid his cloak out on some pieces of firewood, an occupation that sapped his strength, and lay down. Soon Sleep dipped a small branch of poppies into the sweetness of his oblivion and, spraying his eyes with these, made him fall asleep, even though his inner spirit, ever more wakeful, kept a close eye on many things that while his body was awake, it could not be aware of.[142] While he was asleep a light appeared to him, which, spreading sparks, cleared the dark of the shadows that surrounded his soul, a light that kindled, showing in its center a luminous body, as a lit coal appears among bright flames. This was the Messenger of God's will, who had a face of flaming purple, shining hair, and wings that trembled because of the slightness of their feathers. Opening his lips full of heavenly sweetness, he said, "Joseph, servant of the One who tempers with the strength of His power the wind's fierceness, the swelling sea, and nature's harshness, as Herod has died, who sought to kill the Child Jesus, leave Egypt and live in the land of Israel." When he had said this, he disappeared, like the sun when its serene face is obscured by dense clouds. Awakened, the perfect man, thinking of the Mes-

141. Although the story of the massacre of the innocents is related in Book Two, it is included in the summary to Book Three.

142. This refers to the narcotic or sleep-inducing effect of the poppy.

senger who had come, of the Prince who sent him, and of the commandment given him, and withdrawing entirely into himself, thought how great and compassionate divine goodness was, as it did not scorn to make him share the greatness of His secrets. He was similar to a servant who, seeing himself praised by his lord, becomes more inflamed with love for him.

Joseph thanks God. Then, more ardent than ever, kneeling on bare knees, he praised, prayed, and thanked his Maker and God, who had not only made him worthy of seeing, serving, and following His only Son, but also of knowing His hidden and obscure secrets. And he talked with God until Dawn, leaving the gold of her bed, poured from her lap onto mortals the flowers and roses she had grown in the beauty of her gardens. Then, turning his steps, he left prayers in his Lord's hands, and silently went towards the room of the illustrious Queen, where he listened carefully to see whether she was sleeping. Hearing that she was praying to Heaven, he knocked on the door, and when it opened, he told her how the Lord God had sent one of His messengers from the heavenly mansion to tell them that Herod was dead and that they should therefore return to Judea.

Obedient to divine commandments, the Virgin prepared herself, but before leaving she gathered together many things that the Egyptian women had given her for embroidering and quilting. These she returned to them and similarly Joseph did the same with much of the work he had begun. When the Egyptian women, fond of her virtues (which breathed forth other perfumes than branches that the phoenix brings to its pyre),[143] heard that her departure was near, there was not one of them who did not bathe the floor with her tears. Carrying our Salvation on her breast, Mary, mounted on a little donkey with Jesus, went toward Judea, guided by Joseph, leaving the Egyptian places bereft, like the autumn season leaves the earth.[144]

Joseph leads Mary and Jesus to Nazareth. When the glorious Virgin arrived in Nazareth, she was delighted to see the small abode where she had been born, lived, and where the Angel had announced the coming of Christ to her. Having arranged the meanness of her few possessions, she gave herself up to contemplating life and to her soul's spirituality with such fervor in her heart that she could do no more. She was always praying, and praying begged God on behalf of human imperfections.

143. The mythical phoenix, believed to be the only bird of its kind and to have lived in the Arabian desert, burned itself to ashes on its pyre every five hundred years, and rose from its ashes to live through another cycle. In Christian writings, it was often regarded as an image of the Resurrection.

144. The story of the angel's appearance to Joseph and the return to Galilee is in Matthew 2:19–23.

Mary goes with Jesus and Joseph and his relatives to Jerusalem for the festivities of the great Temple. In the meantime, Jesus reached the age of twelve; His beauty, gentleness, and graces I dare not describe. It is enough to say that He was God, and that the sun and moon glorified in seeing Him. As the famous feast day, which took place in the golden Temple of God in Jerusalem, grew nearer, Mary and Jesus, with Joseph and their relations gathered together, set out to go to it.[145] When they had arrived in the holy Temple, the enormous multitude of people assembled was the cause of the young Jesus becoming separated from His Mother, in fact thus permitted by Him, who is the only glory of blessed souls.

Mary realizes that she has lost Jesus. After she had prayed, the Virgin realized that she had lost her dear Son among the groups of people, as well as all His relatives, and, thinking that He had left with them, made the journey with Joseph toward their home. Looking for Him among their relations, and not finding the mainstay of her life, she became troubled in her serene mind, and this truly showed in her face, the lovely demeanor of which was obscured by the clouds of melancholy sorrow and, beading the pink of her cheeks, with tears that competed with each other as they fell from her eyes. I believe that she said to herself:

> Alas, how careless, how foolish I am; as the soul of my limbs has been left elsewhere, do I not feel the loss of it? How is it possible that I went without the Light that gives light to my eyes? Alas, have I lost You, and I know not where? Perhaps, soul of my soul, You have been taken, stolen by the fury and hate that Archelaus inherited together with his father's kingdom?[146] Alas, wretched and unhappy me. This sorrow is surely the point of the sword that will pierce through my heart, foretold to me by Simeon, whose foreseeing spirit mourned the future happenings while he told me of them.

The Virgin seeks her Son. Thus the venerable Lady lamented and, lamenting, was like a pure turtledove that has lost her beloved companion, seeking her hope through the known houses of relations and friends. But as she did not see Him or find Him there, she began to ask everyone if they had seen Him, describing to them His features, the way He walked, His clothes, and

145. The feast day referred to is that of the Passover. Marinella elaborates on the story in Luke 2:41–50 of the loss and finding of Jesus in the Temple.

146. Archelaus, son of Herod the Great, inherited the territories of Judea, Samaria, and Idumea, but was banished to Greece after disturbances in 6 CE.

age, begging them, or their wives, or children, for the love that they bore the Creator of Heaven, that if they knew where He was, they would let her know. Three days later she met someone with a wholly joyful face, who gave her news of Him, saying:

> Glorious Lady, I have seen, not without wonder in my heart, a young boy with a face similar, and way of walking, and wearing clothes similar to the One whom you are seeking, in God's great Temple. He is among a countless multitude of men, who are occupied with the study of the sciences and laws; He is asking questions and answering.

Whereupon everyone who was listening to him was struck by amazement (as I have found it written).

Mary finds her Son among the Doctors in the Temple. These words appeared like a clear ray of sun that considerably lightened the clouds of sorrow that encircled her soul. Accordingly, speeding her steps with righteous Joseph, she reached the lofty house of the One who is the excellence and summit of all things. On entering it, they saw Jesus debating God's providence and wisdom, and saw the priests and doctors, confused by the light of His profound knowledge, look at each other without replying. But they heard them say among themselves, "How could it be that a young boy of such a tender age, who has never studied, could overcome our intellects which have already been tired for so many years by continual reading and research?" And saying to Him, "You are the winner of our holy contest." The Mother, who until now had been silent and to one side, drew near to her Son, her eyes full of tears, and said in the humble voice with which she had replied to Gabriel when she received the Holy Spirit in her breast, "Son, I weep and sigh, because three days have passed since my eyes have not been mirrored in Your blessed face. Therefore my soul, which has been deprived of You, has tasted the food of absence, and borne Your absence wretchedly." Replying, Jesus said with the following, or similar, words, "My duty, beloved Lady, is to make known the greatness, glory, and power of my Father. However, may the heart of your soul be comforted, and rejoice in its own worthiness; its perfection does not need my presence. Therefore calm the sorrows that disturb your mind."[147] Saying this, with His remarkable gentleness and a small smile to cheer her, He dried her eyes with His own hands. His

147. Cf. Luke 2:49. It is interesting to note that Marinella does not refer to Mary and Joseph's not understanding what Jesus says to them ("And they understood not the word that he spoke unto them," v. 50), and chooses to render the scene as one of loving familial reunion.

words etched profoundly into her memory; she encircled His neck with so much love that affection itself could not show the half of it and, taken by tender joy, which touched her to the very core, demonstrated the nature of the fervor of blood ties. Then she joyfully went to Nazareth with her dear Son and her just husband.

The Virgin finds Jesus, and Joseph returns to Nazareth. Joseph, whose goodness—which made him worthy of being chosen by God as guardian of the Virgin and father in name of Jesus—was visible in his appearance, shivering and tired through his exertions and troubles, his shoulders bent under the unbearable weight of his years, felt that he was nearing his last hour. He therefore awaited death to complete his end by closing his eyes that were already almost closed through age. Dropping onto his poor bed, he groaned, and through his groans called in an exhausted and humble voice to the one whom Nature was unable to make proud, and said to her, as might be imagined:

> Daughter and Bride of God, whose ardent prayers turn His anger into peace, I beg the clemency of your goodness that you will make use of it to save my soul, so that it may contemplate in the serenity of His visage the great and immense good we desire. Pray to Him, now that I am dying, holy Virgin, and because my ingratitude has not known how to pay a minimal part of the great debt that I owe God, my soul fears with good reason that He will punish it with eternal damnation, unless your holy intercessions help it; and if I have not been, as I know, as obedient and ready to serve as I should have been toward your Son, and toward you, blessed Mother, I beg you to reconcile Him with me. And I also beg God's only born Son, who is God, and true Messiah, to forgive my weaknesses, to bless me, and that you give me peace with your blessing and commend my spirit to Him, who will sweetly gather it in His longed-for peace.[148]

The just old man finished speaking in a weak voice. Then young Jesus joined them, with His face full of compassion and gentleness. When Joseph saw Him, those few white hairs that sprouted around his brow stood on end through reverence, and, lifting his wrinkled face and weakly raising his arms on which the almost dry skin was stretched, and joining his palms together,

148. This entirely apocryphal speech of Joseph to the Virgin derives ultimately, via Aretino's *Vita di Maria Vergine*, from a much earlier text. See note 150.

he wanted to ask forgiveness if he had not obeyed Him, made reverence, and bowed, as he should have done, and begged Him to forgive him the mistakes caused through his ignorance and weakness. But as he attempted to speak in a trembling voice, he collapsed, incapable of forming words, and stretching out a hand (to further his wish for forgiveness), took the hem of Jesus's garment, and kissing it weakly, gazed at Him with eyes already almost closed with the sign of death in his face.

Mary and Jesus comfort Joseph, who dies after Anna, according to many. Mary and Jesus, full of the mildness of mercy, comforted him and made him secure in the happiness that he would have in Paradise, the reward for perfecting the virtues with which he was endowed, as he had been more like an angel than a mortal. And, then, as he listened attentively, huddled and wrapped in a large piece of coarse sheeting, his life came to an end, his holy soul as beautiful, pure, and shining as he had received it, and he went down to Limbo, and like the simple dove that leaves its nest, so the pure spirit left the stainless body.[149] Then the Virgin was unable to keep back the tenderness that let the tears of sorrow pour from her eyes. Similarly, Jesus, overcome by the love that He felt for the chaste man, spilled the waters from His divine eyes, which, through the strength of His sorrow, sprang from the depths of His heart. Once the perfect man was dead, that holy and stainless person, the worthy relations brought his venerable body to Bethlehem to sleep in the earth near to his other noble ancestors, the very long sleep of the dead.[150]

Jesus goes to the desert where John was. After burying the perfect old man, the only born of the Highest went into the solitude of the desert. There John terrified the horrors of caves and silent woods with loud groans and a fearful voice.

Penitence of John. He had, if we wish to believe many holy men, wild hair, a shaggy beard, and a face that was entirely similar to that of Penitence.[151] His shoulders were covered with the skin of an animal, the purity of which was not dissimilar to that of his own soul. His arms, legs, and feet were bare: he ate bitter herbs and often broke his frequent fasts with locusts, drinking

149. Joseph goes to Limbo, as Christ has not yet opened the gates of heaven.

150. The account of Joseph's death comes from the History of Joseph the Carpenter, a fourth- or fifth-century Egyptian text, probably Greek in origin. See Elliott, *Apocryphal New Testament*, 110–117. His cult was revived in the seventeenth century and became very popular. The reference to Anna in the section heading refers presumably to Anna, mother of the Virgin.

151. The figure of Penitence is usually shown in the visual arts as a gaunt woman with long hair, wearing animal skins and barefooted, similar to a wild woman. John the Baptist is described similarly in the accounts in the New Testament.

water, and resting on a hard, damp rock; with the cries that issued from his heart, he shook the woods and rocks, and, behold, anyone who heard him was terrified.[152]

Seeing Jesus, John withdrew into himself through the reverence that he felt for Him, then said in a loud voice, "Here is the Lamb of God, whose pity and mercy have come to cancel the sins of the world."[153]

Christ has Himself baptized by John. When he had said this, he wished to go up to Christ to sprinkle the most happy water of the fortunate Jordan on the holy head, as some doctors [of the Church] note, during which time the Holy Ghost came down from Heaven, its head of regal purple and wings of flaming beams, and the voice of the Father said, "This is my beloved Son."[154] With the sacrament instituted for all His faithful, Jesus went to the wildest places in the desert, His soul faultless and entirely full of God and, wanting to satisfy the highest Justice, made His body feel the bitterness of penitence through fasting and suffering.[155]

Mary's prayers. While Jesus was in the desert, the Lady of Heaven, who understood with her mind's divinity the penitence her most innocent Son was undergoing, was so moved by such a great example that she never rose from her prayers and, with meditations and contemplation, fed her soul with heavenly food. Nevertheless, she sometimes sighed and wept for her Son's absence with such sweet laments that a harmony could be heard that was similar to the one made by angels. When Jesus had overcome the bitterness of fasting and the persistent temptations of our enemy with ceaseless persistence, He returned to cheer His mother's sorrows.[156]

Jesus and Mary go to the wedding feast in Cana in Galilee. It came to pass not too long after that the blessed Christ and Mother Mary were invited to the magnificent wedding feast being celebrated in Cana in Galilee.[157] The true examples of humanity, they went to the sumptuous home of the newly married couple where, on arrival, the honored gathering sat down. The people saw the tranquility that calms the storms of hearts etched gravely on Jesus's face. Among the women, they saw Mary, resplendent like the sun's face surrounded by dark clouds. The banquet was scarcely halfway through when

152. Mark 1:1–6; Matthew 3:1–6; Luke 3:1–6.

153. John 1:29–34.

154. Matthew 3:13–17; Mark 1:9–11; Luke 3:22.

155. The sacrament alluded to is that of baptism. According to Christian tradition, Christ himself instituted the sacrament (cf. Matthew 28:19 and John 3:5).

156. This refers to the forty days Jesus spends in the wilderness (Mark 1:12–13; Matthew 4:1–11; Luke 4:1–13).

157. The account of the marriage at Cana is in John 2:1–11.

the wine, which makes minds joyful, ran out.[158] Then Mary, who was the fount of mercy, said to her Son, "They have nothing to quench their thirst as there is no wine," and He replied in this fashion, "This is your concern, Lady and dear Mother, and not mine."[159]

Christ makes wine from water. Then to fulfill His dear Mother's request, Jesus ordered the servants to fill six great stone jars with water, which the Jews had placed there, according to their purification rites. When they were full, the One who was to spill His blood to redeem us, said, "Take some of it to the steward to taste." When the steward had tasted it, he reprimanded the bridegroom: "You have acted contrary to normal custom, since everyone puts out the best wine first, and you have served it at the end." All those who saw the water jars being filled declared this to be a miracle. Then because of the strangeness of this marvelous scene, everyone declared Him to be God and the true Messiah. This was the first miracle, which, at the request of the most serene Lady, His power revealed to the world.[160]

Prayers of the Virgin for human sorrow. On their return to Nazareth, the woman who was first Queen of Heaven rather than an earthly woman, distributed her few belongings to others' needs, as she was always sensitive to their misfortunes. And although she was full of divine grace and without the stain of original sin, she did not cease to offer continuous prayers to the great Father, so that she extinguished sin's flames with her mercy's full sea, flames that, continually burning, kill our souls. And sometimes she ate no food other than that taken from God's table for two days at a time.[161]

Miracles of Christ. While she was praying to the King of the World, the sound of her prayers a harmony sweeter than the sound that angels make when turning the eternal heavenly engines,[162] the truth came from Jesus's lips with greater magnificence and more clearly than the sun shows when it springs from Aurora's womb. Beyond this, He showed numerous signs of His superhuman might, so that countless people ran after Him, moved by His teaching and boundless power. The holy Virgin heard all these things and even heard how, at the wonderful sound of His words, the angry sea put aside its overbearing pride that agitated its waves.[163] She heard how He

158. Marinella uses the word *liquore* for wine, possibly the poetic word for a fluid substance.

159. Cf. John 2:4.

160. The miracle of the water and wine is often used to illustrate the power of the Virgin as intercessor, and as instigator of her son's first miracle.

161. That is, spiritual sustenance.

162. The "heavenly engines": the universe was seen as a piece of machinery constructed of concentric spheres.

163. The account of Christ calming the water appears in Matthew 8:23–27.

cured the illness of the centurion's dying servant;[164] how the faith of the great Canaanite woman moved the mercy of the Highest with the voice of her humility;[165] how at Christ's appearance the sea, agitated by winds in its greatest fury, not only soothed its wrath and pride, but was made worthy by Him by feeling the lightness of His divine soles on its back.[166] She heard how at the pool at Bethesda, His goodness cured the man who had been in the grip of illness for seven *lustri* and three years.[167] And how His eminent power drove away the evil spirit from the dumb one, and also the recurring fever that troubled Simon Peter's mother-in-law with its heat and ice.[168] Similarly, she heard how He cured the ten lepers, and the man suffering from dropsy, and raised the lame.[169] She heard how His mercy, having become compassionate toward those who followed His truth, increased the bread and fish to the wonder of the world and honor of Heaven,[170] and how the light coming from His infinite love lit up the shadows that crushed the faculty of sight of the man born blind.[171] The Lady of the Angels heard also how that voice, which would call the souls of the dead on the great day, called the dead son of the weeping widow from his fearful coffin.[172]

Conversion of the Magdalen. She also heard how, through speaking, He struck with words, which seemed like flashes of lightning and thunder, the immodesty and conceit in the heart of the Magdalen, who was absorbed in pride of her great beauty, and how He had turned her entirely to God, removing her wholly and totally from the vanities and lusts of the flesh and the world. And she heard how she, who was entirely vanity, and a nest of all those vices, one of which is powerful enough to make souls fall with their weight into the divine precipice, was converted, offering God the incense of her prayers.[173] [And she heard] how Lazarus, stinking and corrupted, dead

164. The story of the centurion's servant is in Luke 7:2–10.

165. According to Mark (7:25–30), the woman is a Syro-Phoenician; in Matthew (15:22–28), she is a Canaanite.

166. Matthew 14:24–33 (Christ walks on the water).

167. John 5:5–9. A *lustrum* was a period of five years.

168. See Matthew 9:32–33 (the healing of the dumb man); Matthew 8:14–15 (the healing of Simon Peter's mother-in-law).

169. See Luke 17:12–19 (the ten lepers); Matthew 8:2–6 (the man with palsy). There are numerous references to Christ's healing the lame (e.g., Matthew 11:5, 15:31, 21:14; Luke 7:22).

170. Accounts of the feeding of the five thousand appear in Mark 6:30–44; Matthew 14:13–21; Luke 9:10–17; and John 6:1–13.

171. John 9:1–7 (the miracle of the man born blind).

172. Luke 7:12–15 (the raising of the widow's son).

173. The story of Mary Magdalen's conversion, which was the subject of countless paintings, sculptures, poems, and music in the sixteenth and seventeenth centuries, derived from the

for four days already, came out of the terrible tomb, called by Christ's voice, which restored his soul to him, his spirit, and senses, and then returned him alive to the sorrowing sisters Magdalen and Martha, a miracle that was the most immense and greatest of miracles, and how many put all their hopes in Him, having seen such a work worthy of the hand of God only.[174]

The Virgin, on account of Jesus, now troubled, now joyful. Beyond that, the venerable Virgin knew and heard how the scribes and Pharisees, propelled by their shrewd evil and spurred by envy's stinging incitement, now wanted to throw Him down from the boundless height of a mountain; now they sought to kill Him, and now to stone Him.[175] Therefore she was frightened, then she hoped, and fearing and hoping prayed, and praying, praised the One who is alone worthy of praise. Then she heard how her sweet Jesus, entering Jerusalem, was called Son of God by little boys, and was honored with olive branches and palms, signifying victory, which would refer to His death, and she foresaw this with her divine prophetic spirit and knew it by reason of the slanders and outrages directed at her sweet Son by the envious Jews. More sorrowful than any other person within herself, with a tearful face, she went to the noble dwellings of the royal ladies, Magdalen and Martha, who wept at her weeping and grieved at her grieving as if for their own loss.[176] The heavenly Lady remained there for a long time, lamenting and mourning her beloved Jesus's approaching death.[177] And He came into her presence, sorrowful in His heart and joyful in His outward appearance, but with a grave joy, and was soon received as lovingly as possible by the sorrowful Mother

---

amalgamation of her New Testament figure as leading woman disciple and first witness of the resurrected Christ with the woman named a sinner in Luke 7:36–50, who wept on Christ's feet and dried them with her hair before anointing them. From the late sixth century the saint was regarded by the Church of Rome as the repentant sinner par excellence. Her sin, according to the early Church Fathers, was that of her sexuality. The Church's favorite female saint after the Virgin Mary, the tripartite figure was particularly important for Counter-Reformation dogma concerning sin and redemption. See Susan Haskins, *Mary Magdalen: Myth and Metaphor* (New York: Harcourt Brace, 1994), 3–32, 58–97, 134–296, for the evolution of the figure of Mary Magdalen.

174. Mary Magdalen was also identified with Mary, sister of Martha and Lazarus of Bethany (John 11:1–45), who are probably the same Mary and Martha in Luke 10:38–42.

175. John 11:47–53.

176. Mary Magdalen and Martha are given a noble and affluent ancestry in the *Golden Legend* (1:375). This is probably derived from Luke's description of Mary Magdalen as one of the women "who ministered unto [Jesus] of their substance" (8:3), which led early commentators to assume that she was independently wealthy.

177. This long scene of Christ bidding farewell to his mother and Mary Magdalen is apocryphal. It is taken from "How the Lord Jesus Predicted His Death to His Mother" in the *Meditations* (308–309).

and sisterly friends, with every ardor of love, and every kind of friendship and reverence. Mary, gazing with her eyes full of her usual mercy, and already empty of tears, at the tranquility of her loved Son's countenance, in a mournful and weak voice uttered words similar to the following, from her sorrowful breast:

> I understand, I know, and foresee, O only joy of my mind, O only solace of all my sorrows, the envy that rules the hearts of our princes and priests, because of the wisdom You brought from Heaven's heights, and because of the wonder of so many marvels that You show with divine power, that they are seeking, in every way possible, to seize You and wretchedly torture and kill You. Overcome by the strength of this too cruel sorrow, I feel my spirit die a thousand times each hour.

"Put an end to your sorrows, my sweetest Mother," replied the One born to save the world, "because it is necessary for me to die soon, and that I die cruelly. If the first man to stray from the straight path, shown him by the goodness of the eternal Father, was the reason for the death of living souls, therefore, by dying, the Man full of eternal divinity will bring life to the souls over which death now triumphs."[178]

The Virgin's Words to Jesus. And I believe she said as well, trembling weakly:

> I beg You, at least, O Light of my eyes, since it is necessary for You to die violently for the salvation of all, to not deny me this comfort. Which is that it will be many years before You have to suffer the bitter outrages and sorrows of Your death. I do not beg You, O sovereign hope of all my desires, to do it as the reward of the milk sucked from this breast, nor for those long and wearying efforts I bore in the greatest silence of the night, in the most burning heat of the day, nor for those many fears, tremors, and terrors I have already had; nor through an excess of the love that I have given You with every tenderness of love, and give You. But I truly beg You through Your immense and great omnipotence; I beg You through the burning love that, miraculously casting You from Heaven to earth, was the reason You came to bring salvation to the sick world, to revive the dead souls of the

178. In the Christian tradition, the first man, Adam, brought sin, suffering, and death into the world; through his death Christ, the second Adam, brought eternal life.

> world with Your words, which created Heaven out of nothing, but not through Your sufferings.[179] And if this cannot be done thus to please the eternal Father's justice, may the clemency of Your mercy console the afflicted soul languishing in my breast, first with my death, which saddens [my soul], piercing it through, nay killing it, with Your early death.

With these words the divine Virgin became silent, keeping fixedly still her tearful, beautiful eyes, which shone in her face, on the eyes of her Son, and God; and gazing, she knew that His goodness had not bent to her laments.

Grieving words of Mary to her Son. Then more sorrowfully than before (I believe), she began her interrupted supplications again, saying:

> Oh, my Son, the lamenting groans of the disconsolate little widow for her loved son were able to move the goodness of Your divine nature; the centurion's entreating words for his languishing servant; the high priest's tears for his dead daughter; and now maternal prayers, and maternal tears, can they not move the sweet tenderness of Your compassionate breast?[180] Do You not know, who sees and knows all, that it is impossible for a body to live without a soul, and therefore it is impossible for this unhappy Mother to look at the sun's light without You, since You are its soul? But do not let her see Your death, or at least, dying with You, do not let her remain sorrowful forever. Nevertheless, always, and in everything, may Your wish be done, may Your just high will be done, for if it does not please You that I die, living wretchedly in my sorrows, I shall call myself happy obeying Your holy wishes.

Here this dazzling light of glory, flashing with unaccustomed splendor in Heaven's high empire, was silent, her face pale and tearful. Whence one could say that she resembled a rose wounded by the sun's too harsh rays and then softened by sudden rain. On hearing these words, the One who had come to cancel the endless errors of mortal sinners with His blood, no less compassionate in His heart than merciful in His face, looked at her gently

179. The dead souls are all those who died before the coming of Christ, and awaited him in Limbo.

180. See the accounts of the miracles of the widow's son (Luke 7:12–15); the centurion's servant (Matthew 8:5–13); and Jairus's daughter (Mark 5:22–24, 35–43).

and was silent. In the godliness of His appearance, He seemed a spirit happy in the harmonies of peace, even if His breast was tormented by a thousand sorrows.

Words of the Lord to Mary. Hence love for His dear Mother, hence the firm will of the supernal Father, the bitterness of His approaching death, the endless sins of calamitous humankind, all these distressed, even bitterly pierced, the heart and soul of the tormented Christ who, restraining the sorrow of His anguish toward the Virgin Mother, said in a piteous voice, as might be imagined:

> Bring peace to your internal strife, my beloved Mother; bring an end to your so many laments. Assuage the bitterness of your sorrows, the instruments of grief to my grieved breast, because by assuaging them, you will assuage part of that bitterness that distresses my soul for you. Bring an end to your weeping, the cause of general joy.[181]

The Son of the great Ruler of Paradise spoke, consoling His sorrowing and grieving Mother. Then, at a sober feast prepared by faithful Martha, He sat down and near to His goodness, the Queen of the heavenly realms, who, instead of the sweetness of the wine, drank the tears of her sorrows, which ran down her face.[182]

The converted Magdalen, as a loving and charming child, settled herself to sit near her Lord's sacred feet, gathering the sweetness of the flowers of His words with the hand of her enamored soul, and turned her eyes, those eyes formerly flames and arrows of foolish love, into two tearful fountains and reverently washed and kissed the heavenly soles of her beloved Master. Similarly marveling at His kindness, she said to herself, "Accept Lord, receive with favor, O Well-being of my soul, what the penitent heart gives You by means of my eyes," and with her sweet tongue and ringing words, she spoke:

> O Power of the eternal Powers, at the sound of whose great name Heaven bows down, Hell trembles, and the world reverently yields itself, what will be words worthy to give thanks to You, which Your endless kindness merits? Since You wished my eyes, unworthy of looking

181. The cause of the Virgin's sorrow—her son's death—is paradoxically the source of mankind's joy and salvation.

182. Marinella follows the *Meditations* (308–9) in using the episode of Martha and Mary (Luke 10:38–42) for her own scene of the Virgin as the guest of the sisters of Bethany.

at the magnificence of the Sun's flaming face and, despite being misty and weak, to gaze at You, living Sun of Paradise, whom the naked souls worthy of Your realms rejoice in being able to see.

Silent, she thought with her soul's bitterness and sorrow of the filth of sins already committed, and of hell, which had been opened by these, and, thinking of the just punishments, the soul of her soul trembled like a slender reed in the puff of a light breeze. The saving, holy, and kind words that the heavenly Master had said to her when He unburdened her of the heavy load of her countless errors still rang in her heart. The Ruler of the Stars, who saw her closing thoughts with the sharp eyes of His divinity, blessed her and praised her.[183]

When they had finished the sad feast, Jesus consoled His grieving Mother with gentle words. She, however, still believed that she might enjoy her Son for longer on earth. Bidding her farewell and blessing her, He went to pray and then to take the rest that one can imagine that the Son of God would take close to the greatness and cruelty of a most bitter Passion and death, zealous and merciful to the souls who continually fell into the center of the infernal flames.

Jesus has His dear Mother called. Then, the following day, He sat in one of the rooms of the noble ladies of Bethany, His brow veiled by a dark veil of melancholy, and His face pale and afflicted. Somewhat thus lost in Himself, He said to the Magdalen, who was unable to rise from her place at His feet but tasted the sweet honey of His holy words with the tongue of her heart, "Have my dear one, my beloved Mother, come to me, so that before my death, which will take place soon, she can see and hear me." As He said these words, the Magdalen was in the position and paying the kind of attention to hear Him that angels can be imagined to be in to listen to God's commandments. She immediately went to Mary, the woman who before the world's creation was chosen by the supreme King to be the Mother of His only begotten Son, and informed her of Jesus's wish. On hearing it, the Mother went with the weeping Magdalen to where her dear Son was awaiting her, and immediately when she had fixed her blessed eyes on His lofty countenance with trembling heart and saw it full of sorrow and sadness, and the clouded pallor that was painted on the pure serenity of His face, it dispelled every hope in her heart, just as the waters' calm is dispersed by tempestuous puffs of the raging north wind.

183. Marinella has conflated the story of Mary and Martha (Luke 10:38–42) with the scene of the sinner in Luke 7:36–50.

Mary swoons. Assailed by boundless sorrow, her spirits constricted in her heart and, becoming pale, she fainted and fell to the ground before Jesus (as some writers relate, even if others say that she never fainted).[184] Weeping, the beautiful Magdalen and her sister helped her, calling to her, and did all they could to comfort her. Then pity and sorrow seized the sacred breast of the eternal Father's Son with the most recent of her sufferings. Taking His dear Mother by the hand, He raised her and brought her back, making her sit by His side, and to comfort her anguished soul, He showed a spark of joy within the darkness of her distressed brow. One could have compared her face to the sun rising and setting in an instant. The Mother gazed at the Son, the Son His Mother, and they were silent, she taken by too cruel and too bitter anguish, He by compassion and by the tenderness of filial love. If their tongues were silent, they spoke with their eyes, and in the dumb silence the most sublime words of sorrow and lament unfolded.

Jesus consoles the Virgin Mother. Jesus, feeling His Mother's sorrows in His heart and having sealed the abundant springs of her tears, now enclosed in her breast since she was scarcely able to speak, in a low voice and one that was difficult to hear, spoke the following words:

> My beloved Mother, be happy, you have reason not to be unhappy but to truly rejoice as your countless merits are written on the bosom of Paradise. Rejoice in the joy of so many souls who languish in Limbo awaiting my hard and bitter, but longed-for and saving death, since (the moment has now arrived) it is my duty to shed my blood and, by leaving life, to redeem with my death the sons of humankind who have fallen through the Devil's persuasion into God's disgrace, and come into Heaven's hatred. For love of whom the sharp punishments I will not call punishments but sweetest delights. I left Heaven's certain joys and the throne of divine majesty for these disobedient sons, and here on earth I have wanted to suffer wrongs, persecutions, and sorrows. I shall tie the licentious and untamed evil of the proud infernal Angel with strong and unbreakable chains, and shall open Paradise, now for so long closed. And when I have resurrected from death to

184. Marinella was clearly aware of the controversy over the Virgin's fainting, which was first reported in the Gospel of Nicodemus, or Acts of Pilate, an apocryphal writing popular in the Middle Ages (James, *Apocryphal New Testament*, 116). According to Saint Ambrose, she had neither fainted nor wept over her son's fate as she had been a party to and privy to God's salvific plan and knew that he would rise again, and because of her moral nature. See Haskins, *Mary Magdalen*, 202, and note 27.

glorious life, I shall console those many sorrows that pierce the soul of your soul like almost stinging blades.[185]

The Son and the Mother discuss death. Hearing this, the Virgin sighed twice, one sigh interrupting the other, burning ever more with love, and with true love toward humankind; she was silent for a short while as she was unable to speak, prevented by inner anguish. Finally, she said, "My Son, do not deny this favor to Your Mother, who is almost dying. This is, that Your death may happen without bitter torment." "Bring an end to your sorrows, my beloved Mother," He replied (as might be imagined), "since there has never been and never will be a man who has died with so much suffering, so much grief, and such humiliation; so, as it is necessary that I die, all my flesh and bones will be cruelly lacerated, struck, and scourged. Then not only living creatures will be moved to pity, but inanimate things will show clear signs of my countless torments." On hearing these words, the glorious Virgin's spirit gave way, and she fell on the beloved breast and into the dear arms of the weeping Magdalen, her face becoming once more like a pale boss, sprinkled with drops of lukewarm perspiration.[186]

While Jesus was talking with the Virgin, his chosen brothers and disciples arrived, who immediately and simultaneously felt their limbs weaken, bewildered and saddened by her anguish and that of the other women, and by the unbearable sorrow of the heavenly Son, like the melancholy of a group whose harm has been predicted.

The Virgin swoons, according to some. Like people terrified and almost raving, they went to and fro because of their sorrow. Finally, the fainting Virgin, with the kind of fear that someone who dreams of dying awakens with, came to with a tremor of her heart that almost shook the angelic choirs and, wanting to speak, was unable to form the words. Knowing that it was now time to leave, the Son of the Highest, bathing the divinity of His beautiful heavenly eyes with bitter tears, kissed the brow of His afflicted Mother, who rejoiced in seeing Him. Then blessing her, He commended her to Mary Magdalen and Martha and the other Marys, who were there, and left, weeping, with His disciples. Saddened, but strong in sorrow, the Virgin remained, soaking her breast and face with copious tears, and stayed there for a long

185. A reference to Simeon's prophecy.

186. A boss is a sculpted or carved knob or projection placed to cover the intersection of ribs in medieval vaulting. The decoration is often in the form of a human head, as described here.

time as she heard how her Jesus had spent Easter in Jerusalem with His faithful apostles.[187]

Mary sees her Son taken by enemies. Then she not only heard (alas, unhappy news) but saw (alas, wretched sight) how her Son, and her God, was prey to the wicked and prisoner of his own enemies. Then the roses and lilies that adorned her divine face with white and rose changed into a dark pallor and, as she was overcome, she did not weep. Then it was as if her limbs were suddenly wounded, but did not pour forth the blood because it had congealed in her veins.

Mary falls, swooning. She then saw His body, which was whiter than milk and brighter than ivory and, having lost all splendor, was so wretched that it would have been impossible to look upon the cruelty, and while the liquid that nourished His vital spirits poured from His limbs, she mourned and languished like a rose crushed by the shepherd and, becoming pale and fainting, fell in the way that a body does when its life is stolen by the sword's violence. Mary Magdalen and the other sorrowful women who followed her, seized by the strength of their sorrow, were like violets damaged by night frost. Making a bed for her with their arms and breasts, they sprinkled tears instead of rose water onto her face until she regained her senses, which, together with her spirits, had flowed to warm themselves in the center of her heart.[188] And as she was able, she began in a sound worthy of pity and compassion, one of the most heartbroken laments and most sorrowful plaints ever made by a living person. Then she saw the white Lamb and stainless excellent brow, which the rays of His own divinity surrounded, crowned by the pricking thorns.[189] And she saw Him fall under the great weight of the Cross, bloody and almost reaching His last step, and being pulled by the rope, which was tied to that most innocent neck. The faithful Veronica immediately came upon her Savior, and gazing at His torment, was un-

187. The scene of Christ taking leave of his mother comes from the *Meditations*, "Of the Arrival of the Lord in Jerusalem on the Ass: Also How Jesus Is Said to Have Shed Tears in Three Ways" (305–6). Christ does not put his mother into the care of Mary Magdalen and the other women but into Saint John's at the Crucifixion (John 19:26). "Easter in Jerusalem" refers to the Last Supper or Passover feast (Matthew 26:17ff.; Mark 14:1ff.; Luke 22:1ff.; John 13:1ff.).

188. The image of the Virgin falling into the arms of her women companions is nonscriptural but appears in the *Golden Legend* and the *Meditations*, and is depicted in countless scenes of the Crucifixion.

189. The sacrificial lamb of ancient Near Eastern religions, including that of the Hebrews, was taken up by early Christians as representing Christ in his sacrificial role. When John the Baptist was baptizing, he saw Jesus coming toward him and said: "Behold the Lamb of God. Behold him who taketh away the sin of the world" (John 1:29). The "pricking thorns" allude to Christ's crowning with thorns.

able to keep back her tears. Her face suddenly became paler and, terrified in her soul, seized by the strength of pity and mercy, and fixing her eyes, full of sorrowful tears, on the dewy suns and on the bloody face and dripping sweat of her beloved Lord, she was struck and astonished, thinking of the cruelty carried out by the envy of the wicked Jews on the sacredness of that holy body.

Veronica dries Jesus's face. And seeing Him tired and in such a state, only able to stand on His feet with effort, she said to Him with piteous tears, "As I, Your servant, have nothing, I am unable to comfort You with anything. Receive with favor, my sweet Master, please accept, my Salvation, what the unworthiness of Your humble servant can give You in Your last step, of which she of such a name will be worthy and will be able to exalt." Saying this, she took a white veil from the blondeness of her shining hair, and full of fear and reverence, and with devotion, dried the bleeding face of the Ruler of the stars, and spoke in this vein: "Remember me, my Lord. Remember when You are in the eternity of Your glory." And He not only turned the salvation of His divine eyes to His kind maidservant's face, showing that her pity had been welcome, but also left her the sacred image of His divine face imprinted on the white veil, a great and glorious memorial of His sufferings and death.[190] Looking on with tearful eyes at noble Veronica's reverent pity, the Virgin Mother blessed her silently from the depths of her soul since she could not speak for sorrow. She followed the bloody steps of her scourged Son as far as Calvary, the hill on top of which the great bones and entire body of that first disobedient man were laid. As he had not kept the divine commandments, he had been chased from Paradise, once full of peace and joy, into the world of misfortune and the stormy sea of wars, by the heavenly power.[191] Then she looked at Him stretched on the huge wooden Cross and heard the terrible sound of harsh hammers striking the sharp nails that pierced through the powerful right hand, the glorious left, and the most holy feet.

Mary falls swooning again. Then her extremities became like ice again, and her face, turning the color of ashes and her mouth dry, she fell, like a noble plant killed by a violent wind. But the shouts and cheers made by the

190. According to legend, Veronica was a woman who wiped Christ's face with her veil or linen cloth on his way to Calvary. Her name derives from her action, which resulted in the image of Christ's face being imprinted on her veil, the "vera icon," or true image. See Ewa Kuryluk, *Veronica and Her Cloth: History, Symbolism, and Structure of a "True" Image* (New York: Oxford University Press, 1991).

191. Golgotha, "the place of a skull," is the Hebrew name for Calvary. The skull that often appears at the foot of the cross in scenes of the Crucifixion represents Adam's skull.

Hebrew crowds as they raised the boundless One on the Cross, where He lay between the arms as though in the soft feathers of the miraculous pelican, awakened not the Mother but the unhappy semblance of the Mother who, bound up in her sorrows, since she had tearfully gazed at the grieving women who stood around, terrified and blood-stained, turned her eyes toward Jesus, the image of sorrow and fountain of blood.[192] And although her tongue was scarcely able to loosen, I think she spoke in this way:

> *Lament of Christ's Mother.*
> So, O Soul of my soul, have You allowed the humanity that Your goodness made in Your likeness to hammer sharp nails into those hands, which out of nothing created Heaven, into the wood of the Cross? Did You want, O Light enlightening every soul worthy of Your light, Your brow that rises above all Heaven's heights to be crowned by thorns, the brow that blessed souls and celestial rays are proud to encircle? But if I mourn what pleases You, forgive my motherly pity. Even though I know that You alone were able to save humankind, to open Heaven, which has been closed for so many years by its sins, to extinguish with the rivers of Your blood the anger and disdain the supreme Father justly held against the human race, still I cannot prevent my body and soul from collapsing in tears and dissolving in sighs. But as these are the fruits of Your death, I can call these sorrows happy and these tears fortunate.

Mary's words to the crucifiers. While she was saying this, she saw the Jewish rabble, in whom all wickedness seemed to be natural, who wanted to offer hatred and bitterness to the Giver of salvation. Entirely overcome, and almost outside herself, she spoke in this way:

> O, for what purpose do you wish to add this inhuman atrocity to your cruelties? Where has there ever been seen someone who, like Him, went with such decisive steps to His end, denied such poor thanks? I beg you for the joy that you have in His sorrows to sate it with our tears, as He has sated you with His blood. And when your inhumanities deny it to Him, do not refuse to open my veins and, with what comes out of them, quench your greed; or grant me, through the joy

192. Because of its long hooked bill, the legendary pelican of the wilderness (*pelicano solitudinis* in the Latin Vulgate) was believed to revive or feed its offspring with its own blood from its breast. It is one of the symbols of Christ, as the reviver of the dead in spirit through his blood.

that you have in His death, that I may fill a jar with tears that drop from my eyes and offer them to Him to drink; since I have nothing else with which to comfort Him than what I obtain from you, I will not be so sorrowful, nor you so cruel.[193]

Signs of Christ's death. She had scarcely said these words when the sorrow that had left her tongue-tied made her appear like someone lulled to sleep. The sun, seeing pity droop, hid its beauty beneath the frightening dark shadows. All around, Heaven shone listlessly and murmured with unusual thunder, and flashing and murmuring, thundered, and thundering split mountains and made buildings fall. The earth was shaken through the terrifying strength of the earthquake. The great veil of the Temple was ripped from top to bottom: the woods' creaking and trees' collapsing were heard, as they were thrown to the ground by the winds' terrible violence. As Nature's laws were now broken, terrifying tombs opened, out of which came the bodies of saints that had rested in them for a long time. And at the sight of the strange happenings, the entire world knew that God was suffering.[194]

The Magdalen embraces Christ's Cross. At this time the Magdalen showed her heart's bitterness through sighs and laments. Her hair was loose and, without her usual care, spread down over her shoulders; already disgusted by jewels and gold, she covered her body, to which she had formerly given so much delight and now she gave as much pain, with a single garment. Opening her arms, which appeared encircled with the whiteness of snow, she embraced the Cross, and her eyes, which had yielded to lascivious amusements, gave way to tears that bathed her entire face and her entire breast. But between her weeping and sighs, she spoke thus, not with the sound of those voices with which she had formerly charmed her lovers' malleable hearts, but with those that usually gladden Heaven when a soul's wickedness turns into good:[195]

193. For the anti-Semitic sentiments expressed here and below, see volume editor's introduction, 26–27. The scene of Mary's apostrophizing the crucifiers appears in the *Meditations*, "Of the Opening in the Side of Christ" (339). Except for the allusions to the "pricking thorns" (214), "brow . . . crowned by thorns" (216), and "thorny diadem" (219), Marinella makes no reference to the Roman soldiers who of course crowned Christ with the thorns, flagellated him, and drew lots for his robes (Matthew 27:27–37; Mark 15:16–32; Luke 23:26–38; John 18:12ff., 19:1–2, 18–25).

194. These Apocalyptic happenings manifest Christ's sufferings. In Judaism and Christianity God also suffers because of the rebellion of the human race.

195. This description of Mary Magdalen is taken from a well-known sermon given in 591 by Saint Gregory the Great (*Homily* 33), which became a commonplace through the *Golden Legend*. See J.-P. Migne, *Patrologiae cursus completus. Series latina* (Paris: 1844–64), vol. 76, col. 1239.

The Magdalen's words.

O Lord and God, whose mercy full of the usual compassion snatched me from the evil hands of our foe, avenging Yourself with me with the weapons of mercy, when I, Your foolish enemy, raised on the wings of worldly happiness, held Heaven cheaply. Now that I do not believe in offending Your enormous goodness, which created me, I would offer my breast to the lances around me.

As she was saying this, according to some, the blowing wind spread the bright gold of her hair to the foot of the Cross, which was bathed in Jesus's blood.[196]

As Jesus's most holy soul left His tormented and sacred body, full of all sorrows, the evil crowd, ministers of His torments, having already quenched the thirst of its cruelty with His tears and sweat, happy with His pains and death, and bathed in His saving blood, neither wept nor was sorrowful, but laughing and rejoicing came down from the hill and returned to the city, the unhappy city of Jerusalem. Rejoicing in the dark blindness of its ignorance, Jerusalem was unaware of its defects and the errors it had committed, leaving the mortal remains of the pierced-through Christ, which, deformed by His own coagulated and congealed blood, would have been a wretched scene and horrible sight to the cruelest hearts and most atrocious minds.

The Mother contemplates her Son on the Cross. Thus the disconsolate Mother, who with John, the Magdalen, Martha, and the other Marys, was bathed in the blood that dripped from her beloved Son's body, looked one by one at the blows, wounds, and stabs that cruelty's hands had made in the head, hands, and feet of her dead hope, and felt every injury, every wound, and every stab wound pierce her breast with the bitterness of sorrow, as if she had been wounded by the piercing and cruelty of a hundred swords. What torment was yours, O Queen of the most beautiful souls that are worthy of God's presence? While you were by the lofty wood of the tragic Cross, perhaps you were thinking that the birds took sweet rest in their nests, the wolves and the bears in their caves and dens, and that your blessed Jesus had nowhere to rest His wounded and drooping body, which you saw held up only by the hardness of three sharp nails, softness next to the hardness of human hearts. And perhaps you thought that He is the One who clothes the earth with a green mantle painted with a thousand delightful colors,

196. This poetic description reflects countless images of the Crucifixion where the Magdalen's hair is draped round the foot of the cross, and refers to the episode in Luke, chap. 7, where the "sinner," later believed to be Mary Magdalen, wipes Christ's feet with her hair (vv. 37–48).

who covers Heaven with a cloth spangled with golden flowers, and you saw Him with nothing to cover the nakedness of His wounds, and His limbs as if torn to pieces by wolves; and you saw that head, fearful and venerable to the hearts of angels, crowned by the thorny diadem, which had nowhere to lay its tiredness.

And while she was gazing at Him and lost in her anguish, behold a group of proud people arrived, some on foot, and some on strong horses, who came to crush the bones and tear the flesh of the wretched condemned, so that on the Sabbath day (the day revered by Hebrew perfidy) the dead bodies did not remain on the hard scaffolds of the crosses. The sorrowful people were terrified by the rays and flashing light of their shining weapons, and Mary, seeing them, fearful in her sorrows, told herself that they had come to make new lacerations on the stainless body of the supreme Redeemer. On their arrival, they saw the one and the other of the wicked ones enjoy the clear light of day, both the one who knew how to steal Paradise, with the hands of his faith tied on the wood of the Cross, and the other, happy in his damnation. And they broke the bones of both, according to what their sins deserved, and then threw the bodies from a high cliff of a deep gorge.[197]

Mary begs the crucifiers. At this time the Virgin appeared like a lost dove that has ferocious eagles' talons on its head, and her trembling voice was able to make itself heard only with effort. She gently asked the strident angry people not to wish to add new torment to the afflicted body of the already dead Jesus. The poisonous viper listened more to the charms and much more to the sea of prayers of the people troubled by his fury than the wicked men to the sorrow of her piteous words.

Longinus wounds Christ. Among them was a man called Longinus who, despite being blind, nevertheless wanted to enjoy lacerating the body of the sovereign Monarch's Son. O tiger's nature, inhabitant of the Hyrcanian woods, O heart of stone, even of rigid iron, why do you wish to be pitiless towards someone dead, to be cruel to someone dead? Who has ever heard of so great and so much savagery?[198] Taking a lance, in his wickedness he wounded that breast in which the tormented soul of [Christ's] wretched Mother lay in anguished repose, and pierced, with a single blow from the

197. See John 19:31–32 for the breaking of the legs of the robbers crucified with Jesus.

198. The story of the centurion who pierced Christ's side and then believed is in John 19:34–35 (cf. Matthew 27:54; Mark 15:39; Luke 23:47). He is traditionally given the name Longinus, probably from the Greek for lance (*lonchi*); he appears in the apocryphal Acts of Pilate. Hyrcania was an ancient region by the Caspian Sea, noted for its wildness.

sharp weapon, both Jesus's side and His soul, and in wounding the dead Son almost killed the half-alive Mother, who seeing it, trembled, was terrified, and fell, her tired heart oppressed by the heavy weight of her endless sorrow. Pure water came out of the sacred wound, and precious blood, which, flowing along the lance's wood, bathed the hands of the cruel striker who, touching his blind eyes with his soaked hand, regained the faculty that fate had taken from him. O heavenly power, O compassionate wish, O highest divinity, who lives and breathes in the dead body and in those bloodied limbs, on that tormenting Cross, on that lofty wood of sorrow, forgive those who nailed You, harmed You, and humiliated You, and reward whoever wounds You, in ways not used unless by You, divine Wisdom, the greatness of whose knowledge is unknown to our ignorance.

Repentant Longinus. Longinus, touched to the heart by the force of the miracle, full of wonder and marvel, grieving for his sin, did not dismount but threw himself from his horse and abasing the pride of his savage nature with the humility of repentance, loosed the reins of tears in which his heart was melted, and spoke these, or similar, words:

> *Words of Longinus to Jesus.*
> Alas, where will I find mercy, if in my cruelty I have wounded or killed that same mercy? O my Creator, O my Lord, the eyes of this mind, blinder than the eyes of my face, have been unable to know You, God, through hearing the terrible thunder, the frightful earthquakes, the opening of the terrible tombs, and nature's confusion. O clear Light of Paradise, O He who illuminates the stars, the good of whose merciful mercy becomes clearer with the clarity of Your holy light, illuminate not only the eyes of my face but my soul's eyes, which, like those of a blind mole, have been covered with the hard scales of dark ignorance, so that I may gaze at Your light, knowledge of which has humbled my pride and softens the hardness of my heart. Alas, Lord, that I may see behind that great wound that the hand of my iniquity has done to Your breast, relight the living with a flame, even a burning furnace of love. Although I am frightened by the horror of the sin I have committed, I hope in the compassion of Your mercy, which is perpetual spring to the green of our hopes, that You will show joyfully that You forgive me.[199] Now in my soul I feel the sweetness of those fruits that have brought about the bitterness of Your death on the tree of the Cross. Therefore, confused and frightened, my soul, which knows that it has

199. The color green is the symbol of hope because of its association with spring.

been saved by Your compassionate will, does not know how to give You the endless thanks that You are owed.

After he had said this repentantly, he left, amazed by the miracle that he had recognized in himself.

The sorrowful Mother of the dead Lord, moaning and near to fainting, and burning with desire to have her beloved Son's bloody and lacerated body on her breast and in her arms, on taking Him down from the Cross, did not know how to quench the eagerness of her wish and to give Him a worthy sepulcher, one that, if not worthy of Him, at least she could give Him in such a pitiful state.

The day was drawing toward evening when Joseph of Arimathea, a patrician and senator, arrived, and lifted the Maker of the world from the Cross and placed Him in His Mother Mary's lap.[200] There was not a sob left in her, no further sighs, and, having dried her streaming tears, she gazed upon Him and was silent, as though deprived of her tongue. Then she heaved a sigh and like a sleepwalker who spoke, dreaming, she said, "So, spirit of my heart, is it true that You are dead and I am still alive? Alas, life is far fuller of sorrows than death," and kissing His hands again, fainted, and was silent and motionless.[201]

Christ placed in the sepulcher. Joseph and Nicodemus, both just men, placed Christ's sacred body in the sepulcher, which they covered with a heavy stone. Mary, her lost strength regained, envied the stone that closed it, as it seemed to her that the stone's happiness would be great since it contained within its breast the One who makes Paradise beautiful. On her return to her home, the little moisture that remained stopped spilling from her eyes, which had almost been blinded through her tears. And though sorrowful, lost, and cloaked in the clothes and veils that veiled and covered the anguish of widowhood and entirely in disarray, she had lost little of her noble majesty.

Appearance of Jesus to the Mother. Thus she stayed, weeping and sighing, until the resurrecting Jesus, surrounded by the rays of His glory, drove away the darkness of sorrows that veiled the Mother's pitiful face. His face was brighter than the brightness of the sun; the veil that covered Him from the breast downward was whiter than the milk that surged in Aurora's bosom. I

200. In Mark 15:43, Joseph of Arimathea asks Pilate for Jesus's body, which he takes, wraps in linen, and places in a sepulcher. In Matthew 27, Joseph is referred to as a disciple (v. 57), and the tomb is described as his own (cf. Luke 23:51ff.).

201. See volume editor's introduction (29) for the scene of the Pietà, or of the dead Christ lying in his mother's lap.

believe He saw in Mary's face the joy of joy, all the fire of God's spirit, and all the whiteness of the angels' purity. Then, fearful, she said no more than "O my Lord, O my God," and praising, comforting, and blessing her, He disappeared.[202]

Mary's joy. After this, the Empress of the heavenly Kingdom, her venerable face clad in the serenity of joy, cast off the black clothes that had swathed her white body.

The Magdalen laments. Meanwhile, the beautiful Magdalen was alone in the garden near the sacred tomb, which was worthy of gathering the sovereign beauty of the heavenly kingdoms within its cold and hard stones. Believing that her dead Lord had been taken, she wailed bitterly and lamented in such loving ways, with such warm words, and with so sweet a sound that the unfeeling stones, thorn bushes, and tree trunks that were nearby were touched to the heart and moved to pity. She neither moved her eyes, nor said a word, nor moved a step, without permission from the graces that courted her, given to her by nature's kindness.

The Magdalen's beauty. Her hair was beautiful, long, wavy, and loose, and fell over her delicate shoulders; pleasant breezes, playing gently, blew some short hairs around her face, making a bright and quivering crown to the alabaster of her elegant brow. A grace full of divine beauties shone in her demeanor; her shining eyes were beneath two black brows embellished with sweetness and profound seriousness. Two fresh and laughing roses such as Aurora—whence she began to open the doors of her gardens—had never revealed to our eyes, flamed with sweet fire in her beautiful cheeks. Now these graceful beauties, adorned with venerable sanctity, appeared more beautiful than when they had been adorned with foolish vanities. While she was in the garden in the green grass, she was like a lily full of shining dew or a rose at the moment when Aurora triumphs in her golden chariot, while in sweet but sorrowful and weak sound she moved the inanimate stones to the piteousness of piteous compassion and cheered listening Heaven.[203] Sighing deeply, she lowered her eyes, full of flowing tears, to look into the sacred sepulcher. Gazing in, she saw two young men of the age of someone who, having come to the end of his childhood, begins to enter slowly into flower-

202. The scene of the appearance of Christ to his mother is apocryphal. It is related in the *Meditations*, "Of the Resurrection of the Lord and How He First Appeared to His Mother on the Sunday" (359–60). Saint Ambrose of Milan said that although Christ's appearance to his mother was not recorded in the gospels, it was logically necessary, and to be accepted even without scriptural confirmation. See James D. Breckenridge, "'Et prima vidit': The Iconography of the Appearance of Christ to His Mother," *Art Bulletin* 39 no. 1 (March 1957) 9–32, at 16.

203. The description of Mary Magdalen's beauties is indebted to Petrarchan love poetry.

ing youth. She saw these two heavenly inhabitants full of wondrous beauty, with garments so shining and so flaming—as if they were competing with the moon's whiteness—that they dazzled the eyes of the faithful Disciple with their excellence.[204] They had light wings at their shoulders, so delicate and light that they moved at the wind's slightest movement.

The Angel who speaks to the Magdalen. Then one, looking at the weeping young woman with compassionate eyes, said to her in a gentle, heavenly voice, "What bitter sorrow is the cause of your weeping, O Lady loved by Heaven?" from whose words, and from whose countenances, she took a little comfort and then, at his request, she replied, "Alas, my dear Master, my dear Lord, has been stolen from me (O incomparable loss, ah, greatest sorrow). I do not know who has robbed me of Him, nor whom to ask where He has been placed. So my heart, stung by my grievous anguish, pours tears instead of blood."

Jesus appears to the Magdalen. When she finished these words, she turned back and saw Jesus, who was disguised beneath rustic clothes as a gardener, and under His rough appearance were the flaming beauties and flashing lights of His eternal and divine majesty. He said to her in a charming voice (I believe), "Woman, why are you grieving? Why do you weep? Who are you looking for in the loneliness of this garden?" Looking at Him, she thought He was the guardian and caretaker of the gardens, and not the King of Heaven, and that He was the person who had stolen her dead Lord. Gazing into His serene, gentle, and beautiful eyes, with a sweet and soft voice, she replied, "O friend, if Heaven always shows itself kindly to you and always, according to your wishes, favors you with its dewdrops, rain, and sun, and with happy abundance cheers your flowery gardens, tell me where you have put the holiness of that holy body that I left, with my soul, enclosed within this tomb, and that I shall try to retrieve with all my strength?"[205]

204. It is interesting to note Marinella's reference to Mary Magdalen as a disciple of Christ, since at this point in the history of the Church of Rome, the Counter-Reformation, the usual focus on her was as the repentant sinner, symbol of conversion and penance. The allusion to her fidelity refers to the fact that while the male disciples had deserted Christ at the Crucifixion, the women, led by Mary Magdalen, remained present, according to the synoptic accounts. Marinella's narrative of the appearance of Christ to Mary Magdalen is drawn from John 20:1–18.

205. John 20:12–18: "And she saw two angels in white, sitting, one at the head, and one at the feet, where the body of Jesus had been laid. They say to her: Woman, why weepest thou? She saith to them: Because they have taken away my Lord; and I know not where they have laid him. When she had thus said, she turned herself back and saw Jesus standing; and she knew not that it was Jesus. Jesus saith to her: Woman, why weepest thou? Whom seekest thou? She, thinking that it was the gardener, saith unto him: Sir, if thou hast taken him hence, tell me where thou has laid him; and I will take him away. Jesus saith to her: Mary. She turning, saith

Jesus speaks to the Magdalen. Then, His mercy unable to bear concealing Himself from His dear Disciple's eyes, He called her in His usual voice and, in the gentlest sound, uttered the dear name of Mary, and at the same time revealed Himself and showed clear signs of His divinity.

The Magdalen's joy. And recognizing him, she replied, "Master," while her tears flowed, and present joy took in hand past sorrow and, full of humility, she fell at His feet, at those feet that would shortly set in motion the heavenly spheres, and, gazing at them, she saw the wounds—the work of evil will—shining like so many blood-drenched stars. In the way of old habit, she wanted to embrace Him and kiss Him, but the Son of the Highest, although He loved her in His customary way, said, "Do not touch me, Mary, because I have not yet gone up to my Father's kingdom; go from here and tell my dear disciples of what you have heard and seen."[206] Flowers weighed down by the day's rain or night's dew, when the sun appears, rise again no less beautiful and laughing than the sorrowful face of the beautiful young woman at the reappearance of Christ. With chaste looks (as one might imagine), she gazed lovingly upon His venerated face as the true object of her soul. Then her heart rejoiced, in the way of those souls closest to God's power. With a gesture worthy of Himself, Christ blessed the generous penitent, and then, with a thousand flashing lights, even a thousand suns all around displaying His divinity, He vanished. Misty clouds darken Apollo's face less than the clouds of sorrow suddenly darkened the joy in the beautiful young woman's face. Overtaken first by a profound sweetness at His appearance, and then by extraordinary sorrow through His disappearance, she stayed motionless among the beauty of the blossoming flowers and the green of the fresh grasses. To anyone who looked at her, she would have seemed an angel, adorned by celestial beauty and sculpted in white alabaster, sprinkled with the color of pink by Aurora's fingers, if the light breezes blowing gently had not delighted in ruffling her golden mane.

The Magdalen praises Christ's sepulcher. Then she came to herself, lowered her beautiful eyes, full of divine grace, and began to look through the grass for any trace of Christ's sacred feet and, here and there, to find the holy clothes that were His; she kissed the earth in several places, and kneeling by

---

to him: Rabboni (which is to say, Master). Jesus saith to her: Do not touch me; for I am not yet ascended to my Father. But go to my brethren and say to them: I ascend to my Father and to your Father, to my God and your God. Mary Magdalen cometh, and telleth the disciples: I have seen the Lord, and these things he said to me."

206. Marinella's meditation is based on the scene in John 20:1–18 of the *Noli me tangere* (Latin, "Do not touch me"; the Septuagint reads "me mou aptou," and its gentler translation is "Do not seek to hold on to me"), when the resurrected Christ appears to Mary Magdalen (v. 17).

the stone that enclosed the dead Christ (joyful at such a great honor), and the sweetness of her joys exuding through her beautiful divine eyes, then said, kissing the glorious tomb, in all likelihood:

> O how bound am I to give thanks and praise to my blessed Lord, since I can kiss and touch you as much as I want, O stone worthy of being taken from the earth to Heaven's heights. Made fortunate, Christ's friends will consider themselves blessed in years to come, since through what has happened, they can, humbly pious, and piously humble, make you due reverence, as is appropriate to your greatness. If I regard myself as happy through having been able to gaze on the Son of God's revived face with my own eyes, how much happier one ought to call you, since you kept within your breast that body (truly dear and precious burden) replete with the eternal deity. You embraced Him dead, you saw Him return from death to life, and to eternal life; you then saw Him, full of light, spirit, and divinity, raise Himself from your depth, His angels helping Him perhaps, obedient, I believe, to His wishes.

While she spoke these words, the beautiful penitent was soaking the hardness of the rocks of the sacred tomb with her tears, and having kissed it a good thousand times, she left, announcing to Christ's brothers and all the faithful the appearance of her resurrected Lord with so much joy in her voice and with so much happiness in her face that it would be impossible to describe in words.[207] Then she went to the one who had overcome the weight of many sorrows with the strength of her endurance, sorrows that she had undergone through her Son. With joyful tears, the Magdalen told her that she had seen her Lord alive, what He had said to her, of His appearance, and of the brightness of the rays that she saw coming from His divine face. Hearing this, Mary added joy to the sweetness of the happiness she already had.[208] As Christ's Resurrection was made known, she saw countless people raise their hands and give praise to the Ruler of all, people who grew in faith and hope, as roses and lilies planted on banks emerge in beauty and scent.

The Mother of Jesus goes to the Mount of Olives to see the Ascension into Heaven. From day to day, the venerable Lady became more adorned with new joy,

207. Mary Magdalen carries out Christ's injunction to tell the other disciples of his resurrection (John 20:18), thus becoming the herald of the New Life, and first apostle.

208. In the New Testament, Mary Magdalen does not go to inform the Virgin Mary that she has seen the risen Christ.

as she heard from the Apostles of the miracles and appearances that the resurrected Christ made in different ways. And when the time came for His ascension into Heaven, surrounded by her women friends and servants, and accompanied by the eleven brothers, she went up with them onto the Mount of Olives at the time when Aurora embellishes the predicted coming of her lord, the sun, with new beauty, not only arranging her hair and dress at the mirror, but also choosing the most beautiful and most scented roses produced by the heavenly fields. Filling her breast and decorating her hair with these, she moved with weighty steps through the purified tranquility. The Virgin Mother, and all who were with her, knelt, offering prayers to the Creator. Behold, Christ came upon them in the guise of the sun clothed and adorned with heavenly splendor: the snow's whiteness and sun's brightness would have appeared night and darkness in comparison to what flowed from His face.

Christ's words spoken on the Mount of Olives. Turning those blessed eyes to them, the saving look of which gladdened Paradise, He said:

> I go to prepare your places in Heaven; peace I say to the world, and may God be with you. When I reach the right hand of my God, I will send you the spirit of eternal wisdom, which, burning in your breasts, will bring it about that out of love for me, for you alone the stones of pain and martyrdom will be dearer to you than precious gems. Keep in the faith that I have confirmed with my death: remember that I am the way, the life, and the truth, with which and through which you will ascend to the Kingdom of eternal joy.[209]

At the end of these words, His face shone with the clearest light. Then the Queen of the eternal hierarchies, her cheeks bathed in tears of maternal love, and keeping her eyes fixed on Him, probably said, "O Son, why do You not allow me, who am still among the groups of blessed and happy, to come with You to Heaven?"[210]

Christ's Ascension. Then a cloud, which God made from the sun's splendor and the moon's whiteness, passed between Jesus and the eyes of those watching Him, and two angels dressed in white garments, white as their purity, their hair blown by mild puffs of the light breeze, said, "Men of Galilee,

209. Cf. John 14:2–7.

210. The account of the Virgin's wish to go to heaven with Christ occurs in the fourth-century apocryphal Assumption of the Virgin (James, *Apocryphal New Testament,* 222), but takes place just before she dies.

as you have seen the Redeemer of the world ascend to Heaven, so you will see Him descend encircled by the eternal army on the Last Day to give the great Judgment."[211] Having said this, they rose to Paradise to contemplate the divinity of the wounds of Christ, our Salvation.

BOOK FOUR

SUMMARY: *In this fourth book, the Apostles and the Magdalen obtain the benediction of Mary who, full of the kindness of her usual mercy, begs Christ for the salvation of the people and for her desire to die. Then He announces to her through an Angel how He has granted her prayer, and makes the same Angel present her with a palm. With the Angel, she goes up to the Mount of Olives to contemplate God, where she sees with her spiritual eyes the fearfulness of the Day of Judgment. On her return to her home, she announces her death to her relations and friends. The Apostles arrive miraculously in Nazareth. The devil tries to frighten Mary close to her death. In her last hours, Jesus comes down from Heaven. The High Priest wishes to burn her body. Then the miracles made by the Virgin concerning the High Priest's rashness are related. The Apostles bury Mary's body, which rises after three days and goes into Heaven, accompanied by all the beauty and all the venerated of the heavenly dwelling.*

The Virgin leaves the Mount and returns to her house. Leaving the Mount, Mary returned silently to her house, and giving her companions and Jesus's servants permission to leave, attended to her contemplation and to thinking of her longed-for love and cherished hope who, concealing the beauty and immortality of His divine nature beneath His mortal veil, was tormented and dead. As she gazed with a sharp mental eye, and contemplated on the spilt blood, the bitter wounds, and His painful death, the sweetness of the lightest sleep spread into the holiness of her blessed eyes: sleeping, she was like one of those spirits we see in God's great and tremendous presence.[212]

Visions of the Blessed Virgin, and of the martyrdoms of many saints. It seemed to the glorious Virgin, I think, that she saw (still bound in a light sleep), among many other things, a spacious place, like a great theater, in which there were figures in various shapes all cut by swords, with what appeared to her to be the cruelty of tyrants venting their bestial natures on the flesh and bones of those who followed in Christ's divine footsteps. It seemed to her that these filled the fearful theater, firm in the firmness of the faith of

211. Acts 1:9–11. The Ascension is also reported in Matthew 28:16–20; Mark 16:19; Luke 24:50–53. The Virgin does not appear in the Gospel accounts of the Ascension, but popular piety, in its desire to stress Mary's presence throughout her son's life, included her in this event, as witness the *Meditations* (376–77, 379).

212. An angel.

Figure 11. Engraving showing the Angel Giving the Virgin the Palm and Announcing Her Death; the Virgin Contemplating God on the Mount of Olives; the Dormition of the Virgin; the Carrying of the Virgin's Bier; and the Virgin's Assumption. From the 1602 edition of *La vita di Maria Vergine Imperatrice dell'Universo descritta in prosa & in ottava rima da Lucretia Marinella* (fol. 57v). Reproduced by kind permission of the Fondazione Querini Stampalia Onlus, Venice.

the One who wished to make Himself man to make us gods. She saw countless virgins who, at the most beautiful and lovely age and in their beauty, offered their chaste limbs and delicate but strong breasts to swords, arrows, razors, flames, scourges, and poisonous serpents, to the savage talons of wild lions, to the darkness of prisons, to hooks and cords, to the tenacity of hard chains, and who had such open faces in the presence of torments that it appeared to her that they desired more than feared such martyrdoms. She saw many kings who, through love of Christ, recognized that they rejoiced more in seeing themselves girded in chains than adorned in regal purple and crowns.[213]

Saint Columba. She saw among many, many, a young girl in the process of being burned in divine fire, surrounded by true flames, and near her a terrible female bear pitifully quivering, which, softened by the gentleness that came from the young virgin's face, offered its own death to defend the pure modesty of her innocence. Then she heard a voice from Heaven, which called with words very likely like these, "Come, pure dove, come loved Bride, come and enjoy the perfection of the everlasting in Paradise." When these words had come to an end, she saw a wicked executioner raise a shining knife and cut off the fair head.[214]

Saint Catherine, virgin. In the same place, it seemed to the Queen of the Angels that she saw a beautiful young woman of noble bearing and heavenly beauty, and filled with every virtue who, burning in the fire of the Holy Spirit, scorned the empire of Alexandria and royal grandeur; and it seemed to her that she saw her dear Son become the lover of that one by giving her the heavenly ring and taking her as His bride, and receiving from her as dowry the burden of her heroic virtues; then she understood that by the orders of a cruel emperor, her head had been cut off, and instead of purple blood, whitening milk poured out.[215]

Saint Ursula with her happy company. In the same arena, she saw a virgin in the center of 11,000 noble young girls, also a sun crowned by 11,000 stars

213. The Virgin has visions of things to come, as in secular literature a character might similarly see into the future.

214. Saint Columba was a legendary saint, her name a play on words, as the translation of her name, "dove," is a synonym for the Holy Ghost. Marinella had already published a full-length work on Columba (*La colomba sacra: Poema heroico* [Venice: Gio. Battista Ciotti, 1595]). "Come loved bride" is an allusion to the Song of Songs: "Veni Sponsa, veni" (4:8).

215. This is a much-abbreviated life of the legendary Saint Catherine of Alexandria, a virgin martyred in the early fourth century, who underwent a mystical union with Christ, and who is often depicted receiving a ring from Christ.

that, with its splendor, did not diminish their beauty, but rather enhanced all their graces and light.[216]

Saint Laurence. Staying there, she saw, O wretched sight, all the other deaths laid out on the bloody field, into which she gazed at a young man spread out on a large gridiron, and placed on burning lit coals, who neither groaned nor lamented as he felt the bitterness of the cruel pains, but instead praised God and said to his tormentors, "My brothers and friends, turn me to the other side and eat my roast flesh, as I will be sweet through the love of Christ."[217]

Saint Francis. At the same time as she saw Christ's triumphant fellow soldiers end their lives in torment, she saw outside this blood-filled theater a young man wishing to enter. It was he, dressed, indeed adorned, in rough clothes and a hairshirt, and it seemed to her that with his holy and pious words, he frightened hell as much as he secured Paradise by embellishing our souls with gems. He went forth, weeping and singing the sufferings of Jesus. It seemed to her that he knelt on the earth before a man dressed in priestly garments and that he said, his eyes turned towards the serene heavens:

> Lord, and God, the pity of whose compassion rules all with the sovereign of justice and, foreseeing all and providing, governs: as I have rejected not only my comforts and riches, but also paternal and maternal love, I consecrate myself to you. Therefore you receive this young man who, naked, leaves the world full of the darkness of sins and, under the wings of your goodness, covers himself again.

It seemed to her that the priest, praising him and blessing him, said to him:

> So you, brave young man, who are far from any earthly love and vanity, will be able to look upon the radiance of those rays that come from God's marvelous countenance with the eyes of your burning intellect, as the ease and comforts of the world and the love given to one's parents often forbid the possibility of gazing with spiritual eyes at the

216. The legend of the martyr Saint Ursula and her 11,000 virgins became known in the eighth or ninth century. Supposedly a British princess, Ursula went on pilgrimage with her companions, and on their return they were massacred in Cologne, Germany, by the Huns.

217. Laurence was a deacon and martyr (d. 258). One of the seven deacons of Rome, he was martyred under Valerian. According to tradition, he was ordered by the prefect of Rome to hand over the treasure of the Church. He gathered together the poor, to whom he had given the ecclesiastical possessions, and delivered them to the prefect, saying, "These are the treasures of the Church," and was punished by slow roasting on a gridiron.

face that the angels gaze upon, since they veil it, as the thickness of a cloud obscures the luminous rays of the morning star.

It seemed then to the glorious Virgin that she saw him among the hoary snows that whiten the mountains in the Val d'Arno, and then, no differently, her beloved Jesus adorned with five bloody wounds.[218]

Saint Catherine of Siena. A little further away, she saw a gentle young girl, indeed a noble girl, who not only scorning the comforts, pomp, and enticements of the world at her immature age, but caring little for the too affectionate persuasions of her parents, bitterly mortified her tender and growing limbs with hairshirts, fasting, flagellation, and prayer.[219] Instead of crowning herself with roses in her youth, she encircled her serene brow with the pricking crown of sharp thorns in imitation of her beloved Christ. Then Mary saw her drooping, pale and fainting through too bitter penitence, almost next to death, ostentatiously bedecked, not with gold or gems, but embellished with five wounds in her hands, feet, and breast, also with five purple roses more flaming and shining than the sun when it rises out of the sea's depth.[220]

Saint Felicity. The divine mind of Christ's Mother saw in the theater where the friends of Paradise ran joyfully to death, a woman who, cruelly pitiful and with seven sons, encouraged them one by one to death and martyrdom, and was happy to see them fall for Jesus's faith, one by one dead in

218. Marinella had treated the subject of Saint Francis earlier and more fully (*Vita del serafico et glorioso S. Francesco descritta in ottava rime da Lucretia Marinella. Ove si spiegano le attioni le astinenze & i miracoli di esso* (Venice: P. M. Bertani & Fratelli, 1597). Saint Francis (1181/2–1226) was the founder of the Franciscan order of friars. The son of a rich cloth merchant of Assisi, at the age of twenty-two he rejected his worldly life to follow in the footsteps of Christ. Barefoot and clad in a long dark garment, belted with a cord, he set out with a group of companions to save souls. His order was approved by Pope Honorius III in 1223. Marinella's reference to the Val d'Arno is to the retreat in the Apennine mountains called Mount La Verna in the valley of the river Arno, where Francis received the stigmata, the reproduction of the wounds of Christ's Passion in the human body. In the Virgin's vision, Francis's stigmata is no different from that of "her beloved Jesus adorned with five bloody wounds."

219. Saint Catherine of Siena (1347?–80) was a Dominican tertiary. Rebelling against her parents' attempts to persuade her to marry, she spent long hours in prayer and severely mortified her body, joining the Dominican order at the age of sixteen. She took care of the poor and sick and converted sinners. She became so famous that she acted as a mediator not only between local warring factions but even between such elevated entities as Florence and the Papal State. She was canonized in 1461. Marinella was to write a full-length life of her (*De' gesti heroici e della vita maravigliosa della serafica S. Caterina da Siena . . . libri sei* [Venice: Barezzo Barezzi, 1624]).

220. The "five wounds" refer to the stigmata that Saint Catherine received in 1375. In the *Vita* (225), Marinella describes the sun as rising "from the lap of Thetis" ("del grembo della marina Theti"). Thetis was the poetic name for the sea, and for one of the Nereids, or sea nymphs, who was the mother of Achilles.

her presence. Then she was happy to offer her generous breast and unconquered head to the wicked executioners.[221]

Mary awakens from sleep and what she says. Rightly loved by Heaven and revered by the world, and seeing cruelty become arrogant and the sons of humankind destroyed so wretchedly, and overcome by intolerable sorrow, she sighed deeply and, sighing, her heart trembled, and trembling opened her tear-filled eyes. Awakened with her mind's eye, she gazed again at those unconquerable virgins and Christ's triumphant martyrs, and felt wounded in the breast by a thousand pricks of sweet pity and bitter sorrow. Opening her holy lips, which had opened so many times for the salvation of sinful souls, she said:

> O four or six times blessed, those happy souls dying for love of Him who, dying for them on the Cross, gave birth to life. They have scorned the world and its sweet and bitter enticements, so that they will be worthy of being made citizens of the heavenly realms through their unswerving call to virtue. O most sweet and dear punishments, you have not loosed the lives of souls, but rather bound them to God. Why not unleash Your anger on these limbs? O my Son, console this soul with the sweetness of torments, whose joys are the thought of reuniting with You.

Here she was silent, hushed at the wish of the heavenly Good, sympathizing with others' sorrows, praising and blessing her beloved Son and God, spending her days in prayers and fasting, giving alms, and leading straying souls through the wide bosom of this sea of life to the shores of salvation.[222]

When the Lord's brothers received the Holy Spirit, whose virtue spread the sparks of its flames into their breasts, they went before the one who always prays for us and threw themselves at her feet, as some say, not without lamenting her humility.[223] Then they asked for her benediction, as they wished to go and spread the truth in the gospels' pure words. Full of her usual love and humility, she blessed them.

The Magdalen asks for Mary's blessing. Scarcely had the Mother of our hopes

221. Saint Felicity (d. 203) was an African martyr, a companion of Saint Perpetua with whom she was martyred. The Virgin has experienced these visions as a series of tableaux.

222. The sea is often treated as a metaphor for life, with its ebb and flow, calm, storms, rises and falls, choppiness, and indeed anger; in this case the sea is a metaphor of the journey of the soul to redemption.

223. Marinella adds a nice touch concerning the Virgin's humility: the apostles clearly wish to adore Mary, whose modesty makes her flinch from such protestations.

blessed the men, God's trumpets, when the Magdalen fell to her knees before her divine presence and kissed the ground where Mary had placed her foot (the kind of thing that troubled her humility), and said the following words:[224]

> Fount of heavenly virtue, Mother of the Son of the Highest, since I am aware of the gravity of my sins and of the immeasurable grace He has bestowed on me, no less understanding the pleasures the world made to my wanton desire, I should like to settle in the solitude of deserts and caves, and flee the world to live and die in gratitude to Him, and to give Him praise in return for the kindness He showed me. Therefore, Mother of God, give me your benediction with your permission, and remember me, your servant, sometimes in your prayers, which your soul directs toward God.

Having said this, she wanted to kiss the glorious Virgin's holy feet again, or the ground where she had placed them. But she was prevented from so doing by the humility of the one who, blessing and embracing her, spoke words such as these:

> Repentance, daughter, is the way to Paradise, which will bring you near to God and you will accompany angels. Frightening solitude and the caves in which you desire to dwell, wise young lady—the kind of life you wish to lead—will all overcome your desires for magnificence of palaces, the transitory grandeurs in which you so used to delight. I have no hesitation in commending you to my Christ, whose mercy will spread over you the graces that pour on His dearest friends.

When she had said this, she embraced her and kissed her in a way worthy of being written down by angels and not by my clumsy pen,[225] since each of her actions contained that something that, since it is inexpressible in words, remains enclosed in the great sea of marvels.

The Magdalen goes to the desert. After a certain time, the great Lady of Magdala took her leave of the divine Lady and went to the wildness of the deserts. And she remained among the terrors of the woods, among wolves and other animals that lacked all reason. Here she clothed the alabaster of

224. "God's trumpets," that is, the apostles. This passage provides a further, and delightful, reference to the Virgin's troubled humility.

225. This is a typical trope of rhetorical self-deprecation.

her body with the display of her golden hair. She lived, feeding herself with unpalatable grass and quenching her thirst with tasteless water; and she did penance to her soft flesh with frequent and bitter blows. Then the desert's silence and darkness of the caves heard and saw how reverently and with what words the angels exalted the greatness of the Lord who is supreme and excellent perfection.[226]

Mary visits the holy places where Christ suffered. But let us return to her, she who brought in her breast the peace of just souls, and who, all burning with love for God, went (I believe) often with her disciples visiting those places where the immaculate Lamb gave communion to the apostles at the Last Supper; where He prayed; where He was taken; where He was scorned and derided; where He died; and where He rose to His glory. She saw all those places with her eyes bathed in tears, now of joy and then of sorrow. There was no outrage, persecution, injury, or martyrdom given or done to Christ's faithful that she did not experience, or whose strength of anguish she did not feel in her breast. She remained night and day in continuous prayer, meditation, and fasting, teaching with all the feelings of love the way that leads to Heaven. She was continually visited, adored, and revered by groups of women and men; and beyond that, she was loved by God, praised by angels, and feared by devils.[227]

The world is a vanity. She had continually given example to the world with the holiness of her actions and purity of her words, to never entrust itself to its vanities, which, like shadows, are smoke in the most beautiful of its glories and fade away.[228] And she showed how human life does not possess a tranquil moment since, now taking care of daily necessities, then unforeseen misfortune, and now again the spurs to glory, all trouble and afflict both mind and body. She had already converted many people to the true faith of Christ; she had already healed, reinvigorated, illuminated, and with her gaze and by the touch of her most holy hands, put right the sick, those lacking in virtue, the blind and erring. Already hearts, statues, temples, altars, and incense burned and were consecrated to her and for her.[229]

226. The description of the Magdalen's penance in the desert is typical of the Counter-Reformation period (cf. Giambattista Marino's poem "Maddalena di Tiziano" [1620] in *Poesie varie*, ed. Benedetto Croce [Bari: Laterza, 1913], 242; and the epic poem of Erasmo di Valvasone, *Lagrime di S. Maria Maddalena* [Ferrara: Vittorio Baldini, 1586]). It became the most popular Magdalenian theme in art (see, e.g., paintings by Titian, Artemisia Gentileschi, Caravaggio, Guercino, Guido Reni, and Annibale Carracci, and sculptures by Donatello and Bernini).

227. The story of the Virgin's life after the Resurrection is related in the *Golden Legend*, under the heading "The Assumption of the Blessed Virgin Mary" (2:77–97).

228. Ecclesiastes 1:2: "Vanity of vanities, said Ecclesiastes: vanity of vanities, and all is vanity."

229. The Virgin Mary is depicted as the model of good works.

Sixteen years had already gone by since she had seen the One who was her Son, in having been conceived in her, and Father in having created her, go up to Heaven, surrounded by immortal splendors and flashes of glory. She had already lived among the miseries of the world for twelve *lustri* and four years when after her supreme merit, wearied by this stormy sea, she went into the solitude of her little bedroom where she knelt with her hands joined and held outward, and with her eyes fixed on Heaven, gazed and was silent.[230] Her face seemed a composition of milk white and roses, and, although she had already reached old age, wrinkles, which usually render ugliness in the faces of elderly women, dared not make the white softness of her cheeks uneven in the serene gravity of her face.[231] Her every gesture and manner had in themselves the grace that she took with her to Heaven. Whoever saw her could only bow down, adore with the heart of his or her soul, and with the spirit of his or her heart, the revered majesty, which made itself apparent in her divine appearance.

Mary prays for the salvation of humankind and wishes to die. While she contemplated Heaven, every hour she yearned more to enjoy in Paradise the One she had loved, revered, and watched on earth with anguish. So her eyes, still preserving their first splendor of youth, shed the dew of tears, and opening her sweet lips, which now open for our salvation, she said:

> O eternal Light, You who not only embellish the wide and endless galleries of Paradise with the brightness of Your light, but also, for anyone passing, light the stars, and fill with flashing flames the sun's brow. And in all the elements, and in every thing, to which You gave a greater or lesser place in the world, show forth Your ray. But in the small world of our bodies, the light of Your divinity shines so excellently that You pour into it, giving it Intellect, Memory, and Will, for truly, O God, You love humanity because You loved it so much in creating it.[232] Now I intercede for Your clemency, for a gift on humankind's behalf; which is that I may sometimes mediate between Your justice and humanity's weakness and faults regarding their souls and bodies. Also, I beg that my mortal remains, weighed down by so many

230. *Lustrum*, as noted earlier, is Latin for a period of five years; that is, the Virgin was sixty-four years old.

231. Because the Virgin Mary had escaped original sin, she also escaped mortality, the result of original sin, and remained permanently youthful. Most images of her show her as young, even at the Crucifixion. Michelangelo's sculpture of the *Pietà* (1499) is a good example (Saint Peter's, Rome).

232. As would be understood by Marinella's readers, memory, intellect, and will are the three faculties of the soul.

years and by so many sorrows continually experienced in the world, and that my spirit, far away from You, may keep burning with Your love. Loosen the bond, therefore, loved God, set free, loved Son, and set free, loved Father, those ties that keep my soul, almost against its will, in this earthly prison.

When she had finished speaking, some say that Heaven was struck by three claps of thunder, which made the world tremble, and then everything began to be inflamed with heavenly love. Then a Messenger of God, like a golden flame, went toward Mary's small room. She recognized him by his gleaming crown, entwined in his hair, which shone on his rippling curls, and by the flaming purple that ornamented his face. While she was looking at the blessed Ambassador, her tears shone in her face, struck by the angelic light, as Aurora's dew shines in the center of a lily when the sun looks at it fondly. With the most reverent humility ever seen by the people, the Angel knelt before her and spoke thus in a delightful voice:

The Angel's words to Mary.
Your wish—for the good of humankind—has been granted by the One who is God, who did not scorn to live on earth. Similarly, He heard your ardent prayers made through your desire to return to Heaven, which God has allowed you. The unworthy world will enjoy the divine graces of your being for two further days, and then not only your soul, crowned by all the virtues, will rise, but also your body, in the whiteness of whose virginity the Holy Spirit lived.

The Angel gives a palm to Mary. Then (according to some), offering her a beautiful palm, he said, "Take the sign of your victories, glorious Victor. This will be carried by John, the servant of Jesus, before your coffin." He was silent for some time, and then continued, "Follow me, perfect Virgin, so that He who sent me is pleased; so that you see the beauties of Heaven on earth, and what the future centuries enclose in their breasts."[233]

The Queen of Paradise joyfully received the palm and rose from where she was kneeling. She called some of her disciples to her who, when they saw the light that came out of her simple, heavenly body, would have fallen, like a person who falls when a thunderbolt falls nearby, if Mary's grace, comforting them with the light of her eyes, had not restored their strength of

233. The palm is the sign of victory and martyrdom. This scene is related in the *Golden Legend*, 2:78.

heart. She followed the angelic footsteps, together with her women. When the Angel arrived on the summit of the Mount, which takes its name from olives, he halted and the Virgin did the same, and kneeling praised, thanked, and made reverence to her Lord, with both heart and soul. The religious women, who had followed her not far behind, prayed with the fervor of their devoted desires.

Mary contemplates God on the Mount of Olives. When Mary, who gave birth to our Redemption, had adored her Christ, she sat down on the top of the hill from which the whiteness of the cloud had snatched and stolen Christ's miraculous countenance from her sight.[234] Her face burned with the ardor of holy souls, and the diadem of glory encircled her brow. With her heavenly hand placed on her lap, her eyes raised to the serenity of the heavenly realms, I think that, with her soul's eyes, she contemplated her Creator and Son who, being in the Highest of the High, and by the power of His eternity, surrounded by a circle of flashes and rays of salvation and of justice, punished, rewarded, and provided with suffering, favors, and nourishment. The heart of her soul now revived, and rejoicing in the gladness of heavenly joy, she recognized, saw, and heard the magnificence of the temples, the greatness of glories, the clouds of incense, the voices of glory, and holy altars that will be dedicated, burned, and erected to the mercy of her bounty by the devoted belief of mortals to the end of the world. She even saw angels rejoicing in eternal joy. She saw the stars, sparkling sparks of fire and love, show her the desire that their brightness burned to make a crown for the tranquil, pure, and shining gold of her hair. She understood how—thanks to her compassionate mercy—humankind, who took shelter beneath the cape of her sweet kindness, was saved and was freed from plagues, famines, chains, exiles, prisons, and stormy seas, who then, full of joy, thanked her, with joyful cries and pure souls.[235]

Mary sees with her mind's eye what will take place on the Day of Judgment.[236] Then she saw with her mind's eye, as something immediate to her, the world in a horrible mixture of confusion, as the trembling sun hid itself, the moon was terrified, and the stars were frightened. Beyond this, she heard a noise of water and the alarming sound of stones being struck together. She saw the

234. The Ascension traditionally took place on the Mount of Olives, according to Acts 1:12, as the apostles are described as returning "to Jerusalem from the mount called Olivet, which is near Jerusalem."

235. For her role as protectress and intercessor, Mary was designated the "Madonna of Mercy," the "Misericordia," and was depicted standing, usually crowned, her arms outspread supporting a large cloak, under which tiny figures of supplicants knelt.

236. What follows is an imaginative rendering of the Apocalypse.

earth shake, winds blow up, mountains become flattened, woods uprooted, forests collapse. At such frightening visions, she saw the terror and pallor that death spreads on people's faces. She saw the droughts and frightening times being gathered together at the end of time, their falling eyelids concealing the glimmer of light from them.[237] She saw worn-out Nature, having lost the name of mother and reduced to sterility, unable to draw milk from her countless breasts.[238] She saw death and life oppressed by terrifying confusion, as the one tried to raise the dead again and the other to destroy the living: but death, to life's shame, showed itself wholly victorious. She saw the elements lose their natures, and the world become beside itself. Similarly, she heard the clangor—since she had been present at the fearfulness of such an end—the terror, and the sound of the trumpets, given breath by the Lord's wish, and their frightening noise awakened the bodies, already accustomed to rest for so many years, from their deep sleep. These hundred, thousand, and thousand thousand came out of the dark tombs and frightening places.[239]

She saw, as if in a theater, a throne of clouds colored by rays, which issued forth from the pure fires of Heaven, on which Christ was seated, surrounded by radiance and by terrors.[240] He placed His sacred feet on the heads of two little cherubim, who appeared to burn in the vermilion fire of their outspread wings and of their own faces, His face shining with a dazzling and joyful light. She saw the ministers of hell, armed with pride and cruelty, and burning with new rage, vie with each other for brutishness. She saw Fame distressed, her wings plucked of their feathers, with the crowns and palms beneath her feet; and heard and watched God's great, feared, and most just judgment in the form of two arrows, one of salvation and the other of damnation.[241] Then the just, more shining than the sun, surrounded by the imperturbability of beauty, purity, and agility, praised the justice coming from Christ's lips with sweet harmony. But those who delighted in the wickedness of evil works in the world, with terrifying faces, in sounds similar to bulls' bellowing, or to that made by Heaven when thunder roars, blaspheming, cursed the years of the world's existence and similarly the preparations,

237. Mary sees the horrors of the end of the world (cf. Revelation 6:12–17).

238. Nature's "countless breasts": Marinella may have had in mind images of the ancient sculpture of the many-breasted Diana of Ephesus.

239. See the account of the Last Trump (1 Corinthians 15:52). Cf. also Mark 13; Matthew 27:51–54; Luke 17:22–37; Luke 21.

240. Cf. Mark 13:26.

241. The figure of Fame is traditionally shown winged and blowing a trumpet.

labors, and milk foods, which their fathers and mothers had given and made for them. She saw the infernal princes who, the most terrible in their terribleness, doubled fire to conflagration and sorrows to grief with which they surrounded those who died in most just God's anger; and the damned, with tears and wretched cries, revealed the double martyrdom to enraged Lucifer, which came down on their wicked bodies like continual rain.[242]

Mary's prayers to God. At such a terrible sound of feeble and sorrowful voices, Mary, the compassion of mercies, her face the color of violets, her limbs trembling and dismay in her heart, came to herself, and rose from where she was sitting with the haste of a shepherdess who, seeing a serpent close by, arises; then kneeling, she said, in a trembling voice, "O King, O eternal Ruler, who is able to do all, bind our enemy with the strength of Your chains so that in my death (an end nature abhors) he does not come to show his cruel face, proud horns, and fearful countenance to me, Your servant and Mother." Then the Angel, responding to her request, said, "Fear with its ice will not touch your breast, our Queen, since God has granted your request and wishes what you desire."

Mary returns to her house, and leaves the Mount of Olives. After she had venerated Heaven on her knees and in her mind, she turned her steps gracefully toward her home, with the women following her and the Angel escorting them. The beauty of eternal glory showed in her steps and her person, governed by her majestic appearance. On arriving at her ancient house the Angel, kneeling at her feet, venerated her, calling her Temple and Mother of God, Heaven's treasure, glory of Paradise, eye of marvels, light, flame, and fire of charity, faith, and love, and by other names, which I do not know how to express. Having praised her, he spread his wings and flew to the Empyrean spaces to enjoy everlasting good, which lies in the sight of eternal Providence.[243]

Mary shows the closeness of her death to her friends and relations. When the Angel had vanished, Mary called her relations and friends to her and announced to them how the will of the One who cleansed our sins with His blood had sent one of His messengers from the heavenly home to reveal to her that He was calling her to Himself. Her relatives and friends were distressed by the sound of such an announcement, in the way the air's purity is upset by clouds. After a short silence, they gave vent to weeping, sighing, groaning,

242. The "infernal princes" and Lucifer are already in hell. When the souls in hell are united to their bodies, they will suffer doubly, all the more.

243. The Empyrean was thought by the ancients to be the realm of pure fire, and by early Christians to be the abode of God and the angels.

and sobbing, showing that her departure was the reason for that sorrow, and she, made of pity and grace, spoke the following or similar words:

> Sisters and brothers, perfect persons, may my funeral rites be not made by you with sighs and tears; my joys, the achievement of my desires, do not wish for tears or sighs. Death is like a door through which worldly misery passes to heavenly happiness. Therefore rejoice with me because, through dying, I will be reborn to that blessed life that my sweet Jesus is preparing for all those who have trusted in His truth. I will go to my Light, my glory, and my peace, with the Lord's grace, which He prepared for me before the entire creation of the world. If you love me, as I am sure you do, dry your tears and rejoice with me over my gladness, and be delighted by this, that it has pleased God to please me.

When she had finished speaking, she revealed the palm that the angelic hand had given her through its divine commission. The sweetness, the dearness, and lovingness of her words, the brightness, and the scent of the leaves signifying victory, were like a following peace in the air, which suddenly calms storms driven down to earth by winds, and the fury of their struggles in the sea.

Mary's words to her relations. Then, with joy in their faces, the group of women friends praised and thanked the Lord for what He had been pleased to do, and she said to them once more:

> Best of people, whose excellence is loved by heavenly Providence, always keep the memories of Christ's life, death, and resurrection in your souls; His merciful charity took our souls from eternal ruin; embrace poverty, the treasure He loved, and shed tears in asking His grace to be able to scorn the world, which conceals many bitter things beneath a little sweetness. This life is not life, but a journey that leads us to life. But be joyful, and remain in God's grace, and I will not fail to commend you to Him with every kind of prayer.

Having said this, the Queen of Heaven took her leave of the perfect people. Awaited by the angels, her eyes full of mercy and salvation, she was unable to keep back the tears that, in leaving such dear company, spilled her affection. The religious people wept as they were reminded that they would be without such a mother and such a lady; but then thinking that they would have their pious defender near to God, they were consoled. Then, burning with divine love, she began to offer prayers and praises to the Giver of life. While she was contemplating her Christ, with her thoughts on the end of the world, John, the trumpet of divine truth, arrived, who always kept in mind the words that Christ had said to him of the sorrowing Mother, so that he rarely went far from her humble dwelling.[244]

Mary informs John of her death. When Mary saw him, she called him to her, as it has been found written, and with a joyful face and in a clear voice, told him how Christ, the soul of their hopes, had sent her His Angel to inform her of the hour of her approaching death. Telling him this, he rejoiced with her, and she showed him the heavenly palm. On hearing her words, he was taken by a tender lovingness, and then banishing his tender feelings, he said, "I have never sorrowed in your joys nor rejoiced in your sorrows. If you wish me to rejoice, I am happy. But I will truly enter into the sea of sweetness if my soul can follow your footprints and come with you as your servant." And she added, with charming words:

> Hush, O son given me by Christ. When I am dead, watch and defend my body, together with the other eleven apostles, who will be miraculously brought here, so that Jewish wickedness does not cast it in the fire. The care I take of my body is only because it was the dwelling place of Christ, Son of God; and then you will bury it where it pleases Him.[245]

The cloud that brought the Apostles to Nazareth. While she was saying this, they heard, so holy men relate, several claps of thunder, at the noisy roar of which John went out of the door, and looking up at Heaven, saw a great cloud. Its whiteness was greater than the whiteness seen in perfumed privets and, blown by the breath of God's will, it raced, even flew as the arrow flies from the bow, and moved, flashing with extraordinary magnificence. With his hands out before him and his face drawn back, John could scarcely endure the brightness of the light that came from it.[246]

The Apostles' miraculous arrival in Nazareth. It came down from Heaven be-

244. In John 19:26–27, Jesus commends "the disciple . . . whom he loved" to his mother's keeping and his mother into John's keeping.

245. For the source of the legend of the Virgin's death, or Dormition, and Assumption, see volume editor's introduction (26–27). Her fear that her body may be burned is also related in the *Golden Legend*, 2:79.

246. The arrival of the apostles in Nazareth comes from the Assumption narrative attributed to Joseph of Arimathea (James, *Apocryphal New Testament*, 216–17), and also appears in the *Golden Legend*, 2:79.

fore the Virgin's house, and out of it—O miraculous power of God—came the eleven apostles, and then it vanished. John went to meet them and received Christ's amazed brothers, who thought they were dreaming, finding themselves together. But Jesus's beloved disciple[247] told them how the eternal Lord, working His miraculous power, had transferred them to Nazareth so that they would be present at the death of His most holy Mother. On hearing from John what pleased their Leader, they entered the glorious presence of their Queen and with reverent humility praised, blessed, and exalted her. Full of her usual gentleness, she honored them and then sat down with them and said to the holy company:

> And since I know that you have heard the reason why you have been brought here miraculously, I will not explain it to you. I rejoice in knowing that your souls are so straightforward and pure, like those that are freed from impurity and from the weight of our bodies: persevere in your usual labors, always remembering our sweet Jesus, whose life, death, and teachings take us from the enemy's hands. And because I feel near to the end of my life, I bless you in the name of highest God and commend you to Him with my heart's lips.

When she had finished speaking, she lay down on her holy and chaste bed, showing a venerable grandeur in her humble appearance. The palm, which her Son had sent her, lay on her breast, and her hands were crossed one over the other. She was awaiting the voice of the Lord who had created the world out of nothing to call her spirit to Him.[248]

The Devil increases horror in his ugliness to frighten Mary. At that moment the inventor of deceit, as can be imagined, whose power had been bound again in the lowest depths of Hell by Christ's mighty hand, knew that she who had produced life was near to death. Then, to make her more terrified with his fearful appearance, he filled the hands of the poisonous serpent with frosts and chains. Three and four times he opened and tightened his frightening, heavy, and wide open wings, and put all the dark, fire, and terror in his brow, eyes, mouth, and face, and everything frightening in his prison, blackened by smoke, and spreading stinking smoke and terrible flames through his nostrils and ears, went towards her to turn her heart, which was flaming with love of Christ, to ice with his terrifying presence. With his hand of su-

247. This again refers to Saint John the Evangelist. See note 244.

248. This description is close to the many visual images of the Virgin's Dormition throughout Christian art from the early medieval period to the Counter-Reformation.

preme power, Christ struck the daring enemy on the chest, burying him in his own darkness.[249]

Death of the Mother of Christ. After this, her Son, God, and Creator arrived, surrounded by the lively beauty of little cherubim and crowned by virgins and martyrs, to honor the last hour of life of the One who had destroyed death. Together with the twelve brothers, she heard the holy hymns and sweet harmonies of angelic chanting. Kneeling, and disconcerted by the presence of flashing of eternal light, they heard Christ's already many times heard and salvific voice, which said, "Come, beloved daughter, loved Bride and revered Mother, and receive after so many trials the reward that your superabundant merits deserve. Come, Beloved, and enjoy with me the infinite and perpetual for all eternity."[250] Having heard this, they saw the most beautiful, holy, and chaste soul leave through her lips, like a pure and simple dove from its own nest.

Christ's words to the Apostles. As Christ's heroes were soulfully singing the holy obsequies of the glorious soul, they heard a voice that said, according to many writers:

> Keepers of my commandments, carry the holy and pure body of Mary, who was Queen of the Virgins, to the valley of Jehosaphat, which is between the Mount of Olives and Mount Sion, where you will bury it in the newly made marble tomb, and until Aurora has thrice shown the world her beauty's grace, do not leave it since I will awaken it from its deathly sleep.

After he had said this, Jesus ascended with her immaculate soul to the most serene parts of Paradise.[251]

After her death, the twelve brothers were able to do nothing other than weep from sorrow, but the joy of her future resurrection dried their tears.[252] To the apostles, who gazed at her, her face seemed to be that of a person transported by the joy of the sound, and, if they had believed their own eyes, they would have firmly believed that she heard with her bodily ears the verses they sang in her praise. Peter, John, and Andrew reverently and de-

249. The incident with the devil would seem to be Marinella's creation.

250. Cf. Song of Songs 4:8.

251. Christ takes the Virgin's soul, which issues forth from her mouth, to heaven, leaving the body in the bier with the disciples. In art, her soul is usually depicted as a tiny child in Christ's arms.

252. For Marinella's use of the word "resurrection," see below, note 254.

votedly placed the human body of Mary the Virgin in her coffin, and then, with several other of Christ's brothers beneath, they carried the dear burden inside. John carried the palm, God's gift, before the funeral bier, and the others followed him, burdened by the sacred weight, and piously singing sacred hymns in praise of the heavenly Spirit. A multitude of angels encircled the holy coffin and its worthy company with the brightness and purity of their simple natures. Whereupon the singing was heard by the people, but all that could be seen was a very dense light.

The High Priest goes to burn Mary's body. Then the High Priest heard how the chaste Virgin was carried to her fitting sepulcher. As many have written, spurred on by his own stupidity, and with many who followed him, he ran to burn the wonderful body of the divine Virgin. And he went with the wicked people to where the solemn singing of the holy hymns drew him. The mad multitude, on seeing the light encircling the coffin and the disciples, was terrified. But as fear gave way to hate, the evil of their most wicked thoughts changed into rage, in reproaches, curses, and swearing. But God, who wished to reveal His lofty miracles to their wickedness, made the light vanish. Then the weak High Priest saw Christ's heroes and the body of the one who was purer than chastity's whiteness.

Mary's miracles. He immediately ran and seized the happy casket in both hands to throw it to the ground. But through divine will, his wicked hands remained attached to it and detached from his arms. Furthermore, all those who followed him were blinded. The Prince [High Priest] became aware of his mistake and acknowledged Christ as the Son of God and of the most holy Virgin, whom they were carrying to the sepulcher. And the men who had followed him until now in the evil actions, acknowledged the same. The Virgin, who had brought so much joy into the world through her birth, in her death wished no one to be unhappy, and she therefore restored his hands to the rash Prince. And the palm brought by John and placed by Peter on their heads rendered their sight to the blinded people. The enemy rabble of Jesus and Mary therefore became trumpets declaring their great names, and increased belief in Christ's faith and religion.[253]

Angels who concealed and encircled the Virgin's coffin with their brightness. Venerating, the spirits of Paradise surrounded the bier once more, and the perfect Disciples, who had arrived at the Valley of Jehosophat, put down the holy body. Then the angels scattered the sacred tomb with milky violets, white

253. The miracle of the high priest is related in the *Golden Legend* (2:81). It also appears in the Latin narrative of the Assumption of the Virgin by Pseudo-Melito (James, *Apocryphal New Testament*, 214–15).

lilies, and morning roses, the tomb that was to gather such a precious jewel within its breast. Christ's brothers, kneeling around her, venerated her, and then with devoted humility, took the body of the most serene Lady and placed it in the center of the honored sepulcher, putting the rigid stone over it. The valley between the Mount of Olives and Mount Sion, where the happy tomb was, rejoiced, I should like to imagine, in seeing Heaven's joy between their harsh peaks. The heavenly spirits, seated on golden clouds, sang with a harmony so sweet that Christ's just brothers enjoyed the singing within the sacred tomb, singing that must have been heard in Heaven before God's marvelous countenance. In that place, they prayed part of the time, part of the time discussed the royal Lady's virtues, and part of the time the deeds of God, who had covered His divinity with the veil of humanity; now the resurrection of the dead, then the joys of Paradise, and now the punishments tormenting the wicked.

Resurrection of Mary.[254] While they were discussing such things, the time arrived for the resurrection from death of Mary, who gave birth to life. Behold the light of the magnificences, behold the roar of thunder, the lightning and divine spirits that come to honor the resurrection of Christ's holy Mother. Behold, through her the day is more alive, the sun brighter, the air clearer, and the earth more beautiful: hence, and therefore, some clouds spread, made by God of heavenly splendor, which the souls of the blessed held above the density of their brightness.

Coming of Christ. And behold, Christ, from whose great and awesome face came forth rays other than those that encircle the sun's brow, came down from the gates of Heaven. He was seated on the scarlet fire that, flaming, laughs into the faces of the inflamed cherubim. He placed His holy feet on two very bright stars: on His right was the glorious soul of His venerable Mother, accompanied by the majesty of the entire celestial glory. Then a cloud made up of the light that came from the angelic faces, descending rapidly, covered the happy tomb, during which time her immaculate, pure, and noble soul returned to her blessed body. After this, in a merciful and joyful voice, Christ said, "Rise up, loved Mother, mansion of divinity, light of glory, and fount of joy. Rise, my Bride, and show here on earth what you can be in my Kingdom of eternal bliss."[255]

Then the cloud of gold faded away and she who had been awaited by Heaven came out of the sacred casket with her body. The heroes of

254. Marinella uses the word "resurrection," incorrectly, for Mary's "Assumption," presumably to parallel her triumphant ending with Christ's Resurrection.

255. A further reference to the Bride in the Song of Songs 4:8.

Christ, withdrawn into themselves, saw the Queen of the angelic thrones, surrounded by immortality, full of the spirit of life, come out of the hard stone, and they looked at the stars and venerable rays that made a diadem around her serene brow, the veil being broken to them through her grace, the veil that prevents us from seeing the purity and splendor of immaterial bodies. They saw her not only adorned with the purity of her own nature but, surrounded by a dense cloud of sparks and angels, they saw (thanks to the purity of her body, transparent as crystal) all her virtues, which on earth were her guide to Heaven. They heard the melodies of the singing and the sound of well-tempered instruments, which accompanied their Queen to the celestial domain.[256]

Ascension of Mary the Virgin.[257] When they reached the heavenly mansion, each angelic spirit and holy soul was dazzled by gazing at the blazing light that those splendors owed to her, and ordinary sun rays that strike our eyes are darkness and night compared to the brilliance that issued from her majesty. Then she sat at the right hand of the One who raised our humanity above the stars.[258] The angelic intellects, the virgins, the souls of pure innocents, and all the spirits sheltered in Heaven praised, blessed, and exalted her simple, pure, and chaste soul. And again, most serene Virgin, we praise, exalt, and bless your virtues, your wishes, and your mercy, with voices that come from the depths of our souls, and we ask for the compassion of your mercy that you commend the humility of our lowness to the sublime highness of your only begotten Son. And forgive me, heavenly Empress, if this hand, exercised in sin and frivolity, dared write of the stainlessness and holiness of your glorious life.

256. For the Virgin's Assumption, see volume editor's introduction (18–19, 26).

257. Again, Marinella refers incorrectly to the Virgin's "Ascension," rather than Assumption, presumably to link it more closely to Christ's Ascension.

258. As, according to the Nicene Creed, Christ sits at the right hand of God the Father, so the Virgin Mary sits at the honored right hand of Christ.

APPENDIX
THE MAGNIFICAT
(LUKE 1:46–55)

My soul doth magnify the Lord. And my spirit hath rejoiced in God my Saviour.

Because he hath regarded the humility of his handmaid; for, behold, from henceforth all generations shall call me blessed. Because he that is mighty hath done great things to me; and holy is his name. And his mercy is from generation unto generations, to them that fear him. He hath shewed might in his arm; he hath scattered the proud in the conceit of their heart. He hath put down the mighty from their seat and hath exalted the humble. He hath filled the hungry with good things; and the rich he hath sent empty away. He hath received Israel his servant, being mindful of his mercy. As he spoke to our fathers; to Abraham and to his seed for ever.

SERIES EDITORS' BIBLIOGRAPHY

PRIMARY SOURCES

Alberti, Leon Battista (1404–72). *The Family in Renaissance Florence*. Trans. by Renée Neu Watkins. Columbia, SC: University of South Carolina Press, 1969.

Arenal, Electa, and Stacey Schlau, eds. *Untold Sisters: Hispanic Nuns in Their Own Works*. Trans. by Amanda Powell. Albuquerque, NM: University of New Mexico Press, 1989.

Astell, Mary (1668–1731). *The First English Feminist: Reflections on Marriage and Other Writings*. Ed. and introd. Bridget Hill. New York: St. Martin's Press, 1986.

Astell, Mary, and John Norris (1657–1711). *Letters Concerning the Love of God*. Ed. E. Derek Taylor and Melvyn New. The Early Modern Englishwoman 1500–1750: Contemporary Editions. Burlington, VT: Ashgate, 2004.

Atherton, Margaret, ed. *Women Philosophers of the Early Modern Period*. Indianapolis, IN: Hackett, 1994.

Aughterson, Kate, ed. *Renaissance Woman: Constructions of Femininity in England: A Source Book*. London: Routledge, 1995.

Barbaro, Francesco (1390–1454). *On Wifely Duties*. In Benjamin Kohl and R. G. Witt, eds., *The Earthly Republic*, 179–228: translation of the Preface and Book 2. Trans. by Benjamin Kohl. Philadelphia: University of Pennsylvania Press, 1978.

Behn, Aphra (1640–89). *The Works of Aphra Behn*. 7 vols. Ed. Janet Todd. Columbus, OH: Ohio State University Press, 1992–96.

Blamires, Alcuin, ed. *Woman Defamed and Woman Defended: An Anthology of Medieval Texts*. Oxford: Clarendon Press, 1992.

Boccaccio, Giovanni (1313–75). *Corbaccio or the Labyrinth of Love*. Trans. by Anthony K. Cassell. 2nd rev. ed. Binghamton, NY: Medieval and Renaissance Texts and Studies, 1993.

———. *Famous Women*. Ed. and trans. by Virginia Brown. The I Tatti Renaissance Library. Cambridge, MA: Harvard University Press, 2001.

Booy, David, ed. *Autobiographical Writings by Early Quaker Women*. Burlington, VT: Ashgate, 2004.

Brown, Sylvia, ed. *Women's Writing in Stuart England: The Mother's Legacies of Dorothy Leigh, Elizabeth Joscelin and Elizabeth Richardson*. Thrupp, Stroud, Gloceter: Sutton, 1999.

Bruni, Leonardo (1370–1444). "On the Study of Literature (1405) to Lady Battista Malatesta of Moltefeltro." In *The Humanism of Leonardo Bruni: Selected Texts*, 240–51. Trans. and intro. by Gordon Griffiths, James Hankins, and David Thompson. Binghamton, NY: Medieval and Renaissance Studies and Texts, 1987.

Castiglione, Baldassare (1478–1529). *The Book of the Courtier*. Trans. by George Bull. New York: Penguin, 1967.

———. *The Book of the Courtier*. Ed. Daniel Javitch. New York: W. W. Norton & Co., 2002.

Clarke, Danielle, ed. *Isabella Whitney, Mary Sidney and Aemilia Lanyer: Renaissance Women Poets*. New York: Penguin Books, 2000.

Couchman, Jane, and Ann Crabb, eds. *Women's Letters across Europe, 1400–1700: Form and Persuasion*. Women and Gender in the Early Modern World. Burlington, VT: Ashgate, 2005.

Crawford, Patricia, and Laura Gowing, eds. *Women's Worlds in Seventeenth-Century England: A Source Book*. London: Routledge, 2000.

"Custome Is an Idiot": Jacobean Pamphlet Literature on Women. Ed. Susan Gushee O'Malley. Afterword by Ann Rosalind Jones. Chicago: University of Illinois Press, 2004.

Daybell, James, ed. *Early Modern Women's Letter Writing, 1450–1700*. Houndmills, England: Palgrave, 2001.

Domestic Politics and Family Absence: The Correspondence (1588–1621) of Robert Sidney, First Early of Leicester, and Barbara Gamage Sidney, Countess of Leicester. Ed. Margaret P. Hannay, Nowl J. Kinnamon, and Michael G. Brennan. The Early Modern Englishwoman 1500–1750: Contemporary Editions. Burlington, VT: Ashgate, 2005.

Elizabeth I: Collected Works. Ed. Leah S. Marcus, Janel Mueller, and Mary Beth Rose. Chicago: University of Chicago Press, 2000.

Elyot, Thomas (1490–1546). *Defence of Good Women: The Feminist Controversy of the Renaissance*. Facsimile Reproductions. Ed. Diane Bornstein. New York: Delmar, 1980.

Erasmus, Desiderius (1467–1536). *Erasmus on Women*. Ed. Erika Rummel. Toronto: University of Toronto Press, 1996.

de Erauso, Catalina (b. ca. 1592). *Lieutenant Nun: Memoir of a Basque Transvestite in the New World*. Trans. by Michele Stepto and Gabriel Stepto. Foreword by Marjorie Garber. Boston: Beacon Press, 1996.

Female and Male Voices in Early Modern England: An Anthology of Renaissance Writing. Ed. Betty S. Travitsky and Anne Lake Prescott. New York: Columbia University Press, 2000.

Ferguson, Moira, ed. *First Feminists: British Women Writers 1578–1799*. Bloomington, IN: Indiana University Press, 1985.

Galilei, Maria Celeste (1600–34). *Sister Maria Celeste's Letters to Her Father, Galileo*. Ed. and trans. by Rinaldina Russell. Lincoln, NE: Writers Club Press of Universe.com, 2000.

———. *To Father. The Letters of Sister Maria Celeste to Galileo, 1623–1633*. Trans. by Dava Sobel. London: Fourth Estate, 2001.

Gethner, Perry, ed. *The Lunatic Lover and Other Plays by French Women of the 17th and 18th Centuries*. Portsmouth, NH: Heinemann, 1994.

Glückel of Hameln (1646–1724). *The Memoirs of Glückel of Hameln*. Trans. by Marvin Lowenthal. New Introd. Robert Rosen. New York: Schocken Books, 1977.

Harline, Craig, ed. *The Burdens of Sister Margaret: Inside a Seventeenth-Century Convent*. Abr. ed. New Haven: Yale University Press, 2000.

Henderson, Katherine Usher, and Barbara F. McManus, eds. *Half Humankind: Contexts and Texts of the Controversy about Women in England, 1540–1640*. Urbana, IL: Indiana University Press, 1985.

Hoby, Margaret (1570/1–1633). *The Private Life of an Elizabethan Lady: The Diary of Lady Margaret Hoby 1599–1605*. Phoenix Mill, Great Britain: Sutton, 1998.

Humanist Educational Treatises. Ed. and trans. by Craig W. Kallendorf. The I Tatti Renaissance Library. Cambridge, MA: Harvard University Press, 2002.

Hunter, Lynette, ed. *The Letters of Dorothy Moore, 1612–64: The Friendships, Marriage and Intellectual Life of a Seventeenth-Century Woman*. The Early Modern Englishwoman 1500–1750: Contemporary Editions. Burlington, VT: Ashgate, 2004.

Joscelin, Elizabeth (1596–1622). *The Mothers Legacy to Her Unborn Childe*. Ed. Jean LeDrew Metcalfe. Toronto: University of Toronto Press, 2000.

Kaminsky, Amy Katz, ed. *Water Lilies, Flores del agua: An Anthology of Spanish Women Writers from the Fifteenth through the Nineteenth Century*. Minneapolis, MN: University of Minnesota Press, 1996.

Kempe, Margery (1373–1439). *The Book of Margery Kempe*. Trans. and ed. by Lynn Staley. Norton Critical Edition. New York: W.W. Norton, 2001.

King, Margaret L., and Albert Rabil, Jr., eds. *Her Immaculate Hand: Selected Works by and about the Women Humanists of Quattrocento Italy*. Binghamton, NY: Medieval and Renaissance Texts and Studies, 1983; 2nd rev. paperback ed., 1991.

Klein, Joan Larsen, ed. *Daughters, Wives, and Widows: Writings by Men about Women and Marriage in England, 1500–1640*. Urbana, IL: University of Illinois Press, 1992.

Knox, John (1505–72). *The Political Writings of John Knox: The First Blast of the Trumpet against the Monstrous Regiment of Women and Other Selected Works*. Ed. Marvin A. Breslow. Washington: Folger Shakespeare Library, 1985.

Kors, Alan C., and Edward Peters, eds. *Witchcraft in Europe, 400-1700: A Documentary History*. Philadelphia: University of Pennsylvania Press, 2000.

Krämer, Heinrich, and Jacob Sprenger. *Malleus Maleficarum* (ca. 1487). Trans. by Montague Summers. London: Pushkin Press, 1928; reprinted, New York: Dover, 1971.

Larsen, Anne R., and Colette H. Winn, eds. *Writings by Pre-Revolutionary French Women: From Marie de France to Elizabeth Vigée-Le Brun.* New York: Garland, 2000.

de Lorris, William (ca. 1212–ca. 1237), and Jean de Meun (ca. 1237–1305). *The Romance of the Rose.* Trans. by Charles Dahlbert. Princeton: Princeton University Press, 1971; reprinted, University Press of New England, 1983.

Marcus, Leah S., Janel Mueller, and Mary Beth Rose, eds. *Elizabeth I: Collected Works.* Chicago: University of Chicago Press, 2000.

Marguerite d'Angoulême, Queen of Navarre (1492–1549). *The Heptameron.* Trans. by P. A. Chilton. New York: Viking Penguin, 1984.

Mary of Agreda (1602–65). *The Divine Life of the Most Holy Virgin.* Abridgment of *The Mystical City of God.* Abr. Fr. Bonaventure Amedeo de Caesarea, M.C. Trans. by Abbé Joseph A. Boullan. Rockford, IL: Tan Books, 1997.

Moore, Dorothy. *The Letters of Dorothy Moore, 1612–64: The Friendships, Marriage and Intellectual Life of a Seventeenth-Century Woman.* Ed. Lynette Hunter. The Early Modern Englishwoman 1500–1750: Contemporary Editions. Burlington, VT: Ashgate, 2004.

Mullan, David G., ed. *Women's Life Writing in Early Modern Scotland: Writing the Evangelical Self, c. 1670–c. 1730.* The Early Modern Englishwoman 1500–1750: Contemporary Editions. Burlington, VT: Ashgate, 2003.

Myers, Kathleen A., and Amanda Powell, eds. *A Wild Country Out in the Garden: The Spiritual Journals of a Colonial Mexican Nun.* Bloomington: Indiana University Press, 1999.

Ostovich, Helen, and Elizabeth Sauer, eds. *Reading Early Modern Women: An Anthology of Texts in Manuscript and Print, 1550–1700.* New York: Routledge, 2004.

de Pizan, Christine (1365–1431). *The Book of the City of Ladies.* Trans. by Earl Jeffrey Richards. Foreword by Marina Warner. New York: Persea Books, 1982.

———. *The Treasure of the City of Ladies.* Trans. Sarah Lawson. New York: Viking Penguin, 1985. Also trans. and introd. Charity Cannon Willard. Ed. and introd. Madeleine P. Cosman. New York: Persea Books, 1989.

Reading Early Modern Women: An Anthology of Texts in Manuscript and Print, 1550–1700. Ed. Helen Ostovich and Elizabeth Sauer. New York: Routledge, 2004.

Russell, Rinaldina, ed. *Sister Maria Celeste's Letters to Her Father, Galileo.* Lincoln, NE: Writers Club Press of Universe.com, 2000.

Teresa of Avila, Saint (1515–82). *The Collected Letters of St. Teresa of Avila. Volume One: 1546–1577.* Trans. by Kieran Kavanaugh. Washington, DC: Institute of Carmelite Studies, 2001.

———. *The Collected Letters of St. Teresa of Avila. Volume Two: 1578–1582.* Trans. by Kieran Kavanaugh. Washington, DC: Institute of Carmelite Studies, 2007.

———. *The Life of Saint Teresa of Avila by Herself.* Trans. by J. M. Cohen. New York: Viking Penguin, 1957.

Travitsky, Betty, ed. *The Paradise of Women: Writings by Englishwomen of the Renaissance.* Westport, CT: Greenwood Press, 1981.

Weyer, Johann (1515–88). *Witches, Devils, and Doctors in the Renaissance: Johann Weyer, De praestigiis daemonum*. Ed. George Mora with Benjamin G. Kohl, Erik Midelfort, and Helen Bacon. Trans. by John Shea. Binghamton, NY: Medieval and Renaissance Texts and Studies, 1991.

Wilson, Katharina M., ed. *Medieval Women Writers*. Athens, GA: University of Georgia Press, 1984.

———, ed. *Women Writers of the Renaissance and Reformation*. Athens, GA: University of Georgia Press, 1987.

Wilson, Katharina M., and Frank J. Warnke, eds. *Women Writers of the Seventeenth Century*. Athens, GA: University of Georgia Press, 1989.

Wollstonecraft, Mary (1759–97). *A Vindication of the Rights of* Men *and A Vindication of the Rights of Women*. Ed. Sylvana Tomaselli. Cambridge: Cambridge University Press, 1995.

———. *The Vindications of the Rights of Men, the Rights of Women*. Ed. D. L. Macdonald and Kathleen Scherf. Peterborough, Ontario, Canada: Broadview Press, 1997.

Woman Defamed and Woman Defended: An Anthology of Medieval Texts. Ed. Alcuin Blamires. Oxford: Clarendon Press, 1992.

Women Critics 1660–1820: An Anthology. Edited by the Folger Collective on Early Women Critics. Bloomington, IN: Indiana University Press, 1995.

Women Writers in English 1350–1850: 15 volumes published through 1999 (projected 30-volume series suspended). Oxford University Press.

Women's Letters across Europe, 1400–1700: Form and Persuasion. Ed. Jane Couchman and Ann Crabb. Women and Gender in the Early Modern World. Burlington, VT: Ashgate , 2005.

Women's Life Writing in Early Modern Scotland: Writing the Evangelical Self, c. 1670–c. 1730. Ed. David G. Mullan. The Early Modern Englishwoman 1500–1750: Contemporary Editions. Burlington, VT: Ashgate, 2003.

Wroth, Lady Mary (ca. 1586–ca. 1640). *The Countess of Montgomery's Urania*. 2 parts. Ed. Josephine A. Roberts. Tempe, AZ: MRTS, 1995, 1999.

———. *Lady Mary Wroth's "Love's Victory": The Penshurst Manuscript*. Ed. Michael G. Brennan. London: The Roxburghe Club, 1988.

———. *The Poems of Lady Mary Wroth*. Ed. Josephine A. Roberts. Baton Rouge, LA: Louisiana State University Press, 1983.

de Zayas, Maria (1590–1650). *The Disenchantments of Love*. Trans. by H. Patsy Boyer. Albany, NY: State University of New York Press, 1997.

———. *The Enchantments of Love: Amorous and Exemplary Novels*. Trans. by H. Patsy Boyer. Berkeley, CA: University of California Press, 1990.

SECONDARY SOURCES

Abate, Corinne S., ed. *Privacy, Domesticity, and Women in Early Modern England*. Burlington, VT: Ashgate, 2003.

Ahlgren, Gillian. *Teresa of Avila and the Politics of Sanctity*. Ithaca: Cornell University Press, 1996.

Akkerman, Tjitske, and Siep Sturman, eds. *Feminist Thought in European History, 1400–2000*. London: Routledge, 1997.

Allen, Sister Prudence, R.S.M. *The Concept of Woman: The Aristotelian Revolution, 750 B.C.–A.D. 1250*. Grand Rapids, MI: William B. Eerdmans, 1997.

———. *The Concept of Woman, Volume II: The Early Humanist Reformation, 1250–1500*. Grand Rapids, MI: William B. Eerdmans, 2002.

Altmann, Barbara K., and Deborah L. McGrady, eds. *Christine de Pizan: A Casebook*. New York: Routledge, 2003.

Ambiguous Realities: Women in the Middle Ages and Renaissance. Ed. Carole Levin and Jeanie Watson. Detroit: Wayne State University Press, 1987.

Amussen, Susan D., and Adele Seeff, eds. *Attending to Early Modern Women*. Newark: University of Delaware Press, 1998.

Andreadis, Harriette. *Sappho in Early Modern England: Female Same-Sex Literary Erotics 1550–1714*. Chicago: University of Chicago Press, 2001.

Arcangela Tarabotti: A Literary Nun in Baroque Venice. Ed. Elissa B. Weaver. Ravenna: Longo Editore, 2006.

Architecture and the Politics of Gender in Early Modern Europe. Ed. Helen Hills. Burlington, VT: Ashgate, 2003.

Armon, Shifra. *Picking Wedlock: Women and the Courtship Novel in Spain*. New York: Rowman & Littlefield, 2002.

Attending to Early Modern Women. Ed. Susan D. Amussen and Adele Seeff. Newark: University of Delaware Press, 1998.

Backer, Anne Liot. *Precious Women*. New York: Basic Books, 1974.

Ballaster, Ros. *Seductive Forms*. New York: Oxford University Press, 1992.

Barash, Carol. *English Women's Poetry, 1649–1714: Politics, Community, and Linguistic Authority*. New York: Oxford University Press, 1996.

Barker, Alele Marie, and Jehanne M. Gheith, eds. *A History of Women's Writing in Russia*. Cambridge: Cambridge University Press, 2002.

Battigelli, Anna. *Margaret Cavendish and the Exiles of the Mind*. Lexington, KY: University of Kentucky Press, 1998.

Beasley, Faith. *Revising Memory: Women's Fiction and Memoirs in Seventeenth-Century France*. New Brunswick: Rutgers University Press, 1990.

———. *Salons, History, and the Creation of Seventeenth-Century France*. Aldershot and Burlington, VT: Ashgate, 2006.

Becker, Lucinda M. *Death and the Early Modern Englishwoman*. Burlington, VT: Ashgate, 2003.

Beilin, Elaine V. *Redeeming Eve: Women Writers of the English Renaissance*. Princeton: Princeton University Press, 1987.

Bennett, Lyn. *Women Writing of Divinest Things: Rhetoric and the Poetry of Pembroke, Wroth, and Lanyer*. Pittsburgh: Duquesne University Press, 2004.

Benson, Pamela Joseph. *The Invention of Renaissance Woman: The Challenge of Female Independence in the Literature and Thought of Italy and England*. University Park, PA: Pennsylvania State University Press, 1992.

Benson, Pamela Joseph, and Victoria Kirkham, eds. *Strong Voices, Weak History: Early Women Writers and Canons in England, France, and Italy*. Ann Arbor: University of Michigan Press, 2005.

Berry, Helen. *Gender, Society and Print Culture in Late-Stuart England*. Burlington, VT: Ashgate, 2003.

Beyond Isabella: Secular Women Patrons of Art in Renaissance Italy. Ed. Sheryl E. Reiss and David G. Wilkins. Kirksville, MO: Turman State University Press, 2001.

Beyond Their Sex: Learned Women of the European Past. Ed. Patricia A. Labalme. New York: New York University Press, 1980.

Bicks, Caroline. *Midwiving Subjects in Shakespeare's England*. Burlington, VT: Ashgate, 2003.

Bilinkoff, Jodi. *The Avila of Saint Teresa: Religious Reform in a Sixteenth-Century City*. Ithaca: Cornell University Press, 1989.

———. *Related Lives: Confessors and Their Female Penitents, 1450–1750*. Ithaca, NY: Cornell University Press, 2005.

Bissell, R. Ward. *Artemisia Gentileschi and the Authority of Art*. University Park, PA: Pennsylvania State University Press, 2000.

Blain, Virginia, Isobel Grundy, and Patricia Clements, eds. *The Feminist Companion to Literature in English: Women Writers from the Middle Ages to the Present*. New Haven: Yale University Press, 1990.

Blamires, Alcuin. *The Case for Women in Medieval Culture*. Oxford: Clarendon Press, 1997.

Bloch, R. Howard. *Medieval Misogyny and the Invention of Western Romantic Love*. Chicago: University of Chicago Press, 1991.

Bogucka, Maria. *Women in Early Modern Polish Society, against the European Background*. Burlington, VT: Ashgate, 2004.

Bornstein, Daniel, and Roberto Rusconi, eds. *Women and Religion in Medieval and Renaissance Italy*. Trans. by Margery J. Schneider. Chicago: University of Chicago Press, 1996.

Brant, Clare, and Diane Purkiss, eds. *Women, Texts and Histories, 1575–1760*. London: Routledge, 1992.

Briggs, Robin. *Witches and Neighbours: The Social and Cultural Context of European Witchcraft*. New York: HarperCollins, 1995; Viking Penguin, 1996.

Brink, Jean R., ed. *Female Scholars: A Tradition of Learned Women before 1800*. Montreal: Eden Press Women's Publications, 1980.

Brink, Jean R., Allison Coudert, and Maryanne Cline Horowitz, eds. *The Politics of Gender in Early Modern Europe*. Sixteenth Century Essays and Studies, vol. 12. Kirksville, MO: Sixteenth Century Journal Publishers, 1989.

Broude, Norma, and Mary D. Garrard, eds. *The Expanding Discourse: Feminism and Art History*. New York: HarperCollins, 1992.

Brown, Judith C. *Immodest Acts: The Life of a Lesbian Nun in Renaissance Italy*. New York: Oxford University Press, 1986.

Brown, Judith C., and Robert C. Davis, eds. *Gender and Society in Renaissance Italy.* London: Addison Wesley Longman, 1998.

Brown-Grant, Rosalind. *Christine de Pizan and the Moral Defence of Women: Reading Beyond Gender*. Cambridge: Cambridge University Press, 1999.

Burke, Victoria E., ed. *Early Modern Women's Manuscript Writing*. Burlington, VT: Ashgate, 2004.

Burns, Jane E., ed. *Medieval Fabrications: Dress, Textiles, Cloth Work, and Other Cultural Imaginings*. New York: Palgrave Macmillan, 2004.

Bynum, Carolyn Walker. *Fragmentation and Redemption: Essays on Gender and the Human Body in Medieval Religion*. New York: Zone Books, 1992.

———. *Holy Feast and Holy Fast: The Religious Significance of Food to Medieval Women*. Berkeley: University of California Press, 1987.

Campbell, Julie DeLynn. "Renaissance Women Writers: The Beloved Speaks Her Part." Ph.D diss., Texas A&M University, 1997.

Catling, Jo, ed. *A History of Women's Writing in Germany, Austria and Switzerland*. Cambridge: Cambridge University Press, 2000.

Cavallo, Sandra, and Lyndan Warner. *Widowhood in Medieval and Early Modern Europe*. New York: Longman, 1999.

Cavanagh, Sheila T. *Cherished Torment: The Emotional Geography of Lady Mary Wroth's* Urania. Pittsburgh: Duquesne University Press, 2001.

Cerasano, S. P., and Marion Wynne-Davies, eds. *Readings in Renaissance Women's Drama: Criticism, History, and Performance 1594–1998*. London: Routledge, 1998.

Cervigni, Dino S., ed. *Women Mystic Writers. Annali d'Italianistica* 13 (1995) (entire issue).

Cervigni, Dino S., and Rebecca West, eds. *Women's Voices in Italian Literature. Annali d'Italianistica* 7 (1989) (entire issue).

Charlton, Kenneth. *Women, Religion and Education in Early Modern England*. London: Routledge, 1999.

Chojnacka, Monica. *Working Women in Early Modern Venice.* Baltimore: Johns Hopkins University Press, 2001.

Chojnacki, Stanley. *Women and Men in Renaissance Venice: Twelve Essays on Patrician Society*. Baltimore: Johns Hopkins University Press, 2000.

Cholakian, Patricia Francis. *Rape and Writing in the* Heptameron *of Marguerite de Navarre*. Carbondale, IL: Southern Illinois University Press, 1991.

———. *Women and the Politics of Self-Representation in Seventeenth-Century France*. Newark: University of Delaware Press, 2000.

Christine de Pizan: A Casebook. Ed. Barbara K. Altmann and Deborah L. McGrady. New York: Routledge, 2003.

Clogan, Paul Maurice, ed. *Medievali et Humanistica: Literacy and the Lay Reader*. Lanham, MD: Rowman & Littlefield, 2000.

Clubb, Louise George. *Italian Drama in Shakespeare's Time*. New Haven: Yale University Press, 1989.

Clucas, Stephen, ed. *A Princely Brave Woman: Essays on Margaret Cavendish, Duchess of Newcastle*. Burlington, VT: Ashgate, 2003.

Coakley, John W. *Women, Men, and Spiritual Power: Female Saints and Their Male Collaborators*. New York: Columbia University Press, 2006.

Conley, John J., S.J. *The Suspicion of Virtue: Women Philosophers in Neoclassical France*. Ithaca, NY: Cornell University Press, 2002.

Crabb, Ann. *The Strozzi of Florence: Widowhood and Family Solidarity in the Renaissance*. Ann Arbor: University of Michigan Press, 2000.

The Crannied Wall: Women, Religion, and the Arts in Early Modern Europe. Ed. Craig A. Monson. Ann Arbor: University of Michigan Press, 1992.

Creative Women in Medieval and Early Modern Italy. Ed. E. Ann Matter and John Coakley. Philadelphia: University of Pennsylvania Press, 1994. (Sequel to the Monson collection, *The Crannied Wall*, ed. C. A. Monson.)

Crowston, Clare Haru. *Fabricating Women: The Seamstresses of Old Regime France, 1675–1791*. Durham, NC: Duke University Press, 2001.

Cruz, Anne J., and Mary Elizabeth Perry, eds. *Culture and Control in Counter-Reformation Spain*. Minneapolis: University of Minnesota Press, 1992.

Datta, Satya. *Women and Men in Early Modern Venice*. Burlington, VT: Ashgate, 2003.

Davis, Natalie Zemon. *Society and Culture in Early Modern France*, espec. chaps. 3 and 5. Stanford: Stanford University Press, 1975.

———. *Women on the Margins: Three Seventeenth-Century Lives*. Cambridge, MA: Harvard University Press, 1995.

DeJean, Joan. *Ancients against Moderns: Culture Wars and the Making of a Fin de Siècle*. Chicago: University of Chicago Press, 1997.

———. *Fictions of Sappho, 1546–1937*. Chicago: University of Chicago Press, 1989.

———. *The Reinvention of Obscenity: Sex, Lies, and Tabloids in Early Modern France*. Chicago: University of Chicago Press, 2002.

———. *Tender Geographies: Women and the Origins of the Novel in France*. New York: Columbia University Press, 1991.

D'Elia, Anthony F. *The Renaissance of Marriage in Fifteenth-Century Italy*. Cambridge, MA: Harvard University Press, 2004.

Demers, Patricia. *Women's Writing in English: Early Modern England*. Toronto: University of Toronto Press, 2005.

Dictionary of Russian Women Writers. Ed. Marina Ledkovsky, Charlotte Rosenthal, and Mary Zirin. Westport, CT: Greenwood Press, 1994.

Diefendorf, Barbara. *From Penitence to Charity: Pious Women and the Catholic Reformation in Paris*. New York: Oxford University Press, 2004.

Dixon, Laurinda S. *Perilous Chastity: Women and Illness in Pre-Enlightenment Art and Medicine.* Ithaca: Cornell Universitiy Press, 1995.

Dolan, Frances, E. *Whores of Babylon: Catholicism, Gender and Seventeenth-Century Print Culture*. Ithaca: Cornell University Press, 1999.

Donovan, Josephine. *Women and the Rise of the Novel, 1405–1726*. New York: St. Martin's Press, 1999.

Dyan, Elliott. *Proving Woman: Female Spirituality and Inquisitional Culture in the Later Middle Ages*. Princeton: Princeton University Press, 2004.

Early [English] Women Writers: 1600–1720. Ed. Anita Pacheco. New York: Longman, 1998.

Eigler, Friederike, and Susanne Kord, eds. *The Feminist Encyclopedia of German Literature*. Westport, CT: Greenwood Press, 1997.

Engendering the Early Modern Stage: Women Playwrights in the Spanish Empire. Ed. Valerie (Oakey) Hegstrom and Amy R. Williamsen. New Orleans: University Press of the South, 1999.

Erdmann, Axel. *My Gracious Silence: Women in the Mirror of Sixteenth-Century Printing in Western Europe.* Luzern: Gilhofer and Rauschberg, 1999.

Erickson, Amy Louise. *Women and Property in Early Modern England.* London: Routledge, 1993.

Extraordinary Women of the Medieval and Renaissance World: A Biographical Dictionary. Ed. Carole Levin et al. Westport, CT: Greenwood Press, 2000.

Ezell, Margaret J. M. *The Patriarch's Wife: Literary Evidence and the History of the Family*. Chapel Hill: University of North Carolina Press, 1987.

———. *Social Authorship and the Advent of Print*. Baltimore: Johns Hopkins University Press, 1999.

———. *Writing Women's Literary History*. Baltimore: Johns Hopkins University Press, 1993.

Farrell, Michèle Longino. *Performing Motherhood: The Sévigné Correspondence*. Hanover, NH: University Press of New England, 1991.

Feminism and Renaissance Studies. Ed. Lorna Hutson. New York: Oxford University Press, 1999.

The Feminist Companion to Literature in English: Women Writers from the Middle Ages to the Present. Ed. Virginia Blain, Isobel Grundy, and Patricia Clements. New Haven: Yale University Press, 1990.

Feminist Encyclopedia of Italian Literature. Ed. Rinaldina Russell. Westport, CT: Greenwood Press, 1997.

Feminist Thought in European History, 1400–2000. Ed. Tjitske Akkerman and Siep Sturman. London: Routledge, 1997.

Ferguson, Margaret W. *Dido's Daughters: Literacy, Gender, and Empire in Early Modern England and France.* Chicago: University of Chicago Press, 2003.

Ferguson, Margaret W., Maureen Quilligan, and Nancy J. Vickers, eds. *Rewriting the Renaissance: The Discourses of Sexual Difference in Early Modern Europe.* Chicago: University of Chicago Press, 1987.

Ferraro, Joanne M. *Marriage Wars in Late Renaissance Venice.* Oxford: Oxford University Press, 2001.

Fletcher, Anthony. *Gender, Sex and Subordination in England 1500–1800.* New Haven: Yale University Press, 1995.

Franklin, Margaret. *Boccaccio's Heroines.* Burlington, VT: Ashgate, 2006.

French Women Writers: A Bio-Bibliographical Source Book. Ed. Eva Martin Sartori and Dorothy Wynne Zimmerman. Westport, CT: Greenwood Press, 1991.

Frye, Susan, and Karen Robertson, eds. *Maids and Mistresses, Cousins and Queens: Women's Alliances in Early Modern England.* Oxford: Oxford University Press, 1999.

Gallagher, Catherine. *Nobody's Story: The Vanishing Acts of Women Writers in the Marketplace, 1670–1820.* Berkeley: University of California Press, 1994.

Garrard, Mary D. *Artemisia Gentileschi: The Image of the Female Hero in Italian Baroque Art.* Princeton: Princeton University Press, 1989.

Gelbart, Nina Rattner. *The King's Midwife: A History and Mystery of Madame du Coudray.* Berkeley: University of California Press, 1998.

Giles, Mary E., ed. *Women in the Inquisition: Spain and the New World.* Baltimore: Johns Hopkins University Press, 1999.

Gill, Catie. *Women in the Seventeenth-Century Quaker Community.* Burlington, VT: Ashgate, 2005.

Glenn, Cheryl. *Rhetoric Retold: Regendering the Tradition from Antiquity through the Renaissance.* Carbondale, IL: Southern Illinois University Press, 1997.

Goffen, Rona. *Titian's Women.* New Haven: Yale University Press, 1997.

Going Public: Women and Publishing in Early Modern France. Ed. Elizabeth C. Goldsmith and Dena Goodman. Ithaca: Cornell University Press, 1995.

Goldberg, Jonathan. *Desiring Women Writing: English Renaissance Examples.* Stanford: Stanford University Press, 1997.

Goldsmith, Elizabeth C. *Exclusive Conversations: The Art of Interaction in Seventeenth-Century France.* Philadelphia: University of Pennsylvania Press, 1988.

———, ed. *Writing the Female Voice.* Boston: Northeastern University Press, 1989.

Goldsmith, Elizabeth C., and Dena Goodman, eds. *Going Public: Women and Publishing in Early Modern France.* Ithaca: Cornell University Press, 1995.

Grafton, Anthony, and Lisa Jardine. *From Humanism to the Humanities: Education and the Liberal Arts in Fifteenth- and Sixteenth-Century Europe.* London: Duckworth, 1986.

The Graph of Sex and the German Text: Gendered Culture in Early Modern Germany 1500–1700. Ed. Lynne Tatlock and Christiane Bohnert. Amsterdam: Rodolphi, 1994.

Grassby, Richard. *Kinship and Capitalism: Marriage, Family, and Business in the English-Speaking World, 1580–1740.* Cambridge: Cambridge University Press, 2001.

Greer, Margaret Rich. *Maria de Zayas Tells Baroque Tales of Love and the Cruelty of Men.* University Park, PA: Pennsylvania State University Press, 2000.

Grossman, Avraham. *Pious and Rebellious: Jewish Women in Medieval Europe.* Trans. by Jonathan Chipman. Waltham, MA: Brandeis University Press, 2004.

Gutierrez, Nancy A. *"Shall She Famish Then?" Female Food Refusal in Early Modern England.* Burlington, VT: Ashgate, 2003.

Habermann, Ina. *Staging Slander and Gender in Early Modern England.* Burlington, VT: Ashgate, 2003.

Hacke, Daniela. *Women, Sex, and Marriage in Early Modern Venice.* Burlington, VT: Ashgate, 2004.

Hackel, Heidi Brayman. *Reading Material in Early Modern England: Print, Gender, Literacy.* Cambridge: Cambridge University Press, 2005.

Hackett, Helen. *Women and Romance Fiction in the English Renaissance.* Cambridge: Cambridge University Press, 2000.

Hall, Kim F. *Things of Darkness: Economies of Race and Gender in Early Modern England.* Ithaca, NY: Cornell University Press, 1995.

Hamburger, Jeffrey. *The Visual and the Visionary: Art and Female Spirituality in Late Medieval Germany.* New York: Zone Books, 1998.

Hampton, Timothy. *Literature and the Nation in the Sixteenth Century: Inventing Renaissance France.* Ithaca, NY: Cornell University Press, 2001.

Hannay, Margaret, ed. *Silent but for the Word.* Kent, OH: Kent State University Press, 1985.

Hardwick, Julie. *The Practice of Patriarchy: Gender and the Politics of Household Authority in Early Modern France.* University Park, PA: Pennsylvania State University Press, 1998.

Harris, Barbara J. *English Aristocratic Women, 1450–1550: Marriage and Family, Property and Careers.* New York: Oxford University Press, 2002.

Harth, Erica. *Cartesian Women: Versions and Subversions of Rational Discourse in the Old Regime.* Ithaca: Cornell University Press, 1992.

———. *Ideology and Culture in Seventeenth-Century France.* Ithaca: Cornell University Press, 1983.

Harvey, Elizabeth D. *Ventriloquized Voices: Feminist Theory and English Renaissance Texts.* London: Routledge, 1992.

Haselkorn, Anne M., and Betty Travitsky, eds. *The Renaissance Englishwoman in Print: Counterbalancing the Canon.* Amherst: University of Massachusetts Press, 1990.

Hawkesworth, Celia, ed. *A History of Central European Women's Writing.* New York: Palgrave Press, 2001.

Hegstrom (Oakey), Valerie, and Amy R. Williamsen, eds. *Engendering the Early Modern Stage: Women Playwrights in the Spanish Empire*. New Orleans: University Press of the South, 1999.

Hendricks, Margo, and Patricia Parker, eds. *Women, "Race," and Writing in the Early Modern Period*. London: Routledge, 1994.

Herlihy, David. "Did Women Have a Renaissance? A Reconsideration." *Medievalia et Humanistica*, n.s., 13 (1985): 1–22.

Hill, Bridget. *The Republican Virago: The Life and Times of Catharine Macaulay, Historian*. New York: Oxford University Press, 1992.

Hills, Helen, ed. *Architecture and the Politics of Gender in Early Modern Europe*. Burlington, VT: Ashgate, 2003.

Hirst, Jilie. *Jane Leade: Biography of a Seventeenth-Century Mystic*. Burlington, VT: Ashgate, 2006.

A History of Central European Women's Writing. Ed. Celia Hawkesworth. New York: Palgrave Press, 2001.

A History of Women in the West.

Volume 1: *From Ancient Goddesses to Christian Saints*. Ed. Pauline Schmitt Pantel. Cambridge, MA: Harvard University Press, 1992.

Volume 2: *Silences of the Middle Ages*. Ed. Christiane Klapisch-Zuber. Cambridge, MA: Harvard University Press, 1992.

Volume 3: *Renaissance and Enlightenment Paradoxes*. Ed. Natalie Zemon Davis and Arlette Farge. Cambridge, MA: Harvard University Press, 1993.

A History of Women Philosophers. 3 vols. Ed. Mary Ellen Waithe. Dordrecht: Martinus Nijhoff, 1987.

A History of Women's Writing in France. Ed. Sonya Stephens. Cambridge: Cambridge University Press, 2000.

A History of Women's Writing in Germany, Austria and Switzerland. Ed. Jo Catling. Cambridge: Cambridge University Press, 2000.

A History of Women's Writing in Italy. Ed. Letizia Panizza and Sharon Wood. Cambridge: Cambridge University Press, 2000.

A History of Women's Writing in Russia. Ed. Alele Marie Barker and Jehanne M. Gheith. Cambridge: Cambridge University Press, 2002.

Hobby, Elaine. *Virtue of Necessity: English Women's Writing 1646–1688*. London: Virago Press, 1988.

Horowitz, Maryanne Cline. "Aristotle and Women." *Journal of the History of Biology* 9 (1976): 183–213.

Howell, Martha C. *The Marriage Exchange: Property, Social Place, and Gender in Cities of the Low Countries, 1300–1550*. Chicago: University of Chicago Press, 1998.

———. *Women, Production and Patriarchy in Late Medieval Cities*. Chicago: University of Chicago Press, 1986.

Hufton, Olwen H. *The Prospect before Her: A History of Women in Western Europe, 1: 1500–1800*. New York: HarperCollins, 1996.

Hull, Suzanne W. *Chaste, Silent, and Obedient: English Books for Women, 1475–1640*. San Marino, CA: Huntington Library, 1982.

Hunt, Lynn, ed. *The Invention of Pornography: Obscenity and the Origins of Modernity, 1500–1800*. New York: Zone Books, 1996.

Hutner, Heidi, ed. *Rereading Aphra Behn: History, Theory, and Criticism*. Charlottesville, VA: University Press of Virginia, 1993.

Hutson, Lorna, ed. *Feminism and Renaissance Studies*. New York: Oxford University Press, 1999.

The Invention of Pornography: Obscenity and the Origins of Modernity, 1500–1800. Ed. Lynn Hunt. New York: Zone Books, 1996.

Italian Women Writers: A Bio-Bibliographical Sourcebook. Ed. Rinaldina Russell. Westport, CT: Greenwood Press, 1994.

Jaffe, Irma B., with Gernando Colombardo. *Shining Eyes, Cruel Fortune: The Lives and Loves of Italian Renaissance Women Poets*. New York: Fordham University Press, 2002.

James, Susan E. *Kateryn Parr: The Making of a Queen*. Burlington, VT: Ashgate, 1999.

Jankowski, Theodora A. *Women in Power in the Early Modern Drama*. Urbana, IL: University of Illinois Press, 1992.

Jansen, Katherine Ludwig. *The Making of the Magdalen: Preaching and Popular Devotion in the Later Middle Ages*. Princeton: Princeton University Press, 2000.

Jed, Stephanie H. *Chaste Thinking: The Rape of Lucretia and the Birth of Humanism*. Bloomington, IN: Indiana University Press, 1989.

Jones, Ann Rosalind, and Peter Stallybrass. *Renaissance Clothing and the Materials of Memory*. Cambridge, UK: Cambridge University Press, 2000.

Jordan, Constance. *Renaissance Feminism: Literary Texts and Political Models*. Ithaca: Cornell University Press, 1990.

Kagan, Richard L. *Lucrecia's Dreams: Politics and Prophecy in Sixteenth-Century Spain*. Berkeley: University of California Press, 1990.

Kehler, Dorothea, and Laurel Amtower, eds. *The Single Woman in Medieval and Early Modern England: Her Life and Representation*. Tempe, AZ: MRTS, 2002.

Kelly, Joan. "Did Women Have a Renaissance?" In *Women, History and Theory: The Essays of Joan Kelly*. Chicago: University of Chicago Press, 1984. Also in Renate Bridenthal, Claudia Koonz, and Susan M. Stuard, eds., *Becoming Visible: Women in European History*. 3rd ed. Boston: Houghton Mifflin, 1998.

———. "Early Feminist Theory and the *Querelle des Femmes*." In *Women, History and Theory: The Essays of Joan Kelly*.

Kelso, Ruth. *Doctrine for the Lady of the Renaissance*. Foreword by Katharine M. Rogers. Urbana, IL: University of Illinois Press, 1956, 1978.

Kendrick, Robert L. *Celestial Sirens: Nuns and Their Music in Early Modern Milan*. New York: Oxford University Press, 1996.

Kermode, Jenny, and Garthine Walker, eds. *Women, Crime and the Courts in Early Modern England*. Chapel Hill: University of North Carolina Press, 1994.

King, Catherine E. *Renaissance Women Patrons: Wives and Widows in Italy, c. 1300–1550*. New York: Manchester University Press (distributed in the U.S. by St. Martin's Press), 1998.

King, Margaret L. *Women of the Renaissance*. Foreword by Catharine R. Stimpson. Chicago: University of Chicago Press, 1991.

King, Thomas A. *The Gendering of Men, 1600-1700: The English Phallus*. Vol. 1. Madison: University of Wisconsin Press, 2004.

Krontiris, Tina. *Oppositional Voices: Women as Writers and Translators of Literature in the English Renaissance*. London: Routledge, 1992.

Kuehn, Thomas. *Law, Family, and Women: Toward a Legal Anthropology of Renaissance Italy*. Chicago: University of Chicago Press, 1991.

Kunze, Bonnelyn Young. *Margaret Fell and the Rise of Quakerism*. Stanford: Stanford University Press, 1994.

Labalme, Patricia A., ed. *Beyond Their Sex: Learned Women of the European Past*. New York: New York University Press, 1980.

Lalande, Roxanne Decker, ed. *A Labor of Love: Critical Reflections on the Writings of Marie-Catherine Desjardina (Mme de Villedieu)*. Madison, NJ: Fairleigh Dickinson University Press, 2000.

Lamb, Mary Ellen. *Gender and Authorship in the Sidney Circle*. Madison: University of Wisconsin Press, 1990.

Laqueur, Thomas. *Making Sex: Body and Gender from the Greeks to Freud*. Cambridge, MA: Harvard University Press, 1990.

Larsen, Anne R., and Colette H. Winn, eds. *Renaissance Women Writers: French Texts/American Contexts*. Detroit, MI: Wayne State University Press, 1994.

Laven, Mary. *Virgins of Venice: Enclosed Lives and Broken Vows in the Renaissance Convent*. London: Viking, 2002.

Ledkovsky, Marina, Charlotte Rosenthal, and Mary Zirin, eds. *Dictionary of Russian Women Writers*. Westport, CT: Greenwood Press, 1994.

Lehfeldt, Elizabeth A. *Religious Women in Golden Age Spain: The Permeable Cloister*. Burlington, VT: Ashgate, 2005.

Lerner, Gerda. *The Creation of Patriarchy* and *Creation of Feminist Consciousness, 1000–1870*. 2-vol. history of women. New York: Oxford University Press, 1986, 1994.

Levack, Brian P. *The Witch Hunt in Early Modern Europe*. London: Longman, 1987.

Levin, Carole, and Jeanie Watson, eds. *Ambiguous Realities: Women in the Middle Ages and Renaissance*. Detroit: Wayne State University Press, 1987.

Levin, Carole, Jo Eldridge Carney, and Debra Barrett-Graves, eds. *Elizabeth I: Always Her Own Free Woman*. Burlington, VT: Ashgate, 2003.

Levin, Carole, et al. *Extraordinary Women of the Medieval and Renaissance World: A Biographical Dictionary*. Westport, CT: Greenwood Press, 2000.

Levy, Allison, ed. *Widowhood and Visual Culture in Early Modern Europe*. Burlington, VT: Ashgate, 2003.

Lewalsky, Barbara Kiefer. *Writing Women in Jacobean England*. Cambridge, MA: Harvard University Press, 1993.

Lewis, Gertrud Jaron. *By Women for Women about Women: The Sister-Books of Fourteenth-Century Germany*. Toronto: University of Toronto Press, 1996.

Lewis, Jayne Elizabeth. *Mary Queen of Scots: Romance and Nation*. London: Routledge, 1998.

Lindenauer, Leslie J. *Piety and Power: Gender and Religious Culture in the American Colonies, 1630–1700*. London: Routledge, 2002.

Lindsey, Karen. *Divorced Beheaded Survived: A Feminist Reinterpretation of the Wives of Henry VIII*. Reading, MA: Addison-Wesley, 1995.

Lochrie, Karma. *Margery Kempe and Translations of the Flesh*. Philadelphia: University of Pennsylvania Press, 1992.

Lougee, Carolyn C. *Le Paradis des Femmes: Women, Salons, and Social Stratification in Seventeenth-Century France*. Princeton: Princeton University Press, 1976.

Love, Harold. *The Culture and Commerce of Texts: Scribal Publication in Seventeenth-Century England*. Amherst, MA: University of Massachusetts Press, 1993.

Lowe, K. J. P. *Nuns' Chronicles and Convent Culture in Renaissance and Counter-Reformation Italy*. Cambridge: Cambridge University Press, 2003.

Lux-Sterritt, Laurence. *Redefining Female Religious Life: French Ursulines and English Ladies in Seventeenth-Century Catholicism*. Burlington, VT: Ashgate, 2005.

MacCarthy, Bridget G. *The Female Pen: Women Writers and Novelists 1621–1818*. Preface by Janet Todd. New York: New York University Press, 1994. (Originally published by Cork University Press, 1946–47.)

Mack, Phyllis. *Visionary Women: Ecstatic Prophecy in Seventeenth-Century England*. Berkeley: University of California Press, 1992.

Maclean, Ian. *The Renaissance Notion of Woman: A Study of the Fortunes of Scholasticism and Medical Science in European Intellectual Life*. Cambridge: Cambridge University Press, 1980.

———. *Woman Triumphant: Feminism in French Literature, 1610–1652*. Oxford: Clarendon Press, 1977.

MacNeil, Anne. *Music and Women of the Commedia dell'Arte in the Late Sixteenth Century*. New York: Oxford University Press, 2003.

Maggi, Armando. *Uttering the Word: The Mystical Performances of Maria Maddalena de' Pazzi, a Renaissance Visionary*. Albany: State University of New York Press, 1998.

Maids and Mistresses, Cousins and Queens: Women's Alliances in Early Modern England. Ed. Susan Frye and Karen Robertson. Oxford: Oxford University Press, 1999.

Marshall, Sherrin, ed. *Women in Reformation and Counter-Reformation Europe: Public and Private Worlds*. Bloomington, IN: Indiana University Press, 1989.

Masten, Jeffrey. *Textual Intercourse: Collaboration, Authorship, and Sexualities in Renaissance Drama*. Cambridge: Cambridge University Press, 1997.

Matter, E. Ann, and John Coakley, eds. *Creative Women in Medieval and Early Modern Italy*. Philadelphia: University of Pennsylvania Press, 1994. (Sequel to *The Crannied Wall*, ed. C. A. Monson.)

McGrath, Lynette. *Subjectivity and Women's Poetry in Early Modern England*. Burlington, VT: Ashgate, 2002.

McIver, Katherine A. *Women, Art, and Architecture in Northern Italy, 1520–1580*. Burlington, VT: Ashgate, 2006.

McLeod, Glenda. *Virtue and Venom: Catalogs of Women from Antiquity to the Renaissance*. Ann Arbor: University of Michigan Press, 1991.

McTavish, Lianne. *Childbirth and the Display of Authority in Early Modern France*. Burlington, VT: Ashgate, 2005.

Medieval Women's Visionary Literature. Ed. Elizabeth A. Petroff. New York: Oxford University Press, 1986.

Medwick, Cathleen. *Teresa of Avila: The Progress of a Soul*. New York: Doubleday, 1999.

Meek, Christine, ed. *Women in Renaissance and Early Modern Europe*. Dublin-Portland: Four Courts Press, 2000.

Mendelson, Sara, and Patricia Crawford. *Women in Early Modern England, 1550–1720*. Oxford: Clarendon Press, 1998.

Merchant, Carolyn. *The Death of Nature: Women, Ecology and the Scientific Revolution*. New York: HarperCollins, 1980.

Merrim, Stephanie. *Early Modern Women's Writing and Sor Juana Inés de la Cruz*. Nashville, TN: Vanderbilt University Press, 1999.

Messbarger, Rebecca. *The Century of Women: The Representations of Women in Eighteenth-Century Italian Public Discourse*. Toronto: University of Toronto Press, 2002.

Miller, Nancy K. *The Heroine's Text: Readings in the French and English Novel, 1722–1782*. New York: Columbia University Press, 1980.

Miller, Naomi J. *Changing the Subject: Mary Wroth and Figurations of Gender in Early Modern England*. Lexington, KY: University Press of Kentucky, 1996.

Miller, Naomi J., and Gary Waller, eds. *Reading Mary Wroth: Representing Alternatives in Early Modern England*. Knoxville, TN: University of Tennessee Press, 1991.

Monson, Craig A., ed. *The Crannied Wall: Women, Religion, and the Arts in Early Modern Europe*. Ann Arbor: University of Michigan Press, 1992.

———. *Disembodied Voices: Music and Culture in an Early Modern Italian Convent*. Berkeley: University of California Press, 1995.

Mooney, Catherine M. *Gendered Voices: Medieval Saints and Their Interpreters*. Philadelphia: University of Pennsylvania Press, 1999.

Moore, Cornelia Niekus. *The Maiden's Mirror: Reading Material for German Girls in the Sixteenth and Seventeenth Centuries*. Wiesbaden: Otto Harrassowitz, 1987.

Moore, Mary B. *Desiring Voices: Women Sonneteers and Petrarchism*. Carbondale, IL: Southern Illinois University Press, 2000.

Mujica, Bárbara. *Women Writers of Early Modern Spain*. New Haven: Yale University Press, 2004.

Musacchio, Jacqueline Marie. *The Art and Ritual of Childbirth in Renaissance Italy*. New Haven: Yale University Press, 1999.

Nevitt, Marcus. *Women and the Pamphlet Culture of Revolutionary England, 1640–1660*. Women and Gender in the Early Modern World. Burlington, VT: Ashgate, 2006.

Newman, Barbara. *God and the Goddesses: Vision, Poetry, and Belief in the Middle Ages*. Philadelphia: University of Pennsylvania Press, 2003.

Newman, Karen. *Fashioning Femininity and English Renaissance Drama*. Chicago: University of Chicago Press, 1991.

O'Donnell, Mary Ann. *Aphra Behn: An Annotated Bibliography of Primary and Secondary Sources*. 2nd ed. Burlington, VT: Ashgate, 2003.

Okin, Susan Moller. *Women in Western Political Thought*. Princeton: Princeton University Press, 1979.

Ozment, Steven. *The Bürgermeister's Daughter: Scandal in a Sixteenth-Century German Town*. New York: St. Martin's Press, 1995.

———. *Flesh and Spirit: Private Life in Early Modern Germany*. New York: Penguin Putnam, 1999.

———. *When Fathers Ruled: Family Life in Reformation Europe*. Cambridge, MA: Harvard University Press, 1983.

Pacheco, Anita, ed. *Early [English] Women Writers: 1600–1720*. New York: Longman, 1998.

Pagels, Elaine. *Adam, Eve, and the Serpent*. New York: Harper Collins, 1988.

Panizza, Letizia, ed. *Women in Italian Renaissance Culture and Society*. Oxford: European Humanities Research Centre, 2000.

Panizza, Letizia, and Sharon Wood, eds. *A History of Women's Writing in Italy*. Cambridge: Cambridge University Press, 2000.

Parker, Patricia. *Literary Fat Ladies: Rhetoric, Gender and Property*. London: Methuen, 1987.

Pernoud, Regine, and Marie-Veronique Clin. *Joan of Arc: Her Story*. Rev. and trans. by Jeremy DuQuesnay Adams. 1986 (French original); New York: St. Martin's Press, 1998.

Perry, Mary Elizabeth. *Crime and Society in Early Modern Seville*. Hanover, NH: University Press of New England, 1980.

———. *Gender and Disorder in Early Modern Seville*. Princeton: Princeton University Press, 1990.

———. *The Handless Maiden: Moriscos and the Politics of Religion in Early Modern Spain.* Princeton: Princeton University Press, 2005.

Perry, Ruth. *The Celebrated Mary Astell: An Early English Feminist.* Chicago: University of Chicago Press, 1986.

Peters, Christine. *Patterns of Piety: Women, Gender and Religion in Late Medieval and Reformation England.* Cambridge: Cambridge University Press, 2003.

Petroff, Elizabeth A., ed. *Medieval Women's Visionary Literature.* New York: Oxford University Press, 1986.

The Practice and Representation of Reading in England. Ed. James Raven, Helen Small, and Naomi Tadmor. Cambridge: Cambridge University Press, 1996.

Quilligan, Maureen. *The Allegory of Female Authority: Christine de Pizan's "Cité des Dames."* Ithaca, NY: Cornell University Press, 1991.

———. *Incest and Agency in Elizabeth's England.* Philadelphia: University of Pennsylvania Press, 2005.

Rabil, Albert. *Laura Cereta: Quattrocento Humanist.* Binghamton, NY: MRTS, 1981.

Ranft, Patricia. *Women in Western Intellectual Culture, 600–1500.* New York: Palgrave, 2002.

Rapley, Elizabeth. *The Devotés: Women and Church in Seventeenth-Century France.* Kingston, Ontario: McGill-Queen's University Press, 1989.

———. *A Social History of the Cloister: Daily Life in the Teaching Monasteries of the Old Regime.* Montreal: McGill-Queen's University Press, 2001.

Raven, James, Helen Small, and Naomi Tadmor, eds. *The Practice and Representation of Reading in England.* Cambridge: Cambridge University Press, 1996.

Reading Mary Wroth: Representing Alternatives in Early Modern England. Ed. Naomi Miller and Gary Waller. Knoxville, TN: University of Tennessee Press, 1991.

Reardon, Colleen. *Holy Concord within Sacred Walls: Nuns and Music in Siena, 1575–1700.* Oxford: Oxford University Press, 2001.

Recovering Spain's Feminist Tradition. Ed. Lisa Vollendorf. New York: MLA, 2001.

Reid, Jonathan Andrew. "King's Sister—Queen of Dissent: Marguerite of Navarre (1492–1549) and Her Evangelical Network." Ph.D diss., University of Arizona, 2001 (UMI #: 3033623).

Reiss, Sheryl E., and David G. Wilkins, ed. *Beyond Isabella: Secular Women Patrons of Art in Renaissance Italy.* Kirksville, MO: Turman State University Press, 2001.

The Renaissance Englishwoman in Print: Counterbalancing the Canon. Ed. Anne M. Haselkorn and Betty Travitsky. Amherst: University of Massachusetts Press, 1990.

Renaissance Women Writers: French Texts/American Contexts. Ed. Anne R. Larsen and Colette H. Winn. Detroit, MI: Wayne State University Press, 1994.

Rereading Aphra Behn: History, Theory, and Criticism. Ed. Heidi Hutner. Charlottesville, VA: University Press of Virginia, 1993.

Rheubottom, David. *Age, Marriage, and Politics in Fifteenth-Century Ragusa*. Oxford: Oxford University Press, 2000.

Richardson, Brian. *Printing, Writers and Readers in Renaissance Italy*. Cambridge: Cambridge University Press, 1999.

Riddle, John M. *Contraception and Abortion from the Ancient World to the Renaissance*. Cambridge, MA: Harvard University Press, 1992.

———. *Eve's Herbs: A History of Contraception and Abortion in the West*. Cambridge, MA: Harvard University Press, 1997.

Roper, Lyndal. *The Holy Household: Women and Morals in Reformation Augsburg*. New York: Oxford University Press, 1989.

Rose, Mary Beth. *The Expense of Spirit: Love and Sexuality in English Renaissance Drama*. Ithaca, NY: Cornell University Press, 1988.

———. *Gender and Heroism in Early Modern English Literature*. Chicago: University of Chicago Press, 2002.

———, ed. *Women in the Middle Ages and the Renaissance: Literary and Historical Perspectives*. Syracuse: Syracuse University Press, 1986.

Rosenthal, Margaret F. *The Honest Courtesan: Veronica Franco, Citizen and Writer in Sixteenth-Century Venice*. Foreword by Catharine R. Stimpson. Chicago: University of Chicago Press, 1992.

Rublack, Ulinka, ed. *Gender in Early Modern German History*. Cambridge: Cambridge University Press, 2002.

Russell, Rinaldina, ed. *Feminist Encyclopedia of Italian Literature*. Westport, CT: Greenwood Press, 1997.

———. *Italian Women Writers: A Bio-Bibliographical Sourcebook*. Westport, CT: Greenwood Press, 1994.

Sackville-West, Vita. *Daughter of France: The Life of La Grande Mademoiselle*. Garden City, NY: Doubleday, 1959.

Sage, Lorna, ed. *Cambridge Guide to Women's Writing in English*. Cambridge: Cambridge University Press, 1999.

Sánchez, Magdalena S. *The Empress, the Queen, and the Nun: Women and Power at the Court of Philip III of Spain*. Baltimore: Johns Hopkins University Press, 1998.

Sartori, Eva Martin, and Dorothy Wynne Zimmerman, eds. *French Women Writers: A Bio-Bibliographical Source Book*. Westport, CT: Greenwood Press, 1991.

Scaraffia, Lucetta, and Gabriella Zarri. *Women and Faith: Catholic Religious Life in Italy from Late Antiquity to the Present*. Cambridge, MA: Harvard University Press, 1999.

Scheepsma, Wybren. *Medieval Religious Women in the Low Countries: The "Modern Devotion," the Canonesses of Windesheim, and Their Writings*. Rochester, NY: Boydell Press, 2004.

Schiebinger, Londa. *The Mind Has No Sex?: Women in the Origins of Modern Science*. Cambridge, MA: Harvard University Press, 1991.

———. *Nature's Body: Gender in the Making of Modern Science*. Boston: Beacon Press, 1993.

Schofield, Mary Anne, and Cecilia Macheski, eds. *Fetter'd or Free? British Women Novelists, 1670–1815*. Athens, OH: Ohio University Press, 1986.

Schutte, Anne Jacobson. *Aspiring Saints: Pretense of Holiness, Inquisition, and Gender in the Republic of Venice, 1618–1750*. Baltimore: Johns Hopkins University Press, 2001.

Schutte, Anne Jacobson, Thomas Kuehn, and Silvana Seidel Menchi, eds. *Time Space, and Women's Lives in Early Modern Europe*. Kirksville, MO: Truman State University Press, 2001.

Seelig, Sharon Cadman. *Autobiography and Gender in Early Modern Literature: Reading Women's Lives, 1600–1680*. Cambridge: Cambridge University Press, 2006.

Seifert, Lewis C. *Fairy Tales, Sexuality and Gender in France 1690–1715: Nostalgic Utopias*. Cambridge: Cambridge University Press, 1996.

Shannon, Laurie. *Sovereign Amity: Figures of Friendship in Shakespearean Contexts*. Chicago: University of Chicago Press, 2002.

Shemek, Deanna. *Ladies Errant: Wayward Women and Social Order in Early Modern Italy*. Durham, NC: Duke University Press, 1998.

Sibling Relations and Gender in the Early Modern World: Sisters, Brothers and Others. Ed. Naomi Miller and Naomi Yavneh. Women and Gender in the Early Modern World. Burlington, VT: Ashgate, 2006.

Silent but for the Word. Ed. Margaret Hannay. Kent, OH: Kent State University Press, 1985.

The Single Woman in Medieval and Early Modern England: Her Life and Representation. Ed. Dorothea Kehler and Laurel Amtower. Tempe, AZ: MRTS, 2002.

Smarr, Janet L. *Joining the Conversation: Dialogues by Renaissance Women*. Ann Arbor: University of Michigan Press, 2005.

Smith, Hilda L. *Reason's Disciples: Seventeenth-Century English Feminists*. Urbana, IL: University of Illinois Press, 1982.

———. *Women Writers and the Early Modern British Political Tradition*. Cambridge: Cambridge University Press, 1998.

Snook, Edith. *Women, Reading, and the Cultural Politics of Early Modern England*. Burlington, VT: Ashgate Publishing Co., 2005.

Sobel, Dava. *Galileo's Daughter: A Historical Memoir of Science, Faith, and Love*. New York: Penguin Books, 2000.

Sommerville, Margaret R. *Sex and Subjection: Attitudes to Women in Early-Modern Society*. London: Arnold, 1995.

Soufas, Teresa Scott. *Dramas of Distinction: A Study of Plays by Golden Age Women*. Lexington, KY: University Press of Kentucky, 1997.

Spencer, Jane. *The Rise of the Woman Novelist: From Aphra Behn to Jane Austen*. Oxford: Basil Blackwell, 1986.

Spender, Dale. *Mothers of the Novel: 100 Good Women Writers before Jane Austen*. London: Routledge, 1986.

Sperling, Jutta Gisela. *Convents and the Body Politic in Late Renaissance Venice*. Foreword by Catharine R. Stimpson. Chicago: University of Chicago Press, 1999.

Steinbrügge, Lieselotte. *The Moral Sex: Woman's Nature in the French Enlightenment*. Trans. by Pamela E. Selwyn. New York: Oxford University Press, 1995.

Stephens, Sonya, ed. *A History of Women's Writing in France*. Cambridge: Cambridge University Press, 2000.

Stephenson, Barbara. *The Power and Patronage of Marguerite de Navarre*. Burlington, VT: Ashgate, 2004.

Stocker, Margarita. *Judith, Sexual Warrior: Women and Power in Western Culture*. New Haven: Yale University Press, 1998.

Straznacky, Marta. *Privacy, Playreading, and Women's Closet Drama, 1550–1700*. Cambridge: Cambridge University Press, 2004.

Stretton, Timothy. *Women Waging Law in Elizabethan England*. Cambridge: Cambridge University Press, 1998.

Strong Voices, Weak History: Early Women Writers and Canons in England, France, and Italy. Ed. Pamela J. Benson and Victoria Kirkham. Ann Arbor: University of Michigan Press, 2005.

Stuard, Susan M. "The Dominion of Gender: Women's Fortunes in the High Middle Ages." In Renate Bridenthal, Claudia Koonz, and Susan M. Stuard, eds., *Becoming Visible: Women in European History*. 3rd ed. Boston: Houghton Mifflin, 1998.

Summit, Jennifer. *Lost Property: The Woman Writer and English Literary History, 1380–1589*. Chicago: University of Chicago Press, 2000.

Surtz, Ronald E. *The Guitar of God: Gender, Power, and Authority in the Visionary World of Mother Juana de la Cruz (1481–1534)*. Philadelphia: University of Pennsylvania Press, 1991.

———. *Writing Women in Late Medieval and Early Modern Spain: The Mothers of Saint Teresa of Avila*. Philadelphia: University of Pennsylvania Press, 1995.

Suzuki, Mihoko. *Subordinate Subjects: Gender, the Political Nation, and Literary Form in England, 1588–1688*. Burlington, VT: Ashgate, 2003.

Tatlock, Lynne, and Christiane Bohnert, eds. *The Graph of Sex and the German Text: Gendered Culture in Early Modern Germany 1500–1700*. Ed. Lynne Tatlock and Christiane Bohnert. Amsterdam: Rodolphi, 1994.

Teaching Tudor and Stuart Women Writers. Ed. Susanne Woods and Margaret P. Hannay. New York: MLA, 2000.

Teague, Frances. *Bathsua Makin, Woman of Learning*. Lewisburg, PA: Bucknell University Press, 1999.

Thomas, Anabel. *Art and Piety in the Female Religious Communities of Renaissance Italy: Iconography, Space, and the Religious Woman's Perspective*. New York: Cambridge University Press, 2003.

Tinagli, Paola. *Women in Italian Renaissance Art: Gender, Representation, Identity*. Manchester: Manchester University Press, 1997.

Todd, Janet. *The Secret Life of Aphra Behn*. London: Pandora, 2000.

———. *The Sign of Angelica: Women, Writing and Fiction, 1660–1800*. New York: Columbia University Press, 1989.

Tomas, Natalie R. *The Medici Women: Gender and Power in Renaissance Florence*. Burlington, VT: Ashgate, 2004.

Traub, Valerie. *The Renaissance of Lesbianism in Early Modern England*. Cambridge: Cambridge University Press, 2002.

Valenze, Deborah. *The First Industrial Woman*. New York: Oxford University Press, 1995.

Van Dijk, Susan, Lia van Gemert, and Sheila Ottway, eds. *Writing the History of Women's Writing: Toward an International Approach*. Proceedings of the Colloquium, Amsterdam, 9–11 September. Amsterdam: Royal Netherlands Academy of Arts and Sciences, 2001.

Vickery, Amanda. *The Gentleman's Daughter: Women's Lives in Georgian England*. New Haven: Yale University Press, 1998.

Vollendorf, Lisa. *The Lives of Women: A New History of Inquisitional Spain*. Nashville, TN: Vanderbilt University Press, 2005.

Walker, Claire. *Gender and Politics in Early Modern Europe: English Convents in France and the Low Countries*. New York: Palgrave, 2003.

Wall, Wendy. *The Imprint of Gender: Authorship and Publication in the English Renaissance*. Ithaca, NY: Cornell University Press, 1993.

Walsh, William T. *St. Teresa of Avila: A Biography*. Rockford, IL: TAN Books, 1987.

Warner, Marina. *Alone of All Her Sex: The Myth and Cult of the Virgin Mary*. New York: Knopf, 1976.

Warnicke, Retha M. *The Marrying of Anne of Cleves: Royal Protocol in Tudor England*. Cambridge: Cambridge University Press, 2000.

Watt, Diane. *Secretaries of God: Women Prophets in Late Medieval and Early Modern England*. Cambridge, England: D. S. Brewer, 1997.

Weaver, Elissa B., ed. *Arcangela Tarabotti: A Literary Nun in Baroque Venice*. Ravenna: Longo Editore, 2006.

———. *Convent Theatre in Early Modern Italy: Spiritual Fun and Learning for Women*. New York: Cambridge University Press, 2002.

Weber, Alison. *Teresa of Avila and the Rhetoric of Femininity*. Princeton: Princeton University Press, 1990.

Welles, Marcia L. *Persephone's Girdle: Narratives of Rape in Seventeenth-Century Spanish Literature*. Nashville: Vanderbilt University Press, 2000.

Whitehead, Barbara J., ed. *Women's Education in Early Modern Europe: A History, 1500–1800*. New York: Garland, 1999.

Widowhood and Visual Culture in Early Modern Europe. Ed. Allison Levy. Burlington, VT: Ashgate, 2003.

Widowhood in Medieval and Early Modern Europe. Ed. Sandra Cavallo and Lyndan Warner. New York: Longman, 1999.

Wiesner, Merry E. *Working Women in Renaissance Germany*. New Brunswick, NJ: Rutgers University Press, 1986.

Wiesner-Hanks, Merry E. *Christianity and Sexuality in the Early Modern World: Regulating Desire, Reforming Practice*. New York: Routledge, 2000.

———. *Gender, Church, and State in Early Modern Germany: Essays*. New York: Longman, 1998.

———. *Gender in History*. Malden, MA: Blackwell, 2001.

———. *Women and Gender in Early Modern Europe*. Cambridge, UK: Cambridge University Press, 1993.

———. *Working Women in Renaissance Germany*. New Brunswick, NJ: Rutgers University Press, 1986.

Willard, Charity Cannon. *Christine de Pizan: Her Life and Works*. New York: Persea Books, 1984.

Wilson, Katharina, ed. *Encyclopedia of Continental Women Writers*. 2 vols. New York: Garland, 1991.

Winn, Colette, and Donna Kuizenga, eds. *Women Writers in Pre-Revolutionary France*. New York: Garland, 1997.

Winston-Allen, Anne. *Convent Chronicles: Women Writing about Women and Reform in the Late Middle Ages*. University Park, PA: Pennsylvania State University Press, 2004.

Women and Monasticism in Medieval Europe: Sisters and Patrons of the Cistercian Reform. Ed. Constance H. Berman. Kalamazoo: Western Michigan University Press, 2002.

Women, Crime and the Courts in Early Modern England. Ed. Jenny Kermode and Garthine Walker. Chapel Hill: University of North Carolina Press, 1994.

Women in Italian Renaissance Culture and Society. Ed. Letizia Panizza. Oxford: European Humanities Research Centre, 2000.

Women in Reformation and Counter-Reformation Europe: Public and Private Worlds. Ed. Sherrin Marshall. Bloomington, IN: Indiana University Press, 1989.

Women in Renaissance and Early Modern Europe. Ed. Christine Meek. Dublin-Portland: Four Courts Press, 2000.

Women in the Inquisition: Spain and the New World. Ed. Mary E. Giles. Baltimore: Johns Hopkins University Press, 1999.

Women in the Middle Ages and the Renaissance: Literary and Historical Perspectives. Ed. Mary Beth Rose. Syracuse: Syracuse University Press, 1986.

Women Players in England, 1500–1660: Beyond the All-Male Stage. Ed. Pamela Allen Brown and Peter Parolin. Burlington, VT: Ashgate, 2005.

Women, "Race," and Writing in the Early Modern Period. Ed. Margo Hendricks and Patricia Parker. London: Routledge, 1994.

Woodbridge, Linda. *Women and the English Renaissance: Literature and the Nature of Womankind, 1540–1620*. Urbana: University of Illinois Press, 1984.

Woodford, Charlotte. *Nuns as Historians in Early Modern Germany*. Oxford: Clarendon Press, 2002.

Woods, Susanne. *Lanyer: A Renaissance Woman Poet*. New York: Oxford University Press, 1999.

Woods, Susanne, and Margaret P. Hannay, eds. *Teaching Tudor and Stuart Women Writers*. New York: MLA, 2000.

Writing the Female Voice. Ed. Elizabeth C. Goldsmith. Boston: Northeastern University Press, 1989.

Writing the History of Women's Writing: Toward an International Approach. Ed. Susan Van Dijk, Lia van Gemert, and Sheila Ottway. Proceedings of the Colloquium, Amsterdam, 9–11 September. Amsterdam: Royal Netherlands Academy of Arts and Sciences, 2001.

INDEX